# PREMILLENNIALISM

# POSTMILLENNIALISM

# AMILLENNIALISM

# Premillennialism
# Postmillennialism
# Amillennialism

Vinu V Das

Tabor Press

ISBN 978-1-997541-34-9

# Table of Contents

Chapter 1 - Setting the Stage—Why the Millennium Matters ..9

    1.1 Orienting the Reader to the Millennial Question........10

    1.2 Historical Trajectories of Millennial Interpretation...15

    1.3 Hermeneutical Frameworks and Theological Grids...23

    1.4 Theological Stakes and Practical Consequences.........28

    1.5 The Resurrection Question and the Hope of the Church..........................................................................35

    1.6 Temple, Throne, and Sacred Geography (Preview) ...39

    1.7 The Millennium in Popular Culture and Public Imagination .......................................................................43

    1.8 Methodology and Roadmap for the Book...................47

Chapter 2 - Hermeneutical Foundations ..........................51

    2.1 Mapping the Hermeneutical Landscape....................52

    2.2 Literal, Figurative, and Typological Readings............56

    2.3 Covenant, Kingdom, and Dispensational Paradigms .62

    2.4 Interpreting Prophetic Timetables.............................70

    2.5 Reading Revelation—Methodological Touchstones ...77

    2.6 Evaluating Hermeneutical Models .............................83

Chapter 3 - Premillennialism Unpacked ..........................89

    3.1 Historical Development of Premillennial Hope..........90

    3.2 Classic (Historic) Premillennialism.............................96

    3.3 Dispensational Premillennialism .............................102

    3.4 Progressive Premillennialism ...................................109

**3.5 Key Eschatological Sequences in Premillennial Thought** ..................................................115

**3.6 The Millennial Kingdom on Earth** ............................119

**3.7 Theological Distinctives and Systemic Implications** .125

**Chapter 4 - Postmillennialism Explored** ...............................134

**4.1 Foundations of Postmillennial Hope** .........................135

**4.2 The Optimistic Outlook** ............................................138

**4.3 The Golden Age Before the Parousia** .........................143

**4.4 Mechanisms of Kingdom Expansion** .........................147

**4.5 Key Scriptural Trajectories** .......................................152

**4.6 Transition to the Consummation** ..............................158

**4.7 Systemic Implications** ...............................................161

**4.8 Critiques, Challenges, and Rejoinders** ......................167

**Chapter 5 - Amillennialism Clarified** ...................................174

**5.1 From Misconception to Definition** ............................175

**5.2 Hermeneutical Foundations** .......................................178

**5.3 Historical Development of Amillennial Thought** ......181

**5.4 Realized Eschatology in Worship and Sacrament** ....185

**5.5 Consummation without an Earthly Golden Age** .......190

**5.6 Systemic Implications** ...............................................194

**5.7 Critiques, Challenges, and Dialogues** ........................197

**Chapter 6 - Israel and the Nations** .......................................204

**6.1 Premillennial Perspectives on National Israel** ..........205

**6.2 Postmillennial Readings of Israel's Hope** .................209

**6.3 Amillennial Interpretation of "All Israel"** ................214

**6.4 Unity and Diversity in the People of God** .................219

6.5 Comparative Theological Dialogues............................224

Chapter 7 - Temple, Sacrifice, and Sacred Space.................230

7.1 Ezekiel's Vision and Premillennial Rebuilding........231

7.2 Spiritualized Temple in Postmillennial Triumph .....237

7.3 Christ as the True Temple in Amillennial Thought..244

7.4 Typology, Continuity, and Discontinuity.................250

7.5 Historical Trajectories and Architectural
Embodiments ................................................................255

7.6 Sacrifice, Ethics, and Contemporary Mission..........260

Chapter 8 - Resurrection and Judgment...............................266

8.1 Premillennial Two-Stage Resurrection.....................267

8.2 Postmillennial and Amillennial Single Resurrection 272

8.3 Great White Throne and Bema Seat..........................277

8.4 Intermediate State and "Souls Under the Altar"......283

8.5 Degrees of Reward and Punishment (moved per
previous outline order)......................................................286

8.6 New Heavens and New Earth: Cosmic Re-Creation.291

Chapter 9 - The Nature and Scope of Christ's Reign.............296

9.1 Paradigms of Kingship: Political vs. Spiritual .........297

9.2 Duration, Geography, and Administration ...............299

9.3 Cosmic Renewal and Eschatological Shalom ...........301

9.4 Kingdom Ethics and Human Vocation .....................303

9.5 Worship, Sacraments, and Liturgy in Christ's
Kingdom.................................................................................307

9.6 Israel, the Nations, and Inter-faith Relations............311

9.7 Contested Questions and Emerging Syntheses.........315

**Chapter 10 - Comparative Analysis and Critique** ...................318

    **10.1 Hermeneutical Consistency**........................................319

    **10.2 Doctrinal Coherence**....................................................324

    **10.3 Pastoral and Missional Outcomes** ...........................329

    **10.4 Common Ground and Irreconcilable Differences**...334

    **10.5 Methodological Considerations** ................................338

# Chapter 1 - Setting the Stage— Why the Millennium Matters

Throughout the history of the church, Christians have wrestled with the tension between the present reality of Christ's reign and the promise of His future intervention in earthly affairs. The question of whether Jesus will establish a visible kingdom on earth for a defined period, whether the church's spiritual triumph ushers in a golden era, or whether the "thousand years" of Revelation symbolizes the present age has shaped theological reflection from the apostles to the modern academy. At its core, this inquiry touches on how we read sacred Scripture, how we understand God's covenantal promises, and how we live as followers of Christ in a world marred by injustice and suffering. By exploring key biblical passages—such as John's apocalyptic vision in Revelation and Daniel's prophetic dreams— alongside the beliefs that have taken root in the lives of Jewish and Christian communities, this chapter aims to show why the subject of the millennium remains far more than an academic curiosity. Its relevance extends into worship, pastoral care, mission strategy, and even how believers engage the social and political dimensions of our world.

Beyond biblical exegesis, the millennium debate has wielded profound influence on church identity and practice. Whether one anticipates a future earthly reign or holds that Christ's kingdom is already inaugurated in the church, every eschatological stance bears consequences for how we pray, how we minister to the afflicted, and how we work for justice. The various approaches also reflect deeper convictions about God's faithfulness to Israel, the nature of the resurrection, and the scope of cosmic renewal. In examining these themes, this chapter does not merely recount historical milestones or offer definitions; it seeks to equip readers to recognize the high stakes involved, the interpretive choices at play, and the pastoral implications that flow from differing views. In doing so, we lay the groundwork for a charitable yet rigorous engagement with premillennialism, postmillennialism, and amillennialism in the chapters that follow.

## 1.1 Orienting the Reader to the Millennial Question

**1.1.1 Revelation 20 in Canonical Context** The vision recorded by John in Revelation 20 serves as the primary textual locus for most millennial debates, calling readers back to the dramatic unfolding of cosmic history. In this passage, John sees an angel binding Satan for a thousand years, after which believers who have shared in Christ's first resurrection reign with Him during that same period (Revelation 20:1–4). This imagery builds upon Old Testament anticipations of the Messiah's rule, echoing passages such as Daniel 7:13–14, where the "Son of Man" receives dominion, glory, and a kingdom that shall never be destroyed. As John's vision concludes with a final, brief release of Satan (Revelation 20:7–9), the narrative seems to insist upon a historical pause in evil's power before its ultimate defeat. Such a pause resonates with Ezekiel's temple vision (Ezekiel 40–48), which likewise portrays an era of purified worship. When one reads the Gospels alongside Revelation, the Kingdom of God proclaimed by Jesus appears both present and yet to be consummated, making John's thousand-year period a critical hinge between inaugurated and future eschatological realities. Scholars debate whether Revelation 20 reflects a literal chronology or a symbolic framework conveying truths about Christ's supremacy over Satan, but it is impossible to deny the chapter's influence on

Christian hope and doctrinal formation. Early readers of John's text would have connected its language of new heavens and new earth (Revelation 21:1) with Isaiah 65:17 and 66:22, recognizing God's commitment to redeeming the entire cosmos. Likewise, the New Testament epistle of 2 Peter speaks of the day of the Lord coming like a thief, precipitating the dissolution of the present heavens and prompting new creation (2 Peter 3:10–13), which resonates with John's post-millennial vision. Conversely, Paul's epistles, particularly 1 Corinthians 15, teach that Christ's return will bring about the resurrection of the dead, when the last enemy, death, is destroyed (1 Corinthians 15:24–26). Whether John's "first resurrection" in Revelation 20 aligns directly with Paul's "resurrection of the dead" remains a perennial question. That ambiguity helps explain why interpreters have diverged, some opting for a strictly literal chronological reading—seeing a thousand-year reign on earth—while others discern rich symbolism pointing to Christ's heavenly reign over the church age. Even within Revelation 20, details such as the binding of Satan and the souls under the altar crying out in Revelation 6:9–11 evoke sacrificial themes and justice motifs that transcend a purely temporal thousand-year period. Thus, John's vision sits at the nexus of Old Testament prophecy, New Testament fulfillment, and early Christian witness, forming a hermeneutical crossroads. Understanding how Revelation 20 integrates with Daniel's visions, Isaiah's prophecies, and Pauline eschatology is essential for grasping the broader canonical tapestry. This section will therefore prepare the reader to see how differing interpreters—premillennialists, postmillennialists, and amillennialists—each anchor their positions in John's text while appealing to these other scriptural pillars. By acknowledging Revelation 20's complexity and its web of canonical connections, readers can better appreciate why the millennial question ignites enduring theological passion. With that foundation, we turn next to the technical vocabulary that has shaped Christian conversations about the end times.

**1.1.2 Core Terms and Scope** Any exploration of millennialism requires clarity regarding the key terms that practitioners of each position use. The term millennium itself derives from the Latin mille ("thousand") and annum ("year"), drawn directly from the Greek chilioi in Revelation 20:2–3 and 20:7–8. Beyond millennium, words such as tribulation reference periods of hardship often tied to

Daniel's sixty-nine weeks prophecy (Daniel 9:24–27) or Jesus' teaching in Matthew 24 about the sign of the Son of Man (Matthew 24:30–31). Relatedly, parousia (παρουσία), literally "presence" in Greek, denotes Christ's second coming (1 Thessalonians 4:15–17), serving as a keystone for eschatological chronology. When premillennialists speak of a pretribulation rapture, they invoke 1 Thessalonians 4:13–18 to argue for a catching up of the church before the wrath described in Revelation's trumpet and bowl judgments. Meanwhile, postmillennialists focus on the progressive triumph of the gospel, interpreting "first resurrection" (Revelation 20:5–6) in light of Romans 8:19–23, where creation awaits the revealing of the sons of God. Amillennialists often interpret Revelation 20's "binding of Satan" (Revelation 20:2) as Christ's already accomplished work on the cross (Colossians 2:15). Further technical terms include first resurrection versus general resurrection; premillarians distinguish between believers raised at Christ's return before the millennium (Revelation 20:4–5) and the unsaved raised at the great white throne (Revelation 20:12–13), whereas amillennialists see a single general resurrection. The notion of the second death, mentioned in Revelation 20:6 and 20:14, completes the covenant motif of reward and punishment. Kingdom, as used by Jesus in parables (e.g., Matthew 13:31–33) and by Paul in Romans 14:17, has ecclesiological, present, and future dimensions. A millennium "kingdom" may refer to a literal geographic reign in Jerusalem (premill) or a spiritual reign in the hearts of believers (amill). Understanding these distinctions sets the scope of the debate, helping readers navigate when different schools of thought quote the same terms but assign them divergent meanings. Moreover, recognizing that debates over chronology (e.g., whether the tribulation precedes or follows the millennium) hinge on how one defines "millennium" itself prepares readers for the chapters ahead. As we transition to sketching the three major positions that populate our conversation, it is vital to remember that although each camp uses common biblical language, they often disagree on whether such terms should be taken concretely or metaphorically. That hermeneutical divergence lies at the heart of why the millennium matters in every era of Christian life. With terminology in hand, we now survey the three primary positions as a foundation for deeper study.

**1.1.3 Three Primary Positions at a Glance** At its simplest, the spectrum of Christian millennial thought can be divided into three broad categories: premillennialism, which anticipates a literal thousand-year reign of Christ on earth following His return; postmillennialism, which envisions a golden age of Christian influence before Christ's final parousia; and amillennialism, which holds that the millennium is symbolic of Christ's present reign seated at the right hand of the Father, with no separate earthly thousand-year period. Premillennialists generally feel compelled by a surface reading of Revelation 20:4–6 to affirm that Christ must literally return and bind Satan for a thousand years—an era during which the Jewish people are regathered, the temple rebuilt, and Israel restored to its land. Postmillennialists, on the other hand, emphasize texts such as Isaiah 2:2–4 and Matthew 28:18–20, believing that the gospel will permeate the nations until righteous conditions prevail and then Christ will return. Amillennialists, influenced heavily by Augustine's reading of Revelation and the New Testament's teaching that Christ now reigns spiritually (Revelation 1:6; Ephesians 2:6), interpret the "thousand years" symbolically as the entire church age. Those in this camp argue that the binding of Satan has already occurred in Christ's victory on the cross (John 12:31; Colossians 2:15), meaning that Revelation 20 depicts the present reality rather than a future chronology. While these overviews merely scratch the surface, they illustrate why interpreters find themselves at odds when reading the same Bible. For instance, eastern church fathers such as Justin Martyr and Irenaeus often reflected a premillennial hope, whereas Augustine's influence turned the medieval Western church toward an amillennial reading. In the nineteenth century, the rise of dispensational premillennialism further sharpened distinctions as figures like John Nelson Darby and Cyrus Scofield popularized the idea of a secret rapture and a seven-year tribulation preceding the millennium. Meanwhile, postmillennial optimism enjoyed resurgence in the late eighteenth and early nineteenth centuries during revivals in the United States and Britain. Because these positions often rest on different hermeneutical presuppositions—whether one emphasizes continuity or discontinuity between Israel and the church—it becomes crucial to recognize that under each label lies a complex constellation of sub-schools. Understanding such preliminary contours helps readers know what questions to ask: Do we expect Christ's kingdom to be inaugurated fully on earth, or is it already inaugurated and awaiting consummation? Do Old Testament covenants apply literally to modern Israel or find new fulfillment in the church? As we move from this thumbnail sketch into the history of Christian interpretation, it becomes clear that these questions have been argued and reargued from the early church to the present, each era adding its own nuances and controversies. In the next section, we trace how the church's understanding of Christ's reign developed from the New Testament era through patristic, medieval, and modern milestones.

**1.1.4 Why Eschatology Shapes Everyday Discipleship** Eschatology is often mistakenly relegated to academic debate, but how Christians understand the future profoundly influences daily life, worship, and mission. For believers who affirm a premillennial framework, urgency arises from the notion that Christ's imminent return precedes a literal reign; this can foster a sense that social activism is secondary to evangelistic urgency in saving souls before tribulation. Conversely, postmillennialists derive a strong impetus for cultural engagement, believing that through faithful proclamation and social action—including efforts to reform education, government, and the arts—the world will experience an era of unprecedented righteousness before Christ's return. Such optimism undergirds a robust gospel-centered social ethic, as seen in the Social Gospel movement or in certain modern evangelical organizations that push for systemic justice, operating with confidence that societal transformation is part of God's plan. Amillennial believers, acknowledging that Christ's reign is a present spiritual reality, focus on spiritual formation within the church, believing that Christians live in the tension of "already" but "not yet," as they await the essential consummation of all things at the final resurrection (1 Corinthians 15:23–24). From this perspective, the call to holiness becomes a response to Christ's present reign, and the practices of prayer, worship, and sacraments are imbued with eschatological hope (cf. John 17:3–5). In liturgical traditions shaped by amillennial convictions, the weekly Eucharist is often understood as a foretaste of the heavenly banquet (Revelation 19:9). When evangelicals adopt a postmillennial outlook, they tend to embrace expansive mission strategies, believing that the gospel's progressive expansion will eventually usher in conditions conducive to Christ's return; this occasionally leads to alliances with reform-minded political or educational entities in an effort to accelerate cultural renewal. By contrast, those with premillennial convictions might prioritize missionary endeavors aimed at preserving doctrinal purity, lest the world become fully entrapped by Satan during the tribulation, thereby complicating opportunities for gospel witness. Pastoral care flows from these convictions as well: A premillennial pastor may comfort a grieving congregation with promises of a coming physical kingdom in which tears are wiped away (Revelation 21:4), whereas a postmillennial pastor might encourage congregants to labor for societal justice now, trusting that God will use their efforts to advance His kingdom on earth. Meanwhile, an amillennial preacher could emphasize the already-realized reign of Christ, urging believers to submit to Christ in everyday affairs, demonstrating the gospel through compassion, mercy, and sacrificial love (Luke 17:20–21). The shaping of prayer life, hymns, and artistic expressions also bears the mark of one's eschatological convictions: hymns that draw upon the hope of a visible throne in Jerusalem differ greatly in tone from those that celebrate the unfolding of God's kingdom in the heart and community of believers. Ultimately, one's view of the millennium influences one's view of suffering, hope, and mission. Theological teachers must therefore consider eschatology not as peripheral but as central to discipleship, recognizing that how we see the future shapes how we respond to the present. With this conviction established, we turn to the history of millennial interpretation, tracing how these views emerged and evolved over the centuries.

## 1.2 Historical Trajectories of Millennial Interpretation

### 1.2.1 Jewish Apocalyptic Roots and Second-Temple Longings
Before any Christian debate on the millennium could arise, Jewish apocalyptic literature had already set the stage with vivid hopes for a Messianic age. Texts such as Daniel 7 depict four kingdoms replaced by an everlasting dominion given to "one like a son of man," an image that shaped early Jewish and Christian expectations. Intertestamental writings—1 Enoch, 2 Esdras, 4 Ezra, and the Psalms of Solomon—explore themes of cosmic judgment, resurrection, and the vindication of the righteous, all building anticipation for a future golden age. In 1 Enoch 91, the elect are destined to inherit a world made new, while 4 Ezra 7–14 imagines a

vision of Israel's restoration following a period of catastrophic decline. The Dead Sea Scrolls community at Qumran understood itself to be living in the last days of an age defined by evil forces, awaiting a coming Messiah-priest who would inaugurate a righteous kingdom. Their War Scroll (1QM) and Thanksgiving Hymns (Hodayot) reflect a theology that saw history as moving toward a climactic showdown between the forces of darkness and light. Meanwhile, Hellenistic influences and Roman occupation deepened Jewish longing for divine intervention, making the idea of a future reign under God's chosen one all the more urgent. Rabbi Simeon ben Shetach's caution against contact with Gentiles exemplifies how apocalyptic urgency seeped into daily life, intensifying Jewish nationalism and messianic speculation. By the time of Jesus' earthly ministry, these apocalyptic motifs had become embedded in popular piety, as evidenced by His frequent references to the "coming of the Son of Man" (Matthew 24:30; Mark 13:26). Jesus' proclamation that "the kingdom of God is at hand" (Mark 1:15) therefore resonated with audiences expecting a dramatic eschatological shift. When the early church began to write its own apocalypses—such as Revelation—those authors leaned heavily on Jewish precedents, using symbols of beasts, horns, and horns being broken to signal God's final judgment. These Second Temple longings provide the necessary soil from which Christian millennialism sprouted. They also explain why Paul, in 1 Thessalonians 4:13–17, could speak of believers being caught up to meet the Lord, language that presupposes a dramatic divine intervention akin to Jewish apocalyptic hopes. As Christianity moved into Gentile contexts, however, some of those Jewish expectations were reinterpreted in light of Christ's death and resurrection. While some Jewish Christians still hoped for a Davidic throne in Jerusalem, others concluded that Jesus Himself fulfilled those promises, shifting the focus of hope. Understanding these Jewish roots helps us see that Christian views on the millennium did not develop in a vacuum, but emerged from a vibrant matrix of Second Temple Jewish theology and eschatology. With that background, we can better appreciate how the early church fathers received, adapted, or rejected Jewish prophetic motifs in shaping their own millennial outlooks.

**1.2.2 Patristic Chiliastic Hopes and Early Dissent** In the first two centuries of Christian history, many church fathers embraced a chiliastic or literal-millennium perspective, often referred to as "premillennialism" in modern terms. Papias of Hierapolis (c. 70–c. 155) is said to have taught that Christ would reign for a thousand years in Jerusalem, a view that Justin Martyr (c. 100–165) also appears to hold in his Dialogue with Trypho, wherein he speaks of "the thousand years" as a future period when the saints will judge the world (Dialogue 113). Irenaeus (c. 130–c. 202), in Against Heresies, echoes these ideas, describing the earthly reign of Christ and saints with physical inheritance of the land (Against Heresies 5.32.1). These fathers often grounded their views in a straightforward reading of Revelation 20, believing it taught a future, literal kingdom. They likewise affirmed a restored physical temple in Jerusalem, alluding to passages like Ezekiel 40–48 as prophetic maps for that coming era. Church records suggest that many congregations in Asia Minor and Syria anticipated a tangible millennial reign, with some even committing property to Christ's kingdom in the expectation that private ownership would be suspended. Yet, around the late second and early third centuries, dissenting voices emerged. Origen (c. 185–254) brought a more allegorical hermeneutic, treating Revelation's language as symbolic of spiritual truths rather than as literal fulfillment. He suggested that Christ's reign with the martyrs might be understood spiritually rather than through a reconstituted earthly polity. Tertullian (c. 155–c. 240), although once a chiliast, eventually altered his approach, offering ambiguous statements that mix literal and figurative language, perhaps due to his later association with Montanism, which had its own eschatological fervor. By the time of Hippolytus (c. 170–c. 235), we see a tentative shift: while he still affirms a future earthly kingdom, he also begins to read certain details in a symbolic light, anticipating a more nuanced hermeneutic. This ferment contributed to growing debates within the church about whether Revelation's promises applied to a future earthly order or to the current spiritual reign of Christ. Those who questioned literal readings often pointed to Jesus' own parables about the kingdom taking root like a mustard seed (Matthew 13:31–32), suggesting that the kingdom might look quite different from a political kingdom. Despite this dissent, many local churches continued to hold onto chiliastic hopes into the third century, indicating that patristic opinion was far from monolithic. As the church's center of gravity shifted from Antioch and Ephesus to Rome and Alexandria, allegorical methods gained traction, paving the way for new interpretations. In the next subsection, we will see how Augustine's

17

ministry and the medieval church further developed these trends, moving toward a decidedly amillennial posture.

**1.2.3 Augustine, the Medieval Synthesis, and Spiritualized Reigns** The trajectory of Christian eschatology took a decisive turn in the late fourth and early fifth centuries with the influence of Augustine of Hippo (354–430). In his seminal work The City of God, Augustine addressed the millennium question directly, challenging the literal understanding of Revelation 20. He argued that the "thousand years" symbolized the entire era between Christ's first and second comings, during which the righteous reign with Christ in a spiritual kingdom, rather than on a renewed physical earth. Augustine's reasoning leaned heavily on Christ's own statements in Luke 17:20–21, where He indicates that the kingdom of God is not coming with observational signs but is within or among them, suggesting a present spiritual reality rather than a future political reign. By asserting that Satan's binding occurred at the cross (Matthew 12:29; John 12:31) and that martyrs reigning with Christ referred to the church age itself, Augustine effectively reframed the debate. His influence grew throughout the Western church, as Latin became the ecclesiastical lingua franca, and his allegorical and Christocentric approach became normative. The medieval theologians who followed—such as Jerome (c. 347–420) in his Latin Vulgate commentaries and Thomas Aquinas (1225–1274) in the Summa Theologica—further cemented amillennialism by treating Revelation as primarily theological rather than chronological prophecy. During the Middle Ages, monastic spirituality and cathedral liturgies emphasized the heavenly Jerusalem of Revelation 21–22 as a present reality pointing toward future consummation, rather than as a literal city to be rebuilt. Medieval theological schools debated whether the "new heaven and new earth" of Revelation 21 was fully future or partially realized in the church's sacramental life. While the political shape of Christendom during the Carolingian Renaissance resembled an earthly kingdom, theologians generally maintained that any visible Christian empire was an imperfect signpost rather than the outright fulfillment of millennial prophecy. The Crusades (1096–1291) briefly revived eschatological fervor among some, hijacking apocalyptic language to legitimize military campaigns, but even then most church leaders continued to teach Augustine's spiritualized interpretation. By the time of the Scholastics, Augustine's approach had been woven deeply into the fabric of Western orthodoxy, so much so that any advocacy for a literal thousand-year reign was often dismissed as fringe or heretical. Eastern Christianity, by contrast, preserved a greater diversity of millennial perspectives well into the Middle Ages, partially due to differences in how Greek fathers like Gregory of Nyssa (c. 335–c. 395) treated apocalyptic imagery. Nevertheless, the medieval synthesis of spiritualized reign dominated Western Europe, setting the stage for Reformation debates to build upon. As we shift from medieval to Reformation contexts, we will observe how Protestant reformers both inherited and challenged Augustine's legacy, reshaping millennial expectations in light of new theological and political realities.

### 1.2.4 Reformation Diversity: Magisterial versus Radical Streams

The sixteenth-century Reformation erupted as a critique of medieval Catholicism, but it also reopened longstanding debates about eschatology, including millennial expectations. Reformers such as Martin Luther (1483–1546) and John Calvin (1509–1564) generally maintained an amillennial stance, inheriting Augustine's spiritualized reading of Revelation 20. Luther's early writings reflect a belief that the church was living in the end times, but he eventually adopted a more restrained interpretation, suggesting that the kingdom existed in the preaching of the gospel rather than anticipating a future thousand-year reign. Calvin, in his Institutes of the Christian Religion, similarly argued that Christ's kingdom is spiritual, residing in believers' hearts through faith and the word of God (John 3:5–8; 1 Corinthians 4:20). He emphasized that any attempt to assign a specific timeline to Revelation's imagery risked human presumption and detracted from Christ's present work. Yet, the Radical Reformers—Anabaptists, Mennonites, and later the Fifth Monarchists—often revived premillennial hopes. Menno Simons (1496–1561) and Jakob Hutter (1500–1536) believed that the visible church would be purified in the last days, anticipating a tangible reign of Christ on earth. In England, the Puritan preacher Thomas Brightman (1562–1607) wrote Commentaries on the Revelation urging a literal rebuilding of the Jewish temple and a future earthly kingdom. His ideas later influenced Isaac Newton's unpublished theological writings, which predicted that 1666 would mark the millennium's arrival. Meanwhile, John Foxe's Acts and Monuments (1563) narrates martyr stories imbued with apocalyptic fervor, fueling popular hopes for an imminent kingdom. Thus, within Reformed circles, there existed a spectrum: magisterial Reformers leaned toward amillennialism, while certain Puritans and radicals flirted with premillennial or postmillennial ideals. Postmillennialism itself did not coalesce until the seventeenth and eighteenth centuries, but its embryonic seeds appeared as early as the Westminster Assembly (1643–1653), where the notion that gospel advancement would bring about a long period of peace resonated with some members. The political upheavals of the English Civil War (1642–1651) drove various sects to question whether they were living in the eschaton, further complicating the landscape. In France, the millennial debates paralleled civil strife, as the French Wars of Religion (1562–1598) saw Huguenot leaders advocating for a reformed church that would prepare the way for Christ's return. Across Europe, print shops churned out pamphlets debating the timing and nature of the millennium, making eschatology a hotly contested topic well before the Puritan Golden Age. By weaving together these magisterial and radical streams, readers can see that the Reformation did not simply confirm a single, unified view of the millennium. Instead, it opened a more pluralistic conversation that set the stage for the modern explosion of eschatological systems, including dispensational premillennialism and Enlightenment-tinged postmillennial optimism. Moving forward, we will trace how these ideas developed in the eighteenth and nineteenth centuries, especially as North American and British evangelicals wrestled with cultural and political changes.

**1.2.5 Modern Revivals—Dispensationalism, Postmillennial Optimism, Neo-Evangelical Shifts** The eighteenth and nineteenth centuries witnessed an unprecedented flowering of millennial speculation as evangelical revivals, colonial expansion, and the rise of print culture converged. Postmillennial optimism found fertile ground among English and Scottish Presbyterians, who believed that the "golden age" of the gospel would usher in social and moral reforms. Jonathan Edwards (1703–1758) exemplified this optimism, prophesying that, through revival movements like the Great Awakening, the world might experience a protracted era of righteousness before Christ's return. His era saw the formation of missionary societies—such as the British and Foreign Bible Society (founded in 1804)—driven by the conviction that a Christianized world would signal the nearness of the millennium. In contrast, a new school of premillennial thought—dispensationalism—emerged from within the Plymouth Brethren in the mid-nineteenth century. John Nelson Darby (1800–1882) argued that God's redemptive plan unfolded through distinct dispensations, culminating in a secret rapture of the church, a seven-year tribulation for Israel, and then a literal thousand-year reign. Darby's dispensational framework found eager translators in the United States, most notably Cyrus Ingerson Scofield (1843–1921), whose Scofield Reference Bible (1909) popularized dispensational premillennialism among American evangelicals. This approach fueled the rise of Bible conferences, faith-healing movements, and the founding of institutions like Dallas Theological Seminary. Simultaneously, postmillennialism inspired social reform movements, including temperance, abolitionism, and public education, with leaders convinced that God's Spirit would progressively sanctify society. However, the horrors of the American Civil War (1861–1865) and the First World War (1914–1918) shattered many postmillennial hopes, as unprecedented violence convinced some that history was spiraling toward apocalypse rather than toward gradual improvement. In reaction, mid-twentieth-century neo-evangelicals like Carl F. H. Henry and Billy Graham largely embraced dispensational premillennialism, shifting the center of evangelical eschatology toward an expectation of imminent divine intervention rather than cultural triumph. At the same time, some Reformed theologians—represented by O. Palmer Robertson and R. C. Sproul—defended a classic amillennial stance, arguing that history was on a trajectory toward God's final consummation rather than toward a golden age. African-American theologians such as Howard Thurman (1899–1981) interwove apocalyptic hope with civil rights activism, creating a postmillennial-tinged vision of social transformation grounded in gospel witness. By the late twentieth century, the publishing industry, radio, and television had turned books like Hal Lindsey's The Late Great Planet Earth (1970) into bestsellers, demonstrating the enduring appetite for premillennial speculation among the broader public. Meanwhile, the Lausanne Movement (1974 onward) and subsequent global evangelical gatherings brought diverse eschatological views into conversation, prompting renewed scholarly dialogue about the social ethics of each position. This interplay of optimism, pessimism, and realism set the stage for twenty-first-century discussions, which will be the focus of the next subsection.

21

### 1.2.6 Twenty-First-Century Trends and Global South

**Perspectives** Entering the twenty-first century, the landscape of millennial interpretation became more global and more complex. In Western contexts, the rise of the "nones" and growing secularization led some churches to reframe eschatology in terms of present spiritual renewal rather than future geopolitical events. At the same time, global South theologians—particularly in Sub-Saharan Africa, Latin America, and parts of Asia—have developed contextualized eschatological visions that blend traditional biblical exegesis with local concerns about poverty, injustice, and community renewal. African Pentecostal scholars, for instance, often emphasize the Spirit's sovereign work in liberating the oppressed, reflecting a postmillennial confidence that God's kingdom is breaking through present realities in tangible ways. In Latin America, liberation theologians have at times adopted a form of "preferential option for the poor" that resonates with postmillennial themes of social justice as homespun signs of God's inaugurated kingdom. Meanwhile, Chinese house churches—operating under persecution—often take solace in premillennial promises of Christ's imminent return to overthrow oppressive regimes, making Revelation 20's binding of Satan a powerful metaphor for anticipated political transformation. In India, Dalit Christian communities sometimes interpret the millennium through the lens of liberation from caste-based oppression, seeing Christ's coming reign as a promise of radical social equality. At the same time, Western scholars such as N. T. Wright have revitalized amillennial interpretations by emphasizing the "already/not yet" of God's kingdom in Acts and Paul's epistles, suggesting that Christ's resurrection initiated new creation now, with full consummation yet to come. Digital platforms and social media have accelerated the spread of diverse eschatological theories, allowing laypeople from very different cultures to debate the timing of the rapture, the meaning of Daniel's seventy weeks, or the nature of the millennium in live forums. As a result, twenty-first-century church leaders often confront a mosaic of perspectives within their own congregations, necessitating teaching that is both historically informed and contextually sensitive. This global ferment challenges Western Christians to listen to voices from the Global South, recognizing that their suffering and hope may recalibrate inherited eschatological assumptions. It also reminds us that millennial discussions continue to carry real-world consequences, shaping theology, mission strategy, and social engagement. With that contemporary backdrop in mind, the stage is set to explore the hermeneutical frameworks that undergird these diverse positions.

## 1.3 Hermeneutical Frameworks and Theological Grids

### 1.3.1 Literal, Figurative, and Typological Readings of Prophecy

At the heart of any eschatological position lies a hermeneutical question: when Scripture speaks of kings and kingdoms, saints reigning, and beasts rising, should we interpret these images literally, figuratively, or as fulfilling deeper typological patterns? A literal approach, often favored by premillennialists, reads Revelation 20's "thousand years" as a precise chronological marker, expecting a forthcoming thousand-year period in which Jesus dwells on earth, Israel's temple stands, and His followers rule alongside Him. Proponents of this view argue that when Scripture's language of kingship, thrones, and temples aligns closely with Old Testament prophecies—such as Isaiah 9:6–7's promise of an eternal Davidic throne—it warrants a straightforward, concrete expectation. Literal interpreters caution against spiritualizing passages, contending that doing so risks undermining biblical authority and leads to undue speculation. In contrast, a figurative—or symbolic—approach might argue that Revelation's beasts, horns, and numeric images capture spiritual truths about cosmic conflict rather than offering a blueprint for future geopolitics. Amillennialists frequently hold this view, insisting that apocalyptic imagery, by its very nature, surpasses human categories. They see Revelation as a "sacramental" text, conveying the reality of Christ's present reign through vivid pictures that nurture faith and perseverance (Revelation 12:11; 1 John 5:4). Typological readings add another dimension: a typologist might treat Old Testament institutions—such as the Day of Atonement in Leviticus 16—as prefiguring Christ's work in binding Satan (Revelation 20:1–3). Thus, binding Satan may represent the accomplished victory of Christ's death and resurrection (Colossians 2:13–15) rather than a future event. Typology also surfaces in how passages like Daniel 7's four beasts might represent successive empires culminating in God's kingdom, allowing readers to see Revelation's visions as an unfolding of established biblical motifs. Each hermeneutical choice carries implications for how one orders history, values present spiritual experience, and anticipates future events. Hermeneutical decisions also influence how one reads key prophetic texts in the Old Testament. If one insists on literalism, then promises of animal sacrifices in Ezekiel 40–46 may demand the rebuilding of a Temple with renewed sacrificial worship, whereas a symbolic reading might see those chapters as describing how redeemed humanity offers praise in perfected fellowship with God. Likewise, the phrase "the glory of the Lord filled the temple" (Ezekiel 43:5) could be heard as a future apocalyptic event or as describing Christ's presence filling the church through the Holy Spirit. Debates over hermeneutical method have galvanized countless volumes in academic journals and debate stages at Bible conferences. Readers must therefore ask which interpretive commitments they hold and why, recognizing that these choices will shape their entire eschatological framework. As we move into covenantal and dispensational grids, we will see how such hermeneutical orientations underpin broader theological systems. For now, it suffices to note that literal, figurative, and typological readings each bring Scripture into dialogue with history and contemporary church life in distinctive ways.

**1.3.2 Covenant Theology, Classic Dispensationalism, and Progressive Covenantalism** Beyond hermeneutical style, eschatologists often align themselves with larger theological systems that define how they view God's unfolding plan. Covenant theology, for example, understands history through the lens of two or three overarching covenants—works, grace, and often a separate covenant of redemption—emphasizing continuity between Israel and the church. In this view, promises made to Israel find fulfillment in the people of God as a whole, with typological echoes seen in the church's participation in Christ (Galatians 3:29). Covenant theologians typically adopt an amillennial stance, seeing Christ's kingdom inaugurated at Pentecost (Acts 2) as the fulfillment of Davidic and Abrahamic promises (2 Samuel 7; Genesis 12:1–3). Classic dispensationalism, in contrast, divides redemptive history into distinct periods or "dispensations" in which God relates differently to humanity. Dispensationalists argue that God's purposes for ethnic Israel and the church remain separate, anticipating a future fulfillment of Old Testament covenants to Israel in a literal millennium. This approach places great emphasis on the restored land promises, the rebuilding of the Jewish temple, and a distinct program for Israel during the tribulation. Progressive covenantalists seek a middle path: they affirm covenant theology's stress on continuity and typology but allow for some distinct functions in God's unfolding plan, particularly regarding Israel. They might see the church as the new Israel in a foundational sense, yet still affirm that ethnic Israel will one day play a unique role in redemptive history. This nuanced position often results in what some call "new covenant premillennialism," where a future temple and reign in Jerusalem are anticipated, but ultimate fulfillment is understood in covenantal terms. These systems also carry different assumptions about how to read Old Testament prophecies. Covenant theologians might connect Isaiah 11:1–10's shoot from the stump of Jesse to Christ's present reign in the church, whereas dispensationalists insert a future application in which Israel's Davidic king rules in the land. In turn, progressive covenantalists might affirm both senses: Christ as the ultimate fulfillment and a partial restoration that precedes a final heavenly consummation. These divergences extend beyond eschatology into ecclesiology, sacramentology, and ethics; for example, a covenant theologian's view of baptism as sign and seal of covenant grace flows from the same logic that sees a spiritualized kingdom. Meanwhile, a dispensationalist might stress a separation between Israel and the church when it comes to ordinances such as sacraments, seeing them as belonging to the present church age with a future dispensational temple awaiting its own set of rituals. Progressive covenantalists argue for a fuller continuity, suggesting that sacraments anticipate the eschatological banquet in symbolic form but do not require a distinct future temple to validate their significance. As these theological systems demonstrate, one's view of God's covenants and dispensations directly influences how one orders history, reads prophecies, and thereby perceives the millennium. In the next subsection, we will explore how the "already/not yet" tension operates within these frameworks, showing how some see the kingdom as inaugurated, while others await a full consummation.

### 1.3.3 The "Already/Not Yet" Tension and Recapitulation in Revelation

One of the most significant hermeneutical insights of recent theological reflection involves the "already/not yet" tension, a concept popularized by theologians such as George Ladd and N. T. Wright. They propose that many New Testament texts, especially John 5:24–29, Luke 17:20–21, and Ephesians 1:18–23, present the kingdom of God as both a present reality and a future hope. In John

5, Jesus speaks of those who hear His word and believe having eternal life already, while the time is coming when all in the graves will hear His voice, indicating that final resurrection still lies ahead. This duality complicates how we interpret Revelation 20: are the saints "reigning with Christ" now (Revelation 20:4) or is that reign delayed until a future millennium? Recapitulation theories in apocalyptic literature suggest that Revelation does not necessarily follow a linear chronology but rather retells the same cosmic story from varying perspectives, helping readers see the full drama of salvation rather than plotting each event in a strict timeline. According to this approach, one cycle in Revelation might emphasize Christ's victory through the Lamb in the present age (Revelation 5), while another cycle focuses on the final overthrow of Satan and the ushering in of a new creation (Revelation 20–22). By collapsing strict chronological sequences into thematic recapitulations, this method offers a robust way to honor the literary artistry of John's vision and to avoid forcing every image into a future context. Anchoring the "already/not yet" tension in Old Testament passages such as Isaiah 65:17 ("For behold, I create new heavens and a new earth") and Habakkuk 2:14 ("For the earth will be filled with the knowledge of the glory of the Lord"), advocates show that the prophets often held competing visions of present restoration and future consummation simultaneously. New Testament writers lean on those prophetic currents: Paul, in Colossians 1:27, speaks of Christ in you as the hope of glory, suggesting believers already share in the future. Yet, in 2 Peter 3:10, he anticipates a dramatic eradication of the elements. Such tension leads amillennialists to read Revelation 20's "binding of Satan" as present and ongoing, fulfilled at the cross (Matthew 12:28–29; Colossians 2:15), while the future release in Revelation 20:7–9 symbolizes an end-time testing before final judgment. Premillennialists counter that having Christ's throne in present hearts does not preclude a future, visible reign in Jerusalem, so the "already" pertains to spiritual reality, and the "not yet" pertains to political fulfillment. Postmillennialists often see the "already" as the spread of the gospel and the "not yet" as its culmination in global Christian culture preceding the millennium. Recognizing this tension helps explain why hermeneutical methods—whether literal, symbolic, or recapitulative—yield such divergent eschatologies. As we proceed to examine confessional boundaries and doctrinal standards, we will see how various Christian traditions negotiate the "already/not yet" tension differently, each offering its own roadmap for reading apocalyptic texts and understanding the millennium.

**1.3.4 Ecumenical Creeds, Confessional Boundaries, and Doctrinal Method** Eschatological views do not develop in a vacuum; they are shaped and constrained by confessional documents and creedal statements that outline a church's doctrinal commitments. The early ecumenical creeds—such as the Nicene-Constantinopolitan Creed (381)—mention Christ's return, His resurrection of the dead, and the life of the world to come, but deliberately remain silent on specifics regarding any millennium. This deliberate neutrality suggests that early councils aimed to affirm core Christological and Trinitarian affirmations without becoming entangled in millennial minutiae. Later creeds, like the Chalcedonian Definition (451), similarly address the nature of Christ without detailing eschatological timelines. However, regional confessions began to make more explicit statements. The Westminster Confession of Faith (1646), reflecting Puritan influences, teaches that "the end of this world is to be with the last trumpet," at which time Christ will descend visibly to judge inhabitants of the earth (Chapter XXXI). Its silence on a literal thousand-year reign indicates an implicit amillennial posture, even though some Puritan divines privately harbored premillennial hopes. By contrast, the Second Helvetic Confession (1566), adopted by Reformed churches in Switzerland and Scotland, leaves more room for diverse interpretations, urging caution in dogmatizing the millennium since Scripture offers "dark riddles" in the book of Revelation. Lutheran confessions, such as the Augsburg Confession (1530), likewise do not specify a position, although early Lutherans mostly followed Augustine's amillennial approach. In Anglicanism, the Thirty-Nine Articles (1563) speak of Christ's descent into hell, resurrection, and eventual return to judge both the living and dead, but do not privilege any millennial system, reflecting the via media spirit of Anglican theology. As Protestantism splintered into various denominations, some groups—like the Seventh-day Adventists—explicitly adopted a premillennial framework, incorporating it into their doctrinal statements (e.g., the Seventh-day Adventist Fundamental Beliefs). Their emphasis on the investigative judgment, heavenly sanctuary, and an earthly millennium for the 144,000 saints in Revelation 14:1–5 highlights how confessions can shape distinctive eschatological models. Meanwhile, evangelical alliances such as the Lausanne Covenant (1974) and the Manila Manifesto (1989) deliberately avoided specifying eschatology, focusing instead on mission priorities. They recognized that unity in gospel proclamation could exist amid eschatological diversity. The Roman Catholic Magisterium, through documents such as the Catechism of the Catholic Church (1992), describes Christ's reign as inaugurated in the church yet not fully realized until the end, reflecting an amillennial or "realized future" perspective without defining a symbolic timeline. Eastern Orthodox liturgical life, with its weekly celebration of Christ's descent to Hades (Matthew 16:18; 1 Peter 3:18–20), emphasizes the present victory of Christ over death, leaving the chronology of a millennium largely unaddressed in formal liturgy and patristic inheritance. Understanding these confessional boundaries is essential because they frame which eschatological options are deemed acceptable or beyond orthodoxy in various traditions. Doctrinal method also enters here: some churches require that any interpretation of Revelation align with the church's historical exegesis, while others allow more latitude for private judgment. As a result, a minister in a Reformed Presbyterian setting might be constrained to teach amillennialism, whereas a pastor in a Baptist or independent evangelical context might feel at liberty to advocate premillennial or postmillennial views. These confessional contours remind readers that eschatology is not merely an individual intellectual pursuit but also a communal activity, rooted in shared sacramental, liturgical, and doctrinal commitments. With hermeneutical frameworks and confessional contexts established, the book is now poised to delve into the distinctive features of premillennialism, postmillennialism, and amillennialism in subsequent chapters.

# 1.4 Theological Stakes and Practical Consequences

### 1.4.1 Soteriological Horizons—Perseverance, Assurance, and Judgment
How one envisions the millennium directly shapes beliefs about salvation's trajectory, influencing how Christians understand perseverance amid trial. Those holding a premillennial view often stress the imminent return of Christ as the primary guarantee of believer perseverance, teaching that true faith will be vindicated at the parousia (1 Thessalonians 4:14–17). This

immediacy of Christ's coming fosters a sense of urgency to live in holiness, since one anticipates the sudden interruption of human history by divine intervention. For postmillennialists, who foresee a gradually advancing golden age, perseverance is framed within the expectation that gospel influence will steadily transform societies before Christ's return, drawing on Romans 8:18–25's themes of present suffering contrasted with future glory. Their assurance derives not solely from an imminent rescue but also from the unfolding of God's redemptive purposes in history, underscoring that faithfulness to evangelism and social action contributes to a foretold triumph. Amillennial believers, in turn, ground their confidence on texts like Hebrews 6:11–12 and James 1:12, understanding perseverance as a spiritual reality lived out in pilgrim endurance, since Christ's reign is already inaugurated through His work on the cross (Colossians 2:13–15). They affirm that final judgment follows the present church age (Revelation 20:11–15), yet they warn that the certainty of judgment at the end reinforces the urgency of holy living now. All three perspectives agree on the necessity of perseverance but differ on its temporal contours: whether it is secured by an impending physical kingdom, by a gradually unfolding golden age, or by a present spiritual reign culminating in a future consummation. These convictions also affect pastoral counseling: a premillennial pastor might comfort believers by reminding them that persecution is temporary and that Christ will soon appear to set things right (Philippians 3:20–21). A postmillennial pastor might encourage congregants to persevere in social engagement, trusting that each act of justice presses history closer to its divine redemptive goal (Isaiah 2:4). An amillennial pastor will point to Christ's present reigning work in the heart through the Spirit, urging believers to endure gloriously even in conflict, knowing that victory has already been won (Revelation 12:10–11). When it comes to judgment, premillennialists tend to underscore a two-phase resurrection—first of the righteous to reign, then of the wicked for condemnation (Revelation 20:4–6, 20:11–15). Postmillennialists often see a single general resurrection at Christ's return after the millennium, emphasizing that history's arc bends toward judgment only after gospel reign (Acts 24:15). Amillennialists likewise teach a single general resurrection, but stress that the millennium represents the present church age, so the final judgment at the end serves as the culmination of both a present spiritual reign and cosmic renewal (1 Corinthians 15:23–24). Each approach wrestles with how assurance of salvation interacts with eschatological chronology, shaping liturgies, hymns, and catechetical materials accordingly. By understanding these soteriological stakes, readers gain insight into why debates over the millennium are never merely academic—they touch the core of how Christians grasp perseverance, assurance, and coming judgment. As we consider how soteriology interweaves with broader questions of identity, we next turn to how ecclesiology and the Israel–church relationship factor into these millennial frameworks.

### 1.4.2 Ecclesiology and the Israel–Church Question

Eschatological convictions permeate ecclesiology, especially in how one perceives the relationship between ethnic Israel and the church. Premillennial theology typically upholds a clear distinction between God's covenantal promises to Israel and His plans for the church, arguing that many Old Testament prophecies—such as those in Isaiah 11 or Jeremiah 31 regarding Israel's restoration—must be fulfilled literally in a future millennial kingdom. This perspective leads to an ecclesiology in which the church coexists with Israel but is not the fulfillment of all Israel's promises; instead, the church acts as a steward of God's revelation, awaiting a separate program for Israel. In a typical dispensational premillennial scheme, the church will be raptured before a tribulation, during which God turns again to His chosen ethnic people in fulfillment of Davidic and land covenants (Romans 11:25–26). Postmillennialists, meanwhile, often view the church as the means by which nations—both Jew and Gentile—are brought into God's fold, expecting that Israel's restoration occurs in a spiritual sense when large numbers of Jewish individuals embrace faith in Messiah Yeshua (Romans 11:12, 26). They emphasize passages like Isaiah 2:3–4 and Micah 4:1–3 to argue that Israel and the nations will worship together in a golden age preceding Christ's return. In their ecclesiological vision, the church plays a transformative role in gathering both Jew and Gentile into one body (Ephesians 2:14–16), blending Israel and the nations as signs of the kingdom's progress. Amillennial theologians typically stress the continuity between Israel and the church, teaching that the church is the true Israel, inheriting the promises through Christ (Galatians 3:29). They interpret Paul's metaphor of the olive tree (Romans 11:17–24) to indicate that Gentile believers are grafted into the same covenant promises, and that ethnic Israel's future role is either fulfilled in Christ or subsumed into the one people of God.

This ecclesiology underscores that Scripture's temple imagery now centers on the gathered church (1 Peter 2:5), and that physical land promises find their ultimate fulfillment in the new heavens and new earth (Revelation 21:1–3). The role of Israel thus shapes how each tradition defines the church's identity, mission, and eschatological hope. For instance, a premillennial congregation might memorialize Israel's distinct future by praying for Jerusalem as an ethnic and geographical focal point of prophecy (Psalm 122:6), whereas a postmillennial church might emphasize the global nature of the church's mission and celebrate every cultural background as part of God's redeemed people. An amillennial community will often accentuate the unity of saints across history and geography, focusing on the church's present spiritual unity rather than awaiting a separate program for ethnic Israel. Practical consequences flow into liturgical calendars, selection of hymns, and preaching emphases—whether to highlight a future earthly promise to Israel or a present spiritual reality. Recognizing these ecclesiological differences helps readers see that debates about the millennium reflect deeper convictions about what the church is and does in God's redemptive plan. With ecclesiology addressed, we now examine how each view motivates mission, social reform, and—in some streams—Christian Zionism.

**1.4.3 Missional Motivation—Evangelism, Social Reform, Christian Zionism** Eschatology fuels mission by shaping how believers perceive the gospel's urgency and scope. Premillennial adherents often prioritize evangelism with the understanding that Christ's return could occur at any moment, encouraging a "rescue" mentality to reach souls before the great tribulation. Their strategy frequently centers on preaching Christ's imminent coming as the catalyst for conversion, drawing heavily on passages like Matthew 24:14 that link worldwide proclamation with the sign of the end. By emphasizing that "the time is short" (1 Corinthians 7:29), premillennialists foster a sense of urgency that motivates intense evangelistic campaigns, often focusing on personal salvation rather than structural social transformation. However, some premillennialists also partner with Christian Zionist movements, praying for the regathering of Jews to Palestine as a precursor to prophecies in Ezekiel 37 and Zechariah 12, believing that physical events in Israel's restoration signal the approaching millennium. In contrast, postmillennial believers see the Great Commission (Matthew 28:18–20) as both personal and cultural, contending that the spread of the gospel will transform institutions, culminating in a "golden age" of Christian influence. They draw on Isaiah 2:2–4's vision of nations streaming to Zion to learn God's ways, interpreting that passage as a call to social reform—education, political engagement, and economic justice—as integral to advancing the kingdom. This approach yields robust Christian involvement in abolitionism, temperance, and education in the nineteenth century, based on the conviction that Christ's church can progressively shape societies until they reflect gospel values. This same impulse animates modern faith-based non-profit organizations that seek to eradicate poverty, human trafficking, and systemic injustice, believing these efforts herald the approach of a millennial era. In amillennial frameworks, evangelism is likewise vital, but it is often framed as the proclamation of a present spiritual kingdom rather than a future political reign. Amillennialists lean on Luke 17:21's assertion that the kingdom is "in your midst," urging believers to demonstrate Christ's rule through incarnational ministry—charity, mercy, and peacemaking—while awaiting final consummation. They may support social reform efforts as expressions of Christian love without assuming those reforms will produce a final golden age; thus, they temper optimism regarding societal transformation, emphasizing instead the transformative power of the gospel in individual hearts and communities. While amillennial churches occasionally engage in social justice initiatives, they do so with an eye to the brokenness of this age, recognizing that full renewal awaits the return of Christ (Revelation 21:1–4). As for Christian Zionism, amillennial voices tend to view modern political Zionism skeptically, seeing the fulfillment of promises to Israel as already accomplished in Christ and the church (Galatians 3:28–29). Hence, they caution against conflating modern geopolitics with biblical prophecy. By contrast, postmillennialists may applaud Israel's modern flourishing as part of a larger redemptive storyline but often emphasize the church's role in leading the nations to worship rather than focusing on a separate future covenant for Israel. Understanding these missional motivations illuminates why eschatological views influence everything from charitable giving priorities to international political stances. As mission leads into questions of public engagement, we turn next to how political ethics and public theology emerge from millennial convictions.

**1.4.4 Political Ethics—Public Theology, Nationalism, and Peacemaking** Eschatological outlooks carry significant ramifications for how Christians interpret their responsibility toward government, citizenship, and peacemaking. In premillennial circles, the sense that Christ will soon intervene to establish a worldwide kingdom often fosters a posture of political caution or disengagement, encouraging believers to focus on evangelism rather than seeking to transform governments. Passages like Philippians 3:20, describing believers' citizenship as "in heaven," inform a view that earthly political structures are temporary and often complicit in the power of the enemy. For this reason, many premillennialists emphasize prayer for Israel and support for Israel's political security, viewing modern geopolitical events in the Middle East as signs of the approaching tribulation period (Zechariah 12:2–3). Such stances have sometimes led to strong alignments between certain Christian groups and the State of Israel, promoting what is known today as Christian Zionism. Conversely, postmillennial Christians, convinced that Christ's kingdom will progressively advance through society, often embrace robust political engagement as part of faithful kingdom work. They see Romans 13:1–7's teaching on governing authorities as a call for Christians to strive for just and godly governance, believing that laws and policies should reflect biblical principles of justice, compassion, and righteousness. This outlook fosters involvement in political activism, policy formation, and national reform movements, with the expectation that Christian influence can lead to an era of peace and flourishing—an earthly expression of "on earth as it is in heaven" (Matthew 6:10). Postmillennialists may support international peace treaties, economic development initiatives, and legal frameworks that embody biblical conceptions of human dignity. Amillennial theologians, while acknowledging the church's call to be salt and light (Matthew 5:13–16), typically approach political engagement with a posture of realism, recognizing that no earthly system can fully realize God's kingdom until Christ's return. Grounded in texts like Romans 8:20–22, which stress that all creation waits for final liberation, they caution against placing undue hope in political solutions. Instead, amillennial Christians emphasize subsidiarity, local engagement, and peacemaking (Matthew 5:9) as appropriate ways to live out the gospel, pursuing justice while recognizing the limitations of any human institution (Micah 6:8). They advocate a public theology that critiques both secular utopianism and unhealthy nationalism, reminding believers that their ultimate allegiance is to Christ's kingdom, not to any earthly nation. This balanced approach enables amillennial churches to participate in civic affairs—such as voting and community service—without conflating those activities with the imminent arrival of an earthly millennium. By comparing these political-ethical implications, readers see that eschatology profoundly shapes how Christians understand their role as citizens in both local and global contexts. As our discussion of public theology and political engagement draws to a close, we turn toward the pastoral and worship-related consequences of millennial conviction.

### 1.4.5 Pastoral Care—Hope, Suffering, and Worship Formations

Pastors and spiritual leaders often find their sermons, liturgies, and counseling sessions shaped by eschatological convictions, especially in offering hope and comfort amid suffering. In premillennial congregations, preachers frequently emphasize Revelation 21:4's promise that God will wipe away every tear, using the certainty of a future physical kingdom to comfort the bereaved and embattled. They interpret passages like Matthew 24:29–31 as assuring congregants that even the darkest tribulations are preludes to Christ's triumphant return, strengthening believers' resilience. This focus can lead to worship services rich in apocalyptic imagery—sermons on Revelation and songs anticipating "Jesus coming soon"—which foster a sense of anticipation and endurance. Pastoral care in such contexts often involves encouraging personal holiness in light of impending judgment (Hebrews 12:14) and reminding the flock that their citizenship is in heaven (Philippians 3:20), helping them to endure persecution with joy. Postmillennial pastors, by contrast, emphasize the church's hope for societal transformation as a present reality. Sermons may draw on Isaiah 61:1–4, preaching that God's anointed servant brings healing to the brokenhearted and binds up the wounds of the nations, thereby inspiring congregants to serve their communities. Their worship services often blend proclamation of future hope with calls to social action—mobilizing volunteers for community development, feeding programs, or advocacy work—rooted in the belief that the church's faithfulness accelerates the arrival of a millennial age. Under this conviction, pastoral care includes not only spiritual encouragement but also practical training in civic engagement, equipping believers to translate eschatological hope into tangible social impact.

Amillennial pastors typically foster worship that highlights the "already" of Christ's reign in the Word and sacraments, drawing from Romans 6:4 and 1 Corinthians 10:16 to teach that baptism and the Lord's Supper are present participation in the death and resurrection of Christ. Liturgies often feature readings from Revelation 4–5 that depict the heavenly throne, reminding congregations that worship now is a foretaste of the eschatological banquet (Revelation 19:7–9). In pastoral counseling, an amillennial pastor might point a grieving family to 1 Thessalonians 4:13–18, which promises reunion with loved ones at Christ's return, without speculating on the chronology of a future millennium. They emphasize that suffering in the present age aligns believers with Christ's own suffering (Philippians 3:10) and that the church's worship life anticipates the full realization of the kingdom (Revelation 7:9–10). By exploring these pastoral nuances, one sees how ecclesial rhythms—sermons, prayers, hymns—vary across different eschatological convictions, yet each seeks to draw believers forward in hope. As this section transitions toward our next major theme, readers will be ready to engage more deeply with the resurrection question and the hope it offers to the church in every age.

# 1.5 The Resurrection Question and the Hope of the Church

### 1.5.1 Resurrection Sequences across the Three Views The question of "when" and "how" the dead are raised impinges directly upon millennial frameworks, as each tradition constructs its chronology around the order of resurrection events. Premillennialists typically teach a two-stage resurrection: first, the righteous dead are raised at Christ's return to reign during the millennium (Revelation 20:4–6), and second, the wicked are raised after the thousand-year period for final judgment (Revelation 20:11–15). This two-fold sequence finds support in verses like 1 Thessalonians 4:16, where Paul describes the Lord descending from heaven and the dead in Christ rising first, interpreted as aligning with an immediate enthronement period preceding a tribal judgment on unrepentant nations. By building their chronology this way, premillennialists underscore the distinct functions of the resurrection—reward for believers and accountability for the lost—

and highlight the reality of Christ's kingship manifested in bodily form on earth. Postmillennialists, while affirming a resurrection of the dead, envision a single general resurrection at the close of the golden age. They often interpret Daniel 12:2's "many of those who sleep in the dust of the earth shall awake" as referring to the final resurrection occurring when the earth has enjoyed an extended period of righteousness under the church's influence. In their view, 1 Corinthians 15:23's phrase "each in his own order" can refer to one collective resurrection for the righteous and unrighteous alike at the conclusion of history, bypassing the need for a distinct first resurrection in Revelation 20:4–6. Postmillennialists argue that the millennium described in Revelation is a symbolic representation of the present era in which the church's influence gains ascendancy, so the "first resurrection" can be read spiritually as the new birth (John 5:24), with the bodily resurrection reserved for the end. Amillennialists also uphold a single resurrection, reading Revelation 20's first and second death distinctions—"blessed and holy are those who share in the first resurrection" (Revelation 20:6) and "the rest of the dead did not come to life until the thousand years were ended" (Revelation 20:5)—in a symbolic sense. They regard the "first resurrection" as referring to believers' regeneration (Titus 3:5) and union with Christ in His death and resurrection (Romans 6:4), while the "second death" symbolizes eternal separation from God for the unrepentant (Revelation 21:8). Thus, amillennialists maintain that all the dead are raised together at the final judgment, as taught in 1 Corinthians 15:51–52 and 2 Thessalonians 4:16–17. In this scheme, the millennium is the church age during which Christ reigns spiritually, and the bound Satan indicates that his power to deceive nations is held in check until the unified end. Each of these sequences interfaces with pastoral ministry, as church leaders must teach congregations about death, resurrection, and destiny in light of their eschatological convictions. The divergent readings of resurrection events demonstrate why robust biblical exegesis and theological dialogue are indispensable in forming a coherent hope. As we have seen how timing differs across perspectives, we now turn to explore the nature of the bodies raised and the cosmic renewal that follows.

**1.5.2 Nature of Glorified Bodies and Cosmic Renewal** Closely tied to resurrection timing is the question of what kind of bodies resurrected believers will receive and how creation itself is renewed.

Premillennialists often lean on 1 Corinthians 15:42–44, which contrasts the natural body with the spiritual body, to argue that the glorified bodies of believers will be similar to Christ's resurrection body—physical yet imperishable, capable of personal interaction and governance in a restored Edenic environment. They cite Philippians 3:20–21 to affirm that believers' bodies will be transformed "at the coming of Christ," enabling them to participate fully in the earthly kingdom. This transformation, they argue, extends beyond individual bodies to include the land itself, as passages like Isaiah 65:17–25 envision a renewed creation where the wolf lives with the lamb and people build houses without fear of destruction. In their view, the millennial reign will combine a resurrected humanity with a rehabilitated cosmos, fulfilling Genesis 1:28's mandate for human stewardship in its fullest sense. Postmillennialists, while also embracing bodily resurrection for believers, often emphasize that the present earth will experience partial renewal in union with the church's progressive triumph, drawing on Romans 8:19–22, which portrays creation as groaning for liberation. They propose that the church's faithful proclamation and social engagement—guided by passages like Matthew 5:13–16—contribute to tangible improvements in human flourishing and environmental stewardship. Although they acknowledge that full cosmic renewal awaits Christ's ultimate return (2 Peter 3:13), postmillennialists view the church's work in areas such as education, justice, and healthcare as aligning with divine restoration. They highlight Revelation 21:1–2's promise of a new heaven and new earth as culminating the church's redemptive labors, trusting that God will complete what His people begin. Amillennialists stress that Christ's resurrection itself inaugurated a new creation (2 Corinthians 5:17) even as the physical cosmos remains in a state of groaning (Romans 8:22). They read Revelation 21's new heavens and new earth through the lens of inaugurated eschatology, asserting that while church-age believers experience preview glimpses of restoration—such as reconciliation, justice, and mercy—full consummation is deferred until after the final judgment. Passages like Colossians 1:18–20, which declare Christ's reconciling work extends to everything in heaven and on earth, support this tension between present renewal and future perfection. Amillennial theologians caution against overemphasizing environmental renewal before Christ's return, teaching that groaning creation still awaits completion (Revelation 11:18), even as believers practice responsible stewardship now. They often interpret the new creation imagery as primarily symbolic of God's redemptive victory over sin and death, rather than a literal geographic transformation, while affirming that God's plan includes a physical renewal that will be fully manifested in the age to come. By exploring these nuances, readers grasp how views on glorified bodies and cosmic renewal flow from one's overall millennial framework. As our discussion of resurrection and cosmic hope concludes, we transition into the final preview section on temple imagery, sacred geography, and their political implications.

**1.5.3 Pastoral Implications for Grief, Funeral Liturgy, and Future Hope** How churches care for the bereaved often reveals underlying eschatological convictions, since funeral rites and pastoral counseling draw upon beliefs about the afterlife, resurrection, and the world to come. Premillennial congregations frequently design funeral liturgies that highlight Revelation 21:4's promise of a future earth without mourning, teaching families that their loved ones rest until the first resurrection, when Christ returns to establish His earthly reign. In counseling, pastors might lean on 1 Thessalonians 4:14–17 to reassure grieving relatives that death is but a sleep interrupted by Christ's appearing, encouraging a confident hope of bodily reunion. Hymns in such contexts often emphasize longing for heaven and for Christ's visible reign, urging worshipers to "anticipate the day when sorrow flees away." The emphasis on a future physical kingdom shapes how comfort is offered, gently reminding mourners that their ultimate home is not here but in the renewed creation that Christ will inaugurate. Postmillennial churches, while also promising resurrection, focus funeral liturgies on the reality that the deceased now rest in Christ's presence, and on the church's mission to continue till Christ's return inaugurates a golden age. Funeral sermons may draw from Ecclesiastes 3:4 on "a time to weep" and "a time to dance," celebrating the life lived and urging the congregation to honor the deceased through continued faithful labor for God's kingdom on earth. They underscore that, even as individuals pass into Christ's presence (Philippians 1:23), the witness of the living carries forward God's redemptive work in communities, reflecting Isaiah 61:3's call to bind up the brokenhearted. Hymns in postmillennial contexts often blend hope for the future resurrection with calls to active service, encouraging congregants to view each life as contributing to the approaching golden age. Amillennial traditions emphasize the already-ingress of the kingdom into believers' lives, shaping funeral liturgies around texts like 2 Corinthians 5:8—"to be absent from the body and to be at home with the Lord"—while affirming that full resurrection hope awaits Christ's return (1 Corinthians 15:20–23). In bereavement counseling, amillennial pastors often point mourners to Jesus' words in John 11:25–26—"I am the resurrection and the life"— emphasizing that the deceased share in Christ's victory now, though the full consummation awaits the end of the present age. Their hymns frequently balance themes of present comfort with confident future hope, often invoking Revelation 7:9–10 to depict a foretaste of the heavenly worship that unites saints from every tribe, tongue, and nation. In classically liturgical settings, funeral rites incorporate the Lord's Supper as a sign of present communion with the deceased in Christ (1 Corinthians 10:17), while looking forward to the eschatological wedding banquet (Revelation 19:9). Common to all traditions is the conviction that death does not have the final word, but each nuance—whether highlighting a future earthly kingdom, a golden age of gospel triumph, or Christ's present spiritual reign— shapes how the church ministers to the grieving and celebrates the hope of resurrection. As pastoral care cannot be separated from eschatological expectation, congregations learn to navigate grief with words and rituals anchored in their millennial view. Having examined how resurrection and pastoral hope interweave, we now offer a preview of temple imagery, sacred geography, and their ramifications for diverse millennial positions.

# 1.6 Temple, Throne, and Sacred Geography (Preview)

**1.6.1 Biblical Motifs of Sacred Space** Sacred space permeates both Old and New Testament narratives, framing how God's presence dwells among His people. In Genesis 28:10–17, Jacob's vision of a ladder to heaven set in Bethel suggests an early sense that certain locations serve as divine meeting places. As Israel's story unfolds, the tabernacle instructions in Exodus 25 ff. detail a portable holy of holies, signifying that God travels with His people. When Solomon builds the first temple (1 Kings 6–8), he localizes worship in Jerusalem, symbolizing God's settled presence among the twelve tribes. Prophets like Ezekiel then expand on this motif: in chapters

40–48, Ezekiel perceives a future temple and idealized worship system pointing to renewed fellowship between God and humankind. In the New Testament, Jesus refers to His body as a temple (John 2:19–21), indicating that sacred space now resides within His person and, by extension, within the community of believers (1 Corinthians 3:16; Ephesians 2:21–22). The book of Revelation reintegrates temple imagery with cosmic scope—John depicts a heavenly temple from which God's throne issues light (Revelation 21:22–23), uniting sacred space with eschatological fulfillment. These motifs underscore the conviction that where God dwells, life flows differently—holiness is cultivated, worship is transformed, and the boundary between heaven and earth grows thin. Differences in millennial views often stem from how one reads these texts: some see the promise of a rebuilt temple in Ezekiel as a blueprint for a future millennial sanctuary, while others regard Ezekiel's vision as symbolic of Christ's presence and the church's unity. Yet all agree that sacred geography represents the intersection of divine initiative and human response, making the question of when and how a temple appears central to any eschatological framework. With these motifs in view, readers grasp why debates over literal or spiritual temples carry enormous theological weight. In the next subsection, we examine varied proposals about the timing and nature of any future temple.

**1.6.2 Timing of Any Future Temple—Divergent Proposals** The question of whether a future temple will be built, and if so, when it appears, lies at the heart of millennial controversy. Premillennialists who adopt a literal hermeneutic anticipate a third temple constructed in Jerusalem after the tribulation and before Christ's millennial reign. They point to Ezekiel 40–48's detailed measurements and Levitical regulations as evidence that a physical temple is still in God's program, arguing that Zechariah 6:12–13 and Daniel 9:27 further support a rebuilt sanctuary where animal sacrifices will resume during the millennium. Many premillennial writers predict that certain events—such as the Antichrist's desecration of a new temple (Daniel 9:27; 2 Thessalonians 2:4)—must occur before the millennium, making temple reconstruction a critical precondition. In contrast, postmillennialists tend to spiritualize temple references, suggesting that any literal rebuilding either already transpired in Jewish history or serves as a historical curiosity rather than a future necessity. They are more inclined to view the "temple" of Ezekiel as a typological foreshadowing of Christ and the church's corporate worship, echoing Paul's teaching that God's people are God's temple (1 Corinthians 3:16). Accordingly, postmillennial ministers seldom emphasize the rebuilding of a temple, prioritizing instead efforts to establish God's righteousness in society, which they see as a form of 'temple service' in line with Isaiah 56:7. Amillennial theologians almost uniformly deny that a literal temple awaits future construction, contending that prophecies of a temple find fulfillment in Christ's incarnation and atoning work (Hebrews 9:11–12), and that Revelation 21:22's depiction of a holy city without a temple signals the end of temple-based worship. They often argue that passages such as Matthew 24:15, where Jesus warns of the "abomination of desolation" in the holy place, refer to past events (e.g., the Roman destruction of 70 AD) rather than a future rebuilt sanctuary. Thus, amillennial preachers focus on Christ's body and the church as the locus of God's presence (Ephesians 2:19–22), seeing no need for earthly temple construction. Intermediary views also exist, such as those of progressive covenantalists who allow for a modest future restoration of sacrificial signs in a ceremonial sense but deny any separate future era of Israelite temple worship. These divergent proposals illustrate how details about a temple's timing reflect broader hermeneutical commitments: whether one prioritizes a literal future or reads the Old Testament through Christ's completed work. As readers track these differences, they will better appreciate how each millennial position integrates or dissolves the concept of sacred geography. Having surveyed the timing debates, we now turn to the political and inter-religious ramifications that temple expectations carry for the modern world.

**1.6.3 Political and Inter-Religious Ramifications of Temple Expectations** Anticipation of a future temple often spills over into contemporary politics and inter-religious relations, particularly in Jerusalem—a focal point for Jews, Christians, and Muslims alike. Premillennial advocates who support rebuilding a temple frequently align themselves with Jewish groups dedicated to preparing for sacrificial worship, such as the Temple Institute in Jerusalem, which crafts priestly garments and studies rituals in hopes of reestablishing Levitical rites. This involvement has led some Christians to pray for—and even financially support—projects aimed at enabling a third temple, believing that its construction will hasten the fulfillment of end-time prophecy (Zechariah 6:12–13). Such positions can create tension with Muslim communities, which regard the Temple Mount (Al-Haram al-Sharif) as home to the Dome of the Rock and Al-Aqsa Mosque, sacred in Islam as the place of Muhammad's night journey. The prospect of altering the status quo on the Temple Mount therefore carries explosive geopolitical stakes, often inflaming Israeli–Palestinian tensions and drawing in global religious-political actors. Postmillennialists are less invested in literal temple restoration, choosing instead to focus on broad interfaith dialogue and social justice initiatives that promise earthly peace as a foretaste of the kingdom (Isaiah 2:4). They advocate for cooperative efforts—such as advocating for religious freedom, poverty alleviation, and conflict mediation—that bring Jews, Christians, and Muslims together in shared service. By emphasizing common ethical imperatives, they aim to reduce sectarian hostility while still upholding clarity about Christ's unique work. Amillennial believers generally approach political and inter-religious tensions from a perspective that downplays the temple's future political role, stressing that the church is now the vehicle of God's presence and that any attempt to build a new temple risks conflating the church's spiritual reality with geopolitics. They point to Jesus' assertion that "you worship what you do not know" when speaking to the Samaritan woman at the well (John 4:22), suggesting that genuine worship transcends physical location. By focusing on the church as the new temple (1 Peter 2:5), amillennialism encourages believers to engage in peacemaking (Matthew 5:9) without staking faith in physical structures. This orientation often leads amillennial churches to partner with interfaith organizations that pursue social welfare, rather than sponsoring activities aimed at altering the status quo on Jerusalem's Temple Mount. Across all perspectives, however, temple expectations feed into broader questions about Christian responsibility toward global conflict, religious pluralism, and the role of prophecy in shaping political identity. Recognizing these ramifications helps readers see that millennial views extend far beyond abstract theology—they can shape foreign policy, influence charitable priorities, and even affect personal travel decisions when visiting the Holy Land. As this chapter's preview of temple, throne, and sacred geography concludes, readers are well positioned to proceed to the ensuing chapters, where specific millennial systems will be examined in full.

# 1.7 The Millennium in Popular Culture and Public Imagination

**1.7.1 From Left Behind to Literary Utopias** Popular fiction has played a formative role in shaping many Christians' mental images of the end times, often blending biblical motifs with imaginative embellishments. The "Left Behind" series by Tim LaHaye and Jerry B. Jenkins famously propelled premillennial and dispensational ideas into the mainstream, depicting a secret rapture that leaves believers in heaven while the unevangelized experience the terrors of the Tribulation. Readers engage with characters who endure the seven-year period of judgments, wars, and the rise of the Antichrist, forming a vivid narrative that weaves loosely around Revelation 6–19. In contrast, authors such as C. S. Lewis and J. R. R. Tolkien crafted more allegorical or utopian visions grounded in spiritual realities. Lewis's "Space Trilogy" does not depict a literal millennium but imagines worlds where the "true" King has already triumphed, reflecting an amillennial perspective of Christ's reign as a present spiritual reality. Other utopian novels, like John Winthrop's "A Model of Christian Charity" (albeit not fictional), imagine a society ordered by Christian ethics—anticipating a postmillennial hope that faithful communities can birth a transformed society in which gospel values permeate every institution. These literary utopias often draw on Isaiah 65:17–25, weaving narratives in which lions lie down with lambs and child mortality ceases, echoing prophetic images of a restored creation. Meanwhile, dystopian stories such as Cormac McCarthy's "The Road" or Margaret Atwood's "Oryx and Crake" may not explicitly reference the millennium but nevertheless trigger eschatological reflection by casting a vision of desolation absent divine intervention. Such works can unintentionally shape readers' eschatological expectations, invoking fear of environmental collapse or genetic engineering as precursors to tribulation-like conditions. Science fiction novels like Robert A. Heinlein's "Stranger in a Strange Land" subtly engage theological questions by imagining a new Adamic figure who inaugurates a fresh era of human community—resonating with postmillennial hopes of societal renewal through an unexpected intervention. Similarly, Philip José Farmer's "Riverworld" series envisions a literal postmortem resurrection of all humanity at a single moment, echoing Revelation

20:12–13's "book of life" motif. These imaginative retellings force readers to wrestle with the biblical texts behind them, either reinforcing or challenging inherited eschatological frameworks. Even romance and mystery novels may feature characters preparing for the rapture or grappling with prophecy charts, demonstrating how millennial ideas have permeated the wider cultural imagination. Academics note that fiction frequently operates on the "imaginative bandwidth" of biblical literature, giving shape to abstract themes such as judgment and hope. When readers encounter a thriller about an Antichrist figure in control of a global government, they may subconsciously absorb dispensational timelines without ever opening a Bible. Because fictional representations often simplify or sensationalize eschatological concepts, discerning readers must return to Scripture—such as 1 Thessalonians 4:16–17 and Revelation 20:1–6—to measure creative license against canonical teaching. In this way, popular fiction can function as both a bridge and a barrier: it can spark interest in biblical prophecy but also imprint skewed expectations. As one transitions from literary utopias to the silver screen, it becomes clear that movies and television have similarly shaped very public images of the end times, requiring careful discernment to distinguish narrative flourish from faithful exegesis.

**1.7.2 Media, Movies, and Eschatological Fear / Fascination** The film industry has long tapped into apocalyptic fascination, producing blockbusters that draw creatively from biblical eschatology while amplifying suspense and spectacle. Movies such as "The Omen" trilogy (1976, 1978, 2006) reimagine antichrist figures embroiled in supernatural horrors, borrowing imagery from Daniel 7's beasts and Revelation 13's blasphemous horns. Filmmakers often depict the Antichrist as a charismatic world leader whose rise to power fulfills Daniel 9:27's "abomination that causes desolation," though these cinematic portrayals frequently prioritize dramatic effect over careful exegesis. Similarly, "Left Behind: The Movie" (2000) brought LaHaye's premillennial narrative to visual life, featuring scenes of sudden disappearances, collapsing buildings, and global plagues loosely patterned after Revelation's trumpet and bowl judgments (Revelation 8–16). Streaming platforms now host new series like "Apocalypse 10," which merges secular doomsday scenarios with loosely tethered biblical references, illustrating how apocalyptic imagery permeates both religious and secular media.

Audiences watch with a mixture of dread and fascination as movies spotlight global conflagrations, plagues, and cosmic cataclysms—often invoking echoes of Joel 2:30–31's blood and fire imagery or Matthew 24:29's cosmic signs of the Son of Man. Documentaries such as "The 700 Club" segments periodically inform viewers that planetary alignments or ancient Mayan calendars portend imminent tribulation, though such claims often rest on speculative numerology rather than solid hermeneutical analysis. The result is a pervasive sense of eschatological anxiety, where viewers become preoccupied with identifying "signs of the times" in everyday news headlines—wars, natural disasters, political upheavals—interpreting them as fulfillments of Matthew 24:6–8. At the same time, serious filmic efforts such as "The Book of Eli" (2010) and "A Wrinkle in Time" (2018) draw on biblical themes of redemption and cosmic restoration, albeit without explicitly naming the millennium. These creative works illustrate the tension between biblical witness and cultural imagination, challenging viewers to discern how cinematic narratives align with passages like 2 Peter 3:10–13, which teaches that God will one day remake the heavens and the earth in righteousness. Horror films such as "Left Behind II: Tribulation Force" (2002) exploit chapter-and-verse references to Revelation, yet rarely engage readers in the context of the broader canon. Even family-friendly programs like "VeggieTales" have occasionally constructed episodes that nod to end-time themes, softening them with humor and slapstick. Through these varied portrayals, audiences internalize a menu of eschatological motifs—raptures, antichrist villains, prophetic seals—often without understanding their scriptural anchors or theological complexities. As a consequence, many people think of the millennium as a series of blockbuster events rather than as an opportunity to re-evaluate how they live in the present. Discernment requires return to Scripture: with texts like 1 Thessalonians 5:1–2 reminding believers that "times and seasons" are not ours to know, and Revelation 22:18 warning against adding to prophecy. Recognizing the cinematic tropes at work enables one to appreciate creative storytelling while maintaining fidelity to biblical truth. With cinema's influence unpacked, the final subsection turns to how readers can distinguish entertainment from faithful exegesis—ensuring that cultural consumption does not eclipse careful biblical study.

**1.7.3 Discerning Fiction from Faithful Exegesis** Given the profusion of books, movies, and online content inflating eschatological speculation, developing criteria for faithful interpretation is crucial. First, readers should compare any popular claim to the immediate literary context of key biblical passages. For instance, when a novel suggests that Revelation 13's beast imposes a cashless society (Revelation 13:17), a careful exegete will ask how that image aligns with John's broader apocalyptic vision of worldly powers and not reduce it to a single modern phenomenon. Second, it is important to cross-check every detail with multiple biblical texts—recognizing that Revelation's seals, trumpets, and bowls may overlap thematically but do not fit neatly into a linear sequence unless one adopts a particular hermeneutical grid. Third, one must evaluate the hermeneutical method behind a popular portrayal: does the author treat Old Testament prophecies typologically or do they assert a strict literal fulfillment in our time? Those claiming literal accuracy should reconcile their view with passages like Luke 17:20–21, which warn that the kingdom is not coming "with observation", and with Jesus' own passive references to the millennium in Matthew 20:1–16. Fourth, readers should assess whether fictional representations essentialize or oversimplify the roles of Israel, the church, and the nations, carefully weighing those portrayals against Pauline texts such as Romans 11:25–27 on Israel's partial hardening and future restoration. Fifth, historical-critical insights remind us that many apocalyptic images in Daniel, Ezekiel, and Revelation employ symbolic numbers—1260, 144,000, 7—and must be interpreted within their first-century context rather than projected uncritically onto modern technologies or geopolitical alliances. For instance, a best-selling novel that ties 666 to RFID chips must be measured against the Johannine context in which 666 likely functioned as a code for a specific Roman emperor or oppressive regime, not as a futuristic barcode. Sixth, readers should identify whether a work encourages a balanced Christian life or whether it provokes undue fear, anxiety, or sensationalism—bearing in mind that Paul warns against using knowledge "puff up" (1 Corinthians 8:1) and Jesus calls believers to speak "words of eternal life" (John 6:68), not merely preach doom. Seventh, engaging scholarly commentaries provides checks and balances: consulting credible biblical scholars (e.g., G. K. Beale, Grant Osborne, N. T. Wright) ensures that one's understanding of apocalyptic symbolism is anchored in rigorous exegesis. By adopting these practices, one can appreciate creative works while still affirming that "[we] shall know them by their fruits" (Matthew 7:16), testing every spirit by whether it upholds the gospel's core. As readers apply these discernment guidelines to their cultural consumption, they become equipped to navigate the intersection of faith and fiction. With popular culture's role in perspective, the chapter's final section offers a roadmap for using this book itself—guiding readers toward an eschatology of charity and dialogue rather than polarizing stridency.

# 1.8 Methodology and Roadmap for the Book

**1.8.1 Comparative, Multi-Lens Approach (Biblical, Historical, Theological, Pastoral)** This volume undertakes a profoundly comparative methodology, recognizing that no single perspective on the millennium exists in isolation. By starting with Scripture, each chapter will first anchor its discussion in key biblical texts—Revelation 20, 1 Thessalonians 4–5, Daniel 9–12, Ezekiel 37–48—bringing careful exegesis to the fore. Readers will see how each millennial position interacts with the same passages: premillennialists emphasizing a literal chronology, postmillennialists focusing on redemptive progress, and amillennialists finding realized elements in Christ's present reign. Historical analysis follows, tracing how ancient Jewish expectations (e.g., Daniel's "Son of Man" vision, Daniel 7:13–14) shaped early Christian understandings, then mapping shifts through patristic debates, medieval syntheses, Reformation diversity, and modern revivals. This historical lens keeps fresh the insight that our contemporary convictions derive from centuries of theological wrestling, not from isolated private readings of Revelation. The theological layer explores systematic implications—how each position aligns or clashes with doctrines of God, Christ, salvation, and the church—drawing on covenant theology, dispensationalism, and progressive covenant frameworks. By comparing doctrinal loci such as soteriology, ecclesiology, and sacramentology, readers gain a holistic sense of how views of the millennium ripple across Christian belief and practice. Finally, the pastoral dimension invites readers to see how eschatology affects preaching, worship, ethics, and pastoral care. Pastors and church leaders will encounter case studies illustrating how different millennial convictions shape preaching calendars, funeral liturgies, educational resources, and social engagement initiatives. Through this multi-lens approach, the book intends not simply to compare abstract theories but to show how each view makes a tangible difference in Christian life. Readers will be encouraged to move beyond stereotypes—seeing premillennialists as withdrawal-focused, postmillennialists as naïvely optimistic, or amillennialists as disengaged—and instead appreciate the underlying biblical and theological convictions that drive each model. By weaving together biblical exegesis, historical context, systematic theology, and pastoral praxis, this method fosters a comprehensive understanding, enabling readers to reflect critically and charitably. Having outlined our broad comparative approach, we now turn to specific criteria by which millennial models will be evaluated throughout this book.

**1.8.2 Criteria for Evaluating Millennial Models** To assess the strengths and weaknesses of premillennial, postmillennial, and amillennial systems, the book employs several consistent criteria. First, biblical fidelity requires that any model demonstrate coherence with the full counsel of Scripture—not merely isolated proof texts. For example, a model claiming a future earthly reign must reconcile its claims with Matthew 24:30–31, where Jesus speaks of cosmic signs, and 1 Corinthians 15:24–26, where Paul describes the final removal of every opposing force, including death. Second, hermeneutical consistency demands that one apply interpretive principles uniformly: if a model reads symbolic language in Ezekiel 37 as literal, it should not flip to an allegorical reading in Daniel 9 when convenient. Third, theological coherence means that eschatological claims must align with core doctrines—such as the nature of Christ's person and work, the meaning of justification by faith (Romans 5:1), and the relationship between law and grace (Galatians 3). A model that compromises justification by faith in order to support a golden-age paradigm risks undermining the gospel itself. Fourth, historical continuity recognizes that no view springs into existence fully formed in the twenty-first century—each position must show a historical lineage of interpreters, responding to prior debates rather than reinventing the wheel. When a contemporary writer proposes a novel timeline of tribulation events, the question becomes whether that timeline builds on—or abandons—centuries of theological reflection. Fifth, pastoral viability gauges whether a model fosters healthy Christian living, offering hope without fostering escapism, fostering engagement without fostering triumphalism, and fostering realism without fostering despair. This criterion looks closely at how each position forms believers' worship, ethics, and sense of mission. Sixth, missional effectiveness asks whether a given eschatological vision galvanizes believers to share the gospel and serve their neighbors, in line with Jesus' Great Commission (Matthew 28:18–20). Finally, cultural impact assesses how a model interacts with broader society—does it encourage responsible stewardship of creation (Genesis 2:15), advocate for the oppressed (Isaiah 1:17), and cultivate peacemaking (Matthew 5:9), or does it inadvertently promote indifference or coercion? By applying these criteria consistently, readers can measure each millennial model not by rhetoric or popularity but by robust biblical, historical, theological, and practical standards. Having established these yardsticks, we next explain how readers can navigate the structure of this book and make the most of its study aids.

### 1.8.3 How to Use This Book—Reader Pathways and Study Aids

Recognizing that readers approach eschatology from varying starting points—some novices seeking introductory clarity, others pastors wanting sermon illustrations, still others scholars wanting deep research—this volume is designed with multiple navigational pathways. Each chapter begins with a concise overview that orients the reader to its key questions and outlines the learning objectives. For those new to eschatology, "Primer" sidebars appear throughout, offering definitions of essential terms—such as "parousia," "tribulation," and "binding of Satan"—with concise scriptural citations (e.g., 1 Thessalonians 4:16–17; Revelation 20:1–3). Visual timelines and comparison tables illustrate how different models sequence events, enabling visual learners to track distinctions at a glance. For pastors and small-group leaders, each chapter concludes with a "Pastoral Focus" section that highlights practical applications—sermon outlines, worship planning suggestions, and counseling tips—grounded in that chapter's content. Study questions encourage readers to reflect on passages like Daniel 7:13–14 and Revelation 20:4–6, asking how each model's interpretation affects personal devotion and corporate worship. For scholars, extensive footnotes and recommended reading lists provide pathways to deeper exploration, pointing to key works by scholars such as G. K. Beale on Revelation and David Chilton on postmillennialism. Glossary entries at the back of the book define technical terms and list prominent proponents of each view—e.g., John Nelson Darby for dispensational premillennialism or John Owen for historic premillennialism. An interactive online resource (accessible via a QR code) houses updated bibliographies, article discussions, and video interviews with theologians across traditions, enabling readers to stay current as the field evolves. By offering this variety of study aids, the book accommodates seasoned theologians, seminary students, congregational leaders, and lay readers alike. After explaining these reader pathways, the final subsection invites all readers to engage in an eschatology of charity—modeling respectful dialogue and mutual learning across differences.

**Conclusion** Having surveyed the origins and contours of millennial thought—from the apocalyptic yearnings of Second Temple Judaism to the allegorical readings of the medieval church, from Reformation debates to contemporary global perspectives—we gain a clearer sense of why every generation must articulate its hope for the future. The study of the millennium is not an isolated theological sidebar; it is woven into our understanding of God's unfolding redemptive plan, encompassing Israel's calling, Christ's present reign, and the ultimate restoration of all things. By tracing the hermeneutical frameworks that readers bring to Scripture, by reflecting on how eschatology influences personal piety and public engagement, and by charting the ways popular culture both echoes and distorts biblical imagery, we have prepared ourselves to evaluate each millennial model on its biblical fidelity, historical credibility, and pastoral fruitfulness.

As we move forward, the goal is not merely to identify which system best honors the text, but to foster a posture of mutual respect in which believers hold their convictions humbly and listen to one another charitably. The church's unity does not require uniformity of eschatological timelines, but it does call us to lift one another in love as we await the Day when the dead are raised, every tear is wiped away, and Christ's kingdom is fully revealed. With this foundation established, readers are equipped to engage the detailed explorations of premillennialism, postmillennialism, and amillennialism in the chapters ahead—each of which will consider how particular interpretations fulfill biblical promises and shape the life of the redeemed community.

# Chapter 2 - Hermeneutical Foundations

Before embarking on a detailed comparison of premillennial, postmillennial, and amillennial positions, it is vital to recognize that every eschatological system grows out of particular ways of reading Scripture. How one approaches biblical prophecy—whether as plain speech calling for a straightforward fulfillment, rich symbolism inviting multiple layers of meaning, or types pointing forward to Christ—profoundly shapes conclusions about the nature and timing of the millennium. In this chapter, we address the interpretive assumptions and methods that underpin these divergent views, examining how grammatical–historical exegesis, sensitivity to genre, and awareness of canonical context guard against reading texts in isolation or imposing modern ideas onto ancient visions. We explore the tension between literal, figurative, and typological senses, showing how each mode of reading offers both opportunities and pitfalls when handling symbolic apocalyptic texts. We then turn to the larger theological frameworks—covenant and dispensational paradigms—that inform how readers understand God's unfolding purposes for Israel and the church, highlighting how these systems frame prophetic timetables and influence expectations for Christ's reign. Finally, we consider how chronological markers, numeric symbolism, and the book of Revelation's interlocking patterns function within broader literary structures. By laying out these hermeneutical foundations, this chapter aims not to decide every interpretive question in advance but to equip readers with the analytic tools necessary to engage Scripture faithfully, discern how various methods yield different millennial chronologies, and appreciate why these issues matter for worship, mission, and Christian living.

## 2.1 Mapping the Hermeneutical Landscape

**2.1.1 Theological Presuppositions and the Act of Reading** Every act of biblical interpretation begins with theological presuppositions that shape how readers approach the text. These presuppositions include beliefs about the nature of Scripture as divinely inspired (2 Timothy 3:16), the character of God as revealed through both the Old and New Testaments (Isaiah 55:8–9), and convictions regarding the reliability and authority of the biblical authors. Such foundational assumptions influence whether a reader leans toward a more literal or more symbolic understanding of prophecy. For instance, one who presupposes that God's promises to Israel remain valid in a literal sense will read passages like Ezekiel 37 and Amos 9 through a different lens than someone who views those promises as fulfilled typologically in the church. Readers also bring prior beliefs about God's character—His holiness, justice, and mercy— which guide them to expect consistency across biblical genres. Those convinced that God is supremely consistent will be wary of interpretations that seem to present Him acting in contradictory ways in Old Testament versus New Testament contexts. Such readers will insist on continuity in how biblical covenants are understood, even as they wrestle with discontinuities in historical fulfillments. Theological presuppositions further include views on human sinfulness and divine sovereignty, which frame how one interprets passages about Israel's unfaithfulness and God's future restoration. Believing that mankind is incapable of self-redemption without divine intervention (Romans 3:23–24) colors interpretations of prophetic timetables: readers who stress divine sovereignty will see fulfillment unfolding according to God's predetermined plan rather than human agendas. Those who emphasize human agency might focus on the church's role in hastening the millennium by evangelism and social reform. Personal spiritual experiences and denominational loyalties also constitute theological presuppositions that shape reading habits. A pastor who has long preached an imminent rapture may be predisposed to hear Revelation 3 as a call to immediate readiness rather than as symbolic language addressing churches in Asia Minor. Conversely, someone raised in a Reformed tradition might emphasize covenant continuity when reading Daniel's seventy weeks (Daniel 9:24–27) and find it difficult to accept a sharp dispensational break between Israel and the church. Recognizing these underlying assumptions is crucial because they determine which interpretive methods one regards as valid— whether allegorical, literal-historical, or typological. They also affect how readers respond to disputed texts, such as Matthew 24:29–31, where Jesus speaks of cosmic signs. A reader presupposing a symbolic hermeneutic might interpret those signs as metaphors for spiritual realities, whereas someone presupposing a literal future fulfillment might expect actual astronomical disturbances before the Second Coming. The act of reading, therefore, is never neutral; it is filtered through our convictions about who God is, how He has acted in history, and how the Bible should be read. Identifying and reflecting on these presuppositions allows interpreters to test them against Scripture rather than allowing unexamined biases to dictate conclusions. In turn, such self-awareness helps readers navigate controversies, engage respectfully with other perspectives, and adjust their approaches if they discover inconsistencies between their presuppositions and the biblical text. With theological assumptions laid bare, we turn next to the importance of considering the entire canon when interpreting individual passages—a practice that guards against isolated proof-texting and fosters a richer, more coherent understanding of Scripture.

**2.1.2 Canonical Context and Intertextual Echoes** Interpreting any biblical passage responsibly requires situating it within the larger canonical context, recognizing that Scripture is not a collection of disconnected fragments but a unified narrative of creation, fall, redemption, and consummation. When Jesus stands before two disciples on the road to Emmaus and expounds "in all the Scriptures the things concerning himself" (Luke 24:27), He exemplifies intertextual interpretation—showing that Old Testament passages find their true meaning in Him. Similarly, John commends believers to search the Scriptures because they testify of Christ (John 5:39), underscoring that any single text gains fuller clarity when read alongside related passages. This canonical approach discourages proof-texting, where interpreters lift a verse out of context to support preconceived positions. Instead, reading Daniel 7's vision of the four beasts alongside Revelation 13's composite beast fosters a broader understanding of apocalyptic imagery than reading either in isolation. Likewise, recognizing that Revelation 21's "new heavens and new earth" echoes Isaiah 65:17 and 66:22 provides assurance that God's redemptive plan flows consistently from Old Testament prophecy into New Testament fulfillment. Intertextual echoes also operate through typological motifs that span the canon: the exodus narrative in Exodus 12 prefigures Christ's sacrificial death (1 Corinthians 5:7), while wisdom literature's personification of Lady Wisdom in Proverbs 8 informs New Testament depictions of Christ as the Wisdom of God (1 Corinthians 1:24). Reading Psalm 2's description of the Son's enthronement alongside Psalm 110's promise of priestly rule and Hebrews 5's application to Jesus deepens the theological comprehension of Christ's kingly and priestly office. Interpreting prophetic timetables requires weaving together Daniel's seventy weeks (Daniel 9:24–27), Zechariah's visions (Zechariah 14), and New Testament references (Revelation 11:2–3) to discern coherent patterns rather than forcing one text to stand alone. Canonical context highlights how New Testament authors assume their readers know the Old Testament, as seen when Paul invokes Joel 2:28–32 to explain Spirit-baptism in Acts 2:16–21. Similar echoes appear when John's vision of the slain Lamb in Revelation 5 recalls Isaiah 53's suffering servant, showing that John intends his hearers to connect these passages. When interpreting the millennium, such intertextual connections become indispensable: a premillennialist draws on Isaiah 11's promise of a wolf dwelling with a lamb to envision a literal era of peace on earth, while an amillennialist reads Isaiah 11 as fulfilled in Christ's present reign. Postmillennialists might point to Habakkuk 2:14's "the earth shall be filled with the knowledge of the glory of the Lord" as an already-but-not-yet description of the church's mission. In each case, comparing related texts safeguards interpreters from drawing idiosyncratic conclusions divorced from the larger biblical story. Canonical context also includes the recognition that later revelations sometimes recast earlier promises: the New Covenant in Jeremiah

31:31–34 finds definitive fulfillment in the blood of Christ (Luke 22:20; Hebrews 8:6–13), demonstrating that God's people must read prior covenants in light of their Christological culmination. By attending to these intertextual echoes, readers cultivate a hermeneutical posture that honors Scripture's unity and resists fragmentation. As this approach prepares us to handle diverse genres and symbolic language, the next section emphasizes the importance of distinguishing narrative, prophetic, poetic, and apocalyptic forms—a crucial step in reading Revelation and Daniel with sensitivity to genre conventions.

**2.1.3 Genre Sensitivity—Narrative, Prophecy, Poetry, and Apocalypse** Recognizing the genre of a biblical text is essential for determining its interpretive rules. Narrative passages, such as the Exodus account in Exodus 3–14, convey historical events through story, character development, and theological reflection. When reading narrative, interpreters focus on identifying historical context, authorial intent, and theological themes without imposing allegorical or symbolic readings unless the narrative itself indicates such dimensions (e.g., the parable-like character of Jonah's story). By contrast, prophetic literature—such as Isaiah, Jeremiah, and Ezekiel—combines oracles, symbolic actions, and poetic imagery to communicate God's message to Israel and the nations. Prophetic texts often employ metaphorical language (e.g., a "vineyard" representing Israel, Isaiah 5:1–7) to critique covenant unfaithfulness, while simultaneously promising future restoration (e.g., Isaiah 40:1–5). Interpreting prophecy demands attentiveness to both immediate historical situations (e.g., the Assyrian threat in Isaiah 7–8) and dual referents that may include near-term fulfillment and far-off eschatological fulfillment (e.g., Immanuel prophecies in Isaiah 7:14; Matthew 1:23). Poetry, as seen extensively in the Psalms and Song of Solomon, uses parallelism, metaphor, and emotive language to express worship, lament, or wisdom. A psalmist's declaration that "the mountains might flow down at your presence" (Psalm 114:4) should not be taken as a literal description of tectonic activity but as a vivid way of celebrating God's enthronement. Similarly, Proverbs 26:4–5 contains seemingly contradictory injunctions—answering a fool according to his folly, and not answering a fool—teaching that wisdom sometimes requires discerning which proverb applies in a given situation. Thus, genre sensitivity prevents misreading poetic hyperbole as prophecy. Apocalyptic literature, found principally in

Daniel 7–12 and Revelation 1–22, uses highly symbolic imagery—beasts, horns, seals, and number symbolism—to depict cosmic conflict, divine judgment, and ultimate restoration. Apocalyptic texts often resist linear chronological sequencing, instead providing kaleidoscopic visions that reveal heavenly realities (Daniel 7:13–14; Revelation 4–5) and earth's destiny (Daniel 12:1–3; Revelation 21–22). Recognizing that apocalyptic is shaped by near-eastern symbolic patterns—such as the use of "four" to denote universality (Daniel 7:2; Revelation 7:1)—guides interpreters to seek underlying theological truths rather than constructing literal calendars. Without genre sensitivity, an interpreter might read Daniel 7's four beasts as four specific world empires applying precisely to Babylon, Medo-Persia, Greece, and Rome, or as symbolic representatives of all earthly kingdoms in every age. Similarly, one might misread Revelation 13's sea beast rising from the sea as an actual seven-headed monster emerging from the Mediterranean rather than as a symbol of oppressive worldly power. Genre awareness also helps delineate the author's intent: while a narrative author aims to recount events that reveal God's providential activity, a prophetic author seeks to summon repentance or assure future hope, and an apocalyptic author aims to encourage perseverance by unveiling heavenly realities. Each genre calls for different exegetical tools—historical-critical methods for narrative, form criticism for poetry, and symbolic/thematic analysis for apocalyptic. Failing to account for genre can lead to interpretive confusion: e.g., reading Jesus' parable of the wheat and tares (Matthew 13:24–30) as a literal agricultural forecast rather than as an allegory about the coexistence of good and evil until the harvest. By sensitivity to genre, interpreters honor the distinctive voice of each biblical writer, allowing Scripture to speak on its own terms. As we move into section 2.2, this foundational understanding of genre equips readers to apply more precise methods—such as grammatical-historical exegesis, literal sense identification, and symbolic analysis—especially when handling complex prophetic and apocalyptic passages that bear on the millennium debate.

## 2.2 Literal, Figurative, and Typological Readings

### 2.2.1 Principles of Grammatical–Historical Exegesis

Grammatical–historical exegesis seeks to uncover the original meaning of a biblical text by considering its grammar, syntax, vocabulary, and historical context. This method assumes that Scripture is both the Word of God and a product of its time, written in specific historical and cultural circumstances. Applying grammatical-historical exegesis begins with analyzing the text's original languages—Hebrew, Aramaic, and Greek—examining key terms and linguistic structures. For instance, understanding that the Hebrew word "olam" can mean "age," "eternity," or "long duration" informs how one interprets promises in Genesis 9:16 about God's covenant with Noah. Recognizing that Revelation was composed in Koine Greek guides interpreters to consider how first-century readers in Asia Minor would have understood terms like "logos" (Word) or "ekklesia" (church). Historical research is the next critical step: knowing that Daniel was written during the Babylonian exile, for example, helps readers understand the urgency behind chapters 1–6, while chapters 7–12 were likely shaped by Maccabean persecution. By situating texts within their ancient Near Eastern or Greco-Roman contexts, interpreters appreciate why certain images—lion, bear, leopard—evoke memories of Assyria, Babylon, and Persia (Daniel 7:4–7). Applying grammatical-historical principles also requires attention to literary context: identifying the broader section of Scripture—whether Torah, wisdom literature, prophets, gospels, or epistles—guides interpretation. When Paul quotes Isaiah 40:13 in Romans 11:34 to illustrate that no one can fathom God's counsel, recognizing that Isaiah's context in chapter 40 is a message of comfort to exiled Judah helps interpreters see how Paul applies the text to Gentile inclusion. Similarly, noting that Jesus quoted Psalm 118:22–23 in Matthew 21:42 to describe Himself as the rejected stone reveals how the grammatical structure of the psalm sheds light on Christ's messianic identity. Grammatical-historical exegesis remains sensitive to authorial intent: interpreters ask, "What did the original author intend to communicate to the original audience?" In the case of Daniel 9:24–27, the question becomes whether the seventy weeks are presented as a precise timetable for first-century events or a broader prophetic pattern. This approach also insists on internal consistency within Scripture: interpreters avoid interpretations that force a text to contradict clear statements elsewhere. For instance, if Genesis 6:5–7 emphasizes the universality of human wickedness, one cannot invent a reading of Revelation 20:2–3 that suggests many righteous individuals remain hidden during the binding of Satan. Instead, the grammatical-historical approach encourages cross-examination of texts—let scripture interpret scripture (1 Corinthians 2:13). By grounding interpretation in language, context, and literary setting, this method guards against overly speculative readings that read modern concerns back into the text. It also allows interpreters to see texts as living sermons to their original audiences while simultaneously remaining normative for contemporary faith and practice. With these principles clarified, we transition to a detailed examination of what constitutes a literal reading of Scripture, distinguishing it from figurative or symbolic senses.

**2.2.2 Defining the "Literal Sense": Textual Meaning vs. Event Fulfillment** The notion of a "literal sense" has often been misunderstood, with some equating it with insisting that every statement must be physically descriptive—an approach that can hamper recognition of metaphor and symbolism inherent in biblical language. A more nuanced definition understands the literal sense as the meaning intended by the human author under divine inspiration, conveyed through normal semantic and grammatical conventions of the original audience. Thus, when Jesus says, "I am the bread of life" (John 6:35), a literal reading does not interpret this statement as claiming that Jesus is a loaf of wheat, but rather as communicating that He sustains spiritual life in a way analogous to how bread sustains physical life. In this sense, literal reading respects genre and rhetorical devices: recognizing that metaphors, similes, and hyperbole are employed for emphasis without sacrificing authorial intent. Old Testament prophetic texts often combine literal promises with symbolic imagery. When Jeremiah prophesies that "I will gather you out of all the countries where I have driven you" (Jeremiah 29:14), the literal sense acknowledges God's promise of national restoration to geographic Israel. Yet Jeremiah also employs poetic parallelism and kinesthetic imagery—rivers of blessing (Jeremiah 31:12)—that convey blessings tangibly rather than literally requiring water flows. A literal-grammatical reading thus sees the promise as historical or future event that God would act to regather His people (Jeremiah 31:8–9), even if symbolic language enriches the description. Distinguishing textual meaning from event fulfillment also matters when interpreting messianic prophecies. Isaiah 7:14's prophecy of a virgin bearing a son called Immanuel has a literal sense in its immediate context—referring to a young woman whose child served as a sign for King Ahaz—while also carrying a broader fulfillment in Christ's birth (Matthew 1:22–23). This multi-layered fulfillment does not void the original meaning but enlarges it through a "second meaning" (sensus plenior) discovered in the life of Jesus. When interpreting Daniel 9's timeline, a literal description of "seventy weeks" (often understood as seventy sets of seven years) carries a straightforward meaning in the Hebrew text, but interpretive debates arise over whether those "weeks" represent literal years or symbolic periods. A strictly literal chronological approach would insist on counting seventy literal weeks of years, while a more symbolic approach might allow for flexible application. Distinguishing the literal sense helps interpreters avoid the error of pressing symbolic texts into concrete modern events simply because of an assumed necessity for literal fulfillment. For example, Revelation 6's four horsemen—when read literally—would present four actual horses carrying riders representing conquest, war, famine, and death. Yet a more balanced literal-grammatical approach recognizes that John's audience would have understood horses metaphorically as emblems of imperial power (Revelation 6:2, "conquer" as a cavalry commander's banner) rather than as modern military tanks bearing riders with rifles. By contrast, a purely allegorical reading that insists on finding hidden meanings behind every symbol risks inventing interpretations unsupported by the text and ignoring the author's clear statements. A healthy literal sense, then, means seeking the text's plain meaning in its immediate literary and historical context while leaving room for divinely intended layers, such as the prophetic anticipation of Christ. As we move into the realm of apocalyptic literature—with its dense symbolism—we will see how literal-grammatical exegesis helps determine when an image should be read as concrete event, symbolic portrayal, or typological foreshadowing.

### 2.2.3 The Role of Symbolism in Apocalyptic Literature

Apocalyptic literature, by its very nature, communicates divine truths through vivid, often bizarre symbolism intended to transcend temporal boundaries and speak to cosmic realities. Daniel 7's beasts, each with multiple heads and horns, would have reminded first-century readers of powerful, oppressive empires—symbolic portrayals that carry deeper theological messages about human kingdoms under God's sovereign judgment. When Daniel writes that the horn "had eyes like a man and a mouth speaking arrogantly" (Daniel 7:8), he is not offering a zoological description but a literary portrait of a boastful ruler whose cunning authority would oppress God's people. Similarly, John's seven-sealed scroll in Revelation 5 suggests a revelation hidden in heaven's courts, not a literal parchment with seven wax seals. Apocalyptic authors frequently borrow images from earlier prophetic works, reworking them for new audiences. Ezekiel 1's description of living creatures with four faces and wheels within wheels provides a template for John's four living creatures around God's throne (Revelation 4:6–8), both icons pointing to the otherworldly nature of God's heavenly court. Recognizing these intertextual echoes helps interpreters see that symbols resonate with prior scriptural contexts, enriching theological meaning rather than demanding strict literalization. Symbolism in apocalyptic literature often employs numeric imagery to convey theological perfection or judgment. The use of the number seven in Revelation—seven seals, seven trumpets, seven bowls—is not a literal requirement that there be exactly seven objects, but a symbolic signal of completeness or divine orchestration (Revelation 1:4; 21:9). Likewise, the "one thousand years" in Revelation 20:2 can be understood symbolically as a long, complete period under Christ's reign rather than a precise chronological thousand. Interpreters must consider how these numbers function within a literary system designed to reveal spiritual realities beyond human perception. Animals in apocalyptic literature also carry symbolic weight: the lamb with seven horns and seven eyes in Revelation 5:6 symbolizes Christ's perfect power (horns) and knowledge (eyes), not a literal lamb with extra appendages. As readers encounter the dragon in Revelation 12—"that ancient serpent, who is called the Devil and Satan" (Revelation 12:9)—they recognize the dragon as a symbolic embodiment of cosmic evil rooted in Genesis 3's serpent motif. Identifying such symbolic layers requires familiarity with Old Testament imagery and an understanding of how first-century apocalyptic communities communicated under persecution. Without attending to symbolism, readers might mistakenly expect literal dragons to emerge or become preoccupied with physical reconstructions of John's vision. Symbolism also bridges heaven and earth, pointing to realities that lie beyond immediate human experience. When John sees "a new heaven and a new earth" (Revelation 21:1), he communicates the profound truth that God will ultimately renew all creation, even as the metaphor draws on Isaiah 65:17's prophetic vision. Such symbolic language challenges interpreters to discern theological truths rather than to track down literal antecedents. Recognizing the role of symbolism in apocalyptic literature thus guards against misinterpretations that confuse metaphorical imagery with literal events. It also invites readers to engage imaginatively with the text, trusting that symbols invite participation in a cosmic drama whose culmination transcends current human limitations. As we move toward typology, we will see that symbols not only convey meaning in their immediate context but also point forward to deeper fulfillments throughout redemptive history.

**2.2.4 Typology, Analogy, and Extended Metaphor** Typology in Scripture occurs when events, persons, or institutions in the Old Testament prefigure greater realities fulfilled in Christ and the New Testament community. The story of Abraham's near-sacrifice of Isaac (Genesis 22) functions as a type of God the Father offering His own Son (John 3:16). Isaac's willing submission and Abraham's provision of a ram (Genesis 22:8, 13) serve as analogies for Christ's obedience and God's provision of Himself as the substitute sacrifice. Recognizing Isaac as a type clarifies how New Testament writers draw on that story to explain Christ's atoning work (Hebrews 11:17–19; 1 Peter 1:18–19). Similarly, Joseph's betrayal by his brothers (Genesis 37) and subsequent elevation in Egypt anticipate the betrayal and exaltation of Christ. Hebrews 2:10 and Acts 2:36 allude to themes of suffering and exaltation, making Joseph's life a typological lens for understanding Christ. Typological interpretation extends to institutions: Israel's tabernacle or Solomon's temple served as types of God's presence with His people. When Hebrews 8:5 describes the earthly tabernacle as a "copy and shadow of the heavenly things," it signals that the physical structure was intended to point to Christ as the ultimate meeting point between heaven and earth. Likewise, the Day of Atonement ritual (Leviticus 16) becomes a type of Christ's priestly intercession, fulfilling what the high priest symbolically enacted. Readers who attend to typology see how the Old Testament's sacrificial system foreshadows the once-for-all offering of Christ (Hebrews 9:11–14), avoiding attempts to reinstate ritual animal sacrifices in a future millennial temple as though no typological fulfillment had occurred. Analogy operates when Scripture draws parallels without insisting on one-to-one correspondence. For example, David's role as shepherd-king in Psalm 23 serves as an analogy for Christ's shepherding ministry (John 10:14–16), but the analogy does not collapse David and Christ into the same person or timeline. Extended metaphors—such as Paul's portrayal of the church as the body of Christ (1 Corinthians 12:12–27)—build on typological foundations while exploring complex relational dynamics. The "body" metaphor captures unity and diversity simultaneously: each believer has a unique function, yet all share in the life of Christ. Extended metaphors also appear in John 15's "vine and branches" discourse, where Jesus explicates how abiding in Him produces spiritual fruit. The metaphor is not a type in the strict sense but employs agrarian imagery familiar to first-century Galileans to teach profound theological truths about dependence and productivity. Recognizing these rhetorical devices helps interpreters avoid conflating typology with allegory, in which every detail supposedly carries a hidden meaning. Proper typological interpretation honors the historical distinctiveness of types while acknowledging their ultimate fulfillment in Christ and the church. When interpreting passages that bear on the millennium, understanding typology prevents a strictly literal expectation of every Old Testament type reappearing in the same form. For instance, the "booth of David" in Amos 9:11, understood typologically in Acts 15:16–17 as the church's expansion, should not be read as a call to rebuild David's palace in Jerusalem. Similarly, Ezekiel 40–48's temple vision, whether read literally or typologically, must be weighed against New Testament teaching that Christ fulfills the role of the true temple (John 2:19–21; 1 Peter 2:4–5). When interpreters skillfully employ typology, analogy, and extended metaphor, they honor both the text's immediate meaning and its broader redemptive significance. As we prepare to examine a concrete case study of the temple motif across Testaments, readers will see how these hermeneutical tools operate in practice—illustrating how a single theme evolves from a physical structure to a spiritual reality.

## 2.3 Covenant, Kingdom, and Dispensational Paradigms

### 2.3.1 Classical Covenant Theology—Unity of Redemptive History

Classical covenant theology understands redemptive history through overarching covenants that unify the biblical narrative rather than fragment it into distinct epochs. Foundational to this approach are the covenants of works and grace. The covenant of works, implicit in Genesis 2:16–17, sets the terms for Adam's obedience and introduces the principle that life is contingent on perfect adherence to God's commands. When Adam fails, humanity experiences alienation from God, illustrated in Genesis 3. The covenant of grace emerges in Genesis 3:15—the protoevangelium—where God promises that the seed of the woman will crush the serpent's head. This promise marks the beginning of a single Redemptive Covenant that runs through all subsequent covenants: Abrahamic, Mosaic, Davidic, and new covenant, each expressing facets of God's gracious plan to redeem fallen humanity. Covenant theologians emphasize that these covenants are not separate programs for distinct groups but progressive revelations of one unified covenant unfolding over history. For example, the Abrahamic covenant in Genesis 12:1–3 promises land, seed, and blessing, foreshadowing the ultimate blessing in Christ (Galatians 3:16). The Mosaic covenant (Exodus 19:5–6) functions as a covenant of law that highlights human inability to keep God's commands perfectly and points to the need for a greater covenant through Christ (Galatians 3:19). The Davidic covenant (2 Samuel 7:12–16) promises an eternal throne through David's lineage, fulfilled in Jesus (Luke 1:32–33). Finally, the new covenant (Jeremiah 31:31–34; Luke 22:20) seals the work of Christ's atonement, writing God's law on believers' hearts and uniting humanity as God's people. In this model, Israel and the church are seen as one people of God, the former serving as a type of the latter. When Paul writes in 2 Corinthians 3:6 that Christ "has made us competent as ministers of a new covenant," he situates believers within the same covenant framework that began with Abraham, ensuring continuity across Testaments. Covenant theologians argue that promises to Israel find ultimate fulfillment in the church's identity—e.g., Galatians 3:29, "If you belong to Christ, then you are Abraham's offspring, heirs according to promise." This unity of redemptive history rejects the idea that God maintains two separate peoples (Israel and the church) with distinct destinies; rather, he works through the church as the true Israel of God (Galatians 6:16). In covenant theology, eschatological hopes such as resurrection and eternal blessing are applied to all believers—Jew and Gentile—without requiring a future ethnic restoration for Israel alone. Passages like Daniel 7:27's promise of an everlasting kingdom are read in light of Christ's present heavenly reign (Ephesians 1:20–23) and anticipate the ultimate renewal of creation (Revelation 21–22).

As a result, covenant theologians often adopt an amillennial position, seeing the millennium as the church age itself (Revelation 20:1–6) and understanding the "binding of Satan" at the cross (Colossians 2:15) as inaugurating Christ's kingdom in a spiritual sense. Having established the classical covenant framework, we transition to explore how new-covenant theology and progressive covenantalism modify or nuance these unified readings, especially as contemporary scholars seek to honor both continuity and diversity within God's redemptive purposes.

### 2.3.2 New-Covenant Theology and Progressive Covenantalism
New-covenant theology emerges within broader covenantal discussions by emphasizing the primacy of the new covenant inaugurated by Christ (Jeremiah 31:31–34; Luke 22:20). Advocates argue that all previous covenants find their ultimate meaning and fulfillment in the new covenant, reshaping how one reads Old Testament promises. Unlike classic covenant theology, which often posits multiple covenants simultaneously in force (e.g., Abrahamic, Mosaic, Davidic), new-covenant proponents see the new covenant as fulfilling and superseding previous covenant forms. For instance, where classical covenant theology might hold that the Mosaic covenant remains a continuing standard for God's people, new-covenant theology asserts that Christ's atoning sacrifice renders the Mosaic covenant obsolete (Hebrews 8:13). This approach places singular emphasis on Christ as the mediator of the new covenant (Hebrews 9:15), with Old Testament shadows serving purely as typological foreshadows (Colossians 2:16–17). Progressive covenantalism builds on this by acknowledging that while the new covenant is supreme, God's covenants reveal an unfolding economy in which certain elements remain distinct yet complementary. Progressive covenantalists affirm Israel's unique calling under the Abrahamic covenant while maintaining that Gentile inclusion in Christ does not negate ethnic Israel's role in redemptive history. They often point to Romans 11:25–27's promise that "all Israel will be saved" as evidence that ethnic Israel retains a corporate future hope within God's covenantal plan. At the same time, they insist that church and Israel share significantly in covenant blessings—a middle way between classical covenant theology's downplaying of Israel's unique future and dispensationalism's sharp distinction between Israel's covenant and the church's program. In progressive covenantalism, the Davidic covenant's promise of an enduring

throne is understood as fulfilled in Christ's reign over God's people now, yet still anticipating a future revelation of that reign in the new heavens and new earth (Revelation 21:5). This model recognizes that Old Testament genealogies and temple practices functioned to support Israel's typological role, even as the new covenant's inauguration transforms those types into fuller realities (Hebrews 8– 10). Jeremiah 31's promise of a heartfelt law written on Israel's mind and heart (Jeremiah 31:33) becomes normative for both Jew and Gentile in Christ, so that church worship embodies the new covenant worship first promised to Israel. Progressive covenantalism often results in an amillennial or modified postmillennial eschatology, viewing millennial imagery as symbolic of the present age in which Christ reigns from heaven. For example, progressive covenantalists interpret Isaiah 65's vision of a renewed earth as a future reality inaugurated at Christ's return but experienced partially through the church's redemptive mission—an "already/not yet" dynamic. This approach helps reconcile passages like Zechariah 14:9, which speak of the Lord's reign over all the earth, with New Testament texts that describe Christ as reigning now in the church (Ephesians 1:22). By emphasizing the new covenant's centrality, this model encourages Christians to see how Israel's story shapes the church's identity without forcing a redundant future for Old Testament institutions. As we transition to classic dispensationalism, readers will observe how that framework departs radically from these covenantal continuities, insisting instead on a sharp demarcation between Israel and the church.

**2.3.3 Classic Dispensationalism—Epochal Discontinuity** Classic dispensationalism organizes redemptive history into distinct dispensations—administrative periods during which God relates to humanity in different ways. The most common scheme identifies seven dispensations: Innocence, Conscience, Human Government, Promise (Patriarchal), Law, Grace (Church Age), and Kingdom (Millennium). In each dispensation, God tests humanity according to dispensation-specific principles, ultimately finding each generation or covenant community wanting (Romans 3:23). Dispensationalists emphasize that Scripture must be read literally unless context dictates otherwise, applying a "plain sense" approach that anticipates future, literal fulfillment of Old Testament promises to Israel. For example, when God promises land to Abraham's descendants in Genesis 12:7, a classic dispensationalist insists that promise remains unfulfilled until a literal restoration of Israel's land under the millennial kingdom. They argue that passages such as Ezekiel 37's vision of dry bones rising correspond to a future national revival of ethnic Israel rather than a symbolic representation of spiritual regeneration. One hallmark of classic dispensationalism is its radical distinction between Israel and the church. Dispensationalists hold that the church, described in Ephesians 3:2 as part of "the dispensation of the mystery" (i.e., the present Church Age), is a parenthesis in God's plan for Israel—temporarily set aside until the church is raptured, as anticipated in 1 Thessalonians 4:16–17. This "secret rapture" concept, popularized by John Nelson Darby and later by the Scofield Reference Bible, posits that believers will be removed from earth prior to a seven-year tribulation period described in Daniel 9:27 and Revelation 6–19. During the tribulation, Israel experiences God's judgments and redemptive dealings according to the Mosaic Law and the yet-unfulfilled covenants Moses mediated. At the end of the tribulation, Christ returns visibly at Armageddon (Revelation 19:11–21) to defeat the Antichrist and establish a literal thousand-year kingdom in Jerusalem. In this millennial kingdom, Israel experiences the fullness of the Abrahamic and Davidic covenants: the temple is rebuilt (Ezekiel 40–48), animal sacrifices are reinstituted (Zechariah 14:21), and David's throne in Jerusalem becomes the center of global worship (Isaiah 2:3; Zechariah 14:16). Classic dispensationalists often identify the Antichrist with the "little horn" of Daniel 7:8, asserting that his emergence initiates the final week of Daniel 9—a seven-year period culminating in Christ's return. During this time, Israel and the nations face unprecedented judgments until the Messiah's arrival ushers in the millennium. Because dispensationalism treats God's program for Israel and the church as distinct, it rejects the idea that promises to Abraham, Moses, or David find fulfillment in the church. Instead, those promises await a future earthly administration. This sharp discontinuity extends to how dispensationalists read pastoral epistles: they see instructions in 1 Timothy and Titus as applying only to the Church Age, not to Israel's kingdom. Critics argue that this fragmentation neglects the unity of Scripture, but adherents claim that it preserves clarity in God's distinct purposes. As readers move to progressive dispensationalism, they will see how some later dispensational scholars modified these strict boundaries while retaining key elements such as the future millennial kingdom and Israel–church distinctions.

**2.3.4 Progressive Dispensationalism—Overlaps and Adjustments** Progressive dispensationalism arises from mid-twentieth-century efforts to address perceived shortcomings in classic dispensationalism while maintaining its basic structure. It affirms that God works in distinct dispensations but emphasizes that these epochs overlap and flow into one another rather than existing in hermetically sealed compartments. For example, progressive dispensationalists argue that the Abrahamic promises began partial fulfillment in the Old Testament, continued through Christ's earthly ministry, and will reach ultimate fulfillment in the future millennium. In contrast to classic dispensationalism's strict parenthesis view, progressive dispensationalism holds that the Church Age is not an interruption of God's program for Israel but a fulfillment of certain Sandemic promises—such as blessings to the Gentiles—anticipated in Isaiah 49:6 and Genesis 12:3. It posits that during the Church Age, the Messiah already reigns spiritually, as Philippians 2:9–11 foreshadows, but that His full, visible reign awaits a future phase. This model allows for partial, progressive fulfillments of prophecy: for instance, the New Testament church experiences the predicted universality of God's worship (Isaiah 2:2–3; Matthew 28:19), even as complete global worship will wait for the millennium (Zechariah 14:16–19). Progressive dispensationalists also retain a future, literal millennium, including a rebuilt temple and restored sacrificial system, but they nuance the relationship between the present and future temple. They often argue that Ezekiel's temple promises partially find fulfillment in the New Testament temple of believers (Ephesians 2:19–22), and that a future temple, if built, functions as a signpost pointing back to Christ's once-for-all atonement (Hebrews 10:1–10) rather than reinitiating sacrificial atonement. Progressive dispensationalism reframes the "kingdom of heaven" proclamations of Jesus (Matthew 4:17) as inaugurating aspects of the future kingdom today—such as the defeat of demonic powers (Colossians 2:15)—without denying that the consummate physical reign awaits the future. This "already/not yet" perspective mirrors insights from covenant theology while preserving dispensational distinctives like a future tribulation and a millennial temple. On the question of Israel and the church, progressive dispensationalists teach that while the church participates in certain aspects of Israel's program now, ethnic Israel still enjoys a corporate future hope distinct from the church's destiny. Romans 11:25–26's promise that "all Israel will be saved" retains literal force in a future tribulation context, yet the olive-tree metaphor indicates that Gentile believers share in the root of Abraham's promise now (Romans 11:17–18). Progressive dispensationalism therefore resists collapse into one-dimensional continuity or discontinuity, instead offering a dynamic interplay between God's purposes for Israel and the church. As a result, postmillennial or amillennial readers may find common ground in the emphasis on partial fulfillments, even as they maintain different views on the nature and timing of ultimate fulfillment. Having explored these adjustments, we now turn to a close examination of the Israel–church relationship through Paul's olive-tree metaphor in Romans 11.

**2.3.5 Israel–Church Relations and the Olive-Tree Metaphor (Romans 11)** In Romans 11, Paul employs the metaphor of an olive tree to illustrate the relationship between ethnic Israel and the church. He explains that some natural branches—ethnic Israel—were broken off due to unbelief (Romans 11:17), while wild olive shoots (Gentile believers) were grafted in among the remaining natural branches (Romans 11:17–18). This picture conveys both separation and connection: Gentiles share in the rich root of covenant promises originally given to Israel (Genesis 12:1–3). Yet Paul warns that Gentile believers must not boast over the broken branches, for "if God did not spare the natural branches, he will not spare you either" (Romans 11:21). This transition from natural to wild shoots underscores the continuity of salvation history—believers, whether Jew or Gentile, participate in God's covenant through faith. At the same time, Paul signals that the broken branches can be grafted back in if they do not persist in unbelief (Romans 11:23). This prospect of restoration—"all Israel will be saved" (Romans 11:26)—speaks to a future collective redemption of ethnic Israel, suggesting that God's covenant promises to Israel have not been abandoned but are held in abeyance until a future turning of Israel to Christ. Covenant theologians interpret Paul's goal in Romans 11 as confirming that the church is the new Israel, fulfilling Old Testament promises in a broader sense (Galatians 3:29). They emphasize that Gentile inclusion does not nullify Israel's covenant but rather expands it, so that Gentiles become heirs together with

Israel of God's promises (Ephesians 3:6). In this view, the olive tree symbolizes one people of God, united by faith rather than ethnicity. Dispensationalists, however, maintain that the olive-tree metaphor underscores both connection and distinction: while Gentiles share in aspects of God's covenant blessings now, ethnic Israel remains God's chosen people with a separate future plan. The promise that "all Israel will be saved" is linked to a future time of national repentance, often associated with the tribulation's climax or Christ's second coming (Daniel 12:1; Zechariah 12:10). Classic dispensationalists see the entire olive tree as representing Israel in her various covenants, with the church grafted in only temporarily until the imminent rapture. Progressive dispensationalists refine this by teaching that while the olive tree's root remains Israel, the wild olive shoots represent Gentiles who are fully integrated and share in the same root benefits even now. Both dispensational systems insist that the acceptance of Gentiles in the olive tree does not negate the future miraculous regrafting of Israel as a unit, which they locate in Romans 11:26–27 as tied to God's final dealings with the Jewish people. Readers who embrace an amillennial perspective often interpret Romans 11 as affirming one people of God through Christ—Jew and Gentile—so that national Israel's promises are inherited by Christ's church, with no separate future ethnic restoration required. They see Paul's mention of "all Israel" as referring to the elect remnant across history, rather than a future mass conversion of ethnic Jews (Romans 11:5). Under this view, the olive-tree metaphor teaches that God's covenant remains faithful to all who are in Christ, with election understood corporately rather than nationally. The diversity of these readings demonstrates how the same metaphor can undergird sharply different eschatological models. By carefully examining Romans 11 within its rhetorical context and intertestamental background, interpreters can discern how Paul simultaneously upholds God's faithfulness to Israel and affirms the church's identity in Christ. As this subsection concludes, readers will be equipped to see how covenantal and dispensational convictions lead to divergent millennial expectations, shaping everything from temple theology to evangelistic urgency.

## 2.4 Interpreting Prophetic Timetables

**2.4.1 The "Already/Not Yet" Tension** The concept of "already/not yet" serves as a hermeneutical key for understanding how prophetic passages can speak both to present realities and future consummations. Jesus' teaching in Luke 17:20–21 illustrates this tension: when the Pharisees asked when the kingdom of God would come, He replied that "the kingdom of God is not coming in ways that can be observed," because it "is in your midst"—a present spiritual reality. Yet in the same discourse He foretells cosmic signs and a coming revealing of the Son of Man (Luke 17:24–30), signaling an eschatological dimension yet ahead. Paul repeatedly navigates this tension, as when he writes in Colossians 1:27 that Christ is "in you, the hope of glory," indicating present possession of eschatological blessing, while in 1 Corinthians 15:23 he describes a future resurrection sequence—"each in his own order"—that points to a future event. Interpreters must grapple with how Revelation 20's binding of Satan (Revelation 20:1–3) can be understood as having begun in Christ's victory on the cross (Colossians 2:15) yet still await final expression in a future millennium. Likewise, passages such as Romans 8:23—"we wait eagerly for adoption as sons, the redemption of our bodies"—underscore that believers enjoy present spiritual adoption but yearn for bodily redemption in the world to come. Prophetic texts in the Old Testament often reflect this same dynamic: Isaiah 65:17 promises that God will create "new heavens and a new earth," a future reality, yet Isaiah 65:25 speaks of "the wolf and the lamb feeding together" in ways that Scripture's writers sometimes apply to present spiritual harmony (Romans 15:12). Preterist approaches, which see most prophecies as fulfilled in the first century, interpret the "already" as largely realized in Christ's first coming and New Testament era, while futurist interpreters see many prophetic passages as having only partial fulfillment thus far. Some postmillennialists argue that the "not yet" refers to a golden age brought about by evangelistic advance and social reform, reading texts such as Psalm 110:1 ("The Lord says to my Lord: 'Sit at my right hand, until I make your enemies your footstool.'") as a present reality that will become a universal historical reality in stages. Amillennialists often hold that the "already" of Christ's heavenly reign (Ephesians 2:6) is balanced by the "not yet" of final judgment

(Revelation 20:11–15). They read Daniel 7's description of "one like a son of man" (Daniel 7:13–14) as inaugurated now, with "everlasting dominion" to be fully expressed at the end. In each case, staying attentive to how biblical authors themselves switch between immediate context and future consummation guards against readings that either spiritualize everything or literalize everything. It is essential to ask how a given text functions within the redemptive storyline: does it primarily comfort a suffering community with present hope, or does it primarily forecast events still to unfold? The epistemological challenge—knowing that a prophecy can legitimately address both present and future—drives interpreters to weave together New Testament commentary (e.g., Hebrews 10:1–10) with Old Testament expectation (e.g., Malachi 3:1–4). A robust "already/not yet" hermeneutic embodies both tension and promise, affirming that the kingdom balances between what Christ has inaugurated by His death and resurrection and what He will consummate at His return (1 Corinthians 15:24–28). This tension yields a biblical posture of hopeful vigilance—watchfulness (Mark 13:33–37) and faithful service (Luke 19:13) during the present age—while living with eager anticipation of the fullness to come (Titus 2:13). Having explored how prophetic passages evoke this dynamic, the next subsection examines how chronology and literary structure in apocalyptic writings further complicate the task of timeline reconstruction.

**2.4.2 Chronology, Recapitulation, and Literary Structure** One of the central challenges in interpreting apocalyptic timetables lies in distinguishing straightforward chronological sequences from recapitulative or cyclical presentations. In Daniel 9:24–27, scholars debate whether the seventy weeks operate as a continuous 490-year timeline or whether they function typologically, representing eras of fulfillment that overlap and point to Christ's atoning work without demanding a precise day-for-year correspondence. Critics of strict chronological readings point out that Daniel often presents visions as thematic recapitulations—Daniel 7 revisits themes from Daniel 2 (a statue representing successive empires), indicating that Daniel's visions may compress or expand events symbolically rather than strictly sequentially. The interlocking structure of Daniel's visions encourages readers to compare images across chapters—beasts, horns, and fiery thrones—rather than forcing a linear alignment with historical dates. Revelation further complicates chronology through recapitulation: John's vision follows cycles of seven seals, seven trumpets, and seven bowls (Revelation 6–16), with each cycle retelling the same cosmic conflict from different angles. For example, the opening of the seventh seal (Revelation 8:1) leads to the seven trumpets, while the seventh trumpet (Revelation 11:15) ushers in the seven bowls, culminating in the final climactic judgments of Revelation 16. These nested cycles resist being read as consecutive seventy-two-hour periods; instead, they function as theological recapitulations that highlight different facets of divine judgment and redemption. Recognizing this structure prevents misreading Revelation 9's locust-like creatures (Revelation 9:1–12) as an event that chronologically follows Revelation 8's trumpet but precedes Revelation 10's mighty angel; rather, these episodes illustrate God's sovereign authority to judge in stages, focusing on spiritual battles rather than calendar specifics. Authors such as N. T. Wright have emphasized that apocalyptic literature should be read on multiple levels—historical, symbolic, and pastoral—rather than as rigid chronological charts. The red-penned, multi-tiered structure of Revelation affirms that chronology in apocalyptic writing often serves rhetorical and theological purposes. When interpreters assume a straightforward timeline, they risk missing how John uses parallelism—such as contrasting the beast from the sea (Revelation 13:1–10) with the beast from the earth (Revelation 13:11–18)—to underscore different dimensions of antichrist power rather than to suggest two separate chronological events. Good expositional work involves charting the text's literary flow: identifying the introductory prologue (Revelation 1:1–8), the letters to the seven churches (Revelation 1:9–3:22), the heavenly vision (Revelation 4:1–5:14), the unfolding cycles of judgment (Revelation 6–19), and the climactic new creation (Revelation 20–22). This macro-structure reminds readers that Revelation's primary function is to encourage perseverance among persecuted Christians (Revelation 1:9, 3:10) by unveiling the definitive victory of Christ, not to provide a blow-by-blow minute-by-minute account of future events. Psalm 90:4's observation that "a thousand years in your sight are but as yesterday when it is past" can caution interpreters against imposing modern chronological expectations onto ancient apocalyptic sequences. Seen this way, chronology in prophetic timetables serves a thematic purpose—illustrating God's ultimate control over history—while recapitulation and literary structure underscore theological truths. Having addressed how chronology, recapitulation, and literary patterns function, the next subsection considers how prophetic perspectives "telescope" events, collapsing long spans into compressed visions.

**2.4.3 Prophetic Perspective and "Telescoping" of Events** The prophetic "telescoping" technique compresses expansive periods or disparate events into a unified vision, conveying theological emphasis rather than precise historical markers. Isaiah 24–27 exemplifies this by presenting judgment and redemption as occurring in swift sequence—"In that day" passages—without specifying temporal gaps, indicating that the prophet intended to emphasize God's total sovereignty rather than a strict timetable. Ezekiel's vision of Gog and Magog (Ezekiel 38–39) similarly telescopes end-time judgments into a single narrative to underscore Yahweh's triumph, even though the identity of "Gog from the land of Magog" likely operates symbolically to represent hostile nations rather than a specific modern geopolitical configuration. In the New Testament, Jesus' Olivet Discourse (Matthew 24:1–25:46) appears to employ telescoping: He speaks of the destruction of the temple (Matthew 24:2) and then describes signs of cosmic upheaval, the coming of the Son of Man, and the parable of the talents as though these events unfold in rapid succession, yet the Gospel authors seem to understand parts as having near-term fulfillment in 70 AD (Mark 13:14, parallels to Luke 21:20–24) and parts as referencing a more distant final consummation (Matthew 24:29–31). This telescoping challenges interpreters to discern where Jesus shifts from addressing first-century disciples to describing eschatological realities at the close of the age. The telescoping of Daniel's seventy weeks offers another example: rather than insisting on a consecutively counted 490-year period, many Jewish interpreters read the "weeks" typologically, finding partial fulfillments in the rebuilding of Jerusalem under Ezra and Nehemiah, and ultimate fulfillment in the coming of Messiah, as argued by commentators like Keil and Delitzsch. Similarly, Revelation's depiction of a millennial reign in Revelation 20 may telescope the ongoing spiritual reign of Christ with saints (Revelation 20:4–6) and the final defeat of Satan (Revelation 20:7–10) to teach theological truths rather than to demand a rigid chronological interlude. Prophetic telescoping often rests on God's perspective, where time appears compressed—cf. 2 Peter 3:8, which explains that "with the Lord a day is like a thousand years." This divine perspective allows prophets to collapse temporal sequences to convey the urgency of repentance or the certainty of divine intervention. As readers navigate telescoped prophecies, they must ask whether the text signals a shift from immediate circumstances to ultimate fulfillment—such as in Joel 2:28–32, where the pouring out of the Spirit (Joel 2:28–29) finds fulfillment at Pentecost (Acts 2:16–21) yet also points to cosmic cataclysms that accompany the day of the Lord (Joel 2:31). Recognizing telescoping prevents misinterpreting transitional phrases such as "last days" (Acts 2:17) as strictly chronological markers confined to one narrow window. By acknowledging that prophets often share an "eagle-eye" view of history, encompassing multiple epochs within a single vision, interpreters can honor the text's theological intent— emphasizing God's sovereignty and the ultimate triumph of His purposes—rather than forcing passages into neat modern chronologies. As we proceed to examine symbolic numbers, readers should appreciate how prophetic telescoping pairs with numeric symbolism to convey theological weight rather than spatio-temporal precision.

**2.4.4 Symbolic Numbers and Apocalyptic Mathematics (e.g., 1,260; 666; 1,000)** Numbers in apocalyptic literature often carry symbolic or thematic significance rather than representing exact numerical values. The number 1,260 (Revelation 11:3; 12:6) corresponds to "forty-two months" (Revelation 11:2, 13:5) and "1,260 days" (Revelation 12:6), invoking Daniel 7's "time, times, and half a time" (Daniel 7:25) to symbolize a period of trial lasting an indeterminate, divinely appointed duration. Rather than suggesting precisely three and a half calendar years, many interpreters see 1,260 as emblematic of a limited span during which evil forces exert temporary dominion before divine intervention restores justice. The number 666, appearing in Revelation 13:18 as "the number of the beast," has generated myriad interpretive proposals, from identifying Nero Caesar (whose name transliterated into Hebrew yields numeric value 666) to representing the ultimate imperfection—falling short of the divine completeness symbolized by seven (cf. Genesis 2:2–3) and recapturing the fallen state of humanity in rebellion. The variant reading 616 in some manuscripts complicates matters, signaling that early Christians understood the number symbolically rather than literally, adapting it for local contexts. The number 1,000, as used in Revelation 20:2–7 and Psalm 50:10, frequently symbolizes fullness, completeness, or spiritual perfection rather than an exact count. When John speaks of Christ reigning 1,000 years with the saints, many amillennialists see 1,000 as a symbolic figure indicating an indefinite ideal reign—i.e., the church age—in which God's people enjoy spiritual victory. Postmillennialists might understand 1,000 figuratively to represent a long era of gospel triumph without demanding precise duration. Historical-critical scholars note that Hebrew poets often employed numbers for rhetorical effect: the book of Kings and Chronicles uses multiples of seven to indicate completeness (e.g., Solomon's seven-year temple construction, 1 Kings 6:38). Recognizing this poetic-numeric pattern helps interpreters see that Revelation's numeric imagery follows Old Testament precedents, inviting readers to focus on theological meaning rather than precise chronography. The seven trumpets, seven seals, and seven bowls of Revelation 8–16 likewise utilize the number seven to signify divine perfection in judgment, with each cycle intensifying the prophetic message. In Daniel 12:11–12, the 1,290 days and 1,335 days represent extended periods of tribulation before deliverance, but their primary function is to convey that God's timing transcends human schedules. Even John's reference to 144,000 sealed servants of God (Revelation 7:4, 14:1) draws on $12 \times 12 \times 1,000$ to symbolize the fullness of God's redeemed community across the twelve tribes, suggesting completeness rather than a literal headcount. These numeric symbols work in tandem with telescoping, as counting days or months can represent thematic epochs rather than contiguous solar years. Interpreters attuned to apocalyptic mathematics ask how numbers function within the text's literary and symbolic system—whether they reinforce themes of perfection (seven), judgment (three and a half), or fullness (twelve, 1,000). Understanding these numbers' symbolic roles prevents readers from constructing speculative date-setting schemes that claim to pinpoint the day or year of Christ's return. Instead, these numbers call readers to trust God's sovereign timing (2 Peter 3:9), recognizing that any attempt to fixate on numeric precision undercuts the urgency of faithful living in the present (Matthew 24:42–44). Having explored how numeric symbolism patterns prophetic timelines, the next subsection provides a comparative look at two key prophetic systems—Daniel's seventy weeks and Revelation's sequences—illuminating how each text uses symbolic time frames to convey divine purposes.

## 2.4.5 Comparative Charts | Daniel's Weeks, Revelation's Days

Constructing comparative charts can help readers visualize how prophetic literature organizes symbolic time frames, highlighting both parallels and divergences between Daniel's and Revelation's approaches. In Daniel 9:24–27, the seventy weeks are presented as "seventy weeks" decreed for Daniel's people and the holy city, with specific objectives—"to finish transgression, to make an end of sins, to atone for iniquity, to bring in everlasting righteousness." Whether interpreted as seventy literal weeks of years or as seventy symbolic periods, this framework conveys a divine timetable for accomplishing God's redemptive purposes. By contrast, Revelation 11–12 uses multiple markers—1,260 days, forty-two months (Revelation 11:2; 12:6), and "time, times, and half a time" (Revelation 12:14)—to indicate periods of persecution and protection for the faithful. Placing these markers side by side allows readers to see that Daniel's week-based scheme focuses on covenantal fulfillment for Israel, while John's day- and month-based scheme portrays cosmic conflict and church endurance. A second chart might compare how Daniel's forty-two months relates to Revelation's forty-two months: both reference a divinely limited span associated with trial. Daniel 7:25 speaks of persecution "for a time, times, and half a time," while Revelation 13:5 notes that the beast "was given authority to act for forty-two months," indicating a period when evil asserts power before divine judgment. Charting these parallels reveals how early Jewish and Christian authors used time imagery to underscore theological points—namely, that human wickedness temporarily prevails but is ultimately defeated. A third comparative chart could place Daniel's timeline in dialogue with Revelation's cycles: Daniel's four beasts (Daniel 7:3–7) correspond to Revelation's seven seals (each seal unleashing various judgments) and the four living creatures in Revelation 4:6–8, emphasizing recurring motifs of divine sovereignty over earthly powers. While Daniel's beasts represent successive empires, John's living creatures praise God's holiness, redirecting focus from historical kingdoms to heavenly worship. By cross-referencing Daniel 7's "one like a son of man" (Daniel 7:13–14) with Revelation 1:13's Son of Man figure among the lampstands, readers discern how Daniel's chapter shapes John's imagery—both promising ultimate triumph for God's Messiah. A fourth chart might align Daniel 12:1–3's promise of deliverance and resurrection with Revelation 20:4–6's first resurrection, showing how Daniel's vision of awakening "many who sleep in the dust of the earth" (Daniel 12:2) prefigures John's depiction of the risen saints reigning with Christ. Such a comparison highlights the continuity of resurrection hope while noting differences in chronology: Daniel does not specify when these events occur, whereas Revelation places them around the thousand-year sequence. Finally, a chart comparing numeric symbolism—Daniel's seventy weeks (Daniel 9:24) and Revelation's sequenced sevens (seven seals, trumpets, bowls)—demonstrates how both authors use multiples of seven to evoke completeness and divine orchestration. Daniel's seventy weeks symbolize a full period of redemptive action for Israel, while Revelation's cycles of seven images symbolize God's comprehensive judgments and restoration plans. By laying out these comparative charts, readers gain clarity on how divergent texts employ time, numbers, and images to convey coherent theological narratives without demanding simplistic one-to-one alignments. This comparative exercise sets the stage for reading Revelation with methodological maturity, which we explore further in section 2.5.

## 2.5 Reading Revelation—Methodological Touchstones

### 2.5.1 Historicist, Futurist, Preterist, and Idealist Approaches

Revelation's rich symbolism has given rise to four major interpretive paradigms: historicist, futurist, preterist, and idealist. Historicists read Revelation as a panoramic prophecy that unfolds through church history, identifying each symbol with specific historical events or figures. For instance, some historicists see the beast of Revelation 13 as the Roman Catholic papacy or various medieval European powers, tracing Revelation's seals, trumpets, and bowls through events such as the fall of the Western Roman Empire, the Reformation, and the French Revolution. In contrast, futurists argue that almost all of Revelation's chapters 4–22 describe events still future to us, reserving the book's fulfillment for a period immediately preceding and including Christ's return. Dispensational premillennialists often adopt a futurist reading, insisting that the seven-year tribulation described in Revelation 6–19 is yet to come and that the church will be "raptured" before or after those judgments. Preterists contend that most of Revelation was fulfilled in the first century, particularly with the destruction of Jerusalem in

70 AD. They link the "abomination of desolation" (Revelation 11:2; 13:14) to the Roman armies in A.D. 70 (Matthew 24:15), believing that John's audience would have immediately recognized many symbols as references to immediate historical circumstances shaping early Christians under imperial persecution. Idealists interpret Revelation primarily as a timeless allegory of the ongoing spiritual conflict between good and evil. Rather than seeking precise historical or future correspondences, idealists view symbols—such as the dragon (Revelation 12) or the harlot Babylon (Revelation 17)—as representing general principles: cosmic evil opposed to God's kingdom and corrupt worldly systems opposed to divine justice. Each approach highlights distinct facets: historicists emphasize the unfolding of redemptive history; futurists focus on eschatological consummation; preterists underscore near-term vindication for first-century believers; idealists draw lessons for contemporary faithfulness amid universal spiritual struggles. Readers must recognize that each method entails particular hermeneutical presuppositions. Historicism often assumes that biblical prophecy maps onto centuries of church history, leading to detailed charts that identify popes, emperors, or revolutions with specific beasts or judgments. Futurism often depends on a strict literalistic approach, anticipating precise fulfillment of numbers and events. Preterism typically highlights immediate literary and historical context, emphasizing that prophecies addressed a persecuted readership under Roman authority. Idealism prioritizes theological and ethical exhortation, applying Revelation's themes to any era where the church faces adversity. These paradigms are not mutually exclusive; some interpreters adopt mixed approaches— such as partial preterism (which sees early chapters fulfilled but later chapters still future) or moderate futurism (assigning some sections symbolic meanings while retaining literal expectations for others). Evaluating each method's strengths and weaknesses involves assessing biblical fidelity, historical plausibility, theological coherence, and pastoral fruitfulness. Importantly, every approach must wrestle with core passages—Revelation 1:3's blessing for "those who read and hear the words of this prophecy" and Revelation 22:18–19's warning against adding to or taking from the text— reminding readers of the gravity of responsible interpretation. As readers move to explore Revelation's literary features, they will see how interlocking cycles and Old Testament echoes shape our

understanding of Revelation's message for its original audience and for subsequent generations of believers.

**2.5.2 Interlocking Cycles and Parallelism in the Apocalypse**
Revelation's structure is characterized by interlocking cycles and parallel movements that communicate its theological vision through recurring patterns. The most obvious of these are the three cycles of seven: the seven seals (Revelation 6–8), the seven trumpets (Revelation 8–11), and the seven bowls (Revelation 15–16). Each cycle intensifies divine judgments upon the earth, yet they also convey progression: the seals introduce foundational judgments, the trumpets escalate to cosmic woes, and the bowls pour out final plagues. John's use of parallelism—revisiting similar themes (e.g., cosmic disturbances, demonic assaults, God's final victory)—reinforces the certainty of God's sovereignty even when events appear chaotic. For example, earthquakes appear under the sixth seal (Revelation 6:12–14), again under the seventh trumpet (Revelation 11:19), and finally under the seventh bowl (Revelation 16:18), each time signifying escalating divine activity that culminates in the downfall of Babylon (Revelation 18). The parallel cycles encourage readers to note theological patterns: God's judgments are not random but patterned, emphatic, and progressively revealing His purposes. Another example of parallelism is the pairing of the two witnesses in Revelation 11 with the two olive trees and lampstands in Zechariah 4:14. By echoing Maccabean-period prophecy, John intimates that just as God provided for Israel under Antiochus's persecution, He will likewise provide for His people under Roman oppression. Recognizing these intertextual parallels enriches understanding of John's pastoral intent: to assure persecuted Christians that God's deliverance—already promised in Scripture—will come to pass. A third instance of interlocking structure appears in the series of three woes announced in Revelation 8:13, 9:12, and 11:14. Each woe escalates judgment intensity—first trumpet woes, second trumpet woes, and third trumpet woes—culminating in the final woe of Revelation 11:14, which coincides with the sounding of the seventh trumpet (Revelation 11:15). This layered build-up signals to readers that God's wrath moves through distinct stages, culminating in the establishment of Christ's kingdom (Revelation 11:15). Observing these patterns prevents readers from forcing a linear sequence of events where an author intended thematic recapitulation. When apocalyptic scholars such as G. K. Beale

highlight the symmetrical chiastic structures in Revelation's bookends—Revelation 1 (introduction) and Revelation 22 (conclusion), Revelation 2–3 (letters to churches) and Revelation 21 (visions of new creation)—it becomes clear that Revelation is artfully composed to frame its core message: despite persecution, the church's ultimate destiny is to partake in the new creation (Revelation 21:3–4). Understanding how these cycles interlock and echo one another is indispensable for grasping how Revelation conveys its message holistically rather than via isolated vignettes. With awareness of these literary structures, interpreters can better navigate Revelation's complex tapestry—reading symbolic judgments not as chronological checklists, but as layered tableaux depicting various facets of God's redemptive plan. The next subsection delves into how Old Testament echoes and allusions animate John's vision, further enriching the book's theological depth.

### 2.5.3 Old-Testament Echoes and Allusions in John's Vision

John's use of Old Testament imagery in Revelation is both extensive and intentional, inviting readers to connect his apocalyptic vision to the broader biblical narrative. Isaiah's "suffering servant" (Isaiah 53) resonates in Revelation 5, where John sees a Lamb "standing as though it had been slain" (Revelation 5:6). This image merges the messianic expectation of Isaiah 53:7 with the New Testament proclamation that Christ's sacrificial death inaugurates God's kingdom (Luke 4:18–21). Similarly, Ezekiel 1's four living creatures—each with a distinct set of faces—parallel Revelation 4:6–8's living creatures around the throne, suggesting that John draws on Ezekiel's vision as a paradigm for describing heavenly worship. When Ezekiel hears heavenly praise, John also hears "Holy, holy, holy, Lord God Almighty" (Revelation 4:8), echoing Isaiah 6:3, thereby fusing the prophet's temple vision with John's portrayal of Christ's enthronement. These Old Testament echoes demonstrate that John expects his readers—likely first-century Jewish and Gentile Christians—to be familiar with Hebrew Scriptures and to interpret his symbols accordingly. Daniel's ram and goat vision (Daniel 8:3–14) find reflection in Revelation 13's beasts—emblems of imperial power—indicating to vigilant readers that John draws on Daniel's critique of oppressive empires to comfort persecuted churches under Rome. The connection between Daniel 7:9's "Ancient of Days" enthroned amidst heavenly courts and Revelation 4:2–3's vision of one "seated on the throne" reminds readers that God's transcendence and timelessness govern the unfolding drama. Psalm 2's declaration that "You are my Son; today I have begotten you" (Psalm 2:7), interpreted messianically in Acts 13:33, reverberates in Revelation 2:26–27's promise that Christ's faithful followers will "rule with a rod of iron," echoing Psalm 2:9. By weaving these echoes together, John shows that Christ's victory is the culmination of Scriptural promises, giving his readers confidence that their story aligns with the grand narrative of God's redemptive purposes. Old Testament temple language also surfaces in Revelation 11:1–2, where John is told to measure the temple of God and its altar, invoking Ezekiel 40's detailed measurements of a future temple. Even as John measures a literal or symbolic temple, readers hear resonance with Ezekiel's hope of restored worship—yet must discern how John reinterprets "temple" to include the entire city (Revelation 21:22). Isaiah's new covenant prophecy (Isaiah 54:11–17; 65:17–25) informs Revelation 21–22's vision of a new Jerusalem, where "the Lord God will be its temple" (Revelation 21:22) and where there will be "no more death or mourning or crying or pain" (Revelation 21:4). These echoes indicate that John's climax unites Israel's future hope with the church's present identity. Recognizing these biblical allusions requires readers to engage in intertextual analysis: noting how John's use of phrases like "sea of glass" (Revelation 4:6) recalls Exodus 24:10's "paved work of sapphire stone" indicating heavenly sanctity. By tracing these echoes, interpreters can see that when John presents the living creatures offering day and night worship (Revelation 4:8), he is inviting the church into participation in a heavenly liturgy that began in the tabernacle (Leviticus 24:2–3) and finds final expression in the new creation. Having seen how Old Testament echoes enrich John's vision, the next subsection examines how John's rhetorical strategy and pastoral intent shape the book's structure and message.

**2.5.4 Rhetorical Strategy and Pastoral Intent** John's primary goal in Revelation is pastoral rather than encyclopedic chronological forecasting. He seeks to encourage believers enduring persecution under the Roman Empire by unveiling the ultimate triumph of Christ. From his opening address to the seven churches (Revelation 1:4–3:22), John employs rhetorical devices—such as commendations, rebukes, and exhortations—to shape congregational identity and conduct. Each letter's structure mirrors prophetic pattern: addressing the recipient, describing the risen Lamb, commending the community, issuing warnings, and concluding with promises (Revelation 2:1–3:22). These pastoral messages appear tailored: Ephesus receives praise for perseverance but is rebuked for losing first love (Revelation 2:2–4), while Laodicea is critiqued for lukewarm faith (Revelation 3:15–17). John's rhetorical strategy in these letters reflects his concern for spiritual vitality, moral purity, and steadfast witness amid adversity. As John transitions from letters to visions (Revelation 4:1), he frames the subsequent apocalyptic sequences as a revelation "things that must soon take place" (Revelation 1:1). The immediate framing—"Behold, he is coming with the clouds" (Revelation 1:7)—reminds readers that Christ's return is both near and certain, even if its precise timing remains veiled. John's rhetorical move to depict heavenly worship scenes (Revelation 4–5) underscores that Christ's enthronement has cosmic significance; worship in heaven prefigures ultimate victory on earth, bolstering the resolve of believers facing trials. The interlude in Revelation 10:1–11:14, where John eats the little scroll and is told to prophesy again, signals a renewed call for faithful witness, echoing Ezekiel's experience in Ezekiel 2–3, and reflecting Jesus' commission to make disciples of all nations (Matthew 28:19). John's rhetorical use of interludes— such as the temple measurement (Revelation 11:1–2) and the dragon's pursuit of the woman (Revelation 12:1–17)—reinforces the notion that God's people, though oppressed, are under divine protection and destined for final vindication. In his depiction of Babylon's fall (Revelation 17–18), John employs vivid lament language reminiscent of Jeremiah's "Lamentations" (Lamentations 1), warning that imperial arrogance ultimately leads to judgment. This rhetorical strategy serves to strengthen believers' resolve not to compromise with worldly power (Revelation 18:4–5). Finally, John's portrayal of the new Jerusalem descending (Revelation 21:2–3) provides a vision of cosmic renewal that reassures persecuted Christians that God's kingdom will be fully realized, encouraging them to endure with patient faith (Revelation 2:10). Understanding John's pastoral intent—encouragement to persevere, warning against compromise, and assurance of ultimate victory—shapes how interpreters approach Revelation's symbols. It cautions against turning the book primarily into a puzzle demanding exact dates and names, reminding readers that John's rhetorical strategy aims to transform hearts and communities rather than to decode hidden calendars. With Revelation's methodological touchstones in place, we move to evaluating how various hermeneutical models perform in terms of coherence, tradition, and pastoral effectiveness.

## 2.6 Evaluating Hermeneutical Models

**2.6.1 Coherence and Canonical Consistency** A hermeneutical model's credibility depends largely on its coherence with the broader scriptural witness and its consistency across canonical texts. When interpreters propose a particular millennial chronology, they must ensure that their reading of Revelation aligns with Paul's teaching on resurrection (1 Corinthians 15:20–26), Jesus' own words about "the last day" (John 6:40), and other prophetic passages such as Isaiah 65's description of cosmic renewal. A model that renders Daniel 9's seventy weeks as fulfilled entirely in first-century events must still explain how Revelation's later visions—such as the general resurrection in Revelation 20:12–13—intersect with Daniel's prophecies. Likewise, a view that reads Revelation 20's thousand years symbolically must demonstrate how that symbolic reading coheres with Daniel 7's "one like a son of man" receiving "everlasting dominion" (Daniel 7:13–14). If a hermeneutical approach isolates prophetic passages without regard for canonical links—such as disconnecting Ezekiel's temple vision (Ezekiel 40–48) from New Testament temple theology (John 2:19–21; Hebrews 9:11–14)—it risks fragmenting the unified biblical message. Models that fail to account for intertextual consistency—e.g., reading Zechariah 14's "living waters" (Zechariah 14:8) independently from John 7:38's fulfillment in Christ—diminish the coherence of scriptural theology. Canonical consistency also involves reconciling an interpretive model with foundational doctrinal affirmations: if a reading of "binding of Satan" (Revelation 20:1–3) disregards Colossians 2:15's teaching that Christ disarmed spiritual rulers in His death and resurrection, the model creates an apparent contradiction. A robust hermeneutical model proactively engages such potential discrepancies, offering exegetical explanations that honor both texts' integrity. In practical terms, interpreters should conduct "canonical cross-checks" by mapping how a proposed millennial framework aligns with Christ's teachings on future judgment (Matthew 25:31–46), Paul's eschatological references in 1 Thessalonians 4:13–18, and John's apocalyptic vision. By doing so, they demonstrate that their approach does not cherry-pick proof texts but weaves a cohesive theology that arises organically from the entire biblical narrative. Coherence further demands that hermeneutical models respect the progressive unfolding of revelation: early covenants, such as the Abrahamic and Mosaic covenants, must not be treated as fully superseded if New Testament writers affirm their ongoing relevance (Galatians 3:17–29). Thus, interpretive approaches that jettison Old Testament covenants wholesale in favor of New Testament fulfillment risk undermining canonical unity. As we assess different hermeneutical methods, coherence and canonical consistency remain indispensable tests: a model that fails these tests may provide an internally tidy chronology yet falter when confronted with Scripture's multifaceted storyline. Having established this criterion, the next subsection examines how historical tradition and confessional standards further shape—and sometimes constrain—hermeneutical choices.

**2.6.2 The Rule of Faith and Church Tradition** Early church fathers and creeds function as benchmarks in evaluating hermeneutical models, operating under what theologians call the "Rule of Faith" (regula fidei). This rule encompasses core doctrines articulated during ecumenical councils and reflected in the church's creeds, such as the Nicene-Constantinopolitan Creed (381), which affirms Christ's incarnation, resurrection, ascension, and eventual return to judge the living and the dead. While the creed does not specify details about a millennium, it anchors believers in fundamental truths—Christ's bodily resurrection (Luke 24:6–7), His ascension to the Father (Acts 1:9–11), and His future return with glory (Titus 2:13). Any hermeneutical model that undermines these core convictions—by denying a future bodily resurrection, for example—stands at odds with the Rule of Faith. Historical testimonies from the early church—such as Irenaeus's affirmation of a future bodily reign of Christ (Against Heresies 5.32.1)—offer guidance on how the church once read Revelation's promises. While later theologians such as Augustine moved away from a literal millennium, his allegorical approach (The City of God 20) still safeguarded central doctrinal certainties, teaching that Christ's reign is real even if not manifested through a physical temple. A faithful hermeneutical model must therefore account for the breadth of church tradition, weighing how various interpreters—from Justin Martyr and Hippolytus to Aquinas and Reformation theologians—

read apocalyptic prophecy. Confessional documents, such as the Westminster Confession of Faith (1646), summarize biblical teachings on eschatology without endorsing a specific millennium model but affirming that Christ will return, the dead will be raised, and the final judgment will occur (WCF Chapter 32). If a hermeneutical approach conflicts with such confessional affirmations—denying a general resurrection, for instance—it risks fracturing continuity with historic Christian faith. Yet church tradition also recognizes legitimate diversity in non-essential areas; for instance, the Augsburg Confession (1530) does not mandate a particular view of the millennium, demonstrating that early Protestants considered millennial details secondary to core gospel truths. Thus, a hermeneutical model aligned with the Rule of Faith must distinguish between essentials—such as the reality of Christ's future return—and prudential matters, such as whether the millennium is literal or symbolic. Hermeneutical models that ignore or dismiss church tradition altogether risk producing isolated readings detached from the faith once delivered to the saints (Jude 1:3). By contrast, models that engage tradition in humility—acknowledging historical insights while allowing Scripture to speak afresh—demonstrate respect for the church's interpretive heritage. As we proceed to consider pastoral tests in the next subsection, the interplay between tradition and contemporary interpretation remains a vital axis for assessing hermeneutical models.

**2.6.3 Pastoral Test—Fruitfulness for Worship, Ethics, and Mission** Beyond doctrinal coherence and historical fidelity, a hermeneutical model must bear pastoral fruit, shaping worship, ethical conduct, and missional vitality in healthy ways. If a particular millennium framework breeds despair, escapism, or moral indifference—such as suggesting that social engagement is pointless because the world is about to end imminently—then that model fails the pastoral test, even if it maintains biblical coherence. Worship practices reflect eschatological convictions: hymns celebrating the coming reign of Christ (e.g., "Crown Him with Many Crowns") encourage hope and perseverance, while sermons focused on the immediate inauguration of a golden age foster a sense of responsibility to work for justice and compassion in the present age (Ephesians 2:10). Ethical discipleship flows from eschatology: a view that emphasizes Christ's imminent return (premillennial futurism) may inspire personal holiness but discourage systemic engagement, whereas a postmillennial optimism about societal transformation can foster loving activism yet risk legalism or triumphalism if believers presume they can create heaven on earth. Amillennial readings that stress Christ's present reign underscore spiritual formation (Galatians 2:20) and the church's role as God's temple (1 Corinthians 3:16), encouraging sacramental participation and community-building while maintaining a sober awareness that full redemption awaits future consummation. A pastoral hermeneutic examines how a model shapes the church's identity in mission: does it encourage believers to proclaim the gospel to all nations (Matthew 28:19–20), to care for widows and orphans (James 1:27), and to minister compassionately to the poor (Matthew 25:35–40)? Or does it diminish these imperatives by asserting that evangelistic effort or social reform is only of secondary importance to date-setting or monitoring prophecy charts? Pastoral fruitfulness also appears in congregational health: is the model capable of addressing issues such as suffering, grief, and persecution with comfort rooted in Christ's victory (Revelation 1:18; 21:4)? A hermeneutical approach that offers no reassurance to those facing trials or that provides superficial consolation without a robust hope of resurrection (1 Thessalonians 4:13–18) impoverishes pastoral ministry. Additionally, the church's worship calendar—such as celebrating Advent as a season of expectant waiting—depends on eschatological convictions that affirm Christ's coming as both past promise and future fulfillment. If a millennium model undermines liturgical rhythms—suggesting, for example, that Advent or Ash Wednesday hold little relevance—then it compromises the church's spiritual formation. A pastorally sound hermeneutic must therefore cultivate a balanced eschatology that inspires holy living (2 Peter 3:11–12), mobilizes compassionate service (James 1:27), and sustains joyful hope amid trials (Romans 8:18–25). Having considered these pastoral implications, the next subsection explores how ecumenical dialogue and hermeneutical charity further enrich and test interpretive models.

**2.6.4 Ecumenical Dialogue and Hermeneutical Charity** In an age of increasing theological diversity, hermeneutical charity becomes indispensable for sustaining unity amid eschatological differences. Ecumenical dialogue invites believers across traditions to share their interpretive convictions while listening respectfully to other perspectives—recognizing that God's Spirit has guided Christians of different eras to wrestle faithfully with prophecy. When Reformed, Lutheran, Anglican, Pentecostal, and Orthodox interpreters come together to discuss the millennium, they model how the body of Christ can hold diverging eschatological views without fracturing fellowship. Hermeneutical charity means acknowledging that sincere, biblically grounded Christians can and do arrive at different conclusions on non-essential matters, such as whether the millennium is literal, figurative, or a spiritual reality in the church's experience. This charitable posture refuses ad hominem attacks or triumphalist rhetoric, instead focusing on shared commitments—Christ's lordship, the authority of Scripture, the call to holiness, and the mission to make disciples. In ecumenical settings, participants often employ "hermeneutical listening," seeking to understand how each tradition's theological frameworks—covenantal, dispensational, or otherwise—influence their readings of apocalyptic texts. By asking clarifying questions— "How does your emphasis on covenant continuity shape your reading of Revelation 20:1–6?" or "How does your dispensational framework inform your understanding of Daniel 9:24–27?"— dialogue participants foster deeper insights while avoiding caricatures. Ecumenical dialogues also benefit from historical humility, recognizing that early church interpretations—such as those of Irenaeus (Against Heresies 5.28) or Hippolytus (Commentary on Daniel)—provide context for contemporary debates. Acknowledging that traditions such as Eastern Orthodoxy retained a variety of millennial perspectives well into the Middle Ages invites modern Western readers to reassess assumptions about patristic consensus. When theologians like the World Council of Churches convene panels on eschatology, they often emphasize common ground: Christ's ultimate victory, the reality of the final resurrection, and the establishment of God's kingdom in fullness. These ecumenical affirmations serve as touchstones for hermeneutical models, ensuring that no approach strays into heterodoxy. Charitable hermeneutics also demand that participants address theological convictions, not personalities, avoiding dogmatic ultimatums while holding core gospel truths—including justification by faith (Romans 5:1) and salvation through Christ alone (John 14:6). This climate of mutual respect opens space for collaborative study—jointly examining texts such as Revelation 21:1–4 or Daniel 7:13–14, comparing notes on how these passages inform worship, discipleship, and social engagement. By cultivating an ethos of charity anchored in Philippians 2:1–4's exhortation to "do nothing from rivalry or conceit, but in humility count others more significant than yourselves," believers can admit where their own readings may need refinement. Ultimately, ecumenical dialogue and hermeneutical charity remind us that eschatology, while important, must serve the broader imperative of Kingdom unity (John 17:20–23). As we conclude this chapter, readers who have engaged these models will be equipped to assess their own interpretive commitments with both conviction and humility, ready to apply a balanced eschatology in community life and mission.

## Conclusion

Having surveyed the key principles of biblical interpretation—ranging from careful attention to authorial intent and genre conventions to the art of recognizing symbolic numbers and intertextual echoes—we arrive at a more discerning posture for reading prophetic and apocalyptic literature. We have seen that no single passage stands alone; instead, every verse participates in the grand narrative of creation, fall, redemption, and consummation. Covenant and dispensational frameworks, with their divergent emphases on continuity or discontinuity, serve as lenses through which readers organize the Bible's many promises, while prophetic timetables and apocalyptic structures remind us that heavenly realities often eclipse human chronologies. Equipped with these hermeneutical touchstones, readers can now approach the ensuing chapters with greater clarity—evaluating premillennial, postmillennial, and amillennial proposals not merely on the basis of isolated proof texts but within the context of a coherent, historically grounded, and pastorally responsible engagement with Scripture. The tools developed here form the soil in which an informed, charitable, and spiritually fruitful conversation about the millennium can flourish.

# Chapter 3 - Premillennialism Unpacked

The anticipation of Christ's visible return to reign on earth has captivated the hearts and minds of believers from the earliest days of the church. Long before systematic theology distilled premillennialism into neat categories, the promise of a literal, future kingdom shaped worship, fueled missionary zeal, and provided hope in times of trial. This chapter delves into the rich tapestry of premillennial thought, tracing its roots from the early cento of patristic expectations about an earthly reign through the radical ferment of Reformation-era thought, all the way to the diverse expressions that define contemporary evangelicalism. At the heart of premillennialism lies the conviction that the One who conquered sin and death will return bodily to Jerusalem, fulfill God's covenants with Israel, and inaugurate a reign marked by justice, peace, and renewal of creation (Zechariah 14:4–9; Revelation 19:11–16). In exploring these convictions, we will see how early Christian writers read Daniel's apocalyptic visions and John's Revelation as portraits of a coming era when Satan's power is restrained and the righteous serve alongside Christ as co-regents (Revelation 20:4–6). As premillennial thinkers developed their doctrines, questions naturally arose about the church's role during tribulation, the nature of the resurrection(s), and how the promises made to Abraham, David, and the prophets remain unfulfilled until that climactic moment. This chapter invites readers to journey through both classic historic premillennialism—where believers endure persecution and await a post-tribulational advent—and dispensational premillennialism, which introduced the concept of a secret rapture and distinguished God's programs for Israel and the church. We will also engage the contours of progressive premillennialism, which balances "already" and "not yet" in a way that honors present kingdom fruit while holding to a future, tangible fulfillment. As we unpack these strands, our aim is not merely to catalogue differences but to understand how each reading of Scripture influences Christian worship, ethics, mission strategy, and cultural engagement. Through this lens, we will appreciate why premillennial hope has endured—and how it continues to shape the posture of believers as they cultivate holiness, proclaim the gospel, and long for the day when every nation streams to Zion (Isaiah 2:2–4).

## 3.1 Historical Development of Premillennial Hope

**3.1.1 Patristic Chiliastic Expectations** In the earliest centuries of the church, many of the church fathers embraced a chiliastic or literal-kingdom perspective that anticipated Christ's bodily return followed by a thousand-year reign on earth. Papias of Hierapolis, writing in the early second century, referred to the belief that the resurrection would precede a literal earthly kingdom in which the saints would reign alongside Christ, reflecting a straightforward reading of Revelation 20:4–6. Justin Martyr, around the mid-second century, echoed similar views in his Dialogue with Trypho, asserting that Christians would indeed rule with Jesus in Jerusalem after His return and that this period would last a thousand years. For Irenaeus of Lyons, writing circa 180 AD, the millennium was central to his eschatology. In Against Heresies he described a restored earthly order in which the saints would serve as priests for a rebuilt temple, with Zion as the epicenter of global worship. These fathers grounded their chiliastic views in the literal sense of Scripture, holding that John's vision reflected a future chronological epoch rather than a purely symbolic era. The popularity of this perspective among congregations in Asia Minor and Syria manifested in tangible community expectations—some congregations would set aside property or funds in anticipation of the coming kingdom. Theological debates did arise: some argued that John's vision referred primarily to a spiritual reign rather than a geopolitical reality. Yet, until the early third century, premillennial or chiliastic hope was widespread, informing worship hymns that looked forward to "the earth renewed under King Jesus" and prayers petitioning for the hastening of the millennium. Commentary on Daniel 7 and 9 among Eastern fathers reinforced the idea of an imminent temporal kingdom, with Daniel's "Son of Man" vision (Daniel 7:13–14) serving as a cornerstone for the belief in an earthly enthronement. As these patristic testimonies reveal, early Christian communities lived with a keen sense of expectation that history would soon be transformed by Christ's return, ushering in an age of peace and justice. However, as theological sophistication increased and allegorical hermeneutics gained prominence, some church leaders began to question the literal chronology of Revelation 20. This led to subtle shifts that paved the way for later debates, but for centuries, chiliastic hope remained a vibrant force in Christian devotion and eschatological anticipation.

**3.1.2 Mediæval Dormancy and Dissenting Currents** As the medieval church developed, premillennial hope largely receded from mainstream theological discourse, partly because Augustine of Hippo's influential amillennial interpretation of Revelation 20 became normative in the Western church. Augustine argued that the "thousand years" represented the entire present age of the church rather than a future earthly kingdom, effectively reframing earlier chiliastic hopes. Consequently, for much of the early and high Middle Ages, references to a literal millennial reign were considered marginal or heretical, often confined to smaller monastic or mystical circles. Despite Augustine's dominance, some dissenting voices persisted in bearing remnants of premillennial thought. For instance, the writings of Joachim of Fiore in the twelfth century revived interest in a "third age" of the Spirit, which he saw as a spiritual kingdom rather than a literal thousand-year rule, yet his millennial framework nonetheless demonstrated that medieval piety still longed for an eschatological renewal. Likewise, Fra Dolcino's radical sects in the early fourteenth century speculated about an imminent age of perfection based on Christ's return, although their social and political agendas diverged sharply from orthodox expectations. Pilgrim sermons in the late Middle Ages occasionally invoked apocalyptic themes, calling for repentance in light of approaching divine judgment—a rhetorical echo of chiliastic urgency, even if not couched in precise millennial chronology. The broader medieval emphasis remained on sacramental life, monastic asceticism, and eventual entry into the afterlife rather than awaited earthly reign. Art and liturgy focused on the Last Judgment and heaven and hell, with little to no room for imagining a future earthly kingdom lasting a defined thousand years. Yet, medieval mystics such as Hildegard of Bingen and Meister Eckhart occasionally used vivid images of cosmic renewal that harkened back to Isaiah 65–66's visions of a restored earth, hinting at latent millennial hope. These glimpses, while not overtly chiliastic, reveal that medieval spirituality remained sensitive to biblical visions of a renewed creation. As Renaissance humanism and renewed scholarship began to challenge Augustinian allegory, interest in more literal interpretations of prophetic texts gradually resurfaced. The Reformation's recovery of sola Scriptura opened new opportunities for revisiting millennial passages in their original languages and contexts, setting the stage for a revival of premillennial thought among certain reformers and radicals.

**3.1.3 Reformation-Era Revivals and Radical Streams** The sixteenth-century Reformation reignited debates over eschatology as reformers turned to Scripture as the ultimate authority, often bypassing medieval commentarial traditions. While leading magisterial Reformers like Martin Luther and John Calvin generally maintained an amillennial position influenced by Augustine, their renewed focus on exegesis rekindled interest in literal readings of apocalyptic texts among more radical circles. Martin Luther initially wrestled with chiliastic views, at times expressing hope for a visible kingdom in writings such as his early sermons on Revelation, but he ultimately affirmed that Christ's kingdom was spiritual and present in the church. John Calvin, in his Institutes of the Christian Religion, likewise interpreted the "binding of Satan" (Revelation 20:1–3) as fulfilled in Christ's ministry rather than awaiting future chronology. In contrast, some Anabaptist and Radical Reformers embraced premillennial or near-premillennial expectations. Menno Simons and Jakob Hutter, leaders of various Anabaptist movements, taught that Christ's return would inaugurate a thousand-year reign in which the church would be purified and restored. English Puritans such as

Thomas Brightman produced prophetic commentaries arguing that a future earthly temple would be built in Jerusalem and that Christ would reign visibly—positions buttressed by reading Ezekiel 40–48 as a literal blueprint for post-tribulation worship. Thomas Brightman's influential commentaries and sermons laid groundwork for figures like Joseph Mede (1586–1638), whose works on the origin and rise of Antichrist (1627) synthesized Daniel and Revelation to support an imminent premillennial kingdom. During the English Civil War, propaganda pamphlets and treatises forecasted apocalyptic battles aligned with political struggles, suggesting that providential interventions would soon establish Christ's reign on earth. Continental radical sects, including certain Anabaptist factions, anticipated imminent tribulation and a visible millennial rule, though their hopes were often shaped by persecution and political upheaval. In France, Huguenot preachers like Pierre Jurieu linked the Catholic Church's failures to the "antichrist" of Revelation, urging believers to prepare for an approaching kingdom; this apocalyptic fervor provided moral impetus during the French Wars of Religion. Although mainstream Lutherans and Reformed churches largely affirmed amillennialism, the seeds of premillennial revival sown by radical interpreters persisted and would bear fruit in later centuries, setting the stage for the nineteenth-century dispensational resurgence.

**3.1.4 Nineteenth-Century Resurgence: Prophecy Conferences and Mission Societies** The nineteenth century witnessed a pronounced resurgence of premillennial expectation, fueled by the rise of dispensationalism within the Plymouth Brethren and by widespread evangelical revival fervor. John Nelson Darby, a leader among the Brethren, formalized a dispensational framework that integrated historic premillennial belief with a new emphasis on a secret rapture distinct from Christ's visible return. Darby argued that Old Testament covenants remained unfulfilled for ethnic Israel and would be fulfilled literally during a future millennial kingdom. His 1833 series of prophetic lectures for Irish Brethren codified these ideas, presenting a sharp distinction between Israel and the church and mapping out the "seven dispensations" through which God's program unfolds. Cyrus I. Scofield's annotated Bible (1909) brought dispensational premillennialism into American homes, equipping laypeople with charts and notes that illustrated the secret rapture, the seven-year Tribulation, and the literal millennial kingdom.

Meanwhile, prophetic conferences proliferated—beginning with Niagra in 1878—where pastors and laity gathered to study end-times prophecy. Figures such as Dwight L. Moody and D. L. Moody popularized dispensational ideas through revival campaigns and Bible institutes, linking personal piety with heightened interest in eschatological timelines. The establishment of institutions like Dallas Theological Seminary (1924) and Moody Bible Institute provided formal training for pastors committed to dispensational premillennialism, ensuring its transmission to subsequent generations. Parallel to these developments, postmillennial optimism also inspired mission societies aimed at bringing global conversion, yet many missionaries carried premillennial convictions that Christ's visible return must precede any millennial age, tempering cultural optimism with expectations of imminent divine intervention. The Jewish question—renewed interest in Jewish restoration to Palestine—also gained traction as premillennialists saw fulfillment of passages like Ezekiel 37 and Zechariah 12 in the regathering of Jews. Organizations like the British and Foreign Bible Society, while evangelical at heart, included many members who believed that distributing Scripture would prepare the world for Christ's return. This intersection of revival zeal, missionary expansion, and premillennial expectation created a dynamic milieu in which belief in a future earthly kingdom became a defining feature of many evangelical circles. As the twentieth century dawned, dispensational premillennialism had become a major force, influencing not only ecclesiastical teaching but also popular Christian culture and political attitudes toward the Jewish homeland.

### 3.1.5 Twentieth- and Twenty-First-Century Global Expansion

In the twentieth century, premillennialism transitioned from a predominantly Western phenomenon to a global movement, carried by missionaries, printed materials, and later digital media. The rise of fundamentalism in the United States, with its emphasis on biblical inerrancy and eschatological urgency, solidified premillennial belief as normative in many independent Baptist and non-denominational churches. Charles H. Dyer and J. Dwight Pentecost produced influential textbooks—such as Pentecost's *Things to Come* (1958)—that articulated dispensational premillennial theology for both scholarly and lay audiences. Meanwhile, evangelical radio and television broadcasts—most notably by Hal Lindsey's *The Late Great Planet Earth* (1970) and later *The 700 Club*—brought apocalyptic speculation into American living rooms, igniting widespread fascination with Bible prophecy. In parallel, global South Christians adopted premillennial perspectives through translation of these materials and through indigenous prophetic conferences. African evangelical leaders in Kenya and Nigeria began to teach dispensational timelines, connecting local hardships with global end-times narratives. In Latin America, pastors in Brazil and Mexico incorporated premillennial themes into megachurch sermons, linking social justice issues to cosmic battles described in Daniel and Revelation. In Asia, Korean and Filipino Pentecostal congregations integrated chiliastic fervor into their worship, often drawing parallels between spiritual warfare in Revelation 12 and their own experiences of persecution or communal hardship. The proliferation of the internet and social media in the twenty-first century accelerated this global spread: online prophecy blogs, YouTube sermons, and smartphone apps such as Bible prophecy charts and rapture calculators made premillennial speculation instantly accessible. Conferences such as the Global Prophecy Summit attracted thousands of international attendees, featuring speakers from diverse cultural backgrounds united by shared premillennial convictions. Contemporary authors like Tim LaHaye popularized premillennial fiction with the *Left Behind* series, selling millions of copies worldwide and introducing a younger generation to dispensational concepts. Pacific Rim ministries in South Korea and Australia began exporting their own eschatological materials, contributing to a two-way flow of premillennial ideas between North and South. The result has been a melting pot of premillennial expressions—from classic historic premillennial seminaries in Europe preserving early patristic emphases to charismatic megachurches in Africa and Asia infusing millennial hope with Pentecostal exuberance. As we move from this historical overview into a closer examination of distinct premillennial paradigms—classic, dispensational, and progressive—the global dimension of premillennialism underscores that these beliefs continue to evolve in dialogue with local contexts, cultural challenges, and shifting geopolitical realities.

# 3.2 Classic (Historic) Premillennialism

**3.2.1 Tribulation as the Church's Final Purification** Historic premillennialists affirm that the church will endure a final period of intense suffering and persecution—often referred to as the Great Tribulation—before Christ's return. This perspective draws on passages such as Matthew 24:9–14, where Jesus warns His disciples that they will be hated by all nations and that many will turn away from the faith. Historic premillennialists interpret these verses as describing tribulational suffering that Christian communities face, whether in apostolic times under Nero or in subsequent waves of persecution. The tribulation is understood as both a purifying crucible and a fulfillment of prophetic warnings found in Daniel 12:1, where Michael stands up at a time of unprecedented distress. Such interpreters emphasize that the church—even under tribulation—remains on earth, continuing its mission to bear witness to Christ until the Second Advent (Revelation 13:10). This view contrasts with doctrines that remove the church before tribulation, holding instead that enduring suffering cultivates perseverance and faithfulness, consistent with Paul's teaching in Romans 5:3–5 that suffering produces hope tested by endurance. Historic premillennialists often reference Revelation 7:14, interpreting the "great multitude" that comes out of the great tribulation as the church faithful who remain on earth, purified by trials, to be vindicated at Christ's return. The tribulation's purpose, therefore, is not primarily to punish the church but to refine it, undermining the allure of compromise by exposing false religion and reinforcing the reality of Satan's opposition (Revelation 12:17). As in the early church's experience of persecution under local authorities, historic premillennialists believe that modern and future believers will face similar afflictions, culminating in a crescendo of torment under a final Antichrist figure (Revelation 13:7). This ultimate persecution intensifies believers' longing for Christ's coming, transforming tribulation into a catalyst for evangelistic urgency (Matthew 24:14). Historic premillennialists caution against speculating on specific dates, instead urging the church to watch for general conditions—wars, famines, plagues—that signal tribulational intensification (Matthew 24:6–8). They also emphasize the church's call to be salt and light (Matthew 5:13–16) even as unfavorable conditions worsen, demonstrating faith through sacrificial love and prophetic witness.

As the tribulation unfolds, historic premillennialists expect that local and even global evangelical networks will facilitate underground or clandestine expressions of church life, much as early Christian communities met in catacombs or private homes. This endurance ethos roots itself in passages such as 2 Thessalonians 1:4, where Paul commends the Thessalonians for their enduring persecution and afflictions. Ultimately, for historic premillennialists, the tribulation not only refines the church but also sets the stage for Christ's return, demonstrating that opposition will not prevail against His redemptive purposes (1 Corinthians 15:25).

**3.2.2 Post-Tribulational Second Advent** Historic premillennialism maintains that Christ's visible return will occur immediately after the tribulation, inaugurating His thousand-year reign. This post-tribulational understanding asserts that Jesus descends from heaven with power and great glory (Matthew 24:29–30) only when the final outpouring of divine wrath has concluded. Historic premillennialists cite 2 Thessalonians 1:7–10 as a key text: believers who have endured suffering will be relieved "when the Lord Jesus is revealed from heaven," and those who do not know God will face everlasting destruction "at the coming of our Lord Jesus with His mighty angels." The second advent, in this view, marks the end of the church's tribulational endurance and the beginning of Christ's earthly reign. Historic premillennialists often highlight that Revelation 19:11–16 portrays Christ returning as a conquering warrior—"Faithful and True," riding a white horse—to execute judgment and establish His kingdom. They interpret Revelation 19:19–21 as describing the defeat of the beast and false prophet, connecting those events with Daniel 7:11–14's depiction of the Ancient of Days pronouncing judgment on the fourth beast. To historic premillennialists, this climactic conflict precedes the millennium, ensuring that no vestige of Satan's empowered empire remains to challenge Christ's sovereign rule. After the Second Advent, footnotes in classic commentaries often draw on Isaiah 11:6–9's vision of animals living in peace, describing how the healed earth under Christ's rule will reflect God's original design in Eden. Historic premillennialists assert that during this period, resurrected saints will serve as judges and priests, participating in governance (2 Timothy 2:12; Revelation 20:4). Their understanding of this post-tribulational return also affirms that there is only one future bodily resurrection for believers prior to the millennium, after which mortal bodies are transformed into immortal bodies like Christ's (1 Corinthians 15:51–54). This single resurrection ensures that the church's role shifts from faithfulness amid suffering to active participation in Christ's kingdom administration (Revelation 20:4–6). Historic premillennialists critique views that separate the rapture from the Second Advent, arguing that Scripture consistently portrays the resurrection of the dead and Christ's coming as a unified eschatological event (1 Thessalonians 4:16–17). They emphasize that cumulative New Testament passages—such as John 6:39–40, where Jesus speaks of resurrecting all who believe "at the last day"—point to one climactic gathering rather than a two-stage return. By holding to a post-tribulational advent, historic premillennialists stress continuity in Christ's work: His return culminates history, bringing about resurrection, judgment, and kingdom reign in one coherent sequence. The church, having endured tribulation, transitions into its blessed participation in Christ's earthly rule, carrying forward its mission of worship and governance until the final dissolution of the present heavens and earth (Revelation 21:1).

### 3.2.3 Single Resurrection of the Righteous Prior to the Millennium

In the classic premillennial frame, the righteous dead are raised at Christ's return before He inaugurates the millennium, underscoring the intimate connection between resurrection and reign. Historic premillennialists draw on Revelation 20:4–5, interpreting the "first resurrection" as the bodily resurrection of saints who have died in faith, who then reign with Christ for a thousand years. They correlate this "first resurrection" with Paul's teaching in 1 Corinthians 15:23, where "each in his own order" indicates that believers' resurrection aligns with Christ's coming, distinct from the wicked, who rise later to face judgment. This single resurrection event dissolves any notion of a multi-phased resurrection of believers; rather, it consolidates saintly resurrection into a single chronological point at the advent. Historic premillennialists often reference Revelation 11:18, which speaks of rewarding "your servants, the prophets and saints, and those who fear your name, small and great," indicating that reward coincides with resurrection and precedes judgment on the wicked. The concept that resurrected saints immediately assume roles as rulers and priests (Revelation 20:6; 1 Corinthians 6:2–3) flows from this interpretive lens, emphasizing that glorified bodies enable participation in

98

Christ's administration of justice and blessing on earth. Historic premillennialists argue that this teaching on resurrection aligns with Daniel 12:2's promise that "many of those who sleep in the dust of the earth shall awake, some to everlasting life, and some to shame and everlasting contempt," connecting that prophecy to Revelation's two-phase resurrection (the righteous first, the wicked later). They teach that the millennial reign, characterized by peace and righteousness, presupposes the resurrection of saints; without resurrected bodies, the participation in physical governance cannot occur. Historic premillennialists also draw on John 5:28–29, where Jesus declares that "all who are in the tombs will hear his voice and come out, those who have done good to the resurrection of life," further emphasizing that the resurrection to life precedes Christ's rule. During the millennium, resurrected saints exercise judgment (Revelation 20:4) but also enjoy the fullness of God's presence under the new Davidic kingship, which they argue fulfills Psalm 22:27–28's promise that "all the ends of the earth shall remember and turn to the Lord, and all the families of the nations shall worship before you." This unified resurrection model contrasts with dispensational premillennialism's two-phase resurrection (rapture resurrection and great white throne resurrection), asserting instead that Scripture teaches one composite event for the righteous dead. By rooting their understanding in passages such as 1 Thessalonians 4:16–17 and Revelation 20:5–6, historic premillennialists maintain theological coherence, reinforcing that resurrection and the establishment of Christ's kingdom are inseparable in Scripture. As resurrected saints commence their millennium service, they pave the way for the eventual final rebellion and the ultimate establishment of new heavens and a new earth (Revelation 21:1–3).

**3.2.4 Unity of Israel and Gentile Saints in One Kingdom** Historic premillennialists affirm that in the millennium, believing Jews and Gentiles will share equal status in Christ's earthly kingdom, reflecting the multi-ethnic scope of Abraham's covenant promise (Genesis 12:3) and the inclusion of the Gentiles envisioned in Isaiah 2:2–4. This unity flows from New Testament teaching such as Ephesians 2:14–16, which states that Christ has broken down the dividing wall between Jews and Gentiles, creating one new humanity. In the millennium, historic premillennialists envision that redeemed Israel, gathered to her land, will worship with believing Gentiles, thereby fulfilling prophecies like Zechariah 14:16–19, which speak of nations coming to Jerusalem annually to worship the Lord. Historic premillennialists argue that Jesus' own interactions with Gentiles—such as His healing of the Canaanite woman (Matthew 15:21–28) and His declaration that many will come from east and west to recline at table with Abraham, Isaac, and Jacob in the kingdom (Matthew 8:11)—anticipate this inclusive millennial reality. They hold that during the millennium, Israel's covenanted role is restored through direct fulfillment of Davidic and Levitical promises, with Gentile saints enjoying the blessings of royal priesthood alongside them. Passages like Isaiah 19:23–25, which envision Egypt and Assyria becoming a third with Israel in worshiping the Lord, support this multi-national unity. Historic premillennialists further underscore that the division between "people of Israel" and "Gentile nations" in the millennial economy does not entail exclusion but rather reflects different covenant roles—a theme they see in Revelation 21:24, where "the nations walk by its light, and the kings of the earth bring their glory into it." In practical terms, this unity encourages historic premillennial congregations today to maintain robust support for Jewish believers while pursuing global mission, anticipating a future era in which all ethnic groups will stream to Zion in harmonious worship. Historic premillennialists contrast their view with those that see the church as replacing Israel; instead, they affirm that Israel's national identity retains significance in the millennium (Romans 11:26–27), even as Jewish and Gentile saints together serve under Christ's rule. By highlighting texts like Acts 15:14–18, where James speaks of turning "from the Gentiles a people for his name," they emphasize that the church's mission includes drawing from all nations as well as a future restoration of Israel. As this unity of Israel and the church prepares the stage for the literal millennium, historic premillennialists maintain that this corporate identity aligns with God's consistent pattern of fulfilling promises to Abraham—first corporately for Israel, and then extended covenantally to all nations through Christ.

**3.2.5 Key Proponents, Confessions, and Contemporary Advocates** Historic premillennialism has been championed by various theologians and church leaders from early Christianity through to the contemporary era. In the patristic period, Justin Martyr and Irenaeus provided early articulations of a future earthly reign, with Irenaeus's *Against Heresies* (Book 5) offering detailed exposition of Revelation 20 and Daniel 7 as literal prophecies about the millennium. Papias's fragmentary works also attest to a widespread chiliastic expectation among his readers. Augustine's eventual shift away from literal premillennialism in *The City of God* prompted many medieval theologians to adopt amillennial or allegorical approaches, but his writings did not fully extinguish historic premillennial echoes among some monastic circles. During the Reformation, although Luther and Calvin favored amillennial interpretations, a minority of Reformed scholars—such as Thomas Brightman and Joseph Mede—championed historic premillennial or near-premillennial perspectives. Mede's *Clavis Apocalyptica* (1627) offered a recalibration of Daniel's chronology that left space for a future millennium, influencing numerous Puritan divines. As Baptist and Presbyterian confessions spread in the seventeenth century, most confessional statements remained noncommittal or implicitly amillennial, yet commentators like Matthew Poole and Doddridge inserted premillennial comments in their biblical expositions. In the nineteenth century, Anglican premillennialists such as J. N. Darby used their break with the Church of Ireland to propagate historic premillennial ideas within the Plymouth Brethren, though his emphasis on dispensational distinctions pushed many toward what would become dispensational premillennialism rather than classic historic premillennialism. Amid these shifts, figures such as J. Marcellus Kik (1876–1966) and William J. Larkin Jr. (1932–2015) in the twentieth century advanced historic premillennial interpretations, publishing works that emphasized a unified resurrection of the righteous before the millennium and a combined kingdom for Jews and Gentiles. Their writings often responded to dispensational trends by reasserting covenant continuity, arguing that Israel and the church share a single destiny in Christ's future reign. Contemporary advocates of historic premillennialism include theologians such as Robert Gundry, who critiques dispensationalism's separation of Israel and church, and Sam Waldron, who highlights the continuity of covenants in his expositions of Revelation 20. Scholarship from academic contexts—including works by Richard McBrien and Ben Witherington III—examines historic premillennialism in light of early church history, seeking to recover neglected patristic voices. These proponents often gather in organizations like the Evangelical Theological Society, where historical premillennialists interact with dispensational and amillennial scholars, fostering dialogue on eschatological questions.

Though not always represented in major denominational confessions—most of which default to amillennial assumptions—historic premillennialism maintains a vibrant presence through local church teaching, seminary courses, and scholarly monographs. In popular culture, this view influences various independent church movements and online ministries that defend a return to first-century premillennial expectations, encouraging believers to anticipate an earthly kingdom without relinquishing hope in Christ's immediate return. As we transition to explore dispensational premillennialism in the next section, readers should note how classic approaches continue to inform contemporary debates about Israel, covenant, and the nature of Christ's future reign.

## 3.3 Dispensational Premillennialism

### 3.3.1 The Secret Rapture and the 70th Week of Daniel

Dispensational premillennialism, as systematized by John Nelson Darby in the early nineteenth century, introduced the concept of a secret rapture in which the church is caught up to meet Christ in the air before a future seven-year period of tribulation unfolds on earth (1 Thessalonians 4:16–17). This rapture is distinct from the Second Advent, with the former occurring without public apocalyptic signs and the latter presented as a visible, glorious return following tribulation (Revelation 1:7; 19:11–16). Central to this view is the seventy weeks prophecy in Daniel 9:24–27, where Darby and his successors argue that the seventy weeks represent seventy sets of seven years (490 years), with the final "week" yet to be fulfilled. According to this framework, sixty-nine of those weeks are understood to have culminated in the first coming of Christ, leaving the seventieth week as a future period during which a revived focus on national Israel culminates in Christ's second coming. Dispensationalists interpret Daniel 9:27's reference to a covenant made for one week as the signing of a treaty by a future Antichrist with Israel, permitting the rebuilding of the Jerusalem temple and the resumption of sacrificial worship. This treaty marks the beginning of a period known as Daniel's seventieth week, often equated with the seven-year tribulation described in Revelation 6–19. Within dispensational premillennial thought, the secret rapture removes the church from the earth before the tribulation begins, enabling God to turn again to fulfill unfulfilled Old Testament covenants with Israel—especially those regarding the land, the Davidic throne, and temple worship. The church's removal is seen as necessary to avoid being judged under the wrath poured out during tribulation (1 Thessalonians 5:9). Dispensational expositors such as Cyrus Scofield popularized this view in their annotated Bibles, presenting charts and timelines that align Daniel's weeks with modern historical events, often marking the return of Jews to their homeland in 1948 as a further sign that the seventieth week was imminent. This hermeneutical approach relies on a literal reading of prophetic texts, insisting that promises to Israel remain distinct from the church, and thus cannot be spiritualized or fulfilled in the church age. The secret rapture doctrine hinges on verses such as 1 Corinthians 15:51–52, interpreting "we shall not all sleep, but we shall all be changed" as referring to the church's deliverance before the earth endures the tribulation. While dispensationalists find support for the rapture in John 14:1–3—where Jesus says He goes to prepare a place and will come again to receive believers to Himself—they distinguish this event from Christ's return to appear in the clouds (Matthew 24:30). The dispensational framework remains sensitive to signs such as the regathering of Jewish people to Palestine (Ezekiel 36:24) and geopolitical alignments in the Middle East, seeing these as precursors to the start of Daniel's seventieth week. Critics argue that this approach fragments Scripture's unity by creating abrupt discontinuities between Old Testament promises and New Testament fulfillment. Dispensing with such concerns, dispensationalists emphasize the faithfulness of God to keep His distinct promises to Israel, arguing that any attempt to spiritualize those promises undermines God's literal covenants (Genesis 12:7; 2 Samuel 7:12–16). As we transition to explore the timing variants of the tribulation, it becomes clear that dispensational premillennialism offers a finely engineered chronology designed to account for each prophetic detail in Daniel and Revelation.

### 3.3.2 Pre-, Mid-, and Pre-Wrath Tribulation Variants Within dispensational premillennialism, several theories contend over precisely when the church will be raptured in relation to the tribulation's unfolding judgments. Pretribulationalism posits that the church is removed before any part of the seven-year tribulation begins, ensuring that believers avoid all divine wrath poured out upon the earth (Revelation 3:10). This view emphasizes 1

Thessalonians 5:9, where Paul asserts that God has not destined the church for wrath but for obtaining salvation, interpreting "wrath" to refer to the tribulation judgments described in Revelation. Midtribulationalists, in contrast, argue that the rapture occurs at the midpoint of the tribulation, immediately preceding the most intense "Great Tribulation" described in Daniel 7:25 and Matthew 24:21–22. They distinguish between the "beginning of sorrows" (Matthew 24:8) and the abomination of desolation (Matthew 24:15) that marks the halfway point, teaching that the church endures the former but is removed before the latter. Some midtribulational advocates draw on Revelation 11:11–12, where the two witnesses are resurrected after three and a half days—parallel to three and a half years—suggesting the church ascends after a similar timeframe. Pre-wrath rapture proponents modify these positions by placing the rapture between the sixth and seventh trumpets (Revelation 11:15–19), contending that the church will experience much of the tribulation but be spared the outpouring of God's wrath signified by the "bowls" in Revelation 16. They argue that biblical texts indicate a distinction between judgments of the Antichrist and bowls of God's wrath, allowing the church to participate in witnessing through persecution but not in divine retribution. Each variant interprets key texts differently: pretribulationalists read Revelation 3:10's promise of preservation as applying to the entire tribulation, while midtribulationalists see passages like Revelation 11:3–12 as inscribing the church's presence through the first half of tribulation. Pre-wrath advocates rely on Revelation 7:14–17's depiction of a great multitude "coming out of the great tribulation," suggesting that this multitude is the church raptured just before the wrath's full onset. Debates hinge on precise definitions of "wrath" (tháarris in Greek) and which judgments count as God's wrath versus Satan's or human evil, requiring careful exegesis of Revelation's seals (Revelation 6), trumpets (Revelation 8–9), and bowls (Revelation 16). Each timing theory also appeals to Paul's reference to being "caught up" (harpazo) in 1 Thessalonians 4:17, asking whether this event maps onto Christ's appearing or onto sometime after. Despite these nuances, all dispensational variants agree that the church will not be present for God's climactic wrath poured out upon a rebellious earth, preserving the bride from divine judgement. By charting these temporal distinctions, dispensationalists seek to honor both scriptural affirmations of imminent deliverance (Titus 2:13) and warnings about enduring suffering (Revelation 2:10).

### 3.3.3 Distinct Programs for Israel and the Church

Dispensational premillennialism maintains that God operates two distinct redemptive programs—one for ethnic Israel and another for the church—throughout history. This bifurcated perspective derives from a literal reading of Old Testament covenants that promise land, lineage, and national blessings specifically to Israel (Genesis 12:1–3; 2 Samuel 7:12–16). Dispensationalists assert that God's promises to Israel have not been abandoned or spiritually fulfilled in the church, but remain pending a future literal fulfillment during the millennial kingdom. Accordingly, the church age, often termed the "parenthesis" or "Church Dispensation," is a unique epoch in which God's focus extends to Gentile nations, distinct from the preceding "Dispensation of Law" given to Israel at Sinai. During the church age, salvation is offered to all who believe in Christ, Jew and Gentile alike, but this does not nullify the unique program reserved for Israel. In Daniel 9:24–27, dispensationalists see seven weeks of years fulfilled in Old Testament history, with the sixty-ninth week culminating in Christ's first coming, and the seventieth week remaining future; this seventieth week pertains exclusively to Israel—a period of tribulation in which God will renew covenantal dealings with Jerusalem. Dispensational expositors thus interpret Zechariah 12:10–14's promise of Israel's national repentance as yet unfulfilled, awaiting the tribulation's midpoint when the Jewish people recognize their Messiah. The reestablished temple in the millennium (Ezekiel 40–48) symbolizes this renewed program for Israel, with reinstituted Levitical worship and sacrifices pointing back to covenant stipulations in Leviticus. Meanwhile, the church participated in the Age of Grace, distinct from Israel's Law Dispensation. The rapture, in dispensationalism, removes the church before God's tribulation judgments resume focus on unrepentant Israel. After the rapture, God's dealings shift exclusively to Israel, fulfilling promises such as Jeremiah 31:31–34's new covenant within an ethnic context. In the millennium, Israel occupies her land, and the church—having been resurrected with glorified bodies—is not physically present on earth but participates vicariously as Christ's bride. This distinct program model also influences how dispensationalists interpret passages like Romans 11:25–27: they hold that "all Israel will be saved" refers to a future corporate salvation of ethnic Israel during the tribulation and millennium, rather than seeing Paul's olive-tree analogy as indicating a merging of Israel with the church. Dispensationalists argue that Israel and the church coexist simultaneously but in separate spheres: the church age is characterized by the outpouring of the Spirit on all flesh (Joel 2:28; Acts 2), while the Messianic kingdom revolves around Christ's Davidic reign over Israel (Isaiah 9:6–7). This distinction leads dispensational theologians to maintain separate eschatological calendars—one governing church history and another governing Israel's future—ensuring that an interpretation of Old Testament prophecy does not override New Testament revelations concerning the church's destiny. Critics of dispensationalism charge that such strict separation creates an unnecessary fragmentation of Scripture's unity. Proponents reply that the integrity of promises to Israel must be preserved and that God's faithfulness to distinct covenantal recipients is best honored through literal, differentiated fulfillments. As this subsection concludes, readers see how dispensational premillennialism's distinct programs shape its overall eschatological panorama, setting the stage for exploring how judgments and timelines align with its chronology.

### 3.3.4 Judgments: Bema Seat, Sheep-and-Goats, and Great White Throne

Dispensational premillennialism articulates a multi-phase sequence of judgments that address different groups at distinct times, reflecting its emphasis on separate destinies for the church and Israel. The first judgment concerns the church at the Bema Seat of Christ, often placed immediately after the rapture. Drawing on 2 Corinthians 5:10 and 1 Corinthians 3:12–15, dispensationalists teach that believers will stand before Christ to give an account of works, receiving rewards or experiencing loss of rewards according to their service. This judgment does not involve condemnation, since the church has already been justified by faith (Romans 8:1), but it determines degrees of reward, crowns, and positions of authority in the millennial kingdom (2 Timothy 4:8). The second judgment unfolds at the "Sheep-and-Goats" judgment described in Matthew 25:31–46, which historicizes the separation of nations at Christ's Second Advent. In dispensational readings, this judgment occurs after Christ's visible return and resurrection of the church, focusing on Gentile nations' treatment of Israel, believers, and "the least of these" during the tribulation. Those nations who extended mercy and aid to God's children are placed at Christ's right hand—"sheep"—while unmerciful nations are condemned as goats, cast into eternal fire. This judgment underscores dispensationalism's ethical emphasis: human actions toward suffering believers during

106

tribulation carry eternal consequences. The third and final judgment is the Great White Throne judgment of Revelation 20:11–15, which addresses unbelievers—both those who died before and those who died after the tribulation. All the dead stand before the "Ancient of Days," books are opened, and individuals are judged according to works recorded in the books. Those whose names are not found in the Book of Life are cast into the lake of fire, symbolizing eternal separation from God. This last judgment effectively brings closure to the age, separating the wicked from the righteous and paving the way for the creation of the new heavens and new earth (Revelation 21:1–4). Dispensationalists often sequence these judgments thus: (1) rapture, (2) Bema Seat for the church, (3) tribulation for Israel and Gentile believers who were not raptured, (4) Second Advent and resurrection of Old Testament saints and tribulation martyrs, (5) Sheep-and-Goats judgment for nations, (6) millennial reign, and (7) Great White Throne for all unbelievers. This complex arrangement emerges from harmonizing texts such as 1 Corinthians 15:23, which speaks of "Christ the firstfruits, then at his coming those who belong to Christ," with Matthew 16:27, where reward and recompense are distributed "at the Son of Man's coming in His Father's glory." In combining these various judgments, dispensational premillennialists underscore God's justice and the distinct fates awaiting church members, tribulation saints, and the unsaved. This multi-phase scheme raises questions about the nature of reward, the continuity of personal identity after resurrection, and the criteria for national accountability—all topics that receive further exploration in systematic and pastoral theology. As we proceed to examine the figures who popularized these judgments—Darby, Scofield, and others—readers will see how dispensational premillennialism devised a detailed eschatological calendar to guide believers' expectations and conduct.

### 3.3.5 Schofield, Darby, and the Popularization of Prophecy Charts

Cyrus I. Scofield's seminal 1909 Scofield Reference Bible played an instrumental role in popularizing dispensational premillennialism among American evangelicals, providing margin notes, cross-references, and dispensational outlines that made Darby's complex chronology accessible to lay readers. Scofield adopted Darby's distinction between Israel and the church, mapping out prophetic events—including the secret rapture, seven-year tribulation, Second Advent, and millennium—across neatly color-coded charts inserted in his Bible's margins. Pastors and Sunday school teachers quickly adopted this study Bible as a ready-made curriculum, fostering a generation of believers for whom the dispensational timeline became normative. Darby himself, an Anglo-Irish clergyman who formally parted ways with the Church of Ireland to lead the Plymouth Brethren, had earlier circulated his prophetic lectures in the 1830s, but Scofield's institutional platform and the onset of mass printing amplified those ideas exponentially in the United States. Beyond the United States, the Scofield Reference Bible influenced mission training schools in Latin America, Africa, and Asia, embedding dispensational premillennialism within global evangelicalism. Subsequent authors like Lewis Sperry Chafer, co-founder of Dallas Theological Seminary, published *Systematic Theology* (1947–48), which elaborated Darby's and Scofield's thematic structures, adding new charts and diagrams that refined rapture and tribulation distinctions. In the mid-twentieth century, Hal Lindsey's *The Late Great Planet Earth* (1970) brought dispensational ideas into popular culture, selling millions of copies worldwide by interpreting current events—such as Middle East conflicts and technological advances—as signs of the approaching tribulation. Lindsey's reliance on Scofield's charts and his ability to translate biblical symbols into contemporary headlines inspired Christian broadcasting networks and Christian rock musicians to incorporate end-times imagery into their programming and lyrics. The "apocalypse industry," as some critics dubbed it, flourished with daily radio programs and syndicated newspaper columns analyzing geopolitical developments through Daniel and Revelation. In theological education, Dallas Theological Seminary faculty continued to produce textbooks— Charles Ryrie's *Dispensationalism* (1957) and John Walvoord's *The Millennial Kingdom* (1959)—which refined Darby's original outlines, introducing nuanced distinctions such as the pretribulation rapture. These works cemented the secret rapture doctrine as normative in conservative evangelical seminaries. Even as some dispensational scholars began to adjust or soften Darby's rigid dispensational breaks—leading to progressive dispensationalism— Darby's and Scofield's legacy persisted in model curricula: prophecy charts displayed in Sunday school classrooms, end-times study guides in bookstores, and Bible study groups dedicated to "charting the times." This popularization of prophecy charts transformed eschatological speculation into a cultural phenomenon, influencing how believers interpreted news headlines, informed their political views—particularly regarding Israel—and structured church teaching calendars around perceived prophetic milestones. As modern dispensationalists continue to refine and debate Darby's framework, the imprint of Scofield's reference Bible endures in evangelical mentalities, ensuring that dispensational premillennialism remains a powerful lens through which many Christians view the future. Readers are now prepared to explore the nuances of progressive premillennialism, which seeks to integrate some dispensational insights with greater covenant continuity and symbolic flexibility.

# 3.4 Progressive Premillennialism

### 3.4.1 "Already/Not Yet" Nuances within a Premillennial Frame

Progressive premillennialists adopt the view that certain aspects of Christ's millennial rule are already inaugurated in the present church age, while the fullness of His reign awaits His visible return. They trace the "already" dimension to Jesus' earthly ministry when He proclaimed that the kingdom of God had come near (Mark 1:15), viewing His death and resurrection as the decisive victory over evil powers (Colossians 2:15). At Pentecost, the pouring out of the Spirit (Acts 2:17) signals that the Spirit's reign extends Christ's kingship into the world now, producing kingdom realities such as transformation of hearts and multiplication of believers (Luke 17:21). Yet progressive premillennialists insist that the "not yet" remains, for Revelation 20:1–3 indicates that Satan's full binding—preventing him from deceiving the nations—does not occur until Christ's return. In the meantime, demonic activity continues (Ephesians 6:12), temporal conflicts persist, and Christ's rule, though real, remains partially veiled (1 Corinthians 15:25). This tension leads progressive premillennialists to describe the present era as a foretaste of the millennium: signs of growth, peace, and gospel advance point toward a future golden age (Isaiah 9:6–7), even as global injustice and spiritual warfare serve as reminders that the final consummation is still to come (Romans 8:22). They interpret passages like Romans 8:19–23—where creation "awaits its liberation" and believers "wait eagerly for the adoption" of final sonship—as describing both present realities and future hopes. By balancing "already" and "not yet," they maintain that the church participates in Christ's reign now through Spirit-empowered mission, yet the complete restoration of all things will only transpire when Christ physically appears (2 Peter 3:10–13). This perspective contrasts with classic premillennial views that locate virtually all kingdom fulfillment in the future millennium. Progressive premillennialists argue that partial millennial blessings—such as famine relief, increases in justice, and church planting—reflect kingdom seeds sown in the present age (Isaiah 61:1–3). Still, they caution against equating every social advance with the millennium; rather, they see positive cultural shifts as indicators that the gospel is advancing toward its final triumph (Matthew 13:31–33). Even as they affirm present kingdom fruit—church growth, moral reform, and spiritual awakening—they resist claiming that these produce a complete millennial era, preserving the "not yet" of passages like Revelation 20:7–9, where Satan is released for a final rebellion. Consequently, progressive premillennialists encourage believers to invest in social renewal and evangelism as expressions of the kingdom "already," while maintaining fervent longing for Christ's coming to enact the kingdom "not yet" (Titus 2:13). In worship, this view produces a blend of present exaltation—celebrating Christ's reign in believers' hearts—and future anticipation—looking forward to worship in a renewed Jerusalem (Revelation 21:2–4). The "already/not yet" nuance also shapes pastoral ministry: counselors encourage broken families with the assurance that the Spirit now brings comfort (John 14:16–17), even while affirming that full healing awaits Christ's triumphant return (Revelation 21:4). As a result, progressive premillennialism fosters both catalytic cultural engagement—seeking to alleviate suffering now—and patient perseverance—trusting that final victory will only come when Christ appears (James 5:7–9). This dual emphasis distinguishes progressive premillennialists from both classic premillennialists, who tend to postpone cultural hope until the millennium, and from postmillennialists, who place overwhelming confidence in human progress to usher in the kingdom before Christ's return. By embracing "already/not yet" tensions, they navigate a balanced eschatological posture that energizes present mission without discounting future consummation.

### 3.4.2 Partial Fulfillment of Davidic Promises in the Present Age

Progressive premillennialism affirms that certain Davidic covenant promises enjoy partial fulfillment in the present church age, pointing forward to a more complete realization in the future millennium. The Davidic covenant (2 Samuel 7:12–16) promised that David's offspring would have an eternal throne, an explicit reference to Messiah. Progressive premillennialists interpret this promise as inaugurated in Jesus—Israel's Messiah—whose incarnation and resurrection established His present heavenly reign (Luke 1:32–33; Acts 2:36). Thus, Christ fulfills the Davidic promise now, reigning at the Father's right hand (Ephesians 1:20–23) while interceding on behalf of believers (Hebrews 7:25). This present dimension is visible in the Spirit-led expansion of the church, which acts as Christ's body extending His kingship spiritually across the nations (Ephesians 4:15–16). Yet progressive premillennialists also insist that the full manifestation of Davidic rule over the entire earth remains future (Psalm 72:8), to be realized when Christ returns to set up His earthly throne in Jerusalem (Matthew 25:31). This future reign involves resurrected saints serving as co-regents with Christ (Revelation 20:6), administering justice (Psalm 72:1–4) and bringing about peace (Isaiah 11:6–9). In the present age, however, partial fulfillment appears whenever believers exercise spiritual authority over demonic powers (Luke 10:19), display kingdom ethics in community life (Matthew 5:3–12), and work for justice by advocating for the oppressed (Isaiah 1:17). For progressive premillennialists, each instance of gospel-driven social transformation foreshadows the wider millennial administration of David's kingdom on earth. They interpret Amos 9:11–12— promising the restoration of David's fallen "booth"—as finding initial application in the expansion of the church among Jews and Gentiles alike (Acts 15:16–17), while awaiting ultimate physical restoration in the millennial temple. This interpretive stance holds that while the church embodies Davidic values now—shepherding the flock (John 21:15–17), exercising prophetic wisdom (1 Corinthians 12:28)—the authority to implement a world-encompassing reign, replete with political structures and temple worship, awaits Christ's Second Advent. Thus, progressive premillennialists advocate vigorously for contemporary expressions of Davidic justice—feeding the hungry, advocating for the marginalized, and promoting ethical governance—while maintaining that such efforts are foretaste signs rather than full consummations. Their approach contrasts with postmillennialism, which often reads Isaiah 11:1–10 as describing a future social order achieved through widespread Christian influence before Christ's return. Progressive premillennialists maintain that while present culture-shaping efforts are significant, they do not supplant the need for Christ to establish His millennial throne in fulfillment of Davidic covenants. With this understanding of Davidic promises partially fulfilled now and consummated later, progressive premillennialists can appreciate New Testament texts such as Acts 2:29–36, which speak of David's throne ultimately belonging to his descendant, Jesus Christ, even as believers await His visible, worldly reign.

### 3.4.3 Overlap—not Parenthesis—between Israel and the Church

Progressive premillennialism rejects the strict "parenthesis" model of classic dispensationalism that temporarily sets aside God's promises to Israel during the church age. Instead, it proposes an overlapping fulfillment model in which God's covenants to Israel and His global purposes for the church run concurrently, each in distinct ways. This overlap model recognizes that while the church age unfolds under the new covenant inaugurated at Pentecost (Luke 22:20; Hebrews 9:15), God remains at work among ethnic Israel, calling individual Jews to faith in Yeshua the Messiah (Romans 11:25–27). Progressive premillennialists often point to Jesus' directed ministry to "the lost sheep of the house of Israel" (Matthew 15:24) as evidence that Israel retains a corporate role even as the church embraces Gentile nations. Similarly, Paul's statement that he was made "a minister to the Gentiles" while Peter was "a minister to the circumcised" (Galatians 2:7–8) indicates a parallel mission rather than a strict parenthesis. They argue that passages like Romans 11:16–18, which use the olive-tree metaphor, illustrate that Gentile inclusion does not replace Israel but rather grafts Gentiles into existing covenantal promises. In this overlapping model, Israel's national identity, land promises, and temple aspirations maintain relevance for the future without negating the present church's mission. Progressive premillennialists see this approach as supporting a composite fulfillment: for instance, Isaiah 62:1 speaks of salvation in Zion, which they interpret as finding current expression in the church's witness but anticipating fullness when Israel's restoration occurs prophetically in a future millennial temple (Zechariah 8:3). The overlap model also informs how progressive premillennialists read passages such as Ezekiel 36:24–28, which promise national cleansing and new hearts for Israel; they believe these promises already have partial spiritual fulfillment in the hearts of Jewish believers who have embraced the Messiah, yet await complete national fulfillment when "all Israel will be saved" (Romans 11:26). This hermeneutic contrasts with dispensationalism's strict break, which regards the church age as a parenthetic mystery with no overlap of God's redemptive dealings with Israel. Progressive premillennialists affirm that New Testament texts—such as 1 Corinthians 10:32, which admonishes believers not to offend "Jews or Greeks"—reflect this overlapping reality, encouraging simultaneous sensitivity to both communities. Practically, this overlap fosters a dual-focus mission strategy in which churches galvanize evangelical outreach to both Jews and Gentiles, recognizing distinct covenantal pathways without dividing the global church into separate destinies. Such unity-in-diversity is echoed in Revelation 5:9, where a "multitude from every tribe and language and people and nation" stands before the Lamb, implying that Israel and the church share in final worship. Progressive premillennialists therefore encourage believers to anticipate how Israel's future restoration and the church's present mission intersect, fostering prayer for both the Jewish people's national repentance and the Gentile world's transformation. By embracing an overlap rather than a parenthesis model, this view underscores continuity in God's purposes—maintaining covenantal promises to Israel while celebrating the church's global mission—until Christ's Second Advent ushers in the final phase of both programs.

**3.4.4 Ecclesiological and Missional Adjustments** Embracing a progressive premillennial framework prompts significant adjustments in ecclesiology and mission strategy, emphasizing both present gospel expansion and future covenantal fulfillment. Ecclesiologically, progressive premillennialists maintain that the church is the present manifestation of God's kingdom, called to exercise priestly and royal functions now (1 Peter 2:9; Revelation 1:6). This leads to a robust vision of the church's role as a prophetic community, embodying kingdom ethics—justice, mercy, and humility—anticipating millennial realities in community life (Micah 6:8). Worship in progressive premillennial congregations often integrates joyful praise for Christ's present reign with expectant liturgy for His coming reign; psalms of Zion hope (e.g., Psalm 122) are paired with New Testament doxologies affirming Christ's resurrected authority (Revelation 5:12). This ecclesiological model distances itself from triumphalism by insisting that while Christ reigns, believers remain pilgrims in a world still groaning (Romans

8:22), awaiting ultimate renewal. Missional adjustments follow logically: progressive premillennialists emphasize holistic mission, combining evangelism with social engagement. Programs addressing poverty, injustice, and education are regarded as kingdom outposts, reflecting millennial concerns for righteousness (Isaiah 9:7) and social flourishing (Amos 9:13–15). At the same time, evangelistic efforts among both Jews and Gentiles are prioritized, in light of Romans 15:27's reminder that Gentiles share in Hebrew spiritual blessings and Romans 10:1's call for the salvation of Israel. Progressive premillennialism also encourages strategic partnerships with Jewish ministries that witness to their own people, honoring Israel's distinct covenant while maintaining unity in Christ (Ephesians 2:14–16). Recognizing overlapping programs, churches might sponsor synagogue dialogues, fund Hebrew-language evangelistic resources, and support remnant communities of Jewish believers. Simultaneously, they mobilize discipleship initiatives among Gentile populations, trusting that as the gospel flourishes now, it prepares the way for Christ's coming in fulfillment of Isaiah 40:3–5. This dual-front mission resists mono-dimensional activism—avoiding neglect of either the Jewish restoration or Gentile evangelization. In training future leaders, seminaries undergirded by progressive premillennialism integrate courses in Hebrew Old Testament, Jewish cultural literacy, and global missions, equipping graduates to navigate both Jewish and Gentile contexts. Pastoral care in this setting balances hope amid struggle—encouraging congregants with the certainty of Christ's present reign (Colossians 1:13–14) while acknowledging that certain covenantal realities remain future (Zechariah 8:3). These ecclesiological and missional adjustments ensure that progressive premillennialism does not devolve into passive expectation but rather inspires active engagement with both immediate and eschatological dimensions of God's kingdom work. As the church lives out this dual focus, it becomes a foretaste of the harmonious future depicted in Revelation 7:9–10, where a diverse multitude stands unified before the Lamb.

# 3.5 Key Eschatological Sequences in Premillennial Thought

**3.5.1 Order of Resurrection(s) and Judgment(s)** In premillennial frameworks, the sequence of resurrection and judgment reflects careful attention to New Testament texts, ensuring that saintly and unsaintly destinies unfold in a biblically consistent order. Classic historic premillennialists hold to a single resurrection of all righteous dead at Christ's return (1 Thessalonians 4:16–17; Revelation 20:4–6), followed by the thousand-year reign and then a general resurrection of the unrighteous for final judgment (Revelation 20:11–15). Dispensational premillennialists, by contrast, divide the resurrection into two stages: first, the "firstfruits" resurrection of believers at the rapture (1 Corinthians 15:20–23), and second, the general resurrection of both believers and unbelievers after the millennium, followed by the Great White Throne judgment (Revelation 20:5, 11–13). Progressive premillennialists often adopt the historic scheme, citing John 5:28–29's promise that "all who are in the tombs will hear his voice" with separate destinies—some for life, some for judgment—in a way that suggests a single resurrection event rather than multiple phases. They argue that 1 Corinthians 15:51–52 and 1 Thessalonians 4:16–17 describe the same climactic moment when Christ appears, resurrection occurs, and judgment ensues. After the resurrection of the righteous, premillennialists teach that resurrected saints will immediately reign with Christ, exercising judgment roles as indicated in 1 Corinthians 6:2–3. This judgment by saints prior to the millennial reign underscores Scripture's teaching that the righteous judge the world (Revelation 19:11–16) and that believers will share Christ's authority (Revelation 2:26–27). During the millennium, unsaved mortals—those who survived the tribulation but remain unregenerate—face judgment for their rebellion (Matthew 25:41–46), illustrating that Christ's millennial rule includes judicial functions. At millennium's end, Satan is released for a final deception (Revelation 20:7–8), and the "Gog and Magog" rebellion unfolds, followed by Satan's ultimate defeat and the final judgment at the Great White Throne (Revelation 20:11–15). Some premillennialists debate whether these end-of-millennium martially oriented judgments involve a physical resurrection for the unsaved before the final sentence, but consensus holds that a resurrection for the wicked occurs in order to face divine judgment, as taught in Daniel 12:2. Throughout these sequences, passages like Daniel 12:2, John 5:28–29, and Revelation 20:12–13 provide anchor points, ensuring that resurrection and judgment align with biblical chronology. Premillennialists emphasize that the resurrection of the righteous precedes judgment on the wicked to uphold Scripture's teaching that saintly vindication comes before the earth's final cleansing (1 Corinthians 15:24–26). They also affirm that God's justice is meted out with perfect timing: no saint faces condemnation, and no sinner escapes accountability (Romans 14:10–12). This orderly progression reassures believers that resurrection for life comes first, allowing them to anticipate a future reign free from the curse of death (Revelation 21:4). Having clarified the resurrection and judgment sequences, premillennialists turn to examine how nations factor into these events, particularly through the lens of prophecy concerning Gog and Magog.

### 3.5.2 Role of the Nations and the Final Rebellion (Gog & Magog)

Premillennial thought assigns a prominent role to the nations in end-time events, especially regarding the final rebellion led by Gog and Magog at the close of the millennial era. The term "Gog and Magog" originates in Ezekiel 38–39, where Gog, the leader of Magog and various allied peoples, arises from "the far north" to attack a restored Israel. Historic premillennialists interpret Ezekiel's prophecy as corresponding to the millennial kingdom when an alliance of nations, stirred by Satan's release, attempts to overthrow Christ's reign (Revelation 20:7–9). They draw parallels between Ezekiel 38:18–23's cosmic battle imagery—earthquake, hailstones, fiery sulfur—and Revelation 20:9's fire from heaven consuming Gog's forces. Dispensational premillennialists often view Gog and Magog as a distinct end-of-millennium rebellion involving nations such as Russia, Iran, and their allies, reflecting modern geopolitical configurations. They cite passages like Ezekiel 38:2–6 to construct identity lists, seeing Magog as corresponding to Russia, Meshech and Tubal to regions of Turkey, and Persia to Iran (Ezekiel 38:5–6). Progressive premillennialists caution against rigid geographic assignments, arguing that Ezekiel's symbolic language transcends specific modern states, instead representing any human coalition that unites in rebellion against God's rule. They emphasize that Revelation 20:7–9's language—"the nations that are at the four corners of the earth" (Revelation 20:8)—decorates the text with universal scope, indicating that Gog and Magog symbolize a final global uprising of unredeemed humanity. Premillennialists draw on Psalm 2:1–2, where the "nations" and "peoples" "plot in vain against the Lord," to show that this spirit of anti-God coalition recurs at millennium's end. This final rebellion serves two purposes: it exposes the lasting sinfulness in human hearts despite a re-ordered world (Jeremiah 17:9), and it justifies the final judgment of God's wrath, highlighting the necessity of His sovereign victory (2 Thessalonians 1:7–10). After Gog's forces are consumed by divine fire, Satan is thrown into the lake of fire (Revelation 20:10), eliminating any remaining adversarial power. This sequence underscores that the millennium's peace and justice are provisional, contingent on God's restraining work (2 Thessalonians 2:6–7), and that human rebellion will re-emerge without Christ's active rule. Premillennialists often point to Isaiah 66:15–16's language of the Lord coming in fire against all flesh to argue that God's final judgment on Gog's rebellion prefigures the day of the Lord. Moreover, Matthew 25:31–46's separation of nations at the sheep-and-goats judgment affirms that God holds nations morally accountable, even under Christ's millennial rule. By analyzing these passages in concert—Ezekiel 38–39, Revelation 20, Psalm 2, and Isaiah 66—premillennialists construct a cohesive narrative in which God's covenantal promises to Israel and His righteous governance over the nations culminate in a final confrontation that vindicates divine justice. As the rebellion closes the millennial chapter, attention turns to the binding and final defeat of Satan, completing the trajectory of cosmic conflict.

### 3.5.3 Binding, Release, and Ultimate Defeat of Satan A fundamental element of premillennial chronology revolves around Satan's binding at Christ's return, his limited release at the millennium's end, and his final defeat. Historic premillennialists read Revelation 20:1–3 as a literal binding of Satan, during which he is unable to deceive the nations, enabling Christ's reign to proceed unimpeded. This binding is seen as a distinct act that occurs immediately after the Second Advent, aligning with Christ's defeat of Satan on the cross (John 12:31; Colossians 2:15) but fully realized only when Christ returns in glory. During the thousand years, Satan's direct influence is restrained, providing the world an unprecedented period of righteousness and peace (Isaiah 11:9; Micah 4:3–4). Mid-millennium, premillennialists indicate that Satan's binding frees believers to establish a just order, restore

Israel, and initiate worship as prescribed in Ezekiel 40–48. At the millennium's close, Revelation 20:7 describes Satan's release "for a little while," a mandatory, divinely sanctioned permission to test the earth's inhabitants one final time. This release underscores human depravity: despite living under Christ's righteous reign, many persisted in rebellion, demonstrating that genuine submission comes only through transformation at Christ's coming. Progressive premillennialists emphasize that this short release of Satan (Revelation 20:7–8) reveals the depth of sin in human nature, reinforcing Romans 8:20–22's teaching that even a renewed creation still groans for final redemption. The resulting Gog and Magog coalition (Revelation 20:8–9) attempts to surround "the camp of the saints and the beloved city," signifying a direct assault on God's people and the epicenter of worship. Historic premillennialists point to Psalm 2:1–2—"Why do the nations rage and the peoples plot in vain?"—as prefiguring this cosmic insurrection against God's rule, reinforcing the continuity of biblical themes. Satan's ultimate defeat follows swiftly: fire comes down from heaven and consumes his forces (Revelation 20:9), after which Satan is thrown "into the lake of fire and sulfur" to reign there "forever and ever" (Revelation 20:10). This final judgment confirms that any perceived success of evil is a temporary illusion; God's covenant has secured an unassailable victory. Premillennialists draw on 2 Thessalonians 2:8, where the lawless one is destroyed "by the breath of his mouth," to parallel Christ's swift, divine intervention. At this juncture, Satan's binding becomes permanent, and the cosmos proceeds to the "great white throne" judgment (Revelation 20:11–15), culminating in the inauguration of new heavens and a new earth (Revelation 21:1). By tracing Satan's trajectory—from defeated tempter (John 12:31) to bound restrainer (Revelation 20:1–3), to final rebel (Revelation 20:7–9), to consummate prisoner (Revelation 20:10)—premillennialists underscore Scripture's comprehensive portrayal of cosmic conflict and divine sovereignty. This sequence also explains why the millennium is distinct from both the present church age and the eternal state: it is a unique interlude characterized by Christ's visible earthly rule free from Satan's unchecked influence. With Satan's ultimate defeat, biblical eschatology transitions seamlessly into the consummated state of eternal worship, preparing readers to examine the tangible realities of Christ's millennial kingdom on earth.

# 3.6 The Millennial Kingdom on Earth

### 3.6.1 Geographic Center and Davidic Throne in Jerusalem

Premillennialists universally affirm that Jerusalem will serve as the geographic and political center of Christ's millennial kingdom, fulfilling Old Testament prophecies such as Zechariah 14:9, which proclaims, "The Lord will be king over all the earth; on that day the Lord will be one and his name one." They argue that during the millennium, Christ will sit on David's throne in Jerusalem (2 Samuel 7:12–16; Luke 1:32–33), overseeing a theocratic government that extends justice and righteousness (Jeremiah 23:5–6). Historic premillennialists contend that the physical land of Israel, restored to her covenanted borders (Ezekiel 47:13–21), will become the administrative nexus for all nations, as depicted in Isaiah 2:2–4, where "many peoples shall come" to the mountain of the Lord. This reign features a restored Davidic monarchy with Christ as King of kings and Lord of lords (Revelation 19:16), exercising authority through resurrected saints who serve as princes and judges (Revelation 20:4; Daniel 7:22). Dispensational premillennialists emphasize that promises regarding Israel's land—outlined in Genesis 15:18–21—are neither nullified nor spiritualized but will be literally fulfilled when Christ brings His kingdom to earth (Acts 1:6–7). They interpret Zechariah 14:4's description of the Mount of Olives splitting in two as a future, tangible event demonstrating Christ's physical descent and subsequent enthronement in Jerusalem. The resurrected temple described in Ezekiel 40–48 is likewise seen as a literal building reestablished to facilitate worship centered in Jerusalem, with the Davidic throne situated in the temple's inner court (Ezekiel 42:1–5). Progressive premillennialists, while affirming Jerusalem's centrality, sometimes allow for symbolic elements in the city's description—viewing the New Jerusalem imagery in Revelation 21:2 as a heavenly prototype of the millennial city—yet still maintain a physical component to Jerusalem's authority on earth. They reference Psalm 122:6's injunction to "pray for the peace of Jerusalem" as an enduring command that takes on fresh significance during the millennium, when the city's peace represents global harmony under Christ's rule. Pastoral devotion in premillennial churches often emphasizes pilgrimage imagery, encouraging believers to long for the day when all nations will stream to Zion (Isaiah 60:3), evoking Hebrews

12:22–24's depiction of the heavenly Jerusalem in worshipful assembly. The language of "Jerusalem" thus functions both as a present spiritual reality—the gathered community of the redeemed (Galatians 4:26)—and as a future geopolitical epicenter of Christ's reign (Matthew 25:31–34). This dual emphasis ensures that Jerusalem's role in the millennium retains both historical continuity with Israel's heritage and forward-looking hope in Christ's visible rule. As readers consider Jerusalem's centrality, attention then shifts to the socio-political restoration and life under Christ's Davidic administration.

### 3.6.2 Socio-Political Restoration: Justice, Peace, and Prosperity

The millennial kingdom is characterized by a comprehensive restoration of social, political, and economic structures to align with divine justice and righteousness. Premillennialists draw on Isaiah 11:4–5, which prophesies that the Messiah "will judge the poor with righteousness, and decide with equity for the meek of the earth," to depict a government that prioritizes fairness and compassion. Economic systems under Christ's reign will banish poverty in ways described in Amos 9:13–15, where fields yield abundance and "people shall dwell in it without walls, for now I will create security for them." Historic premillennialists envision that resurrected saints, functioning as co-regents, will apply Christ's righteous standards to civil law, adjudicating in ignorance-free conditions since the knowledge of the Lord will fill the earth (Habakkuk 2:14; Jeremiah 31:34). This alignment with prophetic texts ensures that political authority derives directly from Christ's Davidic lineage rather than from human ambition or corruption. Progressive premillennialists emphasize that present expressions of kingdom justice—such as legal reforms, human rights advocacy, and environmental stewardship—foreshadow millennial realities, even as they acknowledge that true and lasting justice will only fully manifest when Christ rules physically. In the social realm, marriage and family structures will be restored to God's design, as suggested by Ezekiel 36:35, which describes a land "enchanted" so that "ruin will not be rebuilt" and "cyphers will not come to mind." Peace, symbolized in Isaiah 2:4's prophecy that "they shall beat their swords into plowshares and their spears into pruning hooks," will prevail as nations no longer "learn war" (Micah 4:3). This literal disarmament contrasts with contemporary peace efforts, which are often temporary and fragile, highlighting the supernatural nature of millennial peace. Prosperity under Christ's rule includes healing of physical ailments (Isaiah 35:5–6) and reversal of ecological curses (Isaiah 35:1–2), fulfilling Genesis 3:17–19's promise that creation groans for restoration. Premillennialists argue that while modern social programs can alleviate immediate suffering, only Christ's direct governance can eradicate systemic injustice and usher in universal well-being. This socio-political utopia will draw scholars, politicians, and church leaders to examine prophetic guidelines—such as Micah 6:8's call to "do justice, love kindness, and walk humbly with your God"—as they envision how resurrected saints will govern under Christ. The present church's mission to advocate for the poor and oppressed (Proverbs 31:8–9) thus participates in preparatory kingdom work, even as premillennialists caution that these efforts cannot realize full millennial prosperity apart from Christ's return. Observers throughout church history have noted that recipe for such universal flourishing requires both divine intervention and human fidelity to kingdom values—affirming that the millennium will be a time when human agency cooperates fully under Christ's righteous rule. As economic and social systems become expressions of God's covenant faithfulness, the millennial kingdom demonstrates how every sphere of life aligns with biblical justice. With socio-political restoration outlined, the focus now turns to temple worship, sacrificial practices, and pilgrimage festivals that define communal worship under Christ's millennial reign.

### 3.6.3 Temple Worship, Sacrificial Memorials, and Pilgrimage Festivals
Premillennialists expect that a physical temple will be built or restored in Jerusalem during the millennium, serving as the locus of worship and sacrifice in continuity with Old Testament prescriptions. They draw primarily on Ezekiel 40–48, where the prophet describes detailed measurements for a future temple, its courts, and sacrificial regulations, as a blueprint for millennial worship practices. According to Ezekiel 43:7–9, the glory of the Lord will fill the temple, signifying God's tangible presence among His people. Historic premillennialists often interpret such passages literally, anticipating that sacrifices—though understood as memorials rather than atoning rituals, since Christ's once-for-all atonement (Hebrews 10:10–14) obviates the need for repetitive blood offerings—will be reinstated as a visible testimony to Christ's redemptive work. See Leviticus 17:11 for the principle that "the life of the flesh is in the blood" which points forward to the

substitutionary death of Christ (1 John 1:7). Dispensational premillennialists, more than classic historic premillennialists, detail how Millennial temple sacrifices will function: they argue that while Christ's sacrifice remains the sole basis for atonement, animal sacrifices during the millennium serve as memorials that teach subsequent generations about the costliness of sin (Ezekiel 43:18–27). Progressive premillennialists acknowledge these memorial sacraments but often stress that the heart of worship belongs to spiritual sacrifices—praising God, reading Scripture, and proclaiming the gospel in the millennial temple courts (Psalm 96:8–9). They cite John 4:23–24 to suggest that true worshipers will worship in spirit and truth, even in a millennial context, thereby integrating continuity with New Testament worship principles. Pilgrimage festivals—Passover, Weeks, and Booths—will be reinstituted as annual celebrations, as foretold in Zechariah 14:16–19, where all nations that survive unconverted "must go up from year to year to worship the King." These festivals will underscore God's sovereignty and Israel's central role in redemptive history, even as Gentile believers join in thanksgiving alongside Jewish participants. The millennial calendar thus reestablishes a sacred rhythm for worship: Passover commemorates Christ's sacrificial death, Weeks (Pentecost) celebrates the outpouring of the Spirit, and Booths (Sukkot) honors God's provision and presence. Historic premillennialists point to Leviticus 23 as a model for these feasts, arguing that Christ's in-gathering of Gentiles before the millennium invites participation in Israel's sacramental life. Economic arrangements during the millennium will ensure that tithes and offerings support the Levites and priests (Leviticus 27:30–34), reinforcing community solidarity and divine provision. The millennial temple's geographical layout—courtyard, inner court, and Most Holy Place—will serve pedagogical purposes, guiding worshipers in understanding their distance from God's holiness and the path of approach made possible by Christ (Hebrews 10:19–22). These temple practices underscore the unity of worship across ethnic lines: Gentiles drawn to Zion (Isaiah 2:2–3) will bring offerings, symbolizing the reconciliation of nations to God. As worship remains central to millennial life, premillennialists envision harmonious gatherings of "a great multitude that no one could number, from every nation, from all tribes and peoples and languages," standing before the throne and before the Lamb (Revelation 7:9). This integration of Jewish feasts and New

Testament spiritual worship demonstrates how temple practices in the millennium fulfill both continuity and fulfillment of biblical worship models. Having detailed temple worship, the chapter now turns to the broader environmental renewal that will accompany Christ's reign.

### 3.6.4 Environmental Renewal: Curse Reversed and Creation's Liberation
Creation's restoration figures prominently in premillennial hope, with the millennium envisioned as an era in which the earthly environment is renewed, and the consequences of the Fall are reversed. Progressive premillennialists highlight Romans 8:19–21, where Paul explains that "creation waits with eager longing for the revealing of the sons of God" because it was subjected to futility—referring to Genesis 3:17–19's curse—and anticipates deliverance at Christ's return. Historic premillennialists emphasize that during the millennium, the ground "shall no more be doomed to production of thorns and thistles" (Isaiah 55:13), aligning with Genesis 3:18's curse wherein the earth yields thorns. Isaiah 35:1–2 describes the desert and parched land blossoming like the crocus, a vivid picture of ecological renewal that will manifest when "the glory of the Lord is revealed, and all flesh shall see it together" (Isaiah 40:5). Dispensationalists point to Ezekiel 47:1–12's vision of water flowing from the millennial temple to bring life to the Dead Sea, turning its waters fresh and teeming with fish. This imagery conveys restoration of aquatic and riparian ecosystems, indicating that environmental healing is both physical and symbolic of Christ's redemptive power. Premillennialists also invoke Isaiah 65:25, which prophesies that "the wolf and the lamb shall feed together" and "no one shall hurt or destroy in all my holy mountain," suggesting a radical reversal of predator-prey dynamics. Such passages inform the premillennial expectation that even animal behavior will reflect peaceful coexistence, reinforcing that the creation itself benefits from Christ's reign. Progressive premillennialists caution against over-allegorizing these images, emphasizing that the text's literal and symbolic elements combine to present an earth-wide renewal that transcends current environmental limitations. They note that Revelation 21:1's promise of a new heaven and new earth follows the closing of the millennial chapter, but many believe that the conditions of the millennium prefigure this final renewal, marking an intermediate stage between present groaning and consummation. Additionally, premillennialists draw on Psalm 104:30, which

portrays God sending forth His Spirit to create and sustain life, as an antecedent to how the Spirit's empowering presence during the millennium will facilitate restoration. This ecology of blessing extends to human stewardship: humans, no longer alienated from the ground, will cultivate and steward creation in ways that reflect God's original mandate in Genesis 1:28. As the curse lifts, premillennialists believe that sustainable agriculture, abundant harvests, and harmonious relationships with flora and fauna will demonstrate God's covenant faithfulness. Social and economic structures during the millennium, such as equitable land distributions (Amos 9:14–15) and Sabbath rest for the land (Leviticus 25:3–7), will also reinforce environmental renewal. By linking creation's liberation with Christ's reign (Romans 8:21), premillennialists underscore that environmental flourishing is not a mere byproduct of human effort but a divine promise fulfilled under Christ's kingdom. As ecological restoration unfolds, the roles of resurrected saints, Israel, and Gentile nations in governance come into focus, leading to an examination of millennial leadership structures.

**3.6.5 Governance: Roles of Resurrected Saints, Israel, and Gentile Nations** Under Christ's millennial reign, governance involves multiple tiers of authority that distribute responsibilities among resurrected believers, national Israel, and Gentile nations. Classic historic premillennialists point to Revelation 20:4–6, where resurrected saints "came to life and reigned with Christ for a thousand years," indicating that believers share in Christ's rule as His co-regents. These co-regents are often portrayed as judges for the nations (1 Corinthians 6:2), administering justice and guiding communities according to Christ's principles. Dispensational premillennialists similarly affirm the saints' co-regency but place strong emphasis on Israel's unique national role, teaching that restored Israel functions as a priestly-kingly nation during the millennium. Isaiah 2:3's vision of many nations streaming to "the house of the God of Jacob" implies that Israel exercises spiritual leadership, instructing Gentile nations in God's ways. Premillennialists teach that tribal territories of Israel, as delineated in Ezekiel 48:1–29, will serve as administrative provinces, each governed by resurrected patriarchs or tribal leaders who coordinate with Christ's kingship on Mount Zion. Progressive premillennialists stress that Gentile leaders, converted to Christ either during tribulation or early in the millennium, will serve under Christ's overarching authority while representing their respective nations (Zechariah 14:16–19). These leaders administer civic responsibilities—law, commerce, and infrastructure—under the ethical frameworks established by Christ and His resurrected saints. Historic premillennialists cite Daniel 7:22, where the "Ancient of Days gave judgment in favor of the saints of the Most High, and the time came when the saints received the kingdom," supporting the notion that saints function as an administrative tier. This multi-tier governance affirms that hierarchy in the millennium reflects divine order: Christ as King, resurrected saints as co-regents, ethnic Israel as priestly intermediaries, and Gentile nations as subject peoples living under God's law (Zechariah 14:16–19). Theocratic jurisprudence will emphasize scriptural precedents—Exodus 21–23's civil codes and Deuteronomy 16:18–20's judicial mandates—though augmented by Christ's own authoritative pronouncements (Matthew 5–7). Economic policies will reflect principles of Jubilee (Leviticus 25:8–22), ensuring equity and preventing generational poverty. Educational systems will center around teaching the Law of the Lord (Isaiah 54:13; Psalm 78:5–7), with resurrected prophets and judges overseeing curriculum to align human flourishing with divine wisdom. By integrating resurrected saints, ethnic Israel, and Gentile nations into a cohesive governance structure, premillennialists illustrate how Scripture's promises coalesce into a functional kingdom that exemplifies justice, mercy, and divine order (Micah 4:1–3). This governance model underscores that the millennium is not simply a prolonged revival of the church age but a novel epoch in which earthly political institutions operate under Christ's visible authority, fulfilling texts such as Zechariah 14:9 and Psalm 2:8–9. As the millennium draws to its close, readers will see how this governance framework gives way to final rebellion, ultimate judgment, and the inauguration of new heavens and earth.

## 3.7 Theological Distinctives and Systemic Implications

### 3.7.1 Hermeneutics: Literal Fulfillment and Prophetic Telescoping Premillennial hermeneutics insist on a predominantly literal reading of prophetic Scriptures, especially those concerning the end times. This approach holds that promises made to Israel—regarding land (Genesis 15:18), temple worship (Ezekiel 40–48),

and the Davidic throne (2 Samuel 7:12–16)—must be fulfilled in a concrete, geographic sense. Advocates point to passages like Zechariah 8:3, which promises "the city shall be inhabited" as evidence that future prophecies describe actual events rather than merely symbolic realities. They argue that Jesus Himself endorsed literal fulfillment when He referred to the temple's stones being thrown down (Matthew 24:2), implying a real destruction and foreshadowing a future literal construction. Literal fulfillment also governs their reading of Revelation 20:1–6; the millennium's "thousand years" are taken as a real chronological span rather than a symbolic period. At the same time, premillennialists recognize that prophetic texts often telescope events—compressing multiple future realities into a single vision to emphasize theological intent. They observe that prophecies like Daniel 9:24–27 illustrate how Daniel's seventy weeks can overlap historical periods, with partial fulfillments in the first century and final fulfillment in a future tribulation context. Similarly, Jesus' Olivet Discourse (Matthew 24–25) weaves together references to the Jewish War of AD 70, the church age, and the final coming in a single extended prophecy. Premillennialists maintain that understanding such telescoping requires careful attention to contextual markers—phrases like "this generation" (Matthew 24:34) versus "immediately after the tribulation" (Matthew 24:29). They argue that only by harmonizing literal expectation with awareness of telescoping can one avoid the pitfalls of overly rigid date-setting or unconstrained allegorization. This dual commitment allows them to affirm that the church will face tribulation (Revelation 7:14) while also looking forward to Christ's physical return to establish His kingdom (Revelation 19:11–16). They find support in 2 Peter 3:8–9, which reminds readers that God's perspective on time differs from ours, so prophetic chronology may exceed human comprehension yet still be literal. Premillennialists often critique allegorical approaches for spiritualizing away Israel's unique identity, contending that Isaiah 65:17's promise of new heavens and new earth demands a literal restoration rather than a purely spiritual metaphor. Their hermeneutical method also involves cross-referencing Scripture with Scripture—using Revelation 21:1–3 to interpret Isaiah 66:22–23, thereby confirming that God's creation renewal encompasses physical geography. This hermeneutic produces detailed eschatological charts that map out a sequence of events from the rapture to the final judgment, aiming for coherence within a literal framework. Critics claim this can lead to forced harmonizations, but premillennialists counter that a disciplined literal reading prevents theological drift and maintains fidelity to God's promises. Ultimately, their hermeneutic of literal fulfillment anchored in prophetic telescoping insists on both historical sensitivity and grammatical–historical exegesis, guarding against eisegesis while embracing the richness of Scripture's timeline.

### 3.7.2 Covenants, Promises, and the Integrity of God's Word

Premillennialism's covenantal framework upholds that God's promises to Israel and to the church remain distinct yet harmonious within a unified redemptive plan. They emphasize that the Abrahamic covenant (Genesis 12:1–3) promised land, offspring, and blessing to all nations through Israel's Messiah, and that these promises have never been revoked. This conviction leads premillennialists to maintain that New Covenant blessings (Jeremiah 31:31–34; Luke 22:20) do not cancel Old Covenant obligations to ethnic Israel; rather, they layer upon one another, allowing Israel's national destiny to unfold alongside the church's spiritual destiny. When Paul writes in Romans 11:29 that "the gifts and the calling of God are irrevocable," premillennialists see this as a clear affirmation that God will fulfill His earlier promises to Israel in the millennium. They argue that Jesus' words in Matthew 5:17—"Do not think that I have come to abolish the Law or the Prophets. I have not come to abolish them but to fulfill them"—should be read as meaning that Christ's fulfillment includes a future fulfillment of Mosaic and Davidic covenants rather than a total abrogation. As a result, premillennialists teach that the land promises found in Deuteronomy 30:1–5 remain binding, guaranteeing Israel's restoration and inheritance at Christ's return. They also highlight passages such as Hebrews 8:6–13, which describe the superior nature of the New Covenant but do not specify that the Old Covenant has no future role. Instead, they see the New Covenant as inaugurating spiritual salvation for both Jews and Gentiles while preserving national covenants for Israel's future earthly administration. This conviction shapes eschatological expectations: the restoration of temple sacrifices (Ezekiel 43:18–27) is not a regression but a memorial enactment that honors the sacrificial system in light of Christ's once-for-all atonement (Hebrews 10:10). Dispensational premillennialists further assert that covenants such as the Davidic covenant (2 Samuel 7:12–16) entail an everlasting throne that must be physically manifested in Jerusalem's political sphere. Progressive premillennialists may soften the sharp division by affirming that New Covenant realities are already at work in the church, yet they maintain that Old Covenant structures find fuller expression in the millennium. This dual-covenantal approach provides theological integrity by refusing to spiritualize away God's literal commitments, thus upholding the veracity of every biblical promise. Critics who charge premillennialists with compartmentalizing Scripture are met with the rejoinder that their framework actually maintains God's faithfulness across dispensations—ensuring that no promise is left unfulfilled. It also underscores the application of Galatians 3:29, where those in Christ are counted as Abraham's seed, while preserving the national identity of Israel in Romans 11:26–27. By demonstrating continuity within diversity, premillennialists argue that the integrity of God's Word remains paramount: divine covenants cannot be selectively nullified without undermining Scripture's unified narrative of redemption.

### 3.7.3 Soteriology and Assurance in a Tribulation Context

Premillennial eschatology intersects robustly with soteriology, influencing how believers understand the security of their salvation amid impending tribulation. Historic premillennialists teach that once a person is justified by faith in Christ, he or she enjoys eternal security grounded in God's irrevocable promise (Romans 8:38–39). They emphasize that this assurance remains steadfast even if the believer endures persecution or falls into sin, because 1 John 5:13 declares, "I write these things to you who believe in the name of the Son of God that you may know that you have eternal life." As tribulation approaches, premillennial pastors often reassure congregations with Christ's words in John 16:33—that in the world, believers will have tribulation, but Christ has overcome the world— affirming that ultimate victory belongs to Christ and His saints. Dispensational premillennialists often emphasize the imminence of the rapture (Titus 2:13), teaching that believers will be removed from the earth before the worst of the tribulation begins, thereby providing comfort that Christ will spare His church from God's wrath (1 Thessalonians 5:9). This doctrine of pretribulation rapture fosters a sense of urgency in holy living (1 John 2:28) and evangelism (1 Thessalonians 4:16–17), since the prospect of Christ's sudden coming motivates ethical obedience and outreach. Historic premillennialists, who affirm a post-tribulation return, emphasize perseverance over escape, calling believers to emulate early Christians under Nero's persecution (1 Peter 1:6–7) while trusting that God will sustain them until Christ's coming. In both classic and dispensational models, soteriology incorporates the concept of a future judgment seat (Bema Seat) for believers (2 Corinthians 5:10), where rewards are dispensed not for salvation but for faithfulness in service. Premillennialists caution against conflating reward with salvation, teaching that while works do not secure justification (Ephesians 2:8–9), they do affect future privileges in the kingdom (1 Corinthians 3:12–15). This secondary judgment underscores the importance of living a faithful life, especially in tribulation, without undermining assurance of eternal life. Progressive premillennialists propose that tribulation will purify the church (Revelation 3:10; 1 Peter 4:12–13), sharpening the community's witness while confirming the genuineness of faith. They draw on James 1:2–4 to argue that trials produce steadfastness, which in turn yields spiritual maturity—attributes that matter at Christ's return. This soteriological framework assures believers that although they may face intense suffering, their salvation is secured by Christ's atoning work (John 10:28–29) and will be fully manifested at the resurrection (1 Corinthians 15:20–23). By integrating these biblical assurances, premillennialists endeavour to cultivate a faith that remains unwavering in the face of tribulation, grounded in the knowledge that Christ's return will vindicate and reward the faithful. As soteriology shapes personal assurance, it also informs how premillennial communities worship, pray, and engage in mission under the shadow of coming tribulation.

### 3.7.4 Ecclesiology: Mission, Sacraments, and Church-State Relations

Premillennial theology impacts ecclesiology in significant ways, shaping how the church understands its mission, administers sacraments, and relates to civil authority. Mission assumes a heightened urgency, for if Christ might return at any moment—or after a short tribulation—the church must proclaim the gospel to all nations (Matthew 24:14; Acts 1:8). Historic premillennialists stress that tribulation intensifies mission by calling believers to serve as witnesses under persecution (Revelation 12:11), while dispensationalists, anticipating a pretribulation rapture, emphasize that the church's work continues unimpeded until Christ appears. In either case, sacraments—baptism and the Lord's Supper—gain eschatological significance as visible markers of

Christ's death and resurrection (1 Corinthians 11:26) and as pledges of future participation in His kingdom (Acts 2:41–42). Premillennial congregations often celebrate the Lord's Supper with special focus on its "proclamation of the Lord's death" until He comes, highlighting the "until He comes" phrase as an eschatological reminder (1 Corinthians 11:26). Baptism is likewise emphasized as a symbolic participation in Christ's death and resurrection (Romans 6:3–4), anticipating the believer's future resurrection in the millennium. Premillennial ecclesiology also addresses church-state relations in light of tribulational scenarios. Historic premillennialists generally advocate for cooperation with government authorities (Romans 13:1–7) while acknowledging that eventual persecution under the Antichrist will put the church at odds with the state (Revelation 13:15–17). They caution that Christ's kingdom is not of this world (John 18:36) and that believers should remain faithful witnesses even if authorities demand allegiance to a global, antichristic regime. Dispensationalists often encourage political disengagement or selective involvement, teaching that since the church's destiny transcends earthly governments, Christians should focus on spiritual preparedness rather than socio-political influence. Progressive premillennialists, emphasizing overlap between the church and Israel, may advocate dual citizenship—earthly and heavenly—encouraging believers to engage civil authorities in ways that reflect kingdom ethics (Matthew 5:13–16) while maintaining loyalty to Christ above all. This perspective draws on Daniel 6:10, where Daniel continues to pray to God despite civil decrees, modeling faithfulness under potential persecution. Sacramental theology in premillennial contexts often incorporates symbolic anticipations of the millennium: baptismal fonts and communion elements may be presented with art emphasizing Christ's return and the coming kingdom. Mission strategies include supporting Jewish evangelism in light of Romans 11:25–26 and encouraging cross-cultural church planting as a foretaste of nations streaming to Zion (Isaiah 2:2–3). As the millennium approaches, premillennial ecclesiology envisions a church purified by tribulation, united with Israel and Gentile converts in worship, and equipped to carry out justice and mercy as signs of Christ's reign (Isaiah 61:1–4). This institutional posture underscores that mission, sacraments, and church-state relations are all imbued with future hope, reminding congregations that their present identity hinges on Christ's coming kingdom rather than solely on current ecclesial structures.

### 3.7.5 Ethics: Holiness, Evangelism, and Social Engagement

Premillennial ethics draws on the expectation of Christ's imminent return to inform personal holiness, evangelistic zeal, and social engagement. Personal holiness is motivated by awareness that Christ could return at any moment, prompting believers to live in anticipation of being found "spotless, blameless, and at peace" (2 Peter 3:14). Historic premillennialists often cite 1 John 3:2–3, teaching that anticipating Christ's appearance purifies one's character—whosoever hopes in Christ purifies himself "just as he is pure." Dispensationalists, emphasizing the rapture's imminence, stress that moral vigilance includes avoidance of compromised finances, pleasures, or idolatrous alliances that could disqualify believers from the Bride's spotless appearance (Revelation 3:5). Progressive premillennialists balance this imminence with an understanding of kingdom growth—pressing believers to engage cultural renewal while maintaining personal integrity (Matthew 5:13–16). Evangelism becomes an urgent imperative for premillennial ethics, grounded in the Great Commission (Matthew 28:18–20) and fueled by the conviction that many remain unreached in the time leading up to Christ's return (Matthew 24:14). Classic premillennialists highlight Jesus' parable of the workers in the vineyard (Matthew 20:1–16) to teach that the invitation to work in the kingdom lasts until the eleventh hour, urging continuous outreach. Dispensationalists, believing in a pretribulation rapture, often emphasize the urgency of warning unbelievers because the opportunity to hear the gospel in the tribulation is limited and fraught with persecution (Revelation 13:10–17). Progressive premillennialists add that present evangelistic efforts have millennial implications; every soul won before Christ's return contributes to the diversity and richness of the saints who will reign with Him (Revelation 7:9–10). Social engagement in premillennial ethics arises from the belief that alleviating suffering and restoring justice prefigures millennial restoration. Historic premillennialists maintain that social programs—feeding the hungry (Matthew 25:35), caring for widows and orphans (James 1:27), and advocating for the oppressed (Isaiah 1:17)—serve as tangible expressions of kingdom values in a world still under the curse. Dispensationalists may prioritize evangelistic work over systemic social change, arguing that the latter cannot fully rectify fallen structures until Christ's direct intervention. Nevertheless, many dispensational congregations support relief efforts and justice ministries, seeing them as opportunities to demonstrate Christ's love (John 13:34–35) and to open doors for gospel witness. Progressive premillennialists affirm that while present social efforts cannot achieve millennial perfection, they participate in the "already" dimension of the kingdom, providing foreshadowing of future harmony with creation's liberation (Romans 8:21). This perspective encourages Christians to exercise responsible stewardship—sustainable use of resources, environmental care, and equitable distribution—reflecting Genesis 2:15's command to "till and keep" creation. As believers anticipate Christ's millennial reign, their ethical choices in holiness, evangelism, and social engagement remain shaped by the conviction that every act of obedience contributes to God's redemptive narrative, poised for ultimate fulfillment at the Second Advent.

**Conclusion** Throughout our exploration of premillennialism, one theme emerges with remarkable consistency: an unwavering confidence that Scripture's promises to Israel, detailed in the covenantal tapestry of the Old Testament prophets, will find literal fulfillment in a future, earthly kingdom. Whether we have followed the historic premillennial vision of the early church fathers, examined the dispensational schema that popularized the secret rapture and the seven-year tribulation, or wrestled with a progressive model that embraces both present and future dimensions of Christ's reign, the central conviction remains that the world as we know it awaits a definitive intervention of the King. This belief has shaped how believers have understood suffering—seeing tribulation as a purifying trial—how they have articulated the order of resurrection and judgment, and how they have envisioned a renewed creation under Christ's Davidic throne in Jerusalem. Along the way, we have seen how brotherhood in the church is bound up with unity with Jewish brethren—an overlap that calls for prayerful engagement and evangelistic fervor among both Jews and Gentiles (Romans 11:25–27). We have also recognized that premillennial ethics flow from an eschatological timetable: the certainty of Christ's return motivates personal holiness, fuels urgent evangelism, and sparks social endeavors that anticipate millennial ideals of justice and restoration. As this chapter closes, readers are invited to measure the insights gained against the broader Christian landscape, noting areas of harmony and tension with postmillennial and amillennial frameworks. In doing so, we prepare to turn our attention to those perspectives—exploring how alternative readings of prophetic and apocalyptic texts give rise to different visions of God's redemptive plan for creation. Ultimately, our journey through premillennialism underscores that the longing for Christ's reign is not mere speculative theology but a dynamic calling: to live as ambassadors of His coming kingdom, stewarding creation's renewal, proclaiming the gospel, and eagerly awaiting the day when every eye sees the returning King (Revelation 1:7).

# Chapter 4 - Postmillennialism Explored

Postmillennialism rests on the conviction that Christ's kingdom, inaugurated at His ascension and empowered by the Spirit at Pentecost, will steadily transform human affairs until the majority of communities reflect gospel values. Rather than anticipating a future age of despair immediately preceding Jesus' return, this perspective sees history moving toward a climactic era of peace, justice, and flourishing under Christian influence. Rooted in the Old Testament's visions of a world reconciled under God's rule and reinforced by Jesus' parables of gradual growth, postmillennialists assert that the same divine power that raised Christ from the dead now works through preaching, sacraments, prayer, and faithful discipleship to reshape families, institutions, and nations. Across church history, revivals and reform movements—from early awakenings in America to global missionary surges—serve as evidence that the Holy Spirit is actively expanding God's reign. Yet this hope coexists with sober recognition of opposition, suffering, and persistent evil, which serve as refining "birth pangs" rather than final verdicts. Throughout this chapter, we explore how postmillennialism derives confidence from covenantal continuity, typological interpretation, and key biblical texts; how it envisions a golden age marked by widespread evangelization, social renewal, and Spirit-empowered institutions; and how it navigates critiques that point to moral decline, persecution, and the risk of triumphalism. By engaging both scriptural promises and historical realities, we aim to show why this optimistic outlook continues to inspire Christians to work for cultural transformation even as they await Christ's glorious return.

# 4.1 Foundations of Postmillennial Hope

### 4.1.1 Kingdom Already Inaugurated: Christ's Present Session

Postmillennialism springs from the conviction that Christ's death and resurrection inaugurated His kingdom here and now, giving the church authority to advance divine rule throughout the world. Jesus' declaration that "the kingdom of God is at hand" (Mark 1:15) is understood not merely as an announcement of a future event but as an announcement that God's restorative reign had arrived in His person. When Christ ascended, He "sat down at the right hand of the Majesty on high" (Hebrews 1:3), signifying the establishment of His kingly session. This session is foundational because it marks the moment when Jesus received all authority in heaven and on earth (Matthew 28:18), enabling the church to share in the mission of expanding that reign. The work of the Spirit poured out at Pentecost (Acts 2:1–4) manifests the kingdom "already," infusing the church with power to preach, heal, and transform lives. As Luke records Jesus saying that He had "overcome the world" (John 16:33), postmillennialists see evidence that Satan's dominion has already been partly broken, even if evil remains. The present church age thus becomes a time of progressive advancement, where gospel truth spreads and Christ's authority grows in human hearts. This inbreaking kingdom contrasts starkly with premillennial assumptions that the church must await a future dispensation before such renewal can occur. Instead, postmillennialists point to passages like Romans 5:17, where Paul speaks of reign in life through Christ, demonstrating that believers already enjoy a foretaste of millennial blessings. The claim that Christ "reigns" (Revelation 19:6) emphasizes that His sovereign rule is not suspended but active. Furthermore, Jesus' teaching in Luke 17:20–21 that "the kingdom of God is within you" highlights an internal dimension, where the reign of Christ transforms believers' ethics and communal life. The church's mission is therefore dual: proclaim the gospel to all nations and foster social structures that reflect kingdom values—justice, mercy, and peace (Micah 6:8). As chapters in this volume will show, postmillennialists build on this present-tense reality to argue that the church's work will bear fruit across society until the majority of humanity experiences kingdom transformation. This expectation does not ignore ongoing suffering or persecution; rather, it holds that such adversity refines the church (1 Peter 1:6–7) even as the Spirit empowers believers to overcome the world. As a result, the kingdom already inaugurated provides both comfort in trials and impetus for vigorous engagement, for the church operates not on human resources alone but on the authority Christ now wields from heaven. This present session thus becomes the launch point for all subsequent optimism about cultural renewal, leading naturally into the theme of covenant continuity and the triumph of grace.

### 4.1.2 Covenant Continuity and the Triumph of Grace

Underpinning postmillennial confidence is a robust theology of covenant continuity that sees God's redemptive plan unfolding steadily from Abraham through the church age to the consummation. When God promised Abraham that "all the families of the earth shall be blessed" (Genesis 12:3), postmillennialists interpret this as a guarantee that the gospel will reach and renew human institutions, culminating in global blessing before Christ's return. The Abrahamic, Mosaic, Davidic, and New Covenants are thus read as progressive revelations that build rather than replace one another. For example, the Sinai covenant's ethical demands (Exodus 20) find renewed expression in Christ's Sermon on the Mount (Matthew 5–7), illustrating continuity in moral vision even as the New Covenant surpasses the Old with its focus on internal transformation (Jeremiah 31:33). When Jesus declared He came to "fulfill the Law and the Prophets" (Matthew 5:17), postmillennialists understand that as signaling not the abrogation of righteous ideals but their deeper realization through love (Romans 13:10). The Davidic promise that David's "throne and the kingdom" would be established forever (2 Samuel 7:16) is taken as assurance that Christ's rule will extend throughout all earth's institutions, not only over individual hearts. New Covenant grace, as described in Hebrews 8:6–13, is regarded as the engine propelling human hearts to embrace kingdom values, equipping the church to reshape political, economic, and cultural structures. For postmillennialists, covenant continuity explains why

Scripture's ethical vision applies universally: God's covenant with Noah (Genesis 9:1–7) addresses all humanity, the Abrahamic covenant primes a global blessing, and the New Covenant empowers believers to pursue justice and mercy across all spheres. This theological scaffolding fuels optimism because it promises that God's purpose to bless the nations through Israel (Galatians 3:8) now finds its ultimate expression through the church's witness under the Spirit. Postmillennialists contrast their view with dispensational readings that strictly separate Israel's covenants from the church's, arguing that such separations undermine God's unified plan. Instead, they highlight passages like Ephesians 2:11–22, where Jew and Gentile are reconciled in one new humanity, demonstrating covenantal unity. They also point to 2 Corinthians 3:6, which calls the New Covenant "ministers of the Spirit," validating that the current age is itself a covenant moment. In sum, the doctrine of covenant continuity assures believers that God's promises are neither suspended nor contingent on human failure; rather, grace ensures that every covenant finds incremental fulfillment, culminating in widespread transformation. This narrative naturally leads to an exploration of the hermeneutical commitments— typology, progressive revelation, and prophetic synergy—that undergird postmillennial confidence.

**4.1.3 Hermeneutical Commitments: Typology, Progress, and Prophetic Synergy** A distinctive feature of postmillennial hermeneutics is the explicit use of typology, a sense of redemptive progress, and an integrative reading of prophetic texts that affirms both immediate and ultimate fulfillments. Typology allows postmillennialists to see Old Testament events as foreshadows of greater New Testament realities while still anticipating final, definitive fulfillments in the days of Christ's visible reign. For example, Israel's exodus from Egypt (Exodus 12) serves as a type of Christian conversion, but it also points forward to a collective exodus of nations turning to Christ during the millennium. The conquest narratives in Joshua (Joshua 1–24) typify the present victory believers enjoy in Christ (Romans 8:37) but also anticipate a literal conquest of cultural strongholds (2 Corinthians 10:3–5) leading to global peace. Postmillennialists see progressive revelation as tracing a path from Jewish prophecy to Christian mission, where Daniel's vision of a "stone that struck the statue and became a great mountain" (Daniel 2:34–35) corresponds to the church's growth into a world-transforming movement (Matthew 16:18). They often cite Matthew 24:14—where Jesus states that "the gospel of the kingdom will be proclaimed throughout the whole world as a testimony to all nations"—as a promise of progressive growth rather than immediate cataclysmic collapse. Prophetic synergy integrates texts such as Isaiah 2:2–4, Psalm 72:8–11, and Micah 4:1–4 to build a composite picture of millennial peace and justice. By weaving these prophecies together, postmillennialists highlight how diverse biblical authors contributed to a single trajectory: the Lord's house established on the highest mountain, nations streaming with weapons turned into tools for cultivation, and the prince of peace reigning over all. The "already/advancing/consummated" framework—wherein the kingdom is already inaugurated, advancing progressively through church mission, and consummated at Christ's return—relies on a hermeneutic that holds texts in tension rather than rigidly forcing them into narrow time frames. This approach allows postmillennialists to account for first-century fulfillments (Luke 4:18–19's partial realization of Isaiah 61:1–2) while maintaining that many promises await fuller realization in history. Their interpretive model also affirms that Scripture's multiple layers—historical, typological, and eschatological—can generate a robust vision of cultural transformation without contradicting any specific text. Critics sometimes charge that this approach "spiritualizes" prophecy, but postmillennialists respond that they maintain literal sense for ultimate fulfillment while recognizing that God often works in stages—double fulfillment—exemplified by prophecies like Joel 2:28–32, which speak of both Pentecost (Acts 2) and cosmic signs yet future. This synergy of typology, progress, and prophetic integration equips the postmillennial hermeneutic to hold together the church's present mission with a hopeful expectation of a golden age preceding the parousia.

## 4.2 The Optimistic Outlook

**4.2.1 Gospel Progress and Cultural Transformation** At the heart of postmillennialism lies the confidence that the gospel's influence will steadily expand, reshaping societies, polities, and cultures. This expectation draws on Matthew 13's parables of the mustard seed and leaven, where small beginnings yield disproportionate growth—signifying that the kingdom's influence, though initially modest, will permeate all dimensions of life. Postmillennialists interpret Jesus' prayer that God's kingdom come and will be done on earth as it is in heaven (Matthew 6:10) not merely as spiritual petition but as a roadmap for cultural renewal. They argue that as believers live out kingdom values—justice, mercy, compassion—these values will incrementally transform legal systems, educational institutions, and economic structures. Passages like Isaiah 42:3–4, which predict that the Servant will bring forth justice to the nations, are understood as ongoing realities until a tipping point is reached where societal norms reflect biblical ethics. From a postmillennial vantage, the abolition of slavery, the expansion of public education, and the rise of human rights movements can be seen as tangible evidence of gospel progress. Abolitionists like William Wilberforce in England and Levi Coffin in America are celebrated as agents through whom the Spirit used Christian convictions to topple cultural strongholds (Romans 16:20). Similarly, the proliferation of Christian hospitals and charitable organizations in the nineteenth century is cited as evidence that the gospel's leaven was permeating society. Postmillennialists do not ignore setbacks—wars, moral decline, or economic crises—but interpret them as part of the "already" that history must traverse as the gospel advances (James 1:2–4). They assert that the principles of Galatians 5:22–23—love, joy, peace, patience—will eventually manifest on a societal scale, producing a civilization marked by genuine human flourishing. This biblical basis for cultural transformation contrasts with secular humanism's attempt to effect change apart from the gospel; where humanistic movements often falter, postmillennialists maintain that Christian foundations yield sustainable renewal. The expectation that "all the ends of the earth will remember and turn to the Lord" (Psalm 22:27) fuels missionary enthusiasm and social activism. Churches invest in educational curriculum, hospitals, and media outreach, aiming to saturate culture with biblical truth. Tactics vary—from establishing Christian schools that integrate faith and learning to championing humane public policies grounded in scriptural justice. Progressive revelation assures postmillennialists that while the kingdom may advance unevenly, the cumulative effect will be unmistakable: poverty alleviated, corruption reduced, and life expectancy increased as stewardship of resources aligns with Genesis 1:28's creation mandate. This confidence in gospel progress undergirds a posture of hope rather than resignation, prompting believers to see every positive cultural development not as secular gain but as evidence of kingdom seeds taking root. As believers witness these shifts, their optimism is reinforced, spurring further engagement rather than retreat, and setting the stage for recounting the historical witnesses and revivals that have embodied this outlook.

**4.2.2 Historical Witnesses and Great Awakenings**
Postmillennialism looks to church history for concrete examples of how the gospel has advanced society, pointing to the Great Awakenings as pivotal moments when revivals catalyzed moral and social reform. The First Great Awakening in eighteenth-century America, led by figures such as Jonathan Edwards and George Whitefield, stirred widespread conversions, leading to declines in alcoholism, dueling, and gambling. Edwards' sermon "Sinners in the Hands of an Angry God" exemplified how the Spirit's convicting power can awaken dormant faith and stimulate community transformation. Postmillennialists highlight that these awakenings produced not only spiritual renewal but also social improvements: as people embraced new life in Christ, philanthropic endeavors like prison reform and care for orphans gained momentum (Proverbs 31:8–9). The Second Great Awakening, spearheaded by evangelists such as Charles Finney and Timothy Dwight, resulted in millions of conversions and directly contributed to the abolitionist movement. Finney's "new measures" of revival preaching drew critique from some quarters, yet postmillennialists credit him with fostering a societal shift that linked personal repentance to moral activism. The Women's Christian Temperance Union and early public education initiatives trace their roots to post-awakening social consciousness. In England, John Wesley's Methodist revivals spawned an ethos that emphasized personal holiness and social reform, leading to improvements in factory conditions and the spread of Sunday schools. Postmillennial historians note that these revivals did not merely inflate church membership but reshaped entire communities—crime rates fell, literacy rates increased, and charitable networks expanded. Global manifestations followed: in nineteenth-century Korea, the Gospel's entrance resulted in a nationwide revival that laid foundations for democracy and human rights. Chinese revivals of the twentieth century, often emerging under persecution, demonstrated that gospel resilience could transform even hostile environments, leading to grassroots healthcare and education in remote regions. Postmillennialists argue that these historical precedents confirm biblical promises like Isaiah

40:5—where all flesh will see God's salvation—and Matthew 24:14—where the gospel of the kingdom is proclaimed to all nations before the end comes. These awakenings provide patterns for modern mission strategy: combine fervent evangelism with holistic ministry to address spiritual and material needs. While not downplaying human sinfulness, postmillennial witnesses underscore that God's Spirit works through ordinary believers to effect extraordinary cultural change. The historical record then becomes a springboard for envisioning how a global awakening in our day could normalize kingdom values across every sphere of life. As churches study these precedents, they glean lessons in evangelistic methodology, pastoral care, and community development. These historical landmarks transition naturally into the role of Israel's restoration and the "fullness of the Gentiles" in advancing the gospel before Christ's return.

### 4.2.3 Conversion of Israel and the "Fullness of the Gentiles"

Postmillennialism frequently incorporates a vision for the conversion of Israel as a key sign that the church age is maturing toward fullness. Romans 11:25–27 speaks of a future fullness of Israel, where "all Israel will be saved," which postmillennialists interpret as corporate Jewish repentance on a wide scale. They see modern Jewish migrations to Israel, as foretold in Ezekiel 36:24, as preparatory steps toward this hope and as precursors to mass movements of Jewish faith in Jesus (Yeshua). This interprets passages like Zechariah 12:10–14 as describing a national awakening among Jews when they "look on him whom they have pierced" and experience collective mourning that leads to faith. Postmillennialists often contrast this projected Jewish revival with premillennial separation, arguing that covenant continuity suggests Jewish and Gentile believers will together form Christ's unified bride before the millennium. Parallel to Israel's conversion, postmillennial theology also anticipates the "fullness of the Gentiles"—a phrase in Romans 11:25 that implies a tipping point in Gentile conversions, where the majority of Gentiles embrace the gospel. As Gentile Christians increasingly populate lands formerly dominated by secularism and syncretism, postmillennialists see promises like Isaiah 49:6—"I will make you as a light for the nations, that my salvation may reach to the end of the earth"—coming to fruition. They cite global church growth statistics as evidence that the gospel now extends into every unreached people group, fulfilling Jesus' commission in Acts 1:8. Moreover, passages such as Matthew 28:19–20 serve as a mandate for the church to disciple nations, reinforcing the belief that Gentile fullness and Israel's conversion will coincide in history's final stages. Contemporary postmillennial advocates point to the establishment of Messianic Jewish congregations worldwide as initial indicators of Israel's movement toward faith. They also celebrate the remarkable expansion of churches in formerly closed countries—China, Iran, and regions of sub-Saharan Africa—as examples of Gentile fullness advancing rapidly. Some postmillennialists draw timelines suggesting that once key demographic thresholds are crossed—such as 20 percent Christian population in a region—social and moral structures shift toward kingdom culture, setting off exponential growth. These calculations, while debated, reflect confidence that prophecy charts are not static but dynamic, responding to missionary breakthroughs and social factors. When Israel's return and Gentile fullness converge, postmillennialists anticipate a global society practicing basic kingdom ethics—charity, peacemaking, and environmental stewardship—before Christ's return, evidencing an extended golden age. This hopeful scenario directly counters pessimistic interpretations of 2 Timothy 3:1–5 or Matthew 24:12 that emphasize moral decline; instead, postmillennialists emphasize God's faithfulness to guide history toward climactic redemption. With this understanding of Israel and the Gentiles converging, attention shifts to the critiques of decline narratives that question whether evil and suffering permanently impede kingdom progress.

**4.2.4 Critiquing Decline Narratives: Evil, Suffering, and Providential Setbacks** Postmillennialism challenges the notion that the world continues in an unstoppable moral and spiritual decline, asserting instead that divine providence weaves setbacks into an overall trajectory of gospel advance. While acknowledging passages like 2 Timothy 3:1–5, which predict that "in the last days there will be terrible times," they interpret such warnings as localized or temporary phenomena rather than as indicators of a final, unbroken downward spiral. The Book of Judges (Judges 2:16–19), for instance, describes cycles of apostasy, oppression, and deliverance among Israel—patterns that postmillennialists see echoed in broader world history. They argue that these cycles do not preclude ultimate progress, as each deliverance brings renewed covenant fidelity and partial restoration. Modern crises—economic downturns, political upheavals, and pandemics—are understood as providential recalibrations rather than as signs that God has abandoned His purpose. When Jesus warns of wars, famines, and earthquakes as "the beginning of birth pains" (Matthew 24:6–8), postmillennialists read this as indicating that these events precede the kingdom's full birth rather than canceling it. They also point to Deuteronomy 28's blessings and curses framework, recognizing that blessings follow obedience and curses follow disobedience, suggesting that revival and reformation are both possible and expected when the church prays, repents, and reforms society's structures. Historical examples like the late-nineteenth-century social gospel movement demonstrate how Christian activism can reverse moral decline, at least temporarily, by attacking social ills such as inequality and neglect of the poor. They also emphasize the role of geopolitics: while global conflicts—World Wars, the Cold War—caused setbacks, the post-World War II era saw unprecedented economic growth and expansion of freedoms, which they link to Christian-influenced Western institutions. Postmillennialists critique stoic fatalism and secular pessimism for underestimating human agency and divine sovereignty working through the church. Scriptures like Isaiah 54:2–3, which promise that barren places will blossom, serve as encouragement that even areas of spiritual barrenness can become fruitful through concerted gospel efforts. They contend that reports of declining church attendance or rising secularism should be met with increased evangelistic zeal rather than surrender, trusting that such downward trends can reverse as the church prays and engages the culture (2 Chronicles 7:14). Moreover, they interpret Revelation 12:11—"they overcame him by the blood of the Lamb and by the word of their testimony"—as an assurance that, despite Satan's assaults, believers will progressively gain ground. Through this lens, societal tragedies are transient, and the church's fidelity corresponds with God's faithfulness to bring renewal. With this critique of decline narratives, postmillennialism turns toward envisioning the golden age that precedes the consummation.

## 4.3 The Golden Age Before the Parousia

### 4.3.1 Timing, Nature, and Duration of the Millennium
Postmillennialists define the millennium not solely by a fixed chronological span but by a qualitative era characterized by gospel-

healing and cultural flourishing. Drawing on 2 Peter 3:8—where "one day is with the Lord as a thousand years"—they maintain flexibility regarding the millennium's duration, emphasizing instead the era's nature: a predominance of righteous influence before Christ's return. Jesus' parable of the wheat and the tares (Matthew 13:24–30) helps illustrate how good and evil coexist until the harvest. Postmillennialists argue that when the wheat fully matures, the kingdom's visible triumph reigns, signaling the nearness of Christ's parousia. Some early postmillennial writers, such as Jonathan Edwards, suggested that key demographic markers—such as a majority of the world professing Christianity—could signal the millennium's advent. Others, like B.B. Warfield, discouraged specific timelines, focusing instead on the qualitative markers: widespread adoption of kingdom ethics and global influence of Christian institutions. Historical postmillennialists like Daniel Whitby in the early 1700s explicitly taught that Christ would return after the world experienced a golden age of righteousness. These optimistic voices drew on Revelation 20:2–7's binding of Satan, reading it as Christ's victory inaugurated on the cross and progressively manifesting as worldly evil loses power. Postmillennialists stress that the nature of this golden age involves peace, justice, and widespread gospel proclamation, aligning with Isaiah 60:1–3's vision of nations coming to the light of Zion. Regarding duration, postmillennialists refrain from specifying that the millennium must be exactly one thousand literal years; rather, they appeal to Revelation 20:7's language of "a little season" after the millennium's close, indicating that the final apostasy—Satan's release and subsequent revolt—marks the transition to Christ's revelation. This era's indeterminate length does not dampen urgency; rather, it infuses mission with expectancy, encouraging the church to work diligently knowing that each advance of the gospel extends the golden age. Postmillennialists contrast their view with amillennial readings that interpret Revelation 20 symbolically as the church age itself, or with premillennial expectations of a separate future kingdom. Instead, postmillennialists maintain a middle ground: the golden age will be recognizably better than present conditions—marked by measurable advances in education, poverty reduction, and moral improvement—yet will still give way to the final rebellion and Christ's return. Texts like Matthew 13:41–43 underscore that at the "end of the age," Christ's angels will separate the righteous from the wicked, implying a definitive endpoint to the golden age. This interpretation of timing, nature, and duration motivates believers to invest in social transformation, confident that such labors align with God's redemptive timeline.

**4.3.2 Peace, Justice, and Global Evangelization** The golden age envisioned by postmillennialists is characterized by an unprecedented diffusion of peace, justice, and global evangelical success—elements they find deeply rooted in biblical prophecy. Passages such as Isaiah 2:4, which forecast that nations "shall beat their swords into plowshares," serve as foundational texts for envisioning how war and violence will wane under Christian influence before Christ's return. Postmillennialists point to historical declines in warfare during periods of robust Christian influence—such as the Pax Britannica in the nineteenth century—as provisional signs that God can restrain violence through faithful witness. Justice, another hallmark of the golden age, draws on Micah 4:3–4's image of nations living securely under God's rule. Postmillennialists argue that Christian jurisprudential principles embedded in common law and modern constitutions, inspired by biblical ethics (e.g., Exodus 23:1–9's statutes on justice), mature over time, yielding legal systems that protect the vulnerable. They note significant abolition of practices like child labor and human trafficking as evidence that biblical norms can transform unjust structures. Global evangelization, meanwhile, constitutes the engine fueling peace and justice: Matthew 28:19–20's Great Commission resonates as a roadmap for missions that establish churches, educational institutions, and healthcare systems worldwide. As indigenous leaders emerge with resources and expertise, postmillennialists see the promise of Mark 13:10—that the gospel will be preached to all nations—drawing nearer. When local churches establish schools, hospitals, and social ministries, they bear witness to the gospel's power to heal both souls and societies. The natural outgrowth of these efforts is a societal landscape where Christian virtues underpin public policy: education systems promote critical thinking and moral integrity, economics emphasize stewardship and generosity (Proverbs 11:25), and healthcare becomes a means of embodying Christ's compassion (Matthew 25:36). Postmillennialists point to modern missions conferences that mobilize millions of laypeople—such as Lausanne (1974) and its subsequent gatherings—as evidence that global evangelization is increasingly coordinated and effective. Critics who cite stubborn pockets of extremism and oppression against Christians respond that these are precisely the areas requiring intensified focus, not reasons for despair. Postmillennialists emphasize Jesus' promise in John 16:33 that believers will "have tribulation" but ultimately conquer through faith. They regard local instances of persecution as sobering reminders of the ongoing presence of evil, but anticipate that widespread gospel advance will undermine oppressive regimes over time. Historical precedents like the decline of persecution under Constantine, while not a template for forced political change, demonstrate how official toleration can follow robust Christian witness (1 Timothy 2:1–4). In this golden age, peace and justice are not passive states but dynamic processes supported by active evangelism. As peaceful institutions flourish, postmillennialists envision a world to which Revelation 21:24–26's description of nations bringing glory and honor to the New Jerusalem corresponds—a vision that simultaneously looks backward to Christ's incarnation and forward to His return. This integrated model of peace, justice, and evangelism sets the stage for understanding how Spirit-empowered institutions will function during the millennium.

**4.3.3 Spirit-Empowered Institutions: Family, Church, State, and Marketplace** Postmillennialism holds that God sustains His kingdom's advance through ordinary means—families, churches, governments, and marketplaces—each empowered by the Spirit to reflect kingdom values. Family, as the foundational social unit, is viewed through Ephesians 6:1–4, where parents are instructed to raise children in the "nurture and admonition of the Lord." Postmillennialists envision families as vital transmitters of faith, instilling biblical ethics that shape future generations into kingdom ambassadors. As children learn values of compassion, stewardship, and service at home, they later contribute to societal transformation—fulfilling Deuteronomy 6:6–7's mandate to teach God's commandments "diligently to your children." The church, meanwhile, functions as Christ's body in the world, governed by New Testament principles of eldership (1 Timothy 3:1–7) and deaconship (Philippians 1:1), ensuring that leadership is defined by character and service. Local congregations serve as centers for discipleship, worship, and social outreach, embodying Acts 2:42–47's model: teaching, fellowship, breaking of bread, prayer, and communal generosity. Through corporate worship and small-group accountability, the church remains connected to Christ's headship

(Colossians 1:18), aligning its ministries with prophetic vision rather than human agendas. Postmillennialists stress that governments—Romans 13:1–7's "ministers of God"—should serve justice, punish evil, and protect the vulnerable while respecting the church's spiritual authority. They cite historical examples where Christian influence informed laws against slavery and injustice, and they advocate for policies promoting religious freedom, social welfare, and economic opportunity. While cautious about theocracy, postmillennialists assert that God's sovereignty over nations means that civil authorities should heed biblical ethics, though without coercive imposition of faith. The marketplace, finally, is viewed as a domain for vocation and stewardship—Genesis 2:15's charge to "till and keep" creation extends to entrepreneurship, innovation, and ethical business practices. Postmillennial thought advances the notion of "creative transformation," where businesses not only generate profit but also foster community development, environmental care, and human flourishing. Examples include community development corporations that operate under Christian principles and microfinance initiatives emanating from faith-based organizations. When the Spirit empowers leaders in each of these spheres, they become agents of holistic transformation—families that nurture faith, churches that equip disciples, governments that enact righteous laws, and businesses that reflect kingdom values. These "Spirit-empowered institutions" together form an ecosystem that nurtures the golden age before Christ's return, providing structural integrity to postmillennial optimism. As each institution fulfills its God-given role, Genesis 12:2–3's promise that "all the families of the earth shall be blessed" begins to see preliminary realization. While acknowledging that no institution is perfect, postmillennialists maintain that under the Spirit's guidance, they can extend the reign of Christ until the final consummation of all things. This comprehensive institutional vision naturally flows into considerations of creation's blessing and environmental stewardship, which will be addressed in subsequent sections.

## 4.4 Mechanisms of Kingdom Expansion

### 4.4.1 Role of the Holy Spirit and Ordinary Means of Grace
Postmillennialism places significant emphasis on how the Holy Spirit works through the ordinary means of grace—preaching,

sacraments, and prayer—to advance God's kingdom. The Holy Spirit, poured out at Pentecost (Acts 2:1–4), empowers the church to bear witness to Christ's lordship in everyday life. Preaching the Word, considered a primary means of grace (Romans 10:14–15), both convicts sinners and instructs believers in righteousness (James 1:21). When sermons faithfully expound Scripture, they serve as channels for the Spirit to regenerate hearts, producing conversions that contribute to cultural renewal. The sacraments of baptism and the Lord's Supper also function as conduits of grace. Baptism signifies entry into the covenant community (Romans 6:3–4) and marks individuals as members of Christ's body. In the Lord's Supper, participants proclaim Christ's death until He comes (1 Corinthians 11:26), reinforcing gospel truth and spiritual unity. Prayer, too, is integral: Jesus promised that whatever believers ask in His name would be granted (John 14:13–14), underscoring that prayer is a vital means through which the Spirit moves providence. Corporate and private prayers for societal transformation—prayers for wisdom, justice, and mercy—invite God's active intervention (1 Timothy 2:1–2). As the church worships and prays, Spirit-anointed ministry flows outward into communities, catalyzing reform in education, healthcare, and public policy. Instances of revival frequently follow focused seasons of prayer (2 Chronicles 7:14), suggesting that the Spirit uses the ordinary means of grace to awaken the church and society. Pastors and church leaders cultivate these means by ensuring robust catechesis, carefully administering sacraments, and gathering congregations for fervent intercession. They also train small groups to pray for specific cultural challenges—poverty, corruption, human trafficking—believing that sustained, Spirit-empowered prayer will yield tangible breakthroughs. As love (Galatians 5:22–23) is poured into hearts by the Spirit (Romans 5:5), believers become agents of reconciliation in families, workplaces, and governments. Through these ordinary channels, what John Owen called "the Spirit's ordinary operations" continue Christ's work of regeneration and sanctification (Titus 3:5), gradually permeating every sphere with kingdom values. This reliance on the Spirit and means of grace sets the stage for more intentional discipleship and worldview transformation, which is the focus of the next subsection.

**4.4.2 Discipleship, Education, and the Transformation of Worldviews** Postmillennialism envisions discipleship and education as strategic levers for transforming worldviews and equipping believers to influence culture. Discipleship involves not only individual mentorship and small-group accountability but also community-based learning that integrates faith with everyday life. Churches frequently establish discipleship pathways—structured curricula that cover biblical literacy, theology, ethics, and practical ministry skills—ensuring that converts are thoroughly grounded in Christ's lordship. Educational institutions, particularly Christian schools and universities, play a crucial role by teaching every subject through a biblical lens. In mathematics classes, for example, instructors illustrate the constancy of truth as reflective of God's unchanging nature (Malachi 3:6), while literature courses explore themes of redemption and moral courage. Science pedagogy in these settings highlights the coherence between creation's order and the Creator's wisdom (Psalm 19:1), countering secular narratives that exclude God from explanations of origin and purpose. By embedding Christian worldview training across disciplines, these institutions prepare graduates to enter the marketplace, technology sectors, and media industries with confidence in integrating faith and vocation. Adult education ministries—seminars on public policy or professional development—equip seasoned professionals to influence legal, medical, and financial systems with kingdom ethics. As faithful disciples model integrity (Proverbs 11:3) in their workplaces, they demonstrate the plausibility of Christian virtue in complex environments, disarming objections that faith and reason cannot cohere. Educational networks often partner with local churches to offer curriculum resources, teacher training, and scholarships, fostering a synergy between ecclesial and academic spheres. By emphasizing the unity of truth—a hallmark of Christian epistemology—postmillennialists contend that transformed worldviews are more durable than mere external behavioral change. Faith renewal, therefore, involves reshaping how people think about politics, art, science, and relationships through a biblical framework. This transformative approach aims not only at personal piety but also at systemic renewal: as Christian graduates occupy leadership roles in various sectors, they instigate incremental reforms—ethical corporate governance, compassionate welfare policies, and culturally sensitive media content. Over time, these educational initiatives catalyze shifts in societal norms, positioning culture to reflect more closely God's cosmic order. With discipleship and education fostering worldview alignment, the church can then press for law and mercy in public policy, a subject explored in the next subsection.

### 4.4.3 Law, Mercy, and Public Policy in a Redeemed Society

Public policy in a redeemed society is shaped by the twin priorities of law and mercy, reflecting Jesus' summary of the Law and the Prophets—loving God and loving neighbor (Matthew 22:37–40). Postmillennialists affirm that governments are ordained by God (Romans 13:1–7) to punish evil and support good, but they also emphasize that civil authorities must operate under biblical constraints: protecting the vulnerable (Psalm 82:3–4), ensuring due process (Deuteronomy 16:18–20), and upholding treaties with justice and equity (Psalm 15:1–5). In practice, this might involve crafting legislation that balances free-market enterprise with regulations preventing exploitation, echoing Proverbs 22:16's warning against oppressing the poor. Laws addressing family protection, such as child welfare statutes and support for mothers, embody Deuteronomy 24:19–21's concern for the marginalized; public policies can be designed to ensure widows and orphans receive medical care and economic assistance. Postmillennialists often advocate for restorative justice models that seek to rehabilitate offenders rather than perpetuate cycles of incarceration (Matthew 25:36). Mercy ministries, often supported by church-state partnerships, provide social services—food banks, counseling centers, and job-training programs—demonstrating God's compassion (Luke 10:30–37) and reducing dependency on punitive systems. Public officials influenced by Christian ethics might implement environmental protections rooted in Genesis 2:15's charge to steward creation, crafting policies that preserve natural resources for future generations. Legislation promoting religious freedom (Galatians 5:1) ensures that churches operate without undue interference, enabling them to continue their witness through social programs. When elected leaders collaborate with faith-based organizations, they facilitate policies that provide safety nets for the poor and encourage adoption and foster care, reflecting James 1:27's call to care for orphans. The integration of law and mercy in public policy thus manifests Jesus' kingdom rule on earth (Isaiah 11:4–5), where justice and compassion form complementary pillars rather than competing priorities. Postmillennialists recognize potential pitfalls: theocracy misused for oppressive ends or welfare systems that stifle personal responsibility. To mitigate these risks, they propose checks and balances grounded in biblical wisdom—honoring human dignity (Genesis 1:27) while promoting accountability (Matthew 18:15–17). With such prudent governance, public policy becomes an instrument of kingdom expansion, fostering societal conditions conducive to gospel progress. As law and mercy converge in a redeemed polity, arts and sciences flourish under the banner of human creativity as kingdom vocation, examined in the next subsection.

**4.4.4 Arts, Sciences, and Human Creativity as Kingdom Vocation** Postmillennialism celebrates human creativity in the arts and sciences as reflections of the Creator's image, calling believers to excel in these fields for God's glory (Genesis 1:27). Artistic expression—painting, music, literature—becomes a means of conveying theological truths, shaping culture, and inviting people into worship. Sacred art traditions, ranging from Renaissance church murals depicting redemption themes to contemporary gospel music lifting Christ's name, serve as evangelistic bridges, drawing hearts toward God's beauty (Psalm 27:4). Christian musicians, inspired by Colossians 3:16's admonition to "let the word of Christ dwell in you richly," compose works that integrate biblical narrative with modern genres, resonating with audiences across demographics. Visual artists embed scriptural motifs in public art installations, sparking curiosity about redemption. In literature, Christian authors craft novels, poetry, and essays that explore themes of sin, grace, and hope, providing avenues for readers to wrestle with existential questions through a biblical lens. The sciences, too, become arenas for kingdom vocation. Postmillennial scientists see their work as expanding humanity's understanding of God's creation, whether through cosmology that reveals the vastness of God's handiwork (Psalm 19:1) or medical research addressing human suffering in line with Christ's healing ministry (Matthew 9:35). Technological innovations—renewable energy, digital communication platforms, and agricultural advancements—are harnessed to alleviate poverty, improve health care delivery, and foster global connectivity. Christian universities often establish research centers focused on ethical biotechnology, exploring how to push forward medical frontiers without compromising moral principles (Proverbs 8:12). As technology reduces barriers to information, postmillennialists leverage digital media for worldwide disciple-making, fulfilling Deuteronomy 6:7's call to teach God's commands everywhere.

Architects and urban planners, guided by Edenic values of harmony between built and natural environments, design sustainable cities that provide green spaces and foster community cohesion, embodying Isaiah 65:17–25's vision of creation's renewal. When creative professionals pursue excellence as sacred calling, they counter the notion that secularization has confined faith to private spheres. Postmillennialists argue that the arts and sciences flourish most fully when grounded in a Christian worldview, demonstrating that Christ's lordship extends over all fields of human endeavor. Through cultural institutions—museums, concert halls, research institutions—believers showcase how their craft contributes to public good, enhancing society's appreciation of human dignity and divine creativity. This robust engagement of arts and sciences as kingdom vocation propels cultural renewal forward, laying groundwork for the scriptural foundations that undergird postmillennial optimism, which we address in the next section.

## 4.5 Key Scriptural Trajectories

**4.5.1 Old-Testament Visions (Psalm 2; Psalm 110; Isaiah 2, 9, 11, 60)** Postmillennial theology draws heavily on Old Testament passages that envision a future age of peace, justice, and the universal recognition of God's rule. Psalm 2's declaration that "the kings of the earth set themselves and the rulers take counsel together" against the Lord's Anointed (Psalm 2:1–2) highlights human rebellion, yet verses 6–8 promise that God will install His King on Zion and give Him "the nations for his inheritance." Postmillennialists interpret this as foretelling an era when Christ's spiritual reign extends globally, bringing nations to worship (Psalm 2:11–12). Psalm 110, which is the most frequently quoted Old Testament passage in the New Testament, speaks of the Messiah as a priest forever after the order of Melchizedek (Psalm 110:4), implying ongoing intercessory rule that empowers the church's witness until the final advent. Isaiah 2:2–4 envisages a day when nations "shall come to the house of the Lord" to receive instruction in God's ways, leading to the transformation of instruments of war into tools for cultivation (Isaiah 2:4). This image resonates with postmillennial confidence that societies will internalize divine wisdom, prioritizing peace over conflict. Isaiah 9:6–7 prophesies the birth of a child called "Wonderful Counselor, Mighty God,

Everlasting Father, Prince of Peace," whose government and peace will have "no end" (Isaiah 9:7). Postmillennialists understand this as signifying a progressive realization of Christ's peace throughout human history, culminating in a world largely aligned with His righteous reign. Isaiah 11:6–9 describes a creation-wide peace where predators and prey coexist harmoniously, reflecting the inbreaking renewal of all things (Romans 8:19–21). Postmillennialists see this as pointing to a gradual but tangible greenlight for ecological stewardship, anticipating environmental restoration under Christian influence even before final consummation. Isaiah 60:1–3 portrays Zion as a light to the nations, drawing wealth and wisdom from distant lands; postmillennialists see modern missionary endeavors and global church growth as initial fulfillments of this promise, as the wealth of nations flows to support biblical institutions and the spiritual wealth of the gospel attracts seekers worldwide. These Old Testament visions form a cohesive trajectory when woven together: they first acknowledge human rebellion, then promise Christ's enthronement, follow with a global outpouring of divine instruction, and culminate in an era of mutual flourishing among nations and creation. Postmillennialists use this multi-author tapestry to argue that the promises of Psalm 2, Psalm 110, and Isaiah will not remain in the future alone but are being progressively realized now through the church's mission and cultural engagement. Having established these Old Testament foundations, readers are prepared to examine how Jesus' parables illustrate kingdom growth in the next subsection.

**4.5.2 Parables of Gradual Growth (Matthew 13; Mark 4)** The parables of the kingdom in Matthew 13 and Mark 4 provide a vivid paradigm for understanding postmillennial optimism: the kingdom starts imperceptibly small but grows into a transformative reality. In the parable of the mustard seed (Matthew 13:31–32; Mark 4:30–32), Jesus compares the kingdom to a tiny seed that becomes the largest of garden plants, "so that the birds of the air come and make nests in its branches." Postmillennialists interpret this as illustrating how the gospel, initially spreading among a handful of disciples, expands over time to create societal structures that shelter and nourish countless people. This parable highlights both the kingdom's humble origins and its eventual grandeur. Likewise, in the parable of the leaven (Matthew 13:33; Luke 13:20–21), a woman hides leaven in three measures of flour until "the whole lump is leavened."

Postmillennialists see this as a metaphor for the pervasive influence of the Holy Spirit throughout all society; just as leaven infiltrates dough invisibly, so the Spirit works through the church to permeate families, institutions, and laws with godly values. The disciples' failure to understand these parables initially (Matthew 13:11) underscores that the kingdom's growth remains largely unseen to outsiders until significant cultural shifts occur. As postmillennialists observe recurring patterns—legal reforms inspired by Christian ethics, educational curricula infused with biblical values, and social norms gradually aligning with God's design—they see parabolic fulfillment. The same texts stress that the kingdom's expansion is not instantaneous. Mark 4:26–29's parable of the growing seed describes a process where "the earth produces by itself" once the seed is sown; the farmer sleeps and rises while the seed sprouts and grows "though he knows not how." Postmillennialists draw a parallel to seed-like gospel planting: once the church preaches the Word, growth continues through Spirit-led processes even when church leaders are unaware of every converted life. This assures them that even in seasons of apparent dormancy, the kingdom continues to advance. Jesus emphasized that kingdom growth should be expected, even if gradual (Mark 4:30, "With what can we compare the kingdom of God?"). Postmillennialists adopt this perspective to counter narratives that portray the world as spiraling downward; instead, they assert that steady, Spirit-empowered work will yield substantive change. These parables also caution against complacency: the farmer must continue sowing seed and maintaining fields, paralleling the church's ongoing mission duty. Postmillennialists thus combine faith in quantitative growth— measured in statistical church growth and moral indicators—with qualitative transformation—profound shifts in individual hearts and community values. The kingdom's parabolic growth informs the comprehensive eschatological framework that unfolds in Pauline writings, explored in the next subsection.

**4.5.3 Pauline Eschatology and Cosmic Reconciliation (1 Corinthians 15; Romans 11)** Postmillennialism finds critical support in Paul's eschatological writings, particularly in 1 Corinthians 15's discourse on resurrection and Romans 11's olive-tree allegory of Israel's future. In 1 Corinthians 15:20–28, Paul affirms that Christ's resurrection is "the firstfruits" of those who have fallen asleep, and that at His coming, "all who are in the tombs" will be raised. Postmillennialists read this as indicating a future event—Christ's visible return—preceded by a process of death's defeat inaugurated in the resurrection. Because Christ "must reign until he has put all his enemies under his feet" (1 Corinthians 15:25), they understand that His reign is an unfolding process extending from His ascension until the final consummation. This supports the notion that Christ's rule, begun at His resurrection, will progressively realize its victory over sin and death across history, culminating in universal reconciliation of creation. Romans 11 develops this theme by explaining God's sovereign plan for Israel and the Gentiles, illustrating cosmic reconciliation. Paul describes Israel as a cultivated olive tree from which some branches (Israel) were broken off because of unbelief and wild olive shoots (the Gentiles) grafted in (Romans 11:17). Postmillennialists interpret this to mean that fulfilling God's purposes involves Gentile believers actively participating in the life of the church as part of God's olive tree, even as Israel's future restoration awaits a later stage. This allegory ensures that Gentile fullness precedes or overlaps with Israel's salvation—affirming both partial Jewish conversion now and a future national repentance (Romans 11:25–27). As the olive tree grows, it symbolizes increasing unity among God's people and a broadening influence across nations. Paul's language of God's "mystery" revealed (Romans 16:25) is taken as evidence that previous partial fulfillments in Christ will flow into a fuller realization of God's redemptive plan, foreshadowing global harmony under Christ's reign. Romans 8:19–23 complements this by depicting creation's eager expectation for the "revealing of the sons of God," linking human redemption with cosmic renewal. This cosmic perspective assures postmillennialists that as believers participate in Christ's resurrection-life now, they contribute to a broader restoration that ultimately manifests in a reconciled creation. These Pauline frameworks, when woven together, provide a robust theological basis for anticipating the golden age described in Old Testament and Jesus' parables, thereby reinforcing confidence in postmillennial expectations. With these Pauline trajectories in mind, readers are poised to explore how Revelation's closing chapters might be read through an optimistic lens.

### 4.5.4 Reading Revelation 19–20 Through an Optimistic Lens
Revelation 19–20 offers dramatic language about Christ's return, the defeat of evil, and a thousand-year reign. Postmillennialists read

these chapters with an optimistic framework, perceiving the binding of Satan (Revelation 20:1–3) as a description of Christ's victory inaugurated at the cross and partially realized throughout church history. They emphasize that the phrase "he seized the dragon" indicates the definitive defeat of Satan's claims, allowing the gospel to advance unimpeded. The thousand-year period, understood symbolically rather than strictly chronologically, signifies an era during which Satan's power is restrained sufficiently for the church to flourish. Postmillennial interpreters often connect Revelation 19:11–16's image of Christ as a warrior triumphing over the beast, reflecting First Corinthians 15:25's declaration that Christ must reign until all enemies are under His feet. This victorious portrayal reinforces the conviction that Christ's triumph will continue to expand until a tipping point of global repentance. The "first resurrection" (Revelation 20:4–6) is seen as the spiritual awakening of believers throughout history, not exclusively a future event, marking contemporary victories of faith over death. The rejoicing in heaven over one soul saved (Luke 15:7) scales up in Revelation's vision, suggesting that every genuine conversion foreshadows the millennium's broader triumph. The final defeat of Satan after the millennium (Revelation 20:7–10) anticipates a brief surge of evil at the era's end, which postmillennialists interpret as a momentary, localized rebellion that fails to derail the kingdom's progress. They underscore that Verses 9–10's immediate consumption of Gog and Magog's forces by fire from heaven demonstrates God's swift vindication of His reign. The subsequent "great white throne" judgment (Revelation 20:11–15) confirms that ultimate justice awaits the wicked, affirming God's character of righteousness. Postmillennialists argue that this sequence—initial victory, protracted reign, brief rebellion, and final judgment—mirrors the church's own historical journey: persecutions flare but ultimately subside as Christ's kingdom advances. The imagery of a new heaven and new earth in Revelation 21:1 resonates with Isaiah 65:17 and 66:22, showcasing continuity between Testaments. Postmillennial readers thus see Revelation 19–20 not as an argument for a short-lived intervention immediately prior to Christ's return but as a panoramic vision of triumph that begins at Pentecost and culminates at the final parousia. This optimistic lens affirms that the church's mission aligns with prophetic intent, inspiring confidence that the closing chapters of Revelation support the postmillennial conviction that the world will experience an extended era of gospel blessing before Christ's final return. As these readings of Revelation propel hope, the "already/advancing/consummated" three-stage framework consolidates the chapter's themes.

**4.5.5 Already/Advancing/Consummated—A Three-Stage Framework** Postmillennial hermeneutics often hinge on a three-stage framework—already, advancing, and consummated—that helps interpret eschatological texts. The "already" stage acknowledges that Christ's kingdom was inaugurated at His first coming (Luke 17:21), confirmed by His resurrection and ascension (1 Peter 3:18). Believers thus experience kingdom blessings now through reconciliation with God (2 Corinthians 5:18) and initial acts of cultural renewal. The "advancing" phase describes the church age during which the gospel progressively extends its influence over hearts, institutions, and cultures. This phase corresponds to passages like Matthew 13's parables of mustard seed and leaven, indicating continual growth until a tipping point. The "advancing" stage also embraces the principle of "birth pangs" (Matthew 24:8), where periods of crisis serve as catalysts for deeper gospel penetration. Historical awakenings, social reforms, and missionary expansions exemplify the "advancing" kingdom in action. The "consummated" phase refers to the final era when the church has overcome widespread resistance, ushering in a golden age of gospel dominance. This phase aligns with Revelation 20's depiction of the binding of Satan and the reign of the saints, indicating that spiritual opposition is largely restrained. During this era, postmillennialists believe that societal norms and institutions increasingly reflect biblical values, fulfilling prophecies like Isaiah 2:4's vision of nations not learning war. This three-stage framework helps postmillennialists read Scripture like Romans 8:18–22's promise of creation's future liberation and 1 Corinthians 15:24–25's affirmation that Christ's reign extends until all enemies are subdued. The framework also equips believers to maintain hope during dark seasons, trusting that setbacks are temporary "birth pangs" within an ongoing process. Jesus' teaching in John 4:34–35—"Lift up your eyes, and look on the fields. They are white for harvest"—reinforces this prophetic timeline. As the church labors in the "already" and "advancing" stages, it anticipates "consummated" fulfillment, culminating in Christ's visible return (Revelation 19:11–16) and the final establishment of new heavens and a new earth (Revelation 21:1–4). This three-stage paradigm thus serves as a compass for postmillennial strategy, guiding mission, worship, and cultural engagement toward a horizon of transformative hope.

## 4.6 Transition to the Consummation

### 4.6.1 Satan's Final Rebellion and the Loosing "For a Little Season"
Postmillennialism holds that after a prolonged golden age, Satan will be permitted a brief release from his binding, resulting in a final, short-lived rebellion against God's kingdom. Revelation 20:7–8 describes this event: "When the thousand years are ended, Satan will be released from his prison and will come out to deceive the nations that are at the four corners of the earth." Postmillennialists interpret the "thousand years" figuratively, emphasizing that it represents an extended era of gospel dominance. As such, the loosing of Satan at the end of this period signifies a momentary reversal rather than a protracted era of evil. This brief uprising resembles the "birth pangs" motif seen earlier in both testaments—a warning that, even after great progress, evil pockets persist. Isaiah 28:21 mentions justice becoming a "strange work" at the end, suggesting a sharp contrast between prevailing righteousness and this final rebellion. Ezekiel 38–39's Gog and Magog narrative parallels Revelation's description, portraying a confederation of nations making war against God's people. Postmillennialists argue that when Satan is loosed "for a little while," he incites remaining pockets of rebellion into a last futile attempt to overthrow God's sovereignty. This rebellion underscores the persistence of human depravity and the necessity of Christ's visible return to quell all resistance. Despite Satan's brief success in amassing his forces, Revelation 20:9–10 records that fire comes down from heaven, consuming his armies and consigning Satan to the lake of fire forever. Postmillennial interpretations of this rebellion highlight its limited scope, reinforcing that it cannot derail the broader kingdom trajectory. Paul's depiction in 2 Thessalonians 2:7–8—where the "restrainer" is taken out of the way, allowing the lawless one to be revealed, before being destroyed by the Lord—provides theological corroboration. This final rebellion thus serves as a divinely ordained signpost, heralding the imminence of Christ's return. Believers are reminded that even in an era of prosperity, vigilance is required: Ephesians 6:11–12 exhorts Christians to put on the helmet of salvation and the sword of the Spirit, preparing for

spiritual warfare until the final victory. The brief nature of this rebellion affirms the sovereignty and faithfulness of God, guaranteeing that His reign endures unchallenged beyond Satan's short-lived insurrection. With Satan's last stand decisively quelled, the stage is set for Christ's visible return and the final judgment.

**4.6.2 Visible Return of Christ, General Resurrection, and Final Judgment** Following the end of Satan's brief rebellion, postmillennialists anticipate the visible return of Christ, a dramatic fulfillment of New Testament promises regarding His parousia. Revelation 19:11–16 portrays Christ as a rider on a white horse, called Faithful and True, whose name is "The Word of God." The armies of heaven accompany Him, signifying that He comes not in secret but with overwhelming power. Postmillennialists link this to 1 Thessalonians 4:16–17, where the Lord descends with a shout and the dead in Christ rise first, followed by living believers being caught up. This event inaugurates the general resurrection, where both the righteous and the unrighteous face bodily resurrection. In John 5:28–29, Jesus explains that "all who are in the tombs will hear his voice and come out"—those who have done good to the resurrection of life, and those who have done evil to the resurrection of judgment. Postmillennialists understand that the resurrection of life aligns with the church and faithful nations participating in Christ's rule, while the resurrection of judgment aligns with the final rebellion's complicit unbelievers facing accountability. Revelation 20:11–15's "great white throne" scene vividly describes the final judgment: the dead stand before God, the books are opened, and each person is judged according to works recorded in the books. Those whose names are not found in the Book of Life are thrown into the lake of fire. Postmillennialists assert that this final judgment underscores that postmillennial progress, however broad, does not annul personal responsibility; each individual stands before the Judge (Ecclesiastes 12:14). The visible return of Christ also fulfills Jesus' promise in Acts 1:11 that He would return "in the same way" as He ascended, reinforcing continuity between first and second comings. As Christ establishes His eternal kingdom, the resurrection and judgment lead directly into the new creation, ensuring that all wrongs are rectified (Revelation 21:4). This visible return contrasts with secret rapture theories, emphasizing biblical depictions of cosmic upheaval—sun darkened, stars falling—as described in Matthew 24:29–30. Postmillennialists find in these apocalyptic details a clear indication that Christ's return will be unmistakable to all. The theological significance of these events lies in their convergence: Christ's return, the resurrection of the dead, and the final judgment all transpire as one majestic moment that consummates redemptive history. With the last echoes of divine judgment completed, the cosmos transitions into its restored state.

### 4.6.3 New Heavens, New Earth, and the Ultimate Sabbath Rest

Once Christ returns, raises the dead, and dispenses final judgment, the stage is set for the inauguration of new heavens and a new earth. Revelation 21:1–2 declares, "Then I saw a new heaven and a new earth; for the first heaven and the first earth had passed away." Postmillennialists interpret this as the ultimate fulfillment of Isaiah 65:17's promise, "Behold, I create new heavens and a new earth; and the former things shall not be remembered." This renovated creation is described as free from death, mourning, crying, or pain (Revelation 21:4), highlighting the comprehensive nature of divine restoration. The New Jerusalem, descending from heaven, becomes the focal point of worship and communion with God (Revelation 21:3). Postmillennialists maintain that while the church anticipates a golden age within history, the new creation transcends all previous eras, fulfilling Romans 8:21–22's vision of creation's liberation from bondage. The eternal state is marked by uninterrupted fellowship with God, as seen when Revelation 21:22 affirms that "I saw no temple in the city, for its temple is the Lord God the Almighty and the Lamb." This emphasizes direct access to God without mediating structures. In this new order, believers experience ultimate Sabbath rest, as envisioned in Hebrews 4:9–10—entering God's rest and ceasing from their own works, for God's works have been completed. Postmillennialists believe that, in anticipation of this ultimate rest, the church's present labors participate in an already-but-not-yet dynamic: they signify future reality while serving immediate needs. The new creation restores human vocation: in Revelation 22:2, the tree of life yields fruit and leaves for the healing of nations, signaling ongoing growth, sustenance, and fellowship. Postmillennialists note that this restoration harmonizes cosmic and moral renewal—evil eradicated, creation healed, human creativity channeled into worship, and eternal fellowship enjoyed. As they transition from the final judgment to eternal Sabbath, postmillennialist hope culminates in the vision of Revelation 22:5, where God's servants "will see his face, and his name will be on their foreheads." This proximity to God underscores the intimacy of the restored relationship that history has been moving toward. By anchoring hope in the new heavens and new earth, postmillennialists affirm that earthly progress—no matter how extensive—remains provisional until the consummation, where faith becomes sight and labor transforms into rest. This completes the eschatological trajectory from the kingdom already inaugurated to the world's final renewal.

## 4.7 Systemic Implications

### 4.7.1 Mission Strategy: From Conversion to Culture-Making

Postmillennial mission strategy extends beyond individual conversions to envision entire cultural arenas shaped by Christian values. This approach builds on the Great Commission (Matthew 28:19–20), not merely to baptize individuals but to nurture disciples who influence families, communities, and institutions. Churches train members in "Kingdom Thinking," encouraging them to view their professions—law, medicine, education, business—as distinct mission fields. Pastors emphasize that ministry does not end with Sunday worship; rather, every workplace and neighborhood is an opportunity to live and proclaim Christ's lordship. Urban church planting movements target city centers, seeking to establish multiethnic congregations that cooperate with social service initiatives to address homelessness, addiction, and illiteracy in light of Isaiah 58:6–10's vision of justice. Denominational mission boards coordinate efforts to translate Scripture, train indigenous pastors, and develop local theological education centers, ensuring that converted communities receive contextualized discipleship aligning with Colossians 1:28's goal of maturity in Christ. Postmillennialists often advocate for integrated mission models where theological training includes courses on public policy, economics, and arts, so that future leaders can carry kingdom-values into every sphere. For example, medical mission teams not only provide health care but also challenge practices like sex trafficking by partnering with law enforcement and educating communities on biblical sexuality (Proverbs 31:8). Agricultural initiatives in impoverished regions aim to teach sustainable farming techniques grounded in stewardship principles (Genesis 2:15), enabling families to escape poverty cycles. Business-as-mission enterprises—enterprises that operate profitably while employing local workers and reinvesting in community development—illustrate how economic empowerment can coincide with gospel witness (Matthew 25:35–36). Throughout these efforts, the church fosters partnerships with like-minded NGOs and educational institutions, sharing resources and expertise to magnify impact. Mission fairs, conferences, and digital platforms facilitate collaboration among churches in different contexts, demonstrating how global networks exemplify the body of Christ working together (1 Corinthians 12:12–27). Regional networks encourage pastors to report on cultural indicators—crime rates, educational attainment, health metrics—highlighting how gospel interventions can correlate with measurable societal improvements. Periodic "Kingdom Summits" bring together government officials, business leaders, and church representatives to craft strategies for legislative reform grounded in biblical ethics (Proverbs 29:2). By maintaining long-term commitments to communities rather than short-term projects, churches ensure sustainable transformation that outlasts seasonal attention. This shift from episodic evangelism to comprehensive culture-making furnishes the church with a sense of vocation that encompasses spiritual renewal and societal well-being. As the church sees neighborhoods revitalized, unemployment decline, and civic life enriched by Christian values, confidence grows that the gospel's impact will extend increasingly until the golden age of the millennium. This mission strategy naturally leads into reflection on liturgical life as a formative practice, which is addressed in the next subsection.

### 4.7.2 Liturgical Life and Sacramental Expectation

Postmillennialism's optimistic vision shapes how congregations view liturgy and sacraments, seeing each service as both a celebration of present redemption and a foretaste of the consummated kingdom. Worship gatherings emphasize confession, praise, prayer, and the Word—elements that align worshipers with the cosmic liturgy described in Revelation 4:8–11, where creatures continually proclaim God's holiness. Preaching sermons that connect biblical narratives to contemporary cultural issues helps congregants understand that their worship has implications beyond Sunday, preparing them to engage society with kingdom values. The Lord's Supper carries eschatological significance: when believers partake of bread and cup, they "proclaim the Lord's death until he comes" (1 Corinthians 11:26), reminding them of Christ's

162

substitutionary atonement and His promised return. This sacramental expectation encourages church members to live in readiness, imbuing daily life with intentional holiness (1 John 3:3). Baptismal liturgies highlight believer's union with Christ in death and resurrection (Romans 6:3–4), signifying that those baptized are called to walk in newness of life, serving as ambassadors in culture-making. Music ministries incorporate hymns and contemporary songs that articulate hope for societal renewal—lyrics that reference prophetic promises of justice and peace, such as "He's Coming Back in Glory" or "Let Justice Roll." Responsive readings that include passages from Isaiah 61:1–3 or Micah 6:8 reinforce the prophetic call to cultural renewal. Pastors often teach that liturgical seasons—Advent, Lent, Easter—serve as rhythms that orient congregations toward both Christ's first and second comings, underscoring that spiritual formation connects with eschatological expectation. When architectural design incorporates community spaces—coffee shops, classrooms, art galleries—church buildings themselves become microcosms of the future kingdom, modeling hospitality and cultural engagement. This encourages laypeople to view homes, workplaces, and public venues as extensions of liturgical space. Churches cultivate a "kingdom culture" by training worship teams and volunteers to practice unity (Philippians 2:1–2), reflecting the eschatological vision of diverse peoples worshiping Christ together (Revelation 7:9–10). Sacramental catechesis includes instruction on how baptism and the Lord's Supper anticipate the new heavens and new earth (Revelation 21:1–4), inspiring worshipers to align their vocational callings with the kingdom mission. Through liturgical consistency—weekly Eucharist or communion celebrations—churches embed the rhythm of remembrance and anticipation into congregational DNA. Pastoral prayer guides connect situational petitions—community transformation, public policy renewal—to biblical promises of shalom (Psalm 122:6–7), fostering a theology of liturgical intercession that carries over into civic prayer initiatives. This sacramental and liturgical life trains the church to reflect and anticipate cultural transformation, preparing believers to embody the kingdom in every aspect of their lives. As these patterns of worship and sacrament feed missionary zeal and ethical alignment, they form a strong foundation for the church's participation in political engagement, which is the focus of the following subsection.

**4.7.3 Politics of Hope vs. Politics of Fear** Postmillennial thought advocates for a politics of hope, wherein Christians engage civic life not out of fear of cultural decline but out of confidence in God's redemptive purposes. Grounded in Jeremiah 29:7's directive to "seek the welfare of the city," believers pursue public office or civic involvement to influence policies that promote human dignity, justice, and welfare. Postmillennial strategists distinguish between the politics of fear—characterized by defensive postures, isolation, and reactive legislating—and the politics of hope, which proposes proactive policies fostering education, healthcare, and economic opportunity. By advocating incremental reforms—such as criminal justice reform informed by restorative justice principles (Matthew 18:15–17)—Christians demonstrate that biblical ethics can generate holistic societal well-being. In many regions, Christian political caucuses form to educate voters on moral issues, organize grassroots advocacy campaigns, and lobby for legislation that protects religious freedom, undergirded by Acts 4:19–20's mandate to obey God rather than men. Postmillennial politicians champion policies that support family integrity, reflecting God's design for marital covenant (Ephesians 5:22–33) while also supporting adoption and foster-care initiatives for children without parents (James 1:27). When Christians capture political office, they are called to exercise servant-leadership (Mark 10:42–45), rejecting power grabs in favor of accountability and transparency. This counters the "kingdom now" pitfalls, where demands for a Christian theocracy overshadow democratic pluralism. By emphasizing servant-hearted governance, Christians in public roles model Jesus' humility, showing that power can be used for the common good rather than personal gain. Politics of hope promote public education systems that prioritize critical thinking and ethical reasoning over indoctrination, drawing from Proverbs 22:6's instruction to "train up a child in the way he should go." With such educational policies, postmillennialists aim to cultivate moral citizens equipped to shape future cultural trajectories. Economic policies—such as tax incentives for businesses that adopt fair wage practices—embody Micah 6:8's mandate to "act justly, and to love mercy," coordinating state-level resources toward human flourishing. Policymakers guided by postmillennial convictions resist fear-driven fracturing, instead advocating inclusive policies that uphold civil discourse and bridge divides (Romans 14:19). In regions where church-state collaboration yields positive outcomes—reduced crime rates through faith-based rehabilitation programs, improved literacy through church-run adult education—politics of hope demonstrate tangible kingdom progress. Even in contexts of opposition, postmillennial leaders maintain a faithful optimism, drawing strength from 1 Timothy 2:2's encouragement to pray for rulers so that the peace of God may facilitate widespread gospel witness. This hopeful political engagement leads naturally into the realm of economic ethics, addressed next.

**4.7.4 Economic Ethics: Stewardship, Generosity, and Structural Justice** Postmillennial economic ethics underpin a vision where Christians steward resources responsibly, practice radical generosity, and pursue structural justice that combats systemic poverty. The biblical principle of stewardship (1 Peter 4:10) asserts that every resource—wealth, time, ability—is entrusted by God for redemptive purposes. Churches therefore teach congregants to manage personal finances through biblically grounded programs emphasizing budgeting, debt reduction, and giving. Tithing and almsgiving, as articulated in 2 Corinthians 9:6–7, become foundations for generosity that fuels community development. Postmillennial communities often establish benevolence funds, microfinance initiatives, and social enterprises, providing loans and training for entrepreneurs in economically marginalized areas. These ventures model Proverbs 31:16's depiction of the virtuous woman who "considers a field and buys it; with the fruit of her hands she plants a vineyard," illustrating how business can reflect God's order. Structural justice, informed by Isaiah 1:17 ("Learn to do good; seek justice, correct oppression; bring justice to the fatherless, plead the widow's cause"), leads churches to partner with local governments and NGOs to reform welfare systems. Instead of fostering dependency, these collaborations provide job training, mentorship, and transitional housing, aligning with James 2:15–16's admonition that true faith manifests in tangible care. Ethical investing— divesting from industries that exploit labor or degrade the environment—reflects Micah 6:8's call to walk humbly and do justly. Postmillennial economic frameworks encourage creation care through sustainable agriculture projects, promoting healthy food access in urban "food deserts" (Genesis 2:15). By demonstrating that biblical economics enhance community well-being, postmillennialists respond to critiques that Christianity's social engagement is utopian; they point to measurable reductions in poverty and crime where such initiatives thrive. Philanthropic networks connect wealthy donors with grassroots ministries, amplifying efforts to alleviate global suffering. Churches hold regular "Kingdom Economics" seminars, equipping members to integrate faith into careers and consumer choices. These economic ethics shape tax-policy advocacy, urging governments to incentivize charitable giving and punish graft, echoing Proverbs 16:8's "better is a little with righteousness than great revenues with injustice." As economic systems align with kingdom principles, rising prosperity fuels further cultural renewal, reinforcing gospel advances that culminate in the millennium's golden age. With economic justice addressed, the chapter now turns to pastoral considerations in an expanding but contested kingdom.

### 4.7.5 Pastoral Care in an Era of Expansion and Opposition

Pastoral care within a postmillennial framework balances vibrant hope with compassionate support for those facing continued persecution and suffering. While churches celebrate gospel advancements—new church plants, social reforms, and community revitalization—they also recognize that pockets of animosity toward Christianity may persist, requiring shepherds to equip believers for trials (2 Timothy 3:12). Pastors provide robust doctrinal teaching to fortify congregations against theological compromise and moral laxity, ensuring that growth does not lead to superficial faith (Matthew 13:21–22). Counseling services address burnout among missionaries and social workers who often confront systemic challenges while seeking to extend blessing (Galatians 6:9). When families navigate economic hardship or cultural pressure—for instance, businesses facing boycotts for public ministry—pastors offer biblical guidance on perseverance, drawing on James 1:2–4's reminder that trials produce steadfastness. Preaching on Romans 8:28 reassures believers that even adverse circumstances serve God's overarching purposes. Care ministries, often integrated with existing community outreach, assist those left behind by societal change—homeless individuals, refugees fleeing conflict, and victims of human trafficking—reflecting Matthew 25:35–40's call to serve "the least of these." Pastoral teams collaborate with healthcare professionals, mental health counselors, and legal advocates to address complex needs sensitively and holistically. Church elders engage in regular "kingdom check-ins," reviewing how the congregation is responding to cultural shifts and identifying areas where people feel disoriented by rapid change. Small-group leaders receive training to facilitate safe spaces where members can share concerns about transformation, seeking biblical wisdom for uncertainty (Philippians 4:6–7). When believers experience cognitive dissonance—joy at societal progress coexisting with dismay at lingering injustices—pastors help them wrestle with the tension, reminding them of 1 Peter 2:12's call to "Keep your conduct among the Gentiles honorable" as testimony to God's truth. Youth ministries emphasize resilience, teaching young people how to engage schools and peer groups with gracious confidence rather than cultural aggression. Pastors also equip intergenerational mentoring programs, pairing younger believers with seasoned Christians who have persevered through earlier waves of persecution, echoing the example of 2 Timothy 1:5. Pastoral prayer gatherings include moments of lament for regions still lacking gospel access, ensuring that gratitude for progress coexists with empathy for those still in darkness (Psalm 34:18). This balanced pastoral approach fosters a church culture that neither descends into triumphalism nor resigns to defeat, but holds tenaciously to postmillennial hope, thus concluding systemic implications and leading into critical evaluations.

## 4.8 Critiques, Challenges, and Rejoinders

### 4.8.1 Exegetical Objections: "Pessimistic" Texts (2 Timothy 3; Matthew 24)

Critics of postmillennialism frequently point to passages describing moral deterioration and tribulation as evidence that societal decline, rather than improvement, characterizes the last days. 2 Timothy 3:1–5 warns that "in the last days there will come times of difficulty" marked by "lovers of themselves, lovers of money, boastful, proud, abusive," suggesting a pervasive moral collapse. Postmillennialists respond by arguing that Paul's words describe conditions during the church age—"last days" being an idiom for the era between Christ's first and second comings (Acts 2:17)—and that God periodically reforms culture through revivals, preventing absolute decline. They highlight 2 Timothy 3:5's phrase "having the appearance of godliness, but denying its power," interpreting it as a warning against hypocrisy rather than a prophecy of unrelenting moral collapse. In Matthew 24, Jesus enumerates signs—wars, famines, earthquakes—that He calls "the beginning of the birth pains" (Matthew 24:8). Critics argue that these signs predict worsening conditions until the end. Postmillennial interpreters counter that birth pangs, by definition, precede new birth and are not indicators of perpetual deterioration. They draw on Matthew 24:14—"this gospel of the kingdom will be proclaimed throughout the whole world as a testimony to all nations, and then the end will come"—to assert that the advance of the gospel brings about a tipping point where kingdom blessing outweighs suffering. This fuller reading emphasizes that the gospel's expansion is as much a sign of the "last days" as are distressing events. When Jesus warns in Matthew 24:12 that "lawlessness will be increased," postmillennialists understand this as describing kinesthetic cycles of evil that intensify until revival overcomes them, rather than as a linear forecast of irreversible decline. They point to Jonah's prophecy in Jonah 3:10, where Nineveh's repentance forestalls judgment, illustrating how God can invert trajectories. Postmillennialists also appeal to Revelation 1:3's bless-edness pronounced upon "those who read and hear the words of this prophecy and keep what is written in it," suggesting that responsible engagement with eschatological texts involves working toward kingdom outcomes rather than retreat. By contending that "pessimistic" texts anticipate both persecution and gospel triumph, postmillennialists assert a balanced hermeneutic that accounts for evil without eliminating hope. This exegetical back-and-forth transitions naturally into historical objections that challenge postmillennial optimism.

**4.8.2 Historical Setbacks: Wars, Persecutions, and Global Catastrophes** Skeptics assert that history's persistent wars, genocides, and global catastrophes refute the postmillennial claim that the world trends toward flourishing before Christ's return. They point to the First and Second World Wars, the Holocaust, and more recent conflicts in Syria and Yemen as evidence of humanity's capacity for evil despite widespread Christian influence. Postmillennial responses emphasize that human depravity exists alongside divine providence: wars and persecutions can serve as catalysts for revival and moral reflection. For instance, the aftermath of World War II saw a surge in Christian humanitarianism— organizations like World Vision and Samaritan's Purse emerged to address global hunger and poverty, embodying Isaiah 58:10's call to feed the hungry. The Cold War's end triggered unprecedented religious freedom in Eastern Europe, resulting in church growth and social transformation that fulfilled proverbs about hidden blessings emerging following trials (Proverbs 20:22). Postmillennialists compare modern catastrophes to earlier eras, such as the Roman persecutions under Nero, which failed to extinguish the church; instead, early Christians saw such trials as "light and momentary affliction" producing "an eternal weight of glory" (2 Corinthians 4:17). They also highlight that global catastrophes have never erased the church's presence; rather, survivors and refugees have pioneered church plants and social services in new regions, testifying to Romans 8:28's promise that God works all things together for good. Economic depressions and famines prompt innovations in food security and economic policy—New Deal–style reforms in the United States or microfinance systems in developing nations—which church partners often drive. Even pandemics, such as the recent COVID-19 crisis, have seen Christian health workers and faith-based organizations on the front lines, exemplifying Matthew 25:36's mandate to visit the sick. Postmillennialists argue that while these events represent moral and physical setbacks, they do not contradict the overarching trajectory of gospel advance. Instead, crises open doors for evangelistic opportunity: South Korea experienced a surge in digital evangelism during the 2015 MERS outbreak, contributing to city-wide revival movements. In each case, the church's faithful witness amid suffering functioned as salt and light (Matthew 5:13–16), reinforcing postmillennial confidence that even in darkness, God's purposes endure. This historical perspective prepares postmillennialists for the next critique—the danger of triumphalism and "kingdom now" excess.

**4.8.3 Triumphalism, Theocracy, and the Charge of "Kingdom Now" Excess** Critics sometimes accuse postmillennialism of veering into triumphalism or theocratic ambition, suggesting that emphasizing societal transformation risks coercing unbelievers or conflating the church's mission with state power. Such critiques point to instances where Christian political movements have pressed for legislation imposing moral standards—controversies over blasphemy laws, religious symbols in public spaces, or "Bible-based" policies—arguing that genuine gospel influence should never coerce but only invite. Postmillennialists respond by clarifying that biblical law and New Covenant ethics must be distinguished: Old Testament theocracy was a specific covenant context with Israel, whereas the church engages pluralistic societies through invitation, persuasion, and service, not compulsion. They emphasize Jesus' statement in John 18:36—"My kingdom is not of this world"— affirming that Christ's kingdom advances through love, not force. When postmillennialists participate in politics, they advocate for policies aligned with natural law and human flourishing—such as criminal justice reform or environmental stewardship—rather than imposing religious rituals or doctrinal tests on civil life. For example, they support religious freedom laws protecting all faith communities, not just Christians, demonstrating a commitment to pluralism. Pastors and theologians in postmillennial circles often preach antithetical to triumphalist attitudes, quoting Micah 6:8's call to "do justice, love kindness, and walk humbly with your God," rejecting any posture of arrogance. They recognize distinctions between "Kingdom Now" theology—which sometimes claims immediate cosmic dominion—and a sober postmillennialism that acknowledges ongoing spiritual battles until Christ's return. By inviting critique from other Christian traditions—such as amillennialists concerned about ecclesial overreach— postmillennialists seek accountability and guard against theocratic excess. They point to Galatians 5:1, which calls believers to freedom, as a safeguard against replacing one oppressive system with another. Moreover, when engaging public policy debates— over abortion, marriage, or poverty—they emphasize compassionate persuasion and evidence-based advocacy, rather than top-down mandates. Churches that practice "servant leadership" in community development projects demonstrate that influence operates through service, not political coercion. Historical examples—like the social reforms of William Wilberforce—are presented as partnerships with legislators rather than attempts to establish a state church. By maintaining these distinctions, postmillennialists reiterate that the gospel's societal impact arises through sacrificial love (John 13:34– 35) and reasoned argument (1 Peter 3:15), rather than through force. With triumphalism addressed, the discussion advances to dialogue with premillennial and amillennial critiques.

**4.8.4 Dialogue with Premillennial and Amillennial Counter-Arguments** Premillennial and amillennial scholars often challenge postmillennial optimism from differing angles. Premillennialists argue that biblical prophecy predicts a literal, catastrophic end-time tribulation that the church cannot avert through cultural engagement (Revelation 6–19). They emphasize verses such as 1 Thessalonians

4:16–17, suggesting the church must await a future rapture rather than labor for global transformation. Postmillennialists respond by highlighting Matthew 24:14, where the sequence of gospel proclamation and the end coincide, implying that widespread Christian influence precedes final events. They also note that Jesus' parables of unknown timing (Matthew 24:36) preclude prescriptive date-setting, redirecting focus to faithful kingdom work. Amillennialists, reading Revelation 20 symbolically, assert that the "binding of Satan" refers to Christ's work on the cross, placing the millennium in the present church age rather than as a future golden age. They also assert that texts about global flourishing are symbolic of spiritual realities, not necessarily material progress. Postmillennialists agree that Christ's cross inaugurated Satan's binding but argue that the full manifestation of this binding unfolds progressively in history, producing tangible cultural renewal. They further contend that amillennial symbolic readings can undercut the call to engage culture practically. Dialogue between these traditions often revolves around Scriptural interpretation: premillennialists emphasize literal fulfillment of promises to Israel, whereas postmillennialists stress covenant continuity—the church now embodies God's kingdom mission. Amillennialists insist that the presence of evil until Christ's return works as a refining fire for believers, while postmillennialists respond that refining and transformation can coexist, allowing for substantial improvements before final victory. Conferences and inter-denominational dialogues provide forums where representatives from each camp present exegeses of key texts—Daniel 9, Revelation 20, and Matthew 24—evaluating the merits of progressive, literal, and symbolic readings. In these settings, postmillennialists emphasize that major historical awakenings demonstrate prophetic tokens of kingdom advance, encouraging premillennial and amillennial interlocutors to consider positive correlations between revival and societal improvement. By engaging such critique charitable, postmillennialists strengthen their case while maintaining respect for differing convictions on non-essential matters, anticipating that unity in core doctrines unites rather than divides. With inter-worldview dialogue advancing understanding, postmillennialism then turns to reframing suffering and martyrdom within its optimistic narrative.

**4.8.5 Reframing Suffering and Martyrdom Within an Optimistic Narrative** Skeptics often challenge postmillennialism by pointing to enduring suffering and martyrdom as evidence against a future golden age. They cite contemporary persecutions—church burnings, assaults on religious freedoms, genocides targeting Christians—as proof that evil remains unchecked. Postmillennialists respond by reframing suffering as part of the "birth pangs" leading to greater victory (John 16:33; Romans 8:18), emphasizing that martyrdom historically has fueled revival and deepened the church's resolve. The early church's experience under Nero, where persecution scattered believers who then preached the gospel widely (Acts 8:1–4), exemplifies how suffering can accelerate evangelistic advance. In more recent times, the Chinese church's growth despite—or because of—state persecution is offered as evidence that adversity can amplify witness. New Testament passages like 1 Peter 4:12–13 assure believers to rejoice insofar as they "share Christ's sufferings" because they may also share in His glory, suggesting that martyrdom itself contributes to the kingdom's glory. Postmillennialists often encourage solidarity with persecuted believers through prayer, advocacy, and resource mobilization, connecting suffering to a larger narrative of redemption. They also differentiate between redemptive suffering—suffering endured faithfully that leads to gospel penetration—and non-redemptive structural injustice, which the church is called to confront. Romans 8:28's promise that God works all things for good reassures postmillennialists that even atrocities can be woven into the tapestry of divine purposes. By celebrating modern martyrs—such as Jim Elliott, killed in Ecuador, or more recently, Christians who died defending their communities in the Middle East—postmillennial churches underscore that testimony often yields conversions among bystanders. When narratives of persecution prompt increased prayer, solidarity, and global missionary funding, postmillennialists see this as evidence that suffering has catalytic, rather than crippling, effects. They assert that a church untested by trials risks complacency, whereas adversity refines faith and intensifies mission. By framing martyrdom as a powerful witness that undergirds gospel advance, postmillennialism maintains an optimistic narrative, even amid undeniable suffering. This compassionate, realistic perspective allows the church to persevere, confident that trials contribute ultimately to the overarching arc of redemption leading to Christ's return.

**Conclusion**

Our examination of postmillennialism has shown that its hope emerges from a coherent reading of Scripture—linking God's promises to Abraham, prophetic visions of peace, Jesus' parables, and Paul's teaching on cosmic reconciliation—and from tangible instances of revival and social reform throughout church history. By emphasizing Christ's present reign, covenant continuity, and the Spirit's use of ordinary means of grace, postmillennialists envision a world in which gospel-infused families, churches, governments, and marketplaces progressively reflect kingdom values. While critics point to wars, moral failures, and persecution as signs of inevitable decline, postmillennial advocates reinterpret these setbacks as temporary "birth pangs" that provoke renewed reliance on God rather than resignation. The result is a holistic approach to mission that encompasses evangelism, cultural engagement, and supralocal cooperation—urging believers to persistently work for justice, mercy, and human flourishing. Yet postmillennialism also acknowledges that a brief final rebellion and Christ's visible coming will ultimately usher in the new creation. As we move forward to examine amillennial perspectives, this chapter's insights will help us compare how different eschatologies balance hope, realism, and anticipation of future consummation, guiding the church's witness in every age.

# Chapter 5 - Amillennialism Clarified

Amillennialism begins by contesting the notion that Revelation's thousand-year reign points to a future geopolitical utopia. Instead, it contends that Christ's victory on the cross inaugurated His reigning kingdom, with Satan's power already curtailed so the church can bear witness amid trials (Colossians 2:15; 1 John 5:19). Far from denying hope or retreating into passivity, amillennial thought affirms that believers now experience a foretaste of the age to come through Word and sacrament, even as they await Christ's return (John 17:21–23; 1 Corinthians 11:26). Drawing on the "already/not-yet" tension woven throughout both Testaments, this perspective reads apocalyptic imagery—beasts, seals, and symbolic numbers— not as literal future events but as rich metaphors describing the church's present pilgrimage (Matthew 24:14; Revelation 12:11). Historically rooted in Augustine's defenses against chiliastic expectations, this view was embraced by Reformers and later refined by modern theologians who emphasized the continuity of God's covenants. By clarifying how the "binding of Satan," the "thousand years," and Israel's promises function within a two-age framework, amillennialism offers a balanced eschatology—one that neither succumbs to utopian optimism nor descends into despair.

## 5.1 From Misconception to Definition

**5.1.1 "No Millennium" vs. "Present Millennium"** Amillennialism is frequently caricatured as denying any millennium, but in truth it affirms a "present millennium" realized spiritually rather than literally. Early critics labeled it "no millennium," assuming that amillennialists dismiss Revelation 20's "thousand years" altogether. In response, amillennial theologians clarify that the thousand years symbolizes the entire church age, from Christ's first coming to His return (Revelation 20:1–3). By reading the text figuratively, they affirm that Christ already reigns from heaven (Hebrews 2:8–9) and that Satan's binding refers to a present restraint on his power to prevent him from deceiving the nations completely (Revelation 20:2–3). Amillennialists emphasize that Scripture often uses symbolic numbers—the seventy weeks of Daniel or the forty days of temptation—to convey theological truths rather than precise calendars (Daniel 9:24–27; Matthew 4:2). Thus, the "thorn in the flesh" (2 Corinthians 12:7) and the "forty years in the wilderness" point to realities that outlast literal spans, underscoring God's purposes. By contrast, some literalist readings insist on a future one-thousand-year earthly reign, but amillennialists argue that such a view can sever biblical unity by requiring two separate reigns of Christ. They cite Ephesians 1:20–23 to show that Christ is already seated at God's right hand, far above every rule and authority, implying His present universal lordship. The idea that there is "no millennium" misses the point that amillennialists see a spiritual flourishing of the kingdom now, evidenced by the global church's growth and the power of the gospel against darkness (Acts 1:8). In this sense, the "present millennium" is visible in the church's witness, sacraments, and corporate life (Colossians 1:13–14). When critics accuse amillennialists of ignoring Revelation 20, proponents respond by demonstrating how apocalyptic literature uses rich imagery—compare Ezekiel 40's temple vision, which functions typologically yet points to Jesus as the true temple (John 2:19–21). Moreover, passages such as Matthew 24:14, where Jesus says the gospel will be preached to all nations before the end comes, align with amillennialism's emphasis on an ongoing church mission rather than a future restoration of Israel alone. As a result, "no millennium" becomes a misnomer; amillennialists uphold a present, spiritual reign of Christ, seeing Revelation's symbolism as describing the church experiencing Christ's victory now. This understanding requires us to examine Christ's passionate advocacy for His people—His heavenly kingship—in greater detail.

**5.1.2 Christ's Heavenly Kingship: Session, Intercession, Triumph** Central to amillennialism is the conviction that Christ's ascension to the right hand of the Father establishes His heavenly kingship, where He presently intercedes and reigns (Romans 8:34; Hebrews 7:25). After His resurrection, Jesus declared, "All authority in heaven and on earth has been given to Me" (Matthew 28:18), inaugurating an age in which He exercises sovereign rule over the church and cosmos. In His session, Christ functions as the once-for-all high priest, presenting the merits of His sacrificial atonement on behalf of believers (Hebrews 4:14–16). Amillennialists stress that this intercessory work undergirds the church's victorious life amid persecution, for in His role as mediator, Christ secures divine provision for His people (1 John 2:1–2). The binding of Satan (Revelation 20:2–3) corresponds with Christ's triumph over demonic powers at the cross (Colossians 2:15), whereby Satan's ability to deceive the nations is limited so that the gospel may advance. This heavenly reign is not static; Christ's royal decrees continually apply, sending the Spirit to empower believers (John 14:16–17; Acts 2:1–4) and dispatching His church with the message of reconciliation (2 Corinthians 5:18–20). The church's victory in spiritual warfare (Ephesians 6:10–18) reflects Christ's rule, eliminating the notion that the millennium is a future earthly reign divorced from current spiritual realities. In His session, Christ also engages in covenantal governance, sowing seeds of His kingdom through the preaching of the cross (1 Corinthians 1:18) and the administration of sacraments that point to heavenly realities (John 6:53–58). Amillennialists point to passages like Ephesians 1:20–23, where Paul says Christ is seated far above all authority and head over the church, indicating that His present reign is global and cosmic rather than geographically confined to Jerusalem or earthly thrones. This heavenly kingship assures believers that their struggle against sin and suffering is undergirded by divine sovereignty, affirming that the church will withstand trials until Christ's return. As we transition into understanding why Revelation's thousand years is therefore symbolic, we grasp that Christ's present rulership from heaven precludes the need for a separate earthly millennium.

### 5.1.3 Symbolic Thousand Years, Satan's Binding, and Mission Advance
Amillennial interpreters regard the thousand years in Revelation 20 as symbolic, representing the entire period between Christ's ascension and His second advent. This perspective relies on understanding the book of Revelation as apocalyptic literature replete with numbers that often carry symbolic rather than literal meaning (Revelation 1:1; 5:1). The use of "ten times ten" (ten squared) evokes fullness or completeness (Leviticus 26:8), suggesting that the "thousand years" marks the complete duration of Christ's spiritual reign through the church. In this context, Satan's binding (Revelation 20:2–3) means his power to deceive Gentile nations is curtailed, facilitating the church's mission to "make disciples of all nations" (Matthew 28:19). Amillennialists highlight that Jesus declared on the cross, "It is finished" (John 19:30), signifying that His decisive victory began restraining Satan even before John penned Revelation. God's design, they argue, is for the gospel to expand unhindered until a future time when Christ returns to judge the world (Acts 17:31). Texts such as 2 Thessalonians 2:6–7 speak of a restraining force preventing the lawless one's revelation until the proper time, aligning with Revelation's depiction of Satan's binding. As the dragon is bound in heaven, the church on earth carries forward the commission, demonstrating that Satan's bondage does not remove demonic activity entirely but limits it in a way that ensures gospel progress (Ephesians 6:12). Amillennialists interpret Revelation 20:7–9's description of a final rebellion "after the thousand years" as Christ's brief permitting of Satan to deceive the nations once more, provoking moral and spiritual apostasy before His return. This temporary release underscores human depravity yet also highlights God's ultimate triumph. By reading these texts as symbolic, amillennialists affirm that no literal earthly reign is necessary; Christ's kingdom operates in the hearts of believers and through the church. Consequently, the church's mission finds motivation in knowing that every conversion advances Christ's rule in history, offering a counterpoint to views that postpone significant kingdom in-breaking to a future millennium.

### 5.1.4 Defeating the Charge of Pessimism: Hope within Realism
Critiques of amillennialism often accuse it of pessimism, arguing

that denying a future earthly golden age leaves believers with no cultural hope. Amillennialists counter that their view fully acknowledges current affliction—war, injustice, suffering—as reality while maintaining hope in Christ's present and eventual triumph. They point to Romans 8:18–25, where Paul affirms that present sufferings are not worth comparing to future glory, suggesting that believers should endure with hope even if societal conditions remain imperfect. Amillennialists emphasize that the church's mission is to proclaim the gospel as a beacon of hope in a fallen world, trusting in God's redemptive purposes despite endemic sin (Luke 4:18–19). They draw on Jesus' words in John 16:33—"In this world you will have trouble, but take heart, I have overcome the world"—to anchor their optimism in Christ's victory rather than in temporal circumstances. By focusing on Christ's heavenly reign, amillennialists contend that true hope lies in the certainty of salvation and the promise of resurrection (1 Corinthians 15:20–28), which transcends any fleeting cultural progress. They resist triumphalism by acknowledging that while the gospel presses onward, evil will not be eradicated completely until Christ returns (2 Thessalonians 2:3–8). This stance fosters a balanced realism: believers pursue justice (Isaiah 1:17), care for the poor (James 1:27), and engage culture (Matthew 5:13–16) while recognizing that full consummation awaits the new heavens and new earth (Revelation 21:1–4). Amillennialists see hope in existing signs of gospel fruit—transformations in individual lives, local communities, and occasional societal reforms—without expecting a universal golden era. They argue that the absence of a future earthly utopia does not negate cultural engagement but rather clarifies that such engagement is faithful stewardship, not a path to ultimate vindication. In this way, amillennialism offers a realistic hope grounded in Christ's redemption, equipping believers to serve faithfully until the day of His return.

## 5.2 Hermeneutical Foundations

### 5.2.1 Apocalyptic Symbolism and Recapitulation in Revelation

Amillennialism's reading of Revelation depends heavily on understanding apocalyptic literature as laden with symbolic imagery and patterns of recapitulation. Apocalyptic texts often use numbers, animals, and cosmic events to convey theological truths (Daniel 7:1–

28; Ezekiel 1:1–28). In Revelation, seals, trumpets, and bowls form recapitulative cycles, with each section retelling divine judgments from different angles (Revelation 6–16). Amillennialists point out that the seven seals culminate in the seventh seal, leading into the seven trumpets, which in turn lead into the seven bowls, demonstrating how John uses repetition to emphasize God's sovereignty and the completeness of His redemptive actions. Recognizing this literary structure cautions against reading every symbol as predictive of unique chronological events. The numerous references to numbers—seven spirits, four living creatures, twelve tribes—carry symbolic significance rooted in Jewish tradition (Revelation 1:4; 4:6–8). For example, the 144,000 sealed servants in Revelation 7:1–8 represent fullness or completeness of God's people (twelve tribes times twelve thousand), not necessarily a literal headcount. By this logic, the thousand-year period in Revelation 20 symbolizes a complete epoch of Christ's reign over Satan rather than a future literal millennium. Comparing Revelation 20:7's "after the thousand years" with prophetic recapitulation in Ezekiel 38–39, amillennialists interpret these chapters as describing events both near and far—historically fulfilled for Israel yet ultimately pointing to final judgment—indicating apocalyptic layers of meaning. Revelation's apostolic context, penned to churches enduring persecution, reinforces the idea that its immediate purpose was encouraging faithfulness under trial rather than instructing them to expect a future earthly golden age. Thus, amillennial hermeneutics prioritize recapitulation and symbolic meaning, recognizing how visionary elements like the beast, the false prophet, and the harlot of Babylon represent recurring patterns of evil rather than precise future figures. This interpretive approach prepares the ground for appreciating how the kingdom unfolds in an "already/not-yet" tension.

### 5.2.2 Already/Not-Yet Tension in New-Testament Eschatology

Amillennial theology builds on an "already/not-yet" framework that sees Christ's kingdom as inaugurated but awaiting consummation. Jesus' ministry inaugurated the kingdom of God (Mark 1:15), yet His definitive reign awaits full revelation at His return (1 Corinthians 15:24–25). Paul's language—Christ "redeemed us to himself" (Titus 2:14) and yet we "wait for our blessed hope" (Titus 2:13)— illustrates this tension. Believers experience kingdom blessings now—justification, sanctification, and spiritual victory over sin

(Romans 8:1–2)—while still wrestling against remaining sin and temptation (Romans 7:14–25). The present ministry of the Spirit (John 16:7–13) empowers the church to live out kingdom ethics, but the new heavens and new earth (Revelation 21:1) remain future. This dynamic explains why amillennialists affirm that Jesus is presently seated at the Father's right hand, interceding for believers (Hebrews 7:25), and yet look forward to His second coming as the moment when all foes will be removed (1 Corinthians 15:26). Biblical texts such as Colossians 1:13–14 highlight that believers have been "delivered from the domain of darkness" now, but the fullness of restoration—"the glory of His inheritance"—is still anticipated. Amillennialists see this tension running through the gospels: Jesus proclaims that "the kingdom of God is in your midst" (Luke 17:21) even as He warns that "the Son of Man will come at an hour you do not expect" (Luke 12:40). John's epistles affirm that believers "are from the devil" no longer (1 John 3:8), yet they "have not yet appeared what we shall be" (1 John 3:2). This has practical consequences: the church engages in sacramental life, preaching, and social action now because the Spirit is present, while remaining humble and watchful in view of judgment to come (2 Peter 3:11–13). Recognizing this "already/not-yet" tension prevents amillennialism from slipping into either extreme of triumphalism—assuming the kingdom is fully realized—or despair—believing Christ's reign is entirely future. This balanced stance, in turn, flows into an appreciation for typology and the broader "two-age" structure of biblical promise and fulfillment.

### 5.2.3 Typology, Promise-Fulfilment, and "Two-Age" Structure
Amillennial hermeneutics emphasize typology and a "two-age" framework distinguishing the present age from the age to come. Typology sees events, persons, and institutions in the Old Testament as anticipatory figures that find wider fulfillment in the person and work of Christ (Colossians 2:17). For example, the Passover lamb (Exodus 12:1–14) prefigures Jesus as the Lamb of God (John 1:29) whose blood secures deliverance from sin. Similarly, Israel's exodus from Egypt (Exodus 14) serves as a type of the believer's spiritual exodus from bondage to Christ's freedom (1 Corinthians 10:1–4). Amillennialists underscore that these types find continuing significance in the church age but culminate in the final consummation when the typological promises—ultimate liberation, unbroken fellowship—are fully realized. The "two-age" structure,

articulated in texts such as Ephesians 1:20–21, contrasts the present age—characterized by sin's dominion and spiritual warfare (Ephesians 6:12)—with the age to come, marked by Christ's universal reign and peace (Revelation 21:3–4). This framework informs how amillennialists read Israel's land promises and temple imagery: they see these as typological precursors to the new covenant realities embodied in the church (Ephesians 2:19–22) and consummated in the new heavens and new earth (Revelation 21:1). Prophetic texts like Isaiah 7:14, which promise a virgin-born child named Immanuel, find partial fulfillment in Isaiah's time but attain full meaning in Jesus' birth (Matthew 1:23). Amillennialists stress that the Davidic covenant's promise of an eternal throne (2 Samuel 7:12–16) is realized in Christ's heavenly session rather than in a future earthly dynasty. By understanding typology in this way, they reconcile Old Testament covenants with New Testament fulfillment, rejecting dispensations that sharply segregate Israel and church. This typological approach sits alongside an awareness that biblical promises unfold through successive layers—initial partial fulfillments in history and ultimate consummation in the age to come—providing a robust hermeneutical scaffolding. From this vantage, amillennialism holds that the church, as a spiritual Israel, participates in the blessings of Abraham (Galatians 3:29) while awaiting their full expression when Christ returns. With these hermeneutical foundations, we now turn to trace how amillennial thought developed historically.

## 5.3 Historical Development of Amillennial Thought

**5.3.1 Augustine's *Civitas Dei* and the Patristic Turn** Augustine's magnum opus, *The City of God*, marks a watershed in amillennial thought, shifting interpretation of the millennium from a literal earthly reign to a symbolic understanding of the church age. In response to pagan accusations that Christianity caused Rome's fall, Augustine reoriented eschatology: instead of expecting a terrestrial utopia, he described two "cities"—the earthly and the heavenly—coexisting in tension until the final judgment (Revelation 20:11–15). Augustine argued that Revelation 20's "thousand years" symbolizes the era in which the saints reign with Christ spiritually from heaven (Revelation 5:10) while the dragon is bound, limiting his power to distract nonbelievers (Colossians 2:15). He maintained that the church does not require an intermediary earthly kingdom, for Christ's kingdom is spiritual (John 18:36) and already present (Luke 17:21). By interpreting Old Testament prophecies such as Ezekiel 40–48 typologically—seeing the temple as pointing to Christ—he closed the door on literalist temple-building schemes, insisting that Christ is the fulfillment of temple and throne promises (John 2:19–21; Acts 2:29–36). Augustine's exegesis of Matthew 24:34—that "this generation" refers to the generation witnessing Christ's coming in judgment on Jerusalem—reinforced his view that Jesus' references to cataclysmic signs applied to first-century events, not to a distant future millennium. His view spread rapidly in both Eastern and Western churches, with Melito of Sardis and John Chrysostom offering similar allegorical readings. This patristic turn shaped medieval theology, where allegorical interpretation predominated, and literalist expectations of a future earthly kingdom declined. Augustine's emphasis on the "already" dimension of the kingdom—believers seated with Christ in heavenly places (Ephesians 2:6)—provided comfort amid Roman political decay and served as a model for understanding Christian life under various earthly regimes. Through his influence, the notion of a future earthly millennium lost traction, replaced by a vision of redemptive history culminating in the new heavens and new earth. As this era progressed, his amillennial framework emerged as the default eschatological paradigm, setting the context for medieval and Reformation developments.

**5.3.2 Medieval and Reformation Consensus: Luther, Calvin, the Confessions** During the medieval era, Augustine's symbolic reading remained normative, and expectations of a literal earthly millennium were largely marginalized. Scholastic theologians such as Thomas Aquinas integrated Augustine's amillennial framework into comprehensive theological systems, affirming that the millennium represents the church age and that Christ reigns spiritually over His people. In the Reformation, leading figures like Martin Luther and John Calvin likewise maintained an amillennial stance, grounded in their return to Scripture over church tradition. Luther's sermons on Revelation emphasized Christ's victory over Satan and the present reality of the kingdom, rejecting literal millennialism as lacking textual warrant. He asserted that Jesus' mention of a "thousand years" in Revelation 20 should not override the numerous texts that situate Christ's kingdom in the hearts of believers (Luke 17:21). Calvin's *Institutes of the Christian Religion* likewise interprets Revelation allegorically, viewing the "binding of Satan" as Christ's work on the cross (Colossians 2:15) and the millennium as the current reign of the church. Calvin taught that Christ's people would "reign" with Him against sin and death now (1 Corinthians 6:2–3) while awaiting final consummation. Reformation confessions—the Augsburg Confession (Art. XVII), the Westminster Confession (CH. 32), and the Heidelberg Catechism (Q&A 52)—echoed these amillennial convictions by describing the millennium as the period of the church's victory over Satan through the Word and sacraments. The Westminster Shorter Catechism's answer to the last things affirms a "visible reign of righteousness" but locates it in the spiritual reign of Christ rather than a future earthly kingdom. Anabaptists and some radical reformers occasionally flirted with chiliastic ideas, but their movements remained marginal compared to the broader magisterial consensus. As these Reformation-era documents spread, amillennialism solidified as the default position in the Reformed and Lutheran traditions, influencing subsequent confessional churches. This medieval-to-Reformation lineage ensured that amillennial thought would shape Protestant eschatology, even as later thinkers revised and expanded upon these foundations.

### 5.3.3 Twentieth-Century Articulations: Vos, Hoekema, Ridderbos

The twentieth century witnessed renewed articulation of amillennial theology through figures such as Geerhardus Vos, Anthony Hoekema, and Herman Ridderbos, who applied historical-critical methods and contemporary scholarship to refine amillennial insights. Vos, often considered the father of Reformed biblical theology, emphasized redemptive history and typological progression, arguing that the Old Testament's promise of a future kingdom finds spiritual fulfillment in Christ's person and work, extending throughout the church age. He taught that Biblical covenants progressively reveal God's plan, culminating in the New Covenant, which obviates any need for a future earthly temple or sacrificial system. Vos's work laid the groundwork for understanding the kingdom in both inaugurated and yet-to-be aspects, demonstrating that Christ's resurrection and ascension inaugurated a new covenant reality (Luke 24:49; Acts 2:17–21). Anthony Hoekema's *The Bible and the Future* offered a systematic, accessible defense of amillennialism, engaging premillennial literalism and postmillennial optimism with exegetical precision. Hoekema argued that Revelation's numerical language must be read symbolically, just as the Beatitudes function as thematic summaries rather than rigid checklists. He demonstrated that the binding of Satan refers to the ritual defeat of the accuser, enabling the church to grow despite opposition. Herman Ridderbos, a Dutch New Testament scholar, contributed a Christocentric interpretation of redemptive history, emphasizing that Romans 5–8's "already/not-yet" dynamic anchors the entire eschatological framework. Ridderbos's commentary on Romans presented the believer's union with Christ as the basis for anticipating full cosmic restoration, underscoring that the church lives as "firstfruits" of the new creation (Romans 8:23). Collectively, these twentieth-century voices refined amillennialism by integrating biblical theology, historical context, and systematic coherence, pushing amillennial thought beyond mere reaction against literalism. Their writings influenced seminary curricula and pastoral teaching, ensuring that amillennial eschatology remained a robust, viable alternative for contemporary churches. As these scholars mentored students and published works, amillennialism gained renewed credibility in academic circles, setting the stage for global appropriations.

### 5.3.4 Global South Appropriations and Ecumenical Statements

In recent decades, amillennialism has found fresh life in majority-world contexts—Africa, Asia, and Latin America—where local theologians integrate traditional Reformed and Catholic insights with their own experiences of persecution and renewal. African theologians such as Kwame Bediako have emphasized how the church's present pilgrimage under Christ's rule resonates with communities enduring social upheaval, interpreting Revelation's symbols in light of ongoing struggles rather than a future earthly utopia. In Latin America, Catholic scholars influenced by Vatican II have emphasized the "now but not yet" of the kingdom, linking social justice movements with eschatological hope while maintaining caution against utopian politics. Asian theologians, writing in contexts where Christians remain a minority, often adopt amillennial perspectives that emphasize the church's witness under suffering (John 15:18–21), drawing strength from Christ's heavenly session rather than expecting a future terrestrial reign. Ecumenical statements—such as the Lausanne Covenant (1974) and the World

184

Evangelical Alliance's statements on end times—often refrain from endorsing any particular millennial view, reflecting amillennialism's broad acceptance across Protestant, Catholic, and Orthodox lines. The joint declaration on justification by the Lutheran World Federation and the Catholic Church (1999) indirectly fostered amillennial approaches by focusing on Christ's atoning work as the central eschatological hope shared by diverse traditions. As seminaries in the Global South train pastors with ceaseless emphasis on mission and discipleship, amillennialism's nonliteral approach to Revelation finds practical resonance: leaders prioritize evangelism and social engagement over speculative timetables. Online platforms and translation efforts have propelled amillennial literature into multiple languages, resulting in grassroots communities—whether in Nigeria or the Philippines—embracing symbolic readings that emphasize Christ's victory rather than calendar-based speculation. These global appropriations underscore amillennialism's flexibility: local churches can articulate their own prophetic readings of social and political realities without forcing them into rigid chronological frameworks. As such, amillennialism continues to evolve, weaving cross-cultural experiences into the tapestry of its theological convictions, and preparing the ground for its practical outworkings in worship, ethics, and mission.

## 5.4 Realized Eschatology in Worship and Sacrament

**5.4.1 Kingdom in Mystery: Word, Table, Baptism as the Powers of the Age to Come** Amillennialism emphasizes that elements of the coming kingdom are already present in the worshiping community through the proclaimed Word, the sacrament of baptism, and the Lord's Supper. When believers gather around Scripture, they encounter Christ Himself, since He is the living Word (John 1:1, 14) who speaks through the apostles' writings (2 Peter 3:2). The preached Gospel functions as a kingdom vector, for Paul declares that "faith comes from hearing, and hearing through the word of Christ" (Romans 10:17). In this way, the church experiences a foretaste of future glory as divine truth penetrates hearts, transforming listeners from spiritual death to life (Ephesians 1:18–19). Baptism signifies incorporation into Christ's body, reflecting Colossians 2:12's teaching that believers are "buried with [Christ] in baptism and raised with him through your faith in the power of God." In the ordinance, water and the Spirit combine as seen in Jesus' promise that one must be "born of water and the Spirit" to enter God's kingdom (John 3:5). Thus, baptism is not merely a memorial but a participation in Christ's death and resurrection, conferring identity with His present reign. The Lord's Supper likewise serves as a mystery, for when believers eat the bread and drink the cup "in remembrance" of Jesus (Luke 22:19; 1 Corinthians 11:24–25), they proclaim His death, affirm His ongoing presence (Matthew 26:26–28), and await Him "in the future" (1 Corinthians 11:26). This Eucharistic anticipation unites worshipers with the eschatological feast described in Isaiah 25:6–9, where God will "swallow up death forever" and wipe away tears. At the table, the church participates in the "powers of the age to come" (Hebrews 6:5), experiencing peace with God (Romans 5:1) and communion with the Triune life even amid suffering. Amillennialists stress that these mysteries engage believers in a foretaste of heavenly realities, forming them into a community where the "firstfruits" of the Spirit give life to a new creation (Romans 8:23). The Word's preaching, baptismal initiation, and Eucharistic communion create a sacramental nexus that sustains the church as a sign and instrument of the kingdom, wielding spiritual power over sin and death (1 Corinthians 10:16–17). In this way, worship and sacrament fuse present participation with future promise, forging a robust ecclesial identity. As churches live out these mysteries week by week, they embody Christ's current reign, simultaneously reminding themselves that full consummation—"the redemption of our bodies" (Romans 8:23)—remains future. This dynamic of "already here but not yet complete" roots believers in both present grace and eschatological hope, equipping them to endure normative trials of faith, which we now examine.

**5.4.2 The Normative Tribulation: Persecution, Perseverance, and Pastoral Care** Amillennial theology recognizes that tribulation characterizes the church age, making persecution and suffering normative rather than exceptional. Jesus warned His disciples that in this world they would have trouble but assured them of His victory (John 16:33), establishing a template for Christian life: facing hardships yet persevering under divine providence. Peter echoed this when he wrote that Christians might suffer "grievous trials" while being refined to genuine faith (1 Peter 1:6–7). For amillennialists, tribulation teaches believers to rely on Christ's righteousness rather than their own, echoing Paul's statement that "we boast in our sufferings for we know that suffering produces endurance, and endurance produces character, and character produces hope" (Romans 5:3–4). Historical examples, such as early church martyrs under Nero or missionary pioneers in closed countries, illustrate how tribulation fuels evangelistic urgency and community solidarity (Acts 6:8–7:60). Pastoral care in this context focuses on nurturing perseverance (Hebrews 12:1–2), offering hope by explicating that trials refine rather than nullify God's promises (James 1:2–4). When believers face social ostracism or economic hardship for their faith, amillennial pastors encourage them with Scripture's manifold assurances—"no temptation has overtaken you that is not common to man" (1 Corinthians 10:13)—underscoring divine faithfulness. Church communities establish support networks: prayer cells that intercede for imprisoned or persecuted members, benevolence funds that aid those losing livelihoods, and counseling ministries that address trauma from hate crimes. Amillennialists stress that such tribulation, while painful, aligns with Christ's own path of suffering (Philippians 3:10), forging deeper conformity to His likeness and witness to the world. They argue that expecting an earthly utopia before Christ's return sets believers up for disillusionment when persecution inevitably resurfaces. Instead, a theology that views tribulation as normative cultivates resilience: Titus 2:11–14's description of Christ giving Himself "to redeem us from all lawlessness and to purify for himself a people for his own possession" frames trials as context for sanctification. By helping congregants understand how Christ's intercession secures strength amid tribulation (Hebrews 7:25), pastors equip them to face opposition without despair. This approach also fosters a global solidarity, as amillennial churches connect with persecuted believers worldwide, sharing resources and testimonies of faithfulness (Revelation 12:11). In sum, the normative tribulation of the church age functions as both a crucible and a catalyst, shaping a faithful witness until the day Christ appears, at which point all tears will be wiped away (Revelation 7:17). As believers persevere, they engage the cosmic conflict in spiritual warfare, which we now explore.

### 5.4.3 Spiritual Warfare and the Already-Defeated Dragon

Amillennialism teaches that the binding of Satan in Revelation 20 represents his present, partial defeat, enabling the church's mission, yet it recognizes that demonic activity continues, requiring vigilant spiritual warfare. When Christ triumphed on the cross, He "disarmed the rulers and authorities" (Colossians 2:15), rendering them powerless over those united with Him. This cosmic victory undergirds the church's ongoing struggle against spiritual forces, as Ephesians 6:12 explains that "we do not wrestle against flesh and blood, but against the rulers, against the authorities... against the spiritual forces of evil in the heavenly places." Amillennialists emphasize that the dragon's inability to deceive the nations entirely (Revelation 20:3) refers to Satan's restricted power to subvert the spread of the gospel, not to his complete eradication. Believers must therefore don the full armor of God—truth, righteousness, gospel of peace, faith, salvation, and the Word (Ephesians 6:14–17)—in order to stand firm. Prayer, especially intercessory prayer, functions as a "strategic weapon" (Ephesians 6:18) that weakens demonic schemes and fortifies the church. Spiritual warfare ministries teach congregants to discern demonic tactics—accusation, deception, and oppression—by studying passages such as 2 Corinthians 2:11, which warns against being "outwitted by Satan." When church leaders anoint the sick and pray for deliverance, they enact Christ's command that believers will "lay hands on the sick, and they will recover" (Mark 16:18), displaying authority over sickness that demonic spirits exploit. Amillennialism also recognizes that demonic forces can subvert Christian communities through false teaching (1 Timothy 4:1) and heresy, so doctrinal vigilance becomes a form of spiritual warfare—guarding the church's unity and purity (Jude 1:3). Contemporary examples include ministries that coordinate prayer networks during periods of persecution, unleashing concentrated spiritual warfare that results in surprising turnarounds, such as church planting movements emerging from previously hostile regions. The practice of corporate confession (1 John 1:9) and mutual encouragement (Hebrews 3:13) sustains believers under demonic assault, reinforcing the community's identity as a fortress of God (Psalm 91:1–2). By recognizing that Christ's victory is both accomplished and applied progressively, amillennialists encourage Christians to live confidently in the "already" of Christ's triumph while anticipating the "not yet" of His final eradication of evil. This balance of spiritual warfare and assured victory flows into mission practices, where the Lamb's authority propels evangelism even amid opposition.

**5.4.4 Mission under the Lamb's Banner: Evangelism amid Suffering** Amillennialism frames mission as the church's participation in Christ's redemptive work, carried out under the banner of the Lamb who has secured victory (Revelation 5:5–6). The "already" of Christ's triumph at the cross dispels the fear that opposition will ultimately prevail, inspiring believers to lionhearted witness (Acts 4:29–31). When the apostle Paul declared that he was "not ashamed of the gospel, for it is the power of God for salvation to everyone who believes" (Romans 1:16), he modeled mission under the Lamb's banner: fearless, Christ-centered, and fueled by divine power. Amillennialists emphasize that mission is inherently incarnational, where each congregation's local outreach reflects the incarnation's logic—God with us (John 1:14). This involves gospel proclamation paired with acts of mercy—feeding the hungry (Matthew 25:35), caring for orphans and widows (James 1:27), and advocating for justice (Isaiah 1:17). Such holistic mission demonstrates the kingdom's present reality and also serves as an apologetic to a watching world (1 Peter 3:15). In hostile environments, amillennial mission strategies include house churches that meet discreetly, underground literature distribution, and digital evangelism that evades censorship, reflecting Jesus' warning that "when they persecute you in one town, flee to the next" (Matthew 10:23). Missionaries trained in amillennial contexts avoid speculative prognostications about political developments, instead grounding their work in theological convictions that Christ is sovereign even over shifting regimes (Daniel 2:21). This posture leads to patience amid slow progress: the parable of the sower (Luke 8:11–15) reminds mission-workers that some seed falls on rocky ground or among thorns, yet persists in sowing because harvest is assured eventually. Mission under the Lamb's banner also entails strategic partnership between majority-world churches and global mission networks, reflecting Revelation 7:9's vision of a diverse multitude "from every nation, from all tribes and peoples and languages" standing before the throne. Collaborative efforts, such as contextualized Bible translation teams, equip local churches to evangelize in culturally meaningful ways, leveraging the Lamb's victory to break ethnic and linguistic barriers (Acts 2:4–11). As the church advances in mission, it does so as a pilgrim people, carrying the Lamb's banner of hope into dark places while trusting that "the light shines in the darkness, and the darkness has not overcome it" (John 1:5). Having explored how realized eschatology informs worship, suffering, spiritual warfare, and mission, we now turn to consider the consummation without an interim golden age.

# 5.5 Consummation without an Earthly Golden Age

### 5.5.1 Single, Universal Resurrection and One Final Judgment

Amillennialism uniformly affirms that there will be one general resurrection of the dead, both righteous and unrighteous, followed by a single final judgment. Jesus' declaration in John 5:28–29—"all who are in the tombs will hear his voice and come out, those who have done good to the resurrection of life, and those who have done evil to the resurrection of judgment"—clearly indicates one resurrection with two destinies. This approach rejects multiple resurrections or separable raptures, emphasizing instead that Christ's return triggers the resurrection of all the dead (1 Corinthians 15:51–53). At that moment, believers will be redeemed from the perishable to the imperishable (1 Corinthians 15:52), while those who remain in unbelief will rise to face eternal separation from God (John 3:36). Revelation 20:5–6 speaks of the "first resurrection" in symbolic or spiritual terms, for amillennialists interpret the technical resurrection language as applicable to all at the same time when Christ returns. The apostolic witness in Acts 24:15, where Paul says he believes in "a resurrection of both the just and the unjust," corroborates this unified model. Scriptural passages such as Matthew 25:31–46 depict Christ shepherding all nations before the throne, separating sheep from goats simultaneously, affirming a single judgment event rather than staggered judgments. Amillennialists teach that this final judgment resolves all moral and cosmic questions in one definitive session, where Christ "hands over the kingdom to God the Father after... destroying every rule and every authority and power" (1 Corinthians 15:24–26). This stands in contrast to dispensational views of separate judgments—the bema seat, the sheep and goats, and the Great White Throne—by maintaining that Scripture presents a cohesive sequence: Christ returns, raises the dead, judges all, and then consummates God's kingdom. Amillennial theology thus guides believers to live with a single eschatological horizon: the day when their eternal destiny is determined once and for all. This awareness shapes the urgency and integrity of Christian life, prompting appeals such as 2 Peter 3:11–12 to live holy and godly lives as we "await and hasten the coming of the day of God." From this climactic judgment, the narrative moves seamlessly into the new heavens and new earth, for which the old order must pass away.

**5.5.2 Cosmic Conflagration and Re-Creation: 2 Peter 3 and Romans 8** Amillennialism's understanding of the new heavens and new earth emerges from texts that emphasize both judgment by fire and subsequent reconciliation of creation. In 2 Peter 3:10–13, Peter vividly describes the "heavens passing away with a roar, and the heavenly bodies being burned up and dissolved," followed by "a new heaven and a new earth in which righteousness dwells." Amillennialists interpret the conflagration literally—cosmic elements undergo a fiery judgment—yet they also recognize Scripture's figurative language to point beyond mere destruction: fire purifies and renews (Isaiah 4:4; Malachi 3:2–3). This cleansing fire removes the curse of sin that infects both humanity and nature, aligning with Romans 8:19–21's promise that creation eagerly awaits its liberation from bondage to decay. Paul's teaching that creation itself will be set free "from its bondage to corruption" (Romans 8:21) underscores the continuity between cosmic redemption and the believer's own deliverance from sin. Amillennialists stress that the eschatological purgation of creation does not annihilate it but re-forms it into a renewed, incorruptible state (Revelation 21:1). This re-creation fulfills Genesis 1's original goodness and Isaiah 65:17–25's visions of peace, where "the wolf and the lamb shall graze together" (Isaiah 65:25) and humans live long lives in harmony. Such language indicates that the new creation will enable full communion between God and His people—a marriage supper of the Lamb (Revelation 19:9) where death, mourning, and pain are no more (Revelation 21:4). This cosmic vision also ties to Revelation 22:1–2's description of the river of water of life flowing from God's throne, with the tree of life on either side yielding fruit for healing the nations. Amillennial theology thus embraces a holistic redemption that reestablishes humanity's stewardship of creation under Christ's lordship (Genesis 1:26; Revelation 22:3). In light of this, environmental responsibility becomes a present duty for believers—not as a way to earn salvation but as participation in creation's redemption (Luke 19:40) and a foretaste of the new earth's harmony. By affirming a cosmic conflagration that purifies and a subsequent re-creation that restores, amillennialists navigate between literalist annihilationism and purely spiritualized readings, holding that Scripture's promises of "new heavens and a new earth" mark a distinctive future reality that transcends the present order. As the renewed cosmos emerges, the church's eschatological hope culminates in unbroken fellowship with God in the age to come, setting the stage for exploring the nuptial imagery of the marriage supper.

### 5.5.3 Marriage Supper of the Lamb: Nuptial Imagery and Eternal Sabbath

Amillennialism frequently draws on nuptial imagery to describe the final consummation, wherein the church, as Christ's bride, celebrates the marriage supper of the Lamb (Revelation 19:7–9). The marriage metaphor permeates Scripture—from the prophetic language of Isaiah 61:10, where the Lord rejoices over His people like a bridegroom, to the New Testament assertion that Christ loves the church "as his own body" (Ephesians 5:29–30). Amillennialists interpret these images not merely as metaphors for future joy but as vital components of the eschatological reality where believers enjoy perpetual communion with God. At the marriage supper, the bride appears in fine linen, bright and pure, representing the righteous deeds of the saints (Revelation 19:8). This attire underscores that the church's readiness is constituted by sanctification, not self-earned merit—"without blemish" because of Christ's atoning work (Ephesians 5:25–27). The Lamb's wedding feast points to the ultimate Sabbath rest—entering into God's rest and ceasing from human labors (Hebrews 4:9–10)—where worship becomes an eternal, unbroken delight (Revelation 21:3–4). Amillennialists emphasize that this banquet transcends all earthly celebrations, for it initiates a timeless age of fellowship where "there will be no night there" (Revelation 22:5), meaning that believers encounter God's unmediated presence without interruption. This consummated fellowship contrasts with the present state of pilgrimage, where faith clings to promises rather than sight (Hebrews 11:1–2). The nuptial imagery also conveys relational themes: just as marriage on earth convenes two persons into one flesh (Genesis 2:24), so the marriage supper unites Christ and the church into a single, eternal community. This eschatological banquet fulfills prophetic allusions such as Isaiah 25:6–8's promise that "the Lord of hosts will prepare for all peoples a feast of rich food" and will swallow up death forever. Amillennialists assert that the consummation embodies humanity's restoration to God's presence—reaffirming creation's purpose as relational, not merely

192

functional. By focusing on the marriage supper and eternal Sabbath, amillennial theology centers its hope on unmediated communion with God, drawing all preceding eschatological events toward this singular, all-transforming banquet.

### 5.5.4 Beatific Vision and the Glory of the Triune God

Amillennialism culminates its anthropology and cosmology in the beatific vision, where believers see God face to face and share in His divine glory (1 Corinthians 13:12; 1 John 3:2–3). This final state, described by Paul in 1 Corinthians 13 as moving from "seeing in a mirror dimly" to seeing "face to face," indicates a shift from partial knowledge to full, immediate apprehension of divine reality. Amillennialists hold that this vision surpasses all earthly and sacramental experiences, revealing God's triune life—Father, Son, and Holy Spirit—in its ineffable majesty (Revelation 4:8–11). The eschaton thus transforms believers into the very image of God (2 Corinthians 3:18), enabling them to reflect divine attributes such as righteousness, holiness, and love. Scripture's language of "making us a kingdom, priests to serve his God and Father" (Revelation 1:6) conveys that this vision is simultaneously relational and functional: priests in the heavenly temple, mediating praise in perfect worship. The beatific vision also reorients human purpose: no longer subject to death, mourning, crying, or pain (Revelation 21:4), believers find their ultimate satisfaction in beholding God rather than in created gifts. This consummated fellowship aligns with Jesus' statement that the Father will give the Spirit of truth to believers, and "you will know him, for he dwells with you and will be in you" (John 14:17), taking that indwelling to its fullest extent. Amillennialists emphasize that this vision is not static. Revelation 21:23–25 describes the Lamb as its lamp, and the nations walk by its light, suggesting that the beatific vision will dynamically illuminate the redeemed community as they grow in knowledge and love. Overarchingly, amillennial theology celebrates that every aspect of salvation—justification, sanctification, glorification—culminates in uninterrupted fellowship with the triune God, fulfilling Jesus' prayer that believers would be "with [Him] where [He] is" (John 17:24). As we move from eschatological consummation to systemic implications, the church's life between Christ's already-won victory and the full outworking of the beatific vision will occupy our attention.

# 5.6 Systemic Implications

### 5.6.1 Ethics of Pilgrimage: Holiness, Humility, and Hope

Amillennialism shapes Christian ethics by emphasizing the church's status as pilgrims in a fallen world, called to holiness, humility, and hope. Seeing the present age as the "already/not-yet" realm means believers must pursue righteous living without assuming total victory over sin has yet arrived. Peter instructs believers to "be holy in all your conduct, since it is written, 'You shall be holy, for I am holy'" (1 Peter 1:15–16), an ethic rooted in ultimate accountability before God at the final judgment. Humility arises from recognizing that no cultural or moral achievement secures the kingdom—only Christ's merits do (Ephesians 2:8–9). Consequently, amillennial Christians avoid triumphalist postures and instead adopt a posture of servant-leadership (Mark 10:42–45), modeling Christ's humility in everyday interactions. Hope fuels perseverance: When Paul states that believers are "saved by hope" (Romans 8:24), amillennialists understand this to mean that present suffering does not extinguish future glory. This hope inculcates resilience: in contexts of political instability or social fragmentation, believers bear witness to God's faithfulness amid uncertainty (Hebrews 10:23). The pilgrimage ethic also includes solidarity with the marginalized: Jesus' beatitudes (Matthew 5:3–10) serve as ethical guideposts, mapping how the poor in spirit, the meek, and the merciful exemplify values reflective of the coming kingdom. Amillennial pastors encourage congregants to integrate these virtues in homes, workplaces, and communities, demonstrating that holiness is practical, affecting social justice initiatives, environmental stewardship (Genesis 2:15), and compassionate charity. By living as pilgrims—temporarily resident, eager for the city whose builder and maker is God (Hebrews 11:10)—Christians balance commitment to cultural engagement with detachment from idolatries of this world (1 John 2:15–17). This pilgrimage perspective shapes how believers approach economics, technology, and politics: each domain is valuable yet provisional, subordinate to the ultimate reality of God's redemptive plan. As amillennial ethics imbues daily life with purpose, it naturally leads to considerations of the church's prophetic witness in the political sphere.

**5.6.2 Politics in the "Time Between": Dual Citizenship and Prophetic Witness** Under amillennialism, Christians acknowledge dual citizenship—citizens of earthly nations and citizens of the heavenly kingdom (Philippians 3:20)—balancing political engagement with ultimate allegiance to Christ. This "time between" perspective means that while believers can participate in democratic processes for justice and mercy (Micah 6:8), they do so with the understanding that secular powers are not the ultimate arbiters of truth. Jesus' teaching in John 18:36—"My kingdom is not of this world"—grounds an approach to politics characterized by prophetic witness rather than domination. Amillennial believers testify to God's sovereignty over all nations, declaring that earthly governments must be judged by divine standards (Isaiah 10:1–3). As Paul instructs in Romans 13:1–7, Christians respect civil authority as God's servant for good, paying taxes and praying for rulers (1 Timothy 2:1–2), yet they resist when laws contravene God's moral imperatives (Acts 5:29). This tension calls for prophetic boldness: just as Jeremiah confronted kings for injustice (Jeremiah 22:13–17), Christians challenge contemporary policies that infringe on human dignity or religious freedom. Civic engagement occurs with humility: amillennialists eschew utopianism, recognizing that no political system can fully eradicate sin. They engage politics as a means to alleviate suffering and foster righteousness, supporting legislation that upholds the sanctity of life and protects the vulnerable. This prophetic stance extends to economics, where amillennial believers critique exploitative practices and advocate for structural reforms. By acknowledging that Christ will "bring to nothing all rule and all authority and power" (1 Corinthians 15:24), they remain critical of political power abused for selfish ends. Dual citizenship also informs prayer: like Daniel, who prayed for his homeland's restoration even as he remained in exile (Daniel 9:3–19), Christians intercede for nations to be "a kingdom of priests" (Exodus 19:6), modeling cross-cultural solidarity. This approach ensures that political involvement does not morph into allegiances that eclipse the lordship of Christ. These principles of dual citizenship and prophetic witness set the stage for addressing how creation care and cultural work fit into amillennial praxis.

**5.6.3 Creation Care and Cultural Work: Good but Not Ultimate**
Amillennialism teaches that creation is inherently good—"God saw everything that he had made, and behold, it was very good" (Genesis

1:31)—and thus calls believers to steward it responsibly, even though the present order remains marred by sin and awaits full redemption. The command in Genesis 2:15 to "till and keep the garden" signifies humanity's enduring vocation to care for the environment, reflecting God's creative purposes. Amillennialists assert that ecological stewardship emerges from love of neighbor (Matthew 22:39), since poorly managed resources disproportionately harm the poor and vulnerable. Practical initiatives—such as church-sponsored recycling programs, community gardens, and conservation education—illustrate how believers participate in creation care. By addressing issues like water scarcity and deforestation, they embody Micah 6:8's call to "do justice, love kindness, and walk humbly" with God's creation. Cultural work in arts, technology, and business aligns with imago Dei, for humans bear God's image in creativity and innovation (Genesis 1:27). Amillennial thinkers encourage Christians to produce art and media that communicate truth, beauty, and goodness, serving as cultural markers that point to the divine Maker. Entrepreneurs develop socially responsible businesses that balance profit with the common good, echoing Paul's instruction in Colossians 3:23 to do everything "as working for the Lord, not for men." Corporate social responsibility initiatives within Christian-run organizations demonstrate how economic activity can uplift communities, provide dignified employment, and diminish unethical labor practices. Yet amillennialists remain cautious not to equate cultural achievements with salvation or to view them as replacements for evangelism. Their perspective holds that while cultural work is commendable and essential, it cannot redemptively solve humanity's deepest problems—that requires the transformational power of the Gospel (Ephesians 2:4–5). This balanced vision counters secular narratives promising utopian futures and affirms cultural work's value within God's redemptive plan while maintaining its subordination to Christ's lordship. This theological stance on creation and culture naturally informs how the church structures its pastoral rhythms, which we turn to next.

### 5.6.4 Pastoral Rhythms: Lament, Longing, and Eucharistic Joy
Amillennial pastoral care weaves together lament over a broken world, longing for Christ's return, and Eucharistic joy in present communion with Him. Lament, rooted in Psalm 42:3's lamenting and Psalm 137:1–6's weeping by the rivers of Babylon, provides a

scriptural model for grieving over sin's consequences and the suffering of creation. Pastors lead congregations in corporate lament, creating liturgical spaces where people can voice their sorrow responsibly rather than default to false optimism. This practice cultivates authenticity and prevents despair by acknowledging God's attentiveness to suffering (Psalm 34:18). Longing follows lament: as believers express hope in Revelation 21:3–4's promise of a new heaven and new earth, they embrace the "maranatha" cry— "Come, Lord Jesus" (1 Corinthians 16:22). Pastoral preaching on Christ's imminent return (Titus 2:13) inspires anticipation that produces holy living (2 Peter 3:11–12) and ignites persistent evangelistic fervor. Eucharistic joy complements lament and longing: when congregations celebrate the Lord's Supper, they taste and see that the Lord is good (Psalm 34:8), proclaiming His death until He comes (1 Corinthians 11:26). This meal encapsulates redemptive history, reminding believers that they are united with Christ and with one another in the new covenant (Luke 22:20). Pastors emphasize the Eucharist as foretaste of the marriage supper of the Lamb (Revelation 19:9), instilling joy that transcends temporal trials. Such pastoral rhythms guard against cynicism and false optimism by balancing honest engagement with suffering, eager expectation of Christ's return, and celebratory proclamation of present redemption. Spiritual disciplines—regular confession (1 John 1:9), communal prayer, worship, and Scripture reading— reinforce these rhythms daily. By embedding lament, longing, and Eucharistic joy in pastoral life, amillennial pastors equip congregations to navigate a world marked by tension between the "already" of salvation and the "not-yet" of consummation. As believers internalize these rhythms, they are fortified to embody Christ faithfully until He finally ushers in the fullness of His kingdom.

## 5.7 Critiques, Challenges, and Dialogues

### 5.7.1 Replying to Premillennial Literalism
Amillennialists respond to premillennial literalism by reaffirming that biblical prophecy must be interpreted in its literary and theological context, rather than imposing a rigid chronological schema. Premillennialists often insist on a future, earthly one-thousand-year reign of Christ where He physically sits on David's throne in Jerusalem, citing

passages such as Revelation 20:4–6. Amillennial interpreters counter that the genre of apocalyptic literature—marked by vivid imagery, metaphoric numbers, and poetic structure—commends a symbolic reading. They point to Daniel's vision of the four kingdoms (Daniel 7:1–28), where beasts represent successive empires, not literal creatures, illustrating how apocalyptic employs symbolic representation. Similarly, Ezekiel's detailed dream of the temple (Ezekiel 40–48) functions typologically, pointing forward to Christ as the true temple (John 2:19–21). Amillennialists argue that insisting on literalism in Revelation 20 risks fragmenting Scripture, for Christ's reign is already inaugurated and presently manifest through the church's global mission (Matthew 16:18; Ephesians 1:22–23). They emphasize that Jesus' own statements—"My kingdom is not of this world" (John 18:36)—preclude a political reign divorced from the spiritual reality of the church age. Premillennialists might cite texts like Isaiah 2:2–4, which speak of nations streaming to Jerusalem, but amillennialists regard these as eschatological patterns fulfilled in Christ's universal priesthood (Hebrews 8:6–13), rather than predictions of a future geo-political center. When premillennial advocates point to prophecies about Israel's land, amillennialists respond by highlighting how New Testament writers reinterpret those promises in Christ (Galatians 6:16; Ephesians 2:14–18), transferring focus from nationalistic fulfillment to spiritual realities. They stress that Paul's olive-tree metaphor (Romans 11:16–27) indicates that Gentile inclusion neither erases nor nullifies Israel but introduces a mystery in which both Jew and Gentile share in Abraham's blessing through faith. Additionally, texts like Matthew 24:34—"this generation will not pass away until all these things take place"—suggest that some prophecies had immediate first-century fulfillments, contradicting a purely futurist timeline. Amillennialists also question the coherence of dividing Christ's return into multiple phases—secret rapture, millennial descent, and final advent—since passages such as 1 Thessalonians 4:16–17 describe one sounding of the trumpet and one return. By holding to a single advent that encompasses resurrection, judgment, and consummation (John 5:28–29; 2 Peter 3:10–13), amillennialists maintain theological and exegetical consistency. Premillennialists sometimes argue that Old Testament covenants guarantee a restored temple and Davidic throne; amillennialists respond that Christ fulfills those covenants in a deeper, spiritual sense, evidenced in passages like Jeremiah 31:31–

34 and Luke 22:20. This approach preserves the unity of redemptive history, showing that Christ inaugurates and embodies the covenantal promises. In sum, amillennial replies to premillennial literalism underscore that prophecy's symbolic language must be understood within the broader scope of biblical theology, avoiding literalism that fragments the text. With these clarifications laid out, amillennialists turn to engage postmillennial optimism in the next subsection.

**5.7.2 Engaging Postmillennial Optimism and Kingdom-Now Excesses** Amillennialism engages postmillennial optimism by acknowledging the kingdom's present advance while cautioning against excessive expectations that cultural transformation will culminate in a golden age before Christ returns. Postmillennialists envision a broad societal shift as the gospel saturates every sphere—political, educational, economic—culminating in a near-universal acceptance of Christian values. Amillennialists agree that the kingdom is already inaugurated and that God calls His people to pursue justice and mercy (Micah 6:8; Matthew 6:10), yet they maintain that Scripture nowhere guarantees a political utopia prior to Christ's return. Passages like 2 Corinthians 4:18, which contrasts the seen with the unseen, instruct that transient cultural gains remain provisional. Amillennial critics highlight Jesus' warning in John 16:2–3, that the world will hate His followers, confirming that opposition and suffering persist until the end. Paul's description of "terrible times" in 2 Timothy 3:1–5 underlines that moral decline frequently accompanies human history, challenging the notion that societal grace extends indefinitely. While postmillennialism points to historical revivals and social reforms—abolition of slavery, temperance movements, educational expansion—amillennialism underscores that every advance has been followed by periods of regression, indicating the enduring bondage of sin (Romans 3:10–18). This perspective encourages believers to promote cultural renewal without presuming that human effort can secure permanent righteousness. Amillennial commentators also note that Revelation's final chapters depict a brief resurgence of evil—Satan's release and Gog and Magog's rebellion—immediately before the final judgment (Revelation 20:7–9), underscoring that any period of relative peace remains provisional. Consequently, amillennialism fosters a balanced posture of hope and realism: rejoice in gospel fruit where it appears, but remain vigilant against pride and impatience that spurn divine timing. Ecclesiastes 3:1–8's reminder that "for everything there is a season" further tempers utopian hopes, reframing cultural efforts as participation in God's sovereign plan rather than engines of final triumph. By preserving both the "already" and "not-yet" dimensions, amillennialists guard against kingdom-now excesses that can lead to coercive politics or abandonment of mission when cultural change stalls. This engagement with postmillennialism paves the way for addressing criticisms that amillennial interpretation "spiritualizes" prophecy, discussed in the next subsection.

**5.7.3 Addressing "Spiritualizing" Accusations** Amillennial interpreters are often accused of "spiritualizing" biblical texts—reducing concrete promises to abstract principles—and thereby neglecting literal fulfillment. Critics cite passages like Isaiah 65:17–25, which depict literal peace and longevity, contending that amillennialism allegorizes these into vague postmortem realities. Amillennialists respond by explaining that biblical prophecy often operates multi-dimensionally: it can have immediate historical fulfillments, typological applications in Christ, and ultimate consummation in the new heavens and new earth. For instance, Isaiah 65's promise of a new creation finds partial fulfillment in Jeremiah's post-exilic temple restorations (Ezra 6:15) and in Christ's inaugurated kingdom, while its ultimate fulfillment awaits final re-creation (Revelation 21:1–4). This threefold movement—historical, typological, and consummative—ensures that prophetic language retains its literal significance while transcending a single earthly horizon. When critics object that Ezekiel's temple vision (Ezekiel 40–48) must signify a future physical temple, amillennialists highlight how Jesus declared Himself the new temple (John 2:19–21), indicating that Ezekiel's language points beyond stones to the living Messiah. Similarly, the Davidic throne promise (2 Samuel 7:12–16) finds messianic fulfillment in Christ's heavenly session (Hebrews 1:3), not in a future earthly monarch. Amillennialists contend that symbolic reading does not negate literal meaning; rather, it discerns the deeper substance of prophecy. The parable of the wheat and tares (Matthew 13:24–30) illustrates how two realities—wheat and tares—coexist until the harvest; likewise, the physical blessings promised to Israel serve as types pointing to greater blessings in Christ's kingdom. Accusations of "spiritualizing" often stem from a limited view of how biblical genres communicate truth; recognizing multifaceted fulfillment prevents reductionism. Furthermore, amillennialists emphasize that apostles like Paul and John frequently applied Old Testament promises to the church (Romans 8:18–23; 1 Peter 2:9–10), showing that early Christians understood these texts in Christocentric and ecclesiological dimensions. This hermeneutical approach upholds the integrity of Scripture while acknowledging the continuity and progression of redemptive history. By clarifying that symbolic interpretation respects literal intent within theological grammar, amillennialists counter "spiritualizing" critiques and maintain fidelity to the whole biblical witness. With these defenses articulated, the discussion naturally leads into martyrs' theology and the church's experience of suffering under amillennial conviction.

**5.7.4 Martyr Theology, Suffering Church, and Global Persecution** Amillennialism's recognition of the church's normative tribulation extends into a robust martyr theology, affirming that suffering and even martyrdom serve God's purposes in redemptive history. When John writes of the souls under the altar in Revelation 6:9–11 calling out for justice, amillennialists interpret these voices as emblematic of persecuted believers throughout the church age, not solely as literal first-century martyrs. The witness of martyrs—both ancient and modern—emphasizes that the kingdom often advances through bloodshed rather than through human power (Revelation 12:11). This perspective aligns with Jesus' promise that "whoever loses his life for my sake will find it" (Matthew 10:39), indicating that suffering can yield eternal gain. Amillennial believers draw courage from Hebrews 11's "hall of faith," which celebrates faithful perseverance under trial—Abel, Enoch, Noah, Abraham, Moses—many of whom endured hardship as they anticipated the city with lasting foundations (Hebrews 11:10). Early church martyrs like Polycarp and Ignatius modeled unwavering trust in Christ's ultimate victory, reinforcing that the church does not look for a future empire to protect it but relies on Christ's sovereign rule even amid adversity. Contemporary persecuted Christians—such as those in North Korea, Iraq, and parts of Africa—embody the same spirit, enduring ostracism, imprisonment, and violence while proclaiming the gospel. Amillennial pastors connect these global stories to Revelation's broader narrative, showing that martyrdom testifies against the world's allegiances, undermining Satan's accusations and revealing Christ's worthiness (Revelation 12:10–11). This theology of suffering also informs pastoral care: counseling ministries assist those traumatized by persecution, reminding them of Romans 8:18's promise that present sufferings are not worth comparing with future glory. Congregations often observe days of remembrance for martyrs, linking contemporary testimonies with historical accounts to foster solidarity and perseverance. Amillennial advocacy groups mobilize prayer chains and relief efforts, recognizing that practical care for persecuted believers aligns with James 1:27's mandate to visit orphans and widows in their affliction. At the same time, amillennial teaching guards against viewing persecution as proof of imminent eschatological collapse, insisting instead that such trials are part of the church's normal experience until Christ returns (John 15:20). By integrating martyr theology with a balanced eschatology—one that foresees persecution alongside present kingdom realities—amillennialism equips believers to stand firm, knowing that suffering often precipitates deeper fellowship with Christ and more compelling witness to the world. This completes the chapter's exploration of critiques and challenges, paving the way for examining contemporary expressions in the following section.

## Conclusion

Amillennialism models an eschatological posture grounded in Christ's present reign and future consummation, guiding believers to live faithfully amid cultural flux and persecution. By interpreting prophetic texts through typology and redemptive history, it upholds the unity of God's promises without fragmenting Scripture into competing earthly scenarios. This approach equips Christians to engage worship and sacrament as genuine encounters with the kingdom "now," while embracing suffering as the church's normative experience (1 Peter 4:12–13). At the same time, it affirms a hope that transcends temporary setbacks, looking forward to the one decisive resurrection and the arrival of new heavens and a new earth (1 Corinthians 15:22; 2 Peter 3:13). In clarifying misconceptions—whether regarding a supposed "no millennium," the nature of Christ's heavenly kingship, or supposed "spiritualizing" of prophecy—amillennialism invites the church to maintain both humility and confidence: humility before mysteries that resist human timelines, and confidence in Christ's sure triumph. As readers move toward a comparative synthesis with premillennial and postmillennial perspectives, this chapter aims to ensure that amillennial convictions remain faithful to Scripture, compassionate toward suffering, and steadfast in hope.

# Chapter 6 - Israel and the Nations

God's purposes for ethnic Israel and the wider world run like a golden thread through both Testaments, calling every generation of believers to wrestle with how divine promises to one people relate to the church's mission among all nations. When Abraham received the covenantal pledge that his offspring would become a blessing to "all the families of the earth" (Genesis 12:3), it launched a redemptive trajectory that intersects with Israel's unique calling and the ultimate inclusion of Gentiles in Messiah. Yet as Scripture unfolds, this convergence of Jew and Gentile becomes a point of vigorous debate: Must Israel's tribal identity continue in every eschatological blueprint, or do her promises find their fullest expression in the church as a multiethnic people? The biblical narrative often shifts seamlessly between prophecies addressed to Jerusalem's temple courts (Isaiah 2:2–3; Zechariah 14:16–17) and horizons extending to "the ends of the earth" (Psalm 2:8; Acts 1:8), demanding a theological framework that honors both dimensions. Questions about land, temple worship, David's throne, and national restoration reappear from Moses through the prophets, and then again in apostolic letters that reinterpret those archetypes in light of Christ (Romans 11; Galatians 3). As modern readers confront geopolitics—Israeli statehood, Palestinian displacement, Messianic

Jewish movements—these ancient texts carry urgent weight. Each eschatological school presses its hermeneutics: one foregrounds a future earthly reign centered on restored Israel, another sees Israel's destiny realized through gospel success among Gentiles, and still others locate Christ's triumph in a heavenly Zion that transcends geography. By jettisoning simplistic caricatures, we can engage these viewpoints beneath the surface, examining how promises to Israel ripple outward to shape the church's call to be "a chosen people, a royal priesthood" (1 Peter 2:9) in a fractured world. In doing so, we remain faithful to Scripture's insistence that "salvation is from the Jews" (John 4:22) even as we embrace the global scope of God's redemptive plan.

# 6.1 Premillennial Perspectives on National Israel

### 6.1.1 Restoration Promises and Land Inheritance
Premillennialists emphasize that God's covenant with Abraham regarding land remains in force until Christ's return. When God told Abraham that his offspring would possess the land from the river of Egypt to the Euphrates (Genesis 15:18), premillennial interpreters understand that promise as perpetual and unconditional, grounded in divine oath rather than human performance. They point out that after the Exodus, the Torah reaffirmed land inheritance as a perpetual statute, instructing Israel to drive out the Canaanite nations and allot territories to each tribe (Numbers 33:50–56; Joshua 21:43–45). Even when Israel fell into exile, prophets like Jeremiah assured the people that the land promise would endure—"this whole land shall be a desolation and a curse, but Judah shall abide forever and Jerusalem shall be inhabited in its place, from generation to generation" (Jeremiah 17:5, 25:11). Premillennialists argue that these promises cannot be nullified by Israel's unfaithfulness (Romans 11:29), for God's gifts and callings are irrevocable. They hold that the modern state of Israel, established in 1948, constitutes a foreshadowing of the greater restoration still to come. During the tribulation, national Israel will suffer and be purified, but at the end of that period, Christ will return to Zion, gathering surviving Jews to the land (Zechariah 12:10–14). At that moment, premillennialists teach, a renewed "covenant of peace" will be established, and Israel will receive full possession of the territorial boundaries described in Ezekiel 47:13–21—restored beyond even the Davidic kingdom's extent. This land

inheritance will not only satisfy physical needs but will also become the center for world redemption, as Gentile nations stream to Jerusalem to worship the Messiah (Isaiah 2:2–3). Thus, the physical geography of Israel retains perpetual significance in God's plan, and premillennialists guard against any reading that spiritualizes away the land promise. They stress that biblical authors consistently distinguish between Israel's inheritance and spiritual blessings given to the church (Romans 11:16–17), maintaining that God's plan includes a future time when national Israel's land inheritance is realized fully. This emphasis on Israel's land leads naturally to questions about Israel's identity during tribulation, which is addressed in section 6.1.2.

**6.1.2 The Tribulation Remnant and the 144,000** Within premillennial schemes, a defining feature is the survival of a believing remnant of Israel during the seven-year tribulation period. Based on Revelation 7:1–8, where 144,000 are sealed—12,000 from each of the twelve tribes—premillennialists see a literal, ethnic Jewish group protected by God from the coming wrath. While some interpreters see the 144,000 as symbolic of totality, classic premillennial thought tends to interpret this number literally, suggesting that during the intense persecution under the Antichrist, many Jews will come to faith under the ministry of two witnesses and the 144,000 themselves (Revelation 11; 12). This remnant confesses Jesus as Messiah, leading to large-scale conversions within Israel (Romans 11:25–26), and their witnessing serves as a catalyst for the wider ingrafting of Jewish believers into the eschatological harvest (Matthew 24:14). Premillennialists argue that God's protective seal (Greek: sphragizo) indicates judicial protection rather than exemption from all suffering—those sealed may still endure hardship, but they will be preserved from the Second Coming's wrath "like a hen gathers her chicks" (Matthew 23:37). They point out that Old Testament figures such as David experienced God's preserving protection despite national calamity (Psalm 23), illustrating that a remnant always remains faithful. This remnant then organizes under Christ's return, serving as priestly mediators for Israel and Gentile survivors in the millennium (Ezekiel 44:11–14). Progressive premillennialists, while affirming a Jewish remnant, sometimes emphasize that the 144,000 symbolize a core group rather than a precise census, focusing on the qualitative nature of their witness rather than numerical literalism. In either case, the notion of a tribulation remnant underscores God's faithfulness to preserve a believing Jewish presence, fulfilling prophetic texts like Zechariah 13:8–9, which speak of two-thirds in the land being cut off and the remaining third refined. This refined remnant then participates in the millennial kingdom as co-regents under Christ (Revelation 20:6), fulfilling Ezekiel's vision of the restored tribes worshiping at a millennial temple (Ezekiel 44:15–31). The remnant's identity and function lead observers to inquire about the reestablishment of temple worship under the Davidic throne, which we explore in section 6.1.3.

**6.1.3 Millennial Temple, Sacrifices, and Davidic Kingship** In premillennial thought, the millennial kingdom includes a restored temple in Jerusalem, complete with sacrificial worship and Davidic kingship. Prophecies in Ezekiel 40–48 provide detailed architectural and liturgical blueprints, which dispensational premillennialists, in particular, interpret literally. They anticipate that after Christ returns, a physical temple will be constructed on the temple mount, featuring courts, chambers, and offerings that adhere to Ezekiel's specifications (Ezekiel 41:1–26; 43:1–12). In this view, animal sacrifices become memorial offerings that point back to Christ's once-for-all atonement (Hebrews 10:10–14), teaching future generations about sin's seriousness. Priests and Levites, descended from surviving lines of Aaron and Levi, will resume their cultic duties, managing daily offerings, grain offerings, and festival celebrations—Passover, Weeks, and Tabernacles—yearly drawing nations to worship (Zechariah 14:16–19). The restored temple reflects the Davidic throne's relocation to the heart of millennial worship, for Christ, as Son of David, will rule from Jerusalem (Luke 1:32–33; Revelation 19:16), enforcing divine justice and righteousness (Isaiah 32:1–2). Under classic premillennialism, David himself is resurrected to serve as prince of Israel alongside Christ (Ezekiel 37:24), demonstrating the continuity of covenantal monarchy. Progressive premillennialists sometimes allow for symbolic elements, seeing the temple as representing Christ's corporate body, yet even they anticipate literal temple worship in the millennium, emphasizing that liturgy shapes societal ethics. The sacrificial system will no longer serve atonement—Christ's death has achieved that—but will function pedagogically, illustrating how God forgives through shedding of blood (Leviticus 17:11; 1 John 1:7). By reinstating Davidic kingship, premillennialists underscore

207

that Christ's rule encompasses civil, religious, and environmental restoration, fulfilling promises such as Psalm 72's vision of all nations serving Him. This return to mosaic and Davidic structures contrasts starkly with the present church age, raising questions about how Israel and the church relate, a topic examined in 6.1.4.

**6.1.4 Israel-Church Distinction in Classic vs. Progressive Premillennialism** A central debate within premillennialism concerns the nature of Israel's distinction from the church. Classic (historic) premillennialism generally views the church age as a temporary parenthesis between Israel's program and its ultimate fulfillment. In this view, God paused the land and kingdom promises to Israel during a "mystery" period (Ephesians 3:5–6), focusing on building the church until the fullness of Gentiles is reached (Romans 11:25). After that, God resumes His program with ethnic Israel. Progressive premillennialists reject the strict parenthesis, instead advocating for an overlapping model in which Israel and the church operate concurrently. They point to Paul's argument in Romans 11 that Gentiles are "grafted in" (Romans 11:17) without permanently severing natural branches (Romans 11:18), implying that God works with both communities simultaneously. This overlap view holds that Jewish believers have always been part of the church—but national promises to ethnic Israel still await future fulfillment. Classic premillennialists maintain a clear temporal and programmatic distinction, taught as a "mystery" not revealed until Christ's first coming (Colossians 1:26), whereas progressive premillennialists see a more fluid relationship, where the church is a multiethnic body that includes believing Israelites currently, but national Israel's status remains unique. The debate has practical repercussions: classic premillennialists often adopt a dispensational hermeneutic with detailed distinctions between Israel and the church—calling Gentile Christians to support a Jewish national future—while progressive premillennialists encourage simultaneous evangelistic efforts among Jews and Gentiles, emphasizing unity in worship (Revelation 5:9–10) even amid distinct future destinies. This ongoing discussion sets the stage for exploring how Israel's hope is reinterpreted in postmillennial contexts, which we address in section 6.2.1.

**6.1.5 Contemporary Zionism and Prophetic Expectations** Modern political Zionism and the reestablishment of the State of Israel in 1948 have become integral elements in many premillennial frameworks. Premillennialists see these events as initial fulfillments of prophetic scriptures like Ezekiel 36:24–28, promising a "regathering" of Israel to its land and divine renewal of heart. They interpret the United Nations' partition plan (1947) and subsequent Jewish immigration as the fulfillment of Isaiah 49:22, where broken nations's strength brings sons and daughters to Zion. While acknowledging secular motivations behind Zionism, premillennial believers regard these geopolitical shifts as God providentially preparing the stage for end-time events. The Six-Day War (1967) and Israel's recapture of the temple mount region further bolster their conviction that the pieces are aligning for future prophetic fulfillments, such as the rebuilding of the third temple (Daniel 9:27; Zechariah 14:4). Some dispensational schools produce detailed timetables correlating modern events with Daniel's seventy weeks, arguing that the "prince who is to come" (Daniel 9:26–27) will imminently arise from a revived Roman Empire or a comparable coalition. Progressive premillennialists emphasize caution, recognizing that political developments often deviate from simplistic prophetic charts, but they still see national restoration as a vital sign of God's faithfulness. This intertwining of modern Zionism with eschatological expectation raises ethical and political questions about Christian support for Israeli government policies, the treatment of Palestinians, and the broader Middle Eastern context. Premillennial writers often engage in conferences and publications analyzing how current events resonate with biblical prophecy, providing local churches with frameworks for prayer and advocacy. While some promote unconditional support for Israel as a non-negotiable prophetic alliance, others temper this view by reminding believers of the broader biblical mandate to seek justice and peace for all peoples (Jeremiah 29:7; Isaiah 61:1–3). The complexity of contemporary Zionism thus both energizes premillennial conviction and necessitates careful theological reflection, bridging into postmillennial evaluations of Israel's hope.

## 6.2 Postmillennial Readings of Israel's Hope

### 6.2.1 Conversion and the "Fullness of the Gentiles" (Romans 11:12–27) Postmillennialists commonly interpret Romans 11:12–27 as a roadmap for Israel's future, emphasizing that the "fullness of the Gentiles" precedes a national conversion of the Jewish people.

They understand Paul's olive-tree metaphor to mean that Gentile believers have been grafted in among natural branches, while some natural branches—ethnic Israel—were broken off due to unbelief. However, Paul assures the Romans that if the Gentiles do not continue in unbelief, God will graft back the natural branches (Romans 11:23), implying a future restoration for Israel alongside continued Gentile faithfulness. Postmillennial thinkers point to global church growth statistics as evidence that Gentile churches are reaching levels Paul would call "fullness," fostering optimism that a tipping point is near (Matthew 24:14). At that tipping point, they believe, large-scale Jewish conversions will take place, fulfilling passages like Isaiah 49:6—"I will make you as a light for the nations, that my salvation may reach to the end of the earth"—but now with Israel as a progressive witness among Gentiles rather than a separate program. In this reading, the church does not simply replace Israel; rather, the church's global advance prepares the way for Israel's collective turning to Messiah (Romans 11:26). Postmillennialists thus see Israel's national restoration not as a precondition for global gospel success, but as an outcome of that success. This optimistic reading connects with historical revival precedents: when the church reached critical influence in nineteenth-century Europe and America, mission societies prioritized Jewish evangelism, sending missionaries and setting up Hebrew-language ministries, hoping to fulfill Paul's promise. Postmillennial advocates argue that as modern methods—digital outreach, Messianic music, and cross-cultural partnerships—allow the gospel to saturate Jewish communities worldwide, an increase in Jewish faith is a foreseeable development. They note that passages like Zechariah 12:10 and 13:1–2, predicting a national weeping that leads to turning, will find application when Jewish individuals and communities see evidence of the Messiah's work among Gentiles. Yet they caution that any Jewish conversion sequence emerges from Spirit-empowered preaching and contextualized ministry—aligning with Acts 2:21—rather than geopolitical pressures or artificially created theocratic structures. This dynamic interplay between Gentile fullness and Jewish restoration then naturally transitions into a more extensive look at postmillennial views of covenant continuity.

### 6.2.2 Covenant Continuity: Abrahamic Blessing to the Nations
In postmillennial theology, God's covenant with Abraham (Genesis 12:1–3) forms the bedrock for understanding Israel's destiny. When

God promised Abraham that "in you all the families of the earth shall be blessed," postmillennialists see this as a twofold guarantee: first, that ethnic Israel would be the channel through which the Messiah would come, and second, that the Messiah's reign—extended through the church—would bless all nations. Consequently, postmillennialists argue that attempts to extract Israel out of the church age distort the unity of covenant promises. They maintain that Jesus' affirmation that He came to fulfill the Law and the Prophets (Matthew 5:17) includes bringing Old Testament hope to its appointed climax in the church's global mission. When Jeremiah announced a "new covenant" (Jeremiah 31:31–34), postmillennial interpreters see this as extending the Abrahamic blessing, transforming individual hearts but also empowering the church as the new "Israel of God" (Galatians 6:16). They contend that the promises regarding land remain typological, pointing to the church's worldwide mandate rather than a future geographical inheritance for ethnic Israel alone. For instance, Psalm 2's declaration that "you shall break them with a rod of iron" (Psalm 2:9) finds ultimate fulfillment in the church's spiritual authority over evil powers, not necessarily in a physical kingdom. This covenantal continuity undergirds postmillennial social ethics: just as Old Testament laws promoted justice and care for the orphan and widow (Deuteronomy 10:18), so Christians working to reform legal and economic structures participate in fulfilling Abraham's promise to bless all families. In this light, the birth of the United Nations or the enactment of global human rights declarations can be seen as echoes of covenantal progress. Postmillennialists affirm that while ethnic Israel remains significant as the root from which the church has been grafted (Romans 11:17), the church's global expansion represents the outworking of Abrahamic blessing in real time. When the nations receive the gospel en masse, they participate in the blessings originally promised to Abraham, reflecting Deuteronomy 4:6–8's vision that God's statutes confer distinctive wisdom upon those who obey them. This understanding moves smoothly into an exploration of how postmillennialism envisions Israel's role in a Christianized world, which we address in the next subsection.

### 6.2.3 Great-Commission Mechanisms: Gospel to the Jew First

Postmillennial strategy for engaging Israel's hope hinges on prioritizing Jewish evangelism "to the Jew first" (Romans 1:16; Matthew 10:5–6). Postmillennialists argue that because Israel was the initial covenant community and original recipient of divine revelation, the gospel's global advance must never neglect Jewish outreach. This conviction drives mission boards to invest in Hebrew-language resources, train Messianic Jewish pastors, and support local fellowships that cultivate Jewish believers as ambassadors to their own communities. They often point to Paul's example—he consistently traveled to synagogues first (Acts 17:1–3; Romans 2:17)—as the apostolic model for reaching Israel. Postmillennial churches host "Feasts of Weeks" celebrations in line with the Jewish festival of Shavuot (Acts 2:1–4), integrating traditions such as reading Joel's prophecy alongside explaining its New Testament fulfillment in the Spirit's outpouring. Through these practices, they seek to honor Israel's heritage while proclaiming Christ as the ultimate antitype of Old Testament promises. When prominent figures like Andrew Brunson returned from persecution in Turkey, postmillennial leaders highlight his testimony to encourage Jewish evangelism even in hostile climates. They maintain that as the church grows in influence among Gentiles, reaching the 20–30 percent mark of a region's population—a threshold some sociologists identify as tipping points—Jewish communities become more receptive to the gospel (Acts 6:7; 11:21). Campaigns focus on establishing congregations in cities with significant Jewish populations—Jerusalem, Tel Aviv, New York—intending to cultivate networks that can replicate globally as diaspora contexts shift. This strategy aligns with Revelation 7:9–10's vision of a "great multitude from every nation, from all tribes and peoples and languages," suggesting that Jewish believers will stand alongside Gentiles in final worship. By emphasizing "gospel to the Jew first," postmillennialists see how Israel's national turning complements the fullness of Gentiles described in Romans 11:25–26. This gospel thrust naturally transitions to a vision of Israel's integrated role in a millennial-like golden age, discussed in 6.2.4.

**6.2.4 Golden-Age Integration: Israel's Role in a Christianized World** Postmillennialism envisions a golden age in which global society increasingly reflects Christian values, with Israel assuming a distinctive yet integrated role. In this perspective, as nations embrace Christ's lordship, Jewish believers re-emerge not as a separate political entity but as vibrant participants in a transformed global culture. Prophecies such as Isaiah 2:2–4—where many nations "shall go and say, 'Come, let us go up to the mountain of the

LORD'"—are understood as depicting a world that, through the church's missional efforts, hears and heeds God's instruction. In that era, postmillennialists anticipate Jewish cultural contributions—literature, music, scholarship—reinforcing Christian worldview initiative within a renewed society. Educational institutions founded by Jewish believers and other renewed communities collaboratively shape curricula that integrate biblical wisdom with scientific knowledge, fulfilling Isaiah 60:3's promise that Gentiles will come to Israel's light. Israel's diaspora communities, while geographically scattered, function as hubs of prophetic insight, helping to interpret and apply ancient scriptural wisdom within modern contexts (Romans 11:4–6). The festival calendar—Passover, Weeks, Tabernacles—takes on renewed significance as cultural celebrations that unite Jewish and Gentile believers in year-long cycles of worship, reflecting Zechariah 14:16–19's expectation that all who survive will annually worship the King. Economic alliances among postmillennial Christian and Messianic Jewish entrepreneurs foster marketplaces that model generosity, ethical labor, and compassion for the poor, echoing Deuteronomy 14:28–29's sabbatical provisions. In these ways, Israel contributes to the golden age without reverting to exclusive nationalism, demonstrating that covenantal identity can find harmonious integration with global culture under Christ's sovereignty. Contemporary media networks, streaming Jewish-Christian educational content worldwide, exemplify how Israel's story informs a culture oriented toward the kingdom (Acts 26:22–23). As this integrated vision matures, society experiences unprecedented declines in violence, poverty, and moral decay, surpassing earlier revivals. Yet postmillennialists remain aware that human responsibility must accompany divine sovereignty, ensuring that cultural success does not breed complacency or neglect the urgency of ongoing mission. This optimistic integration of Israel into a Christianized world shifts attention to how Israel's modern political movements fit into postmillennial hopes, which is explored in section 6.2.5.

**6.2.5 Evaluating Modern Aliyah Movements through an Optimistic Lens** Postmillennialists approach contemporary Jewish aliyah—immigration to Israel—from both a theological and missional perspective, seeing such movements as opportunities rather than mere political developments. They note that the biblical pattern of return (Ezekiel 36:24) often unfolds in unexpected ways, and modern aliyah aligns with prophetic motifs without necessitating a dispensational reading. When Jews in North Africa, the former Soviet Union, and elsewhere move to the land, postmillennial churches view this as a call to accompany them with the gospel, offering Hebrew-language New Testaments, Messianic worship gatherings, and social services that demonstrate Christ's love. They believe that God can use aliyah to concentrate Jewish populations in a center where targeted evangelism can bear fruit, fulfilling Zechariah 8:23's vision that "many peoples and strong nations shall come to seek the LORD of hosts in Jerusalem." While recognizing complex geopolitical realities, postmillennial advocates seek alliances with Messianic Jewish organizations to facilitate humanitarian aid for new immigrants—shelter, language training, job assistance—reflecting James 2:15–16's call to address physical needs alongside spiritual outreach. They regard aliyah as a time-sensitive window for sharing Christ's love and doctrinal truth, believing that God's purposes for Israel's restoration include the offer of Messiah. As aliyah accelerates, postmillennialists leverage digital platforms—social media, webinars, Hebrew-language podcasts—to share personal testimonies of Jewish believers, demonstrating that Jewish identity and Christian faith coexist. These narratives cultivate cultural credibility and open doors for deeper conversation about Messiah in communities that might otherwise remain closed. Postmillennial thinkers caution against conflating political support for the State of Israel with endorsement of every policy; rather, they advocate advocacy for peace and justice grounded in Scripture's standards (Micah 6:8). By weaving aliyah into a broader missional tapestry, postmillennialists see it as part of the church's unfolding vocation—serving as Abraham's seed to bless the nations—while preserving balanced critique and compassionate engagement. This nuanced perspective on aliyah leads directly into amillennial interpretations of "All Israel" in Romans 11, which we explore in section 6.3.1.

# 6.3 Amillennial Interpretation of "All Israel"

### 6.3.1 Corporate Election vs. Ethnic Fulfillment in Romans 9–11
Amillennialists approach Romans 9–11 by emphasizing corporate election and typological continuity rather than a strict future ethnic fulfillment of every covenant promise to Israel. When Paul laments

that "Israel has failed to obtain what it seeks" (Romans 9:6), amillennial interpreters explain that Paul is not denying God's faithfulness to Israel's covenant but rather reiterating that elect Israel is defined by covenant faithfulness, not mere ethnic descent (Galatians 3:7). They interpret Paul's statement that "not all who are descended from Israel belong to Israel" (Romans 9:6) as distinguishing between physical lineage and spiritual lineage—those who trust in Messiah. In this light, "all Israel" in Romans 11:26 does not necessitate every ethnic Jew's conversion; rather, it points to the corporate unity of God's people culminating in a final, eschatological ingathering. This view aligns with Old Testament prophecies like Isaiah 49:6, anticipating that "kings shall shut their mouths because of Him" as the faithful remnant fulfills its role in the nations' salvation. Amillennialists observe that Paul's vine-and-branches analogy (Romans 11:17–24) emphasizes that Gentile inclusion does not nullify God's covenant with true Israel—whosoever is "in" Christ is heir to the promises. When Paul writes that "all Israel will be saved" (Romans 11:26), amillennial interpreters view this as a corporate, representative reference to the elect community—a "remnant chosen by grace" (Romans 11:5), rather than a promise of every single Jewish individual's faith. They draw parallels with Old Testament usage, such as in Daniel 9:24, where seventy weeks conclude with "the end of sins" yet only need a faithful remnant to fulfill God's purposes. This corporate reading maintains Paul's continuity with promises given to Abraham's seed (Galatians 3:29), seeing the church as the new Israel—"the Israel of God" (Galatians 6:16). Yet amillennialists also acknowledge the ongoing significance of ethnic Israel in God's redemptive heritage, affirming that Jewish believers share equally in Messiah's blessings (Romans 11:11–12). This tension between corporate election and ethnic particularity underpins amillennial exegesis, preparing the way for explaining the olive-tree metaphor in 6.3.2.

**6.3.2 One Olive Tree: Grafting, Pruning, and Eschatological Mercy** The olive-tree metaphor in Romans 11:16–24 serves as a central image for amillennialists understanding Israel and the church. Paul describes Israel as a cultivated olive tree that had natural branches broken off because of unbelief, allowing wild olive shoots—Gentile believers—to be grafted in. Amillennialists interpret this as demonstrating God's mercy and sovereignty: He can prune unfruitful branches and graft in others to produce spiritual abundance. The metaphor underscores that the root—God's covenant promises—remains the same, sustaining both believing Jews and Gentile believers alike. Amillennial theology asserts that grafting signifies incorporation into the covenant community of promise, where faith in Messiah is the criterion rather than ethnicity (Galatians 3:7–9). When some Gentile branches begin to flourish in godliness, they serve as catalysts for the natural branches' jealousy, prompting God's mercy toward Israel (Romans 11:11–12). This reading affirms the present reality of the church as a multiethnic body of believers, unified under one root and nourished by the same divine sap. It also explains why amillennialists envision God preserving a believing Jewish remnant within the church rather than segregating them for a future program. The metaphor's warning—"if you do not continue in his kindness, you too will be cut off" (Romans 11:22)—applies to all branches, emphasizing the universal call to faithfulness. In this framework, election remains conditional upon faith in Christ, ensuring that ethnic Israel's promises can be fulfilled in the collective experience of believers, Jew and Gentile alike. By viewing Israel and the church as one olive tree, amillennialists bridge both Testaments—seeing the church as the climax of prophetic expectation rather than a replacement or a temporary parenthesis. This unified tree eventually produces "life from the dead" (Romans 11:15), signifying that God's long-term purpose culminates in the restoration of all things under Messiah's headship. With this metaphor in view, attention turns to how amillennialists treat Israel's typological land and temple promises in 6.3.3.

### 6.3.3 Typological Land and Temple: Christ as the New Zion

Amillennial interpreters understand Old Testament promises of land and temple as typological anticipations fulfilled in Christ rather than as literal future events to be realized by ethnic Israel. When Moses instructed the Israelites to enter Canaan, he spoke of "a land flowing with milk and honey" (Exodus 3:8), signaling a fulfilled principle in the abundant spiritual life offered through Jesus (John 10:10). Similarly, Davidic promises such as "I will set up your seed after you" (2 Samuel 7:12) point to Jesus as the ultimate Son of David reigning from heaven, rather than a future earthly descendant reigning over a physical kingdom. Amillennialists see the temple's destruction (Matthew 24:2) and Jesus' claim that He is the living temple (John 2:19–21) as key indicators that God intended believers to look forward to a spiritual realization of Israel's worship. The church is thus viewed as the true house of God, "built on the foundation of the apostles and prophets, Christ Jesus himself being the cornerstone" (Ephesians 2:19–22). Passages like Hebrews 8:1–6 reframe the old covenant temple as a "copy and shadow" of heavenly realities, situating the church as the locus of divine presence. Amillennialists argue that Revelation's new Jerusalem (Revelation 21:2–3) signifies the eschatological city where God dwells with humanity, not a rebuilt earthly city, reinforcing that typology culminates in Christ's person. This perspective retains respect for Israel's sacred history while relocating its ultimate expression in the church's identity. It also clarifies why amillennialism resists constructing a future temple: doing so would undermine the sufficiency of Christ's priestly work, which the writer to Hebrews affirms as "once for all" (Hebrews 10:10). By seeing Christ as the apex of Israel's land and temple promises, amillennial theology maintains covenant continuity while avoiding the pitfalls of literalist frameworks. As this typological vision completes the transition from Israel's physical program to Christ's spiritual reality, it leads into a broader consideration of the "two-age" structure of realized eschatology in section 6.3.4.

**6.3.4 Israel within the Two-Age Schema: Now, Not-Yet, and Consummation** Amillennial theology situates Israel's promises within a "two-age" framework, distinguishing between the present age—where Christ's kingdom is active but incomplete—and the age to come, when all things are perfected. In this schema, ethnic Israel's historical role played out in Old Testament redemptive history, setting the stage for Jesus' incarnation, death, and resurrection. Amos 9:11–12's promise to restore the "booth of David" finds its initial fulfillment in Christ's establishing of the church, echoing Acts 15:16–17. Yet Amos's broader vision still awaits full realization in the age to come, where all nations "call upon the name of the LORD," demonstrating that Israel's future hope lies beyond earthly borders. Prophecies about land and temple function in the present as signs pointing to the heavenly reality—Hebrews 12:22–24 describes Mt. Zion as the assembly of the firstborn and the mediator of a new covenant. Amillennialists teach that believers now dwell in the "new creation" dimension spiritually (2 Corinthians 5:17), experiencing early fruit of Israel's promises, while awaiting the final consummation when there will be "new heavens and a new earth"

(Isaiah 65:17; Revelation 21:1). This cumulative tension prevents amillennial theology from minimizing Israel's past significance or coupling it exclusively with geography, while also warning against imagining a separate future program in which promises to Israel are fulfilled apart from Christ and His bride. Instead, the two-age schema emphasizes that Israel's historical narrative continues in the church's life until the consummation, ensuring covenants progress organically. The present age provides time for the nations to be discipled (Matthew 28:19–20), whereas the consummation age rewards faithful endurance (Matthew 25:23). By situating Israel within these two ages, amillennialism fosters a balanced eschatology that neither nullifies Israel's unique role nor isolates it from the universal purposes of God. This framework paves the way for exploring pastoral sensitivities when teaching about Israel in section 6.3.5.

**6.3.5 Pastoral Sensitivities When Teaching Difficult Texts** When amillennial pastors and teachers address Israel-related texts, sensitivity is crucial to avoid alienating Jewish believers and to prevent anti-Semitic misapplications. For instance, Romans 11's language about broken-off branches can be misunderstood as God's rejection of all Jewish people, leading to theological anti-Semitism. Amillennialists stress that Paul's argument centers on a faithful remnant and reciprocal grafting rather than unconditional tribal condemnation. Pastors must clarify that Judaism as a religious system does not inherit covenant promises apart from faith in Messiah (John 1:12–13), but that individual Jewish persons who trust in Jesus apply to Paul's gracious olive-tree paradigm (Romans 11:23). Discussions of "partial hardening" (Romans 11:25) require explaining that God's patience with Israel's unbelief is not final, and His mercy extends to Jewish communities in the present age. When preaching prophetic imagery—such as Ezekiel's vision of the dry bones (Ezekiel 37:1–14)—pastoral teachers need to balance encouragement for Jewish restoration with caution against presenting secular Jewish nationalism as guarantee of divine favor. Emphasizing that true "Israel" in the New Testament sense comprises those in Christ (Galatians 3:29) helps congregations avoid conflating Jewish ethnicity with automatic covenantal standing. Similarly, amillennial pastors must handle texts on eschatological violence—such as Isaiah 63:1–4—with care to prevent endorsing modern militancy. Instead, they teach that ultimate judgment belongs to God alone (2 Corinthians 5:10), calling believers to pray for peace in Jerusalem (Psalm 122:6–7) while maintaining prophetic critique of injustice. These pastoral sensitivities ensure that teaching on Israel in amillennial contexts fosters hope for genuine spiritual renewal among Jewish people without veering into political partisanship or theological indifference. By modeling humility and empathy, pastors can facilitate constructive conversations on Israel, preparing the church to engage both Jewish and Gentile neighbors in ways that reflect the unity and diversity of God's people.

## 6.4 Unity and Diversity in the People of God

**6.4.1 Olive-Tree Metaphor and Ecclesiology** The olive-tree metaphor in Romans 11 provides a vivid image of how Jewish and Gentile believers coexist within one covenantal community, undergirding a robust ecclesiology that transcends ethnic divisions. Paul's illustration of natural branches being broken off and wild branches grafted in underscores that both groups share the same root, representing God's irrevocable promises to Abraham (Romans 11:16–18). This root supplies spiritual nourishment equally to those of Jewish descent who embrace Messiah and to Gentile believers, indicating that covenant membership depends on faith rather than genealogy (Galatians 3:7–9). The metaphor's warning—that grafted branches can be pruned if they do not persevere in faith (Romans 11:22)—applies to the entire church, reminding all believers that spiritual privileges carry the responsibility of holiness (1 Peter 1:16). By depicting the olive tree as one living organism, Paul dissolves any notion of a future dual-covenant economy where Israel and the church pursue separate destinies. Instead, he envisions a single, multiethnic community that will ultimately experience the fullness of God's mercy when Messiah returns (Romans 11:25–26). This unity carries practical ecclesiological implications: congregations must welcome Jewish believers not as outsiders but as integral branches, affirming their unique heritage while fostering shared identity in Christ (Ephesians 2:19–22). Pastors and church planters consequently design liturgies that incorporate Jewish feasts— Passover reflections or Sukkot symbols—to honor the olive tree's heritage without segregating practices. When Orthodox Jewish believers join a predominantly Gentile congregation, the community serves as a microcosm of the olive tree, where differing cultural

219

traditions converge under the same vine (John 15:5). This unity also demands sensitivity to particular struggles Jewish believers may face—such as anti-Semitic persecution or family estrangement—requiring pastoral care that upholds their dignity while nurturing mutual understanding (Romans 12:15). Ultimately, the olive tree's ecclesiological vision paves the way for Ephesians 2's portrayal of one new humanity, which we examine next.

**6.4.2 Ephesians 2 and the One New Humanity** Ephesians 2:11–22 highlights the revolutionary nature of the church as a reconciled community whose membership transcends ethnic, cultural, and religious barriers. Paul describes Gentile believers as once "alienated from the commonwealth of Israel and strangers to the covenants of promise" (Ephesians 2:12), yet he rejoices that Christ has broken down the dividing wall of hostility, creating in Himself one new man from the two (Ephesians 2:14–15). This "new humanity" implies that distinctions between Jew and Gentile, once sharpened by law and tradition, no longer determine divine favor or communal standing. Instead, both groups are "members of the household of God" (Ephesians 2:19), built upon the apostles and prophets, with Christ Jesus serving as the cornerstone. The implication is that the church embodies a foretaste of eschatological unity envisioned in prophetic passages such as Isaiah 56:6–7, where foreigners who join themselves to the Lord are accepted. In practical terms, congregations reflecting this unity structure their leadership teams to include both Jewish and Gentile voices, ensuring that decision-making honors the diverse heritage of the olive tree. Worship settings often integrate Hebrew and Greek liturgical elements—Scripture readings in both languages, use of Jewish melodies alongside Gentile hymnody—to manifest Ephesians 2's vision. This one new humanity also transforms how churches approach social outreach: feeding programs and community development initiatives deliberately enlist teams of Jewish and Gentile volunteers, signaling to the world that the church's heart beats with a reconciled rhythm (2 Corinthians 5:18–19). Additionally, theological education programs incorporate courses on Jewish history, Rabbinic hermeneutics, and New Testament apologia, teaching future pastors that ministry effectiveness requires understanding the roots of Ephesians 2's reconciliation. This reconciled community transcends political alliances; even when nations clash, local churches remain steadfast in their unity under

Christ. By actualizing Ephesians 2's vision, the church anticipates a future where the olive tree's groaning finds perfect peace (Romans 8:22–23). As this one new humanity gathers, Messianic Judaism emerges as a tangible expression of united identity, which we explore in the next subsection.

### 6.4.3 Messianic Judaism: Bridge Community or Parallel Track?

Messianic Judaism occupies a unique position as both a bridge between Jewish and Christian traditions and, at times, a perceived parallel track that challenges ecclesiastical boundaries. Messianic congregations affirm Jewish identity—observing festivals such as Sukkot and Shavuot—while proclaiming Yeshua (Jesus) as the Messiah, thus embodying Ephesians 2's new humanity (Romans 11:26). This dual allegiance often raises questions: Are Messianic Jews simply a subculture within the church, or do they represent a distinct movement with its own theological emphases? Many Messianic Jewish leaders view themselves as fulfilling Isaiah 42:6's calling to be "a light for the nations," reaching Jewish communities with contextualized worship and teachings that resonate with Hebrew scriptures. As a bridge community, they facilitate dialogue between synagogue and church, creating opportunities for Jewish families to encounter the gospel without initially abandoning cultural norms. For example, Messianic Bible studies in Israel or the diaspora often use Hebrew Scriptures (Tanakh) alongside the Apostolic Writings (B'rit Chadasha), allowing participants to trace threads of Messianic expectation from Genesis to Revelation. Yet some of their practices—such as calling themselves "Jewish Christians" and maintaining separate ecclesiastical structures—lead to perceptions of parallelism, prompting debate within broader church circles about ecclesial unity. Critics argue that separate structures risk reinforcing divisions rather than dissolving them, while proponents contend that Messianic communities provide essential cultural safety for Jewish believers navigating faith in predominantly Gentile church settings. This tension mirrors the olive-tree metaphor: while valuing Jewish distinctiveness, Messianic Jews must remain grafted into the larger olive tree of the church (Romans 11:17–18). Theologically, Messianic Judaism challenges both Jewish leaders—who may view it as a departure from covenant faith—and Gentile congregations—who may see it as an unnecessary ethnic particularism. Successfully navigating this requires embracing Philippians 2:4's call to consider the interests of others above one's own, fostering mutual learning rather than suspicion. As Messianic congregations grow, they contribute to the olive tree's fruitfulness by producing worship resources—Hebrew-language Messianic songs, theological commentaries bridging Talmudic insights with biblical revelation—that enrich the global church. Their apologia ministries, engaging Jewish skepticism with historical and scriptural evidence, serve as exemplars of 1 Peter 3:15's call to give a defense for one's hope with gentleness and respect. In light of these dynamics, attention turns to how Messianic identity interacts with the modern state of Israel and the Palestinian situation, which we consider in the following subsection.

### 6.4.4 Implications for the Modern State of Israel and the Palestinians

The establishment of the modern State of Israel presents both opportunities and challenges for the unified people of God, as envisioned in chapters such as Ephesians 2 and the olive-tree metaphor. For Messianic Jews and their Gentile partners, Israeli statehood offers a tangible homeland that aligns with Old Testament covenants (Isaiah 11:11–12), yet the political realities often complicate the church's calling to be a reconciler among nations (Matthew 5:9). Churches must balance support for Israel's security and right to exist with compassion for Palestinian neighbors, who often face displacement and humanitarian crises. Scripture's witness—"let justice roll down like waters, and righteousness like an ever-flowing stream" (Amos 5:24)—challenges believers to advocate for the dignity and well-being of all peoples under God's image (Genesis 1:27). Practically, this means Chrstian organizations partner with Israeli NGOs providing medical care to both Jews and Palestinians, demonstrating Micah 6:8's ethic of justice and mercy. Interfaith reconciliation initiatives—like shared Hebrew-Arabic worship gatherings—exemplify the Ephesians 2 vision by creating spaces where Jewish, Palestinian Christian, and Muslim neighbors jointly pray for peace in Jerusalem, reflecting Psalm 122:6's exhortation to "pray for the peace of Jerusalem." Additionally, theological reflection on passages like Galatians 3:28—"There is neither Jew nor Greek"—urges church leaders to reject any ethnocentric nationalism that elevates one group over another in God's covenant people. Messianic congregations in Israel often run outreach programs bridging Jewish and Palestinian communities: vocational training for disadvantaged youth, interethnic summer camps, and micro-loan initiatives supporting Arab and Jewish entrepreneurs working side by side. These grassroots efforts resonate with Jesus' teaching that the greatest commandment is to love God and neighbor (Mark 12:29–31), transcending political fault lines. Pastors addressing the Israeli-Palestinian conflict in sermons must navigate biblical narratives of conquest (cf. Joshua 1:1–9) while firmly grounding contemporaneous ethics in New Testament commands to peace and reconciliation (2 Corinthians 5:18–19). This balanced approach prioritizes human dignity over geopolitical allegiances, embodying Jeremiah 29:7's call to seek the welfare of the city for all its citizens. Through prayer movements—such as the International Day of Prayer for the Peace of Jerusalem—churches globally highlight Ephesians 2's reconciled community, demonstrating solidarity with both Jews and Palestinians in Christ. These complex dynamics of modern politics and ethnicity flow into discussions about interfaith dialogue, evangelism, and how to avoid supersessionist pitfalls, which is the subject of section 6.4.5.

### 6.4.5 Interfaith Dialogue, Evangelism, and the Charge of Supersessionism

Engagement with Jewish communities inevitably raises questions about how evangelism coexists with interfaith respect, particularly given accusations of supersessionism—the idea that the church has entirely replaced Israel in God's plan. Amillennialists insist that supersessionism misrepresents biblical teaching, because God's covenant with Israel remains genuine, albeit fulfilled in Christ (Romans 11:29). Accordingly, Christians engaging in interfaith dialogue with Jews must clarify that evangelism is not about cultural eradication but about offering the Messiah as the fulfillment of Jewish hope (John 4:22; Romans 1:16). This requires deep humility, recognizing that Jewish believers maintain a unique scriptural heritage and that the Old Testament Scriptures belong to both communities (Luke 24:44). Evangelistic methods normally include building genuine relationships—sharing meals during Passover Seders to highlight how Jesus instituted the Lord's Supper in continuity with Jewish tradition (Luke 22:15–20). When discussing key texts such as Isaiah 53, evangelists interpret the Suffering Servant's language as pointing to Jesus' atoning work, while acknowledging that Jewish rabbinic interpretations differ, thus fostering respectful conversation rather than dogmatik proselytism. Interfaith dialogue forums—joint Torah study groups, scholarly conferences—create settings in which theological differences can be examined in academic depth, preventing simplistic conflations that fuel supersessionist attitudes. Pastors and evangelists often use John 17:21—the prayer for unity among believers—as a guiding principle, aiming for mutual enrichment rather than mere numerical growth. They emphasize that God's gifts to ethnic Israel include a seasoned understanding of Scripture's narrative arc, which can inform the church's own proclamation and practice. By actively listening to Jewish critiques—such as the argument that Christian readings of Isaiah 53 misappropriate Jewish suffering—believers demonstrate James 1:19's call to be quick to hear and slow to speak. This posture not only wards off supersessionism but also secures a more credible witness, for Jesus taught that love would be the distinguishing mark of His followers (John 13:35). When engaging in online dialogues—webinars, social media discussions—Christian participants commit to using respectful language, avoiding hyperbolic claims that dismiss Jewish interpretations wholesale. Historical awareness about Christian antisemitism further tempers evangelistic zeal, ensuring that approaches remain sensitive to Jewish collective memory of persecution (Matthew 23:29–36). As the church refines its evangelistic and dialogical methods, it can better embody Ephesians 2's vision of one new humanity while preparing hearts for the diverse people of God to worship together in fullness at the consummation (Revelation 7:9–10). Transitioning from unity and diversity to a side-by-side comparison with other frameworks, the chapter now turns to examine comparative theological dialogues in section 6.5.

# 6.5 Comparative Theological Dialogues

### 6.5.1 Literal vs. Typological Approaches to Land Promises
Comparative dialogue begins by contrasting literal and typological interpretations of Old Testament land promises. Premillennialists maintain that texts like Genesis 15:18–21—where God delineates specific geographical boundaries for Israel—are binding covenants that require fulfillment in a literal, historical sense. They argue that numbers in these passages correspond to real territories, as demonstrated by Joshua's conquest narrative (Joshua 1:3; 13:1–7). In contrast, postmillennial and amillennial approaches view these promises as typological: physical land boundaries prefigure a spiritual inheritance in Christ (Romans 4:13). Postmillennialists argue that the Abrahamic land promise, "to your offspring I will give

this land," finds full expression in Christ's worldwide kingdom rather than in specific real estate (Galatians 3:16, 29). Amillennialists similarly assert that the vineyard imagery—Israel as God's vine (Psalm 80:8–16)—points to Christ as the true vine (John 15:1–5), and the land metaphor extends to the new heavens and new earth (Isaiah 65:17; Revelation 21:1). While premillennialists counter that typology can obscure clear covenantal commitments (Isaiah 49:8–9), typologists respond that New Testament authors themselves applied these promises spiritually—Acts 7:5 emphasizes that Abraham was "a stranger in the land," indicating temporary use until a heavenly city is realized (Hebrews 11:10–16). This dialogue raises questions about hermeneutical categories: when does allegory enhance understanding, and when does it undermine textual fidelity? A balanced mediating view might suggest that certain promises have both historical and theological dimensions, yet defining that boundary remains a point of contention. Understanding these differing approaches helps believers appreciate underlying assumptions about how God's covenants unfold, setting the stage for examining "kingdom geography" in the next subsection.

**6.5.2 Kingdom Geography: Earthly Jerusalem, Heavenly Zion, or Both?** The question of kingdom geography hinges on whether New Testament passages refer to a renewed literal Jerusalem, an entirely heavenly city, or some combination of both. Premillennialists affirm that Revelation 21–22's new Jerusalem descends from heaven to earth, thus restoring earthly geography in a perfected state, fulfilling Ezekiel 48:35's prophecy that Jerusalem's name will be "from generation to generation." They view the consummated Zion as a physical metropolis where Christ's saints dwell with bodies of flesh and bone (Revelation 21:3–4), aligning with Luke 24:39's account of the risen Lord's physical body. In contrast, amillennialists interpret the new Jerusalem typologically, seeing it as representing the perfected church—the Eschatological Zion—rather than a tangible city. Hebrews 12:22 locates believers in "Mount Zion and the city of the living God" in a present spiritual sense, suggesting that heavenly Zion is already accessible to the church. Postmillennialists often affirm both aspects: earthly Jerusalem functions as a symbolic locus for Jewish evangelism, but ultimate fulfillment lies in the spread of kingdom ethics globally, producing a cultural landscape that anticipates Zion's peace (Isaiah 2:2–4). They point to Matthew 5:3–10, the Beatitudes, as invitations to participate in Zion's blessings now through ethical transformation rather than geographic change. Amillennialists further note that Jesus stated in John 4:21–24 that true worshipers will worship "in spirit and truth," loosening the tie between Jerusalem's temple and access to God. Yet they do not entirely dismiss the hope of a renewed earth with Jerusalem as a focal image, recognizing Revelation 21's city as a powerful eschatological archetype. This diversity of kingdom geography reflections illustrates how each framework balances literal, symbolic, and present-tense dimensions, leading into debates over sacrifice and temple in section 6.5.3.

### 6.5.3 Sacrifice and Temple: Memorial, Symbolic, or Obsolete?

Differing views on sacrifice and temple worship reveal deeper theological commitments about continuity and discontinuity between covenants. Premillennialists assert that Ezekiel's temple (Ezekiel 40–48) provides a blueprint for literal millennial worship, including daily burnt offerings, sacrifices for atonement, and Levitical priesthood (Ezekiel 44:1–16). They argue that Hebrews 8:7–13 only replaces the sacrificial system's efficacy—pointing to Christ's once-for-all atonement—while not nullifying the statutory aspects intended for Jewish ethnic practice under God's specific timetable (Hebrews 10:1–2). Sacrifices in the millennium, in this view, function pedagogically, reminding Israel of Christ's redemptive work. Postmillennialists, however, see sacrificial language as primarily symbolic, fulfilled in the Eucharist, which they interpret as a continuity of temple worship (Luke 22:19–20). They maintain that Christ's body and blood offered on the cross inaugurate a new temple reality (John 2:21), and every Eucharistic celebration reenacts the ultimate sacrificial once-for-all (1 Corinthians 11:26). Amillennialists similarly emphasize Hebrews 10's theme that Christ's sacrifice rendered temple offerings obsolete; they view the church as the new temple (1 Corinthians 3:16–17) where living stones—believers—represent perpetual spiritual worship (Romans 12:1). This suggests that Old Testament temple structures become typological foreshadows rather than future literal blueprints. In their view, references to temple in Revelation—such as "there will be no more sea" (Revelation 21:1, 21)—signal the dissolution of temple imagery and ceremony, replaced by direct access to God (Revelation 21:22). Yet amillennialists also honor Old Testament sacrifices as pointing to Christ's work and include occasional liturgical elements—like Passover Seders—to acknowledge their theological significance. This variety in understanding sacrifice and temple prompts deeper reflection on when and how Israel's promises reach their eschatological peak, leading into the next subsection on eschatological sequences.

**6.5.4 Eschatological Sequences: When Do Israel's Promises Peak?** Comparing premillennial, postmillennial, and amillennial eschatological sequences raises questions about the chronology of Israel's promises—whether they culminate before, during, or after a collective turning of the nations. Premillennialists depict a clear sequence: first, a literal Jewish tribulation and restoration; next, Christ's millennial reign over ethnic Israel; finally, the new heavens and new earth (Revelation 20:4–6, 21:1–4). In this model, Israel's promises reach their peak during the millennium with temple worship and Davidic rule, restoring covenant fidelity in an earthly kingdom (Jeremiah 33:14–26). Postmillennialists rearrange the sequence: widespread Gentile conversion heralds a golden age in which Israel's fulfillment emerges through a corporate turning in response to global Christian influence (Romans 11:25–26). Israel's peak thus coincides with the church's cultural transformation of society rather than a distinct centuries-long reign in the land. Amillennialists contend that Israel's promises find their climax in Christ's first coming—His resurrection inaugurates the new covenant—and ultimately in the new creation when all believers, Jew and Gentile, worship together forever (Revelation 21:2–4). They argue that passages like Psalm 110:1–2, which speak of the Messiah's ascension and reign, apply to Christ's present heavenly session, illustrating that Israel's covenants reach their apex in spiritual reality rather than a future physical kingdom. These divergent sequences reflect differing hermeneutical priorities: literalist chronology for premillennialists, covenant continuity for postmillennialists, and typological fulfillment for amillennialists. Engaging these sequences together fosters humility and mutual learning, encouraging believers to discern how chronological reading influences theological expectations and practical engagement. This discussion naturally transitions into considering whether any convergence or mediating views are possible, addressed in section 6.5.5.

**6.5.5 Can the Frameworks Converge? Prospects for a Modified "Mediating View"** Given the diversity of interpretations, some theologians propose a "mediating view" aiming to integrate strengths from premillennial, postmillennial, and amillennial perspectives. Such a view might affirm the ongoing sequence of covenants—acknowledging Israel's unique role—while also embracing the church's participation in God's purposes (Romans 11:17–24). For example, it could hold that God's land promises have historical literal fulfillment in ancient Israel, partial spiritual fulfillment in the church, and future consummation in the new heavens and new earth—synthesizing literal and typological approaches. This model allows for a future messianic banquet symbolized liturgically now while avoiding rigid calendars that predict specific dates. Similarly, a mediating view could maintain that Christ's present reign from heaven reflects His Davidic kingship and that Revelation 20's thousand years describes both present spiritual reality and anticipatory fulfillment preceding consummation. Postmillennial optimism concerning gospel advance becomes a present imperative, motivating the church while still remaining open to divine surprises and geopolitical developments. Amillennial caution about over-literalizing prophetic texts ensures that mediating interpretations resist reductionist tendencies. Such a framework encourages mission strategies that prioritize Jewish evangelism "to the Jew first" (Romans 1:16) without assuming that every Jewish individual must convert before Christ returns. Additionally, it fosters ecumenical respect, permitting Messianic Jewish congregations to flourish alongside Gentile churches as branches of the one olive tree (Romans 11:17). Critics argue that a mediating view risks compromising doctrinal clarity by avoiding definitive stances on key passages, but proponents counter that nuanced theology mirrors the complexity of God's redemptive plan as revealed progressively across Scripture (2 Peter 1:20–21). Churches adopting a moderating approach emphasize unity amid diversity, embodying Psalm 133:1's vision of brothers dwelling together in harmony, while awaiting the day when God will gather all tribes and tongues in unbroken fellowship (Revelation 7:9–10). This optimism regarding convergence sets the stage for exploring practical implications and missional strategies in the next chapter.

**Conclusion** Our exploration of Israel and the nations has revealed that no single eschatological model exhausts the depth of God's covenantal design. Whether one anticipates a literal fulfillment of land and temple promises under a messianic Davidic king, sees

Israel's hope flowering through the church's worldwide influence, or discerns those promises fulfilled spiritually in Christ's present reign and final consummation, all approaches wrestle with the same Scriptures speaking of Zion's blessing and Abraham's seed. At stake is not only our interpretation of prophetic texts but also our posture toward Jewish neighbors, the ethics of political advocacy in the Middle East, and the manner in which liturgy and evangelism engage shared heritage without coercion. As we have seen, the olive-tree image (Romans 11) calls us to recognize a single community rooted in Abraham, where believing Jews and Gentile believers grow together under the same divine care. Ephesians' vision of "one new humanity" (Ephesians 2:15) reminds us that God's end goal is not ethnic triumphalism but the reconciliation of "both ... in one body" so that "the world might know" His wisdom (Ephesians 2:16–17). While each millennial framework carries strengths—premillennialism's attentiveness to literal covenant continuity, postmillennialism's confidence in gospel progress, amillennialism's focus on present spiritual realities—none can fully claim to erase the tension of texts that speak simultaneously to Israel's land and the nations' spiritual destiny. By holding these tensions faithfully, the church can embody Jesus' prayer "that they may all be one" (John 17:21), serving as a sign of what Zion will one day become: a people composed "from every tribe, language, people, and nation" (Revelation 7:9). As we press forward into integrative reflections and pastoral applications, may our shared conviction—that Jesus is Israel's long-awaited Messiah and the world's true Redeemer—shape a posture of humility, love, and hopeful anticipation for what God will yet accomplish among both Jew and Gentile.

# Chapter 7 - Temple, Sacrifice, and Sacred Space

Throughout Scripture, images of sacred architecture and sacrificial systems convey profound truths about God's presence among His people. From the early tabernacle repairs in the wilderness to the opulent stones of Solomon's temple, these structures served as earthly meeting places where heaven intersected earth. As the prophets peered forward, they envisioned a renewed sanctuary whose waters would flow to heal nations, symbolizing the rippling impact of divine blessing. In the New Testament, Jesus both claimed to fulfill and transcend these physical edifices, asserting that His very body served as the ultimate temple in which the fullness of deity dwells. Over centuries, Christian communities have debated whether future millennial realms will witness rebuilt altars and revived animal offerings, or whether all such practices pointed to a once-for-all sacrifice that renders cultic rites obsolete for eternity. Alongside these theological discussions, human creativity in worship spaces—cathedrals soaring toward heaven, simple meeting halls stripped to their bare essentials, and even digital interfaces—reveals how believers adapt temple concepts to changing contexts. This chapter explores how each millennial framework understands temple and sacrifice: one anticipates a tangible rebuilding under a Davidic prince, another senses a spiritualized global "temple" in advancing gospel influence, and a third identifies Christ as the definitive sanctuary, rendering future cultic structures unnecessary. By tracing these divergent visions, we gain insight into how concepts of holiness, ritual, and sacred geography shape worship, ethics, and mission across ages.

# 7.1 Ezekiel's Vision and Premillennial Rebuilding

**7.1.1 Architectural Details and Levitical Order** Ezekiel's vision of the future temple is described with meticulous precision, underscoring the importance of divine patterns rather than purely human design (Ezekiel 40:2–4). Walls, doorways, and inner chambers are measured with a reed in hand (Ezekiel 40:5), indicating that God alone supplies the exact dimensions, reminding readers that any millennial structure must conform to divine specification rather than human preference. The outer court spans 500 cubits by 500 cubits (Ezekiel 42:20), roughly equivalent to 750 feet square, emphasizing not mere grandeur but precise symbolism—each measurement correlates to completeness or holiness. Within these courts are chambers for priests, located on the north, south, and west sides (Ezekiel 40:46; 44:19), illustrating how ministry zones surround the central sanctuary. The inner courts ascend in elevation, with steps leading to the inner sanctuary (Ezekiel 41:11–12), conveying theological layers: as one moves deeper into the temple, one draws nearer to God's presence. Levitical chambers line the courts, their doors opening eastward (Ezekiel 40:41–44), symbolizing readiness to receive God's glory coming from the east (Ezekiel 43:1–5). The gates—east, north, and south—each feature guardrooms to secure sacred precincts (Ezekiel 40:6–18), demonstrating that holiness requires both invitation and protection. Inside, the inner sanctuary (holy of holies) measures 20 cubits square (Ezekiel 41:4), matching Solomon's temple (1 Kings 6:20) yet differing in that no mercy seat or cherubim are specified; God's glory enters directly (Ezekiel 43:4–7). The threshold of the vestibule is one cubit high (Ezekiel 41:6), suggesting that stepping into God's presence requires humility. Measurements extend to the altar, which stands fifteen cubits square with a height of six cubits—taller than Solomon's (Ezekiel 43:13–17)—signifying intensified sacrificial symbolism during the millennium. The priests' chambers (thirty on each side) accommodate Zadokite priests and their families (Ezekiel 44:10–14), teaching that worship requires continuity and community. Each chamber is equipped with a window facing the sanctuary (Ezekiel 41:8–9), conveying that all ministry tasks—sacrifice preparation, Torah instruction, musical training—remain oriented toward divine worship. Levitical chambers also include storerooms for grain, oil, and wine (Ezekiel 45:11), ensuring that sacrificial and celebratory meals are sustained without interruption. The temple precinct includes a separate annex for the Levites (Ezekiel 45:1–8) to maintain purity in gatekeeping, teaching, and sanitation duties, underscoring how the millennium's worship is communal yet distinct. By situating these chambers around the sanctuary, Ezekiel's design integrates practical ministry with theological purpose: the temple exists not as a static monument but as a living institution where God's holiness shapes every aspect of life. Understanding these architectural and Levitical details equips believers to anticipate how divine order will manifest in the future kingdom, leading into how tribal allocations and geographical boundaries intersect with these sacred spaces.

**7.1.2 Geographical Boundaries and Tribal Allotments** Ezekiel's millennial temple vision extends beyond architecture into a reimagined land distribution, affirming God's redemptive restoration for Israel's tribes (Ezekiel 48:1–29). Beginning in the north and proceeding clockwise—east, south, west—Ezekiel delineates each tribal territory, with Judah in the south and Benjamin in the east (Ezekiel 48:1–7). The central portion stretching from Dan in the north to Reuben and Gad in the south (Ezekiel 48:8–15) includes a sacred district measuring five hundred by five hundred rods, reserved for the sanctuary and Levites (Ezekiel 48:8–14). This sacred district separates different tribal holdings, ensuring that worship remains at the heart of communal life, physically and spiritually. The territory of Joseph is divided into two: Ephraim in the west and Manasseh in the east, each adjoining the sacred district (Ezekiel 48:16–22). This dual allotment honors Joseph's preeminence while distributing land equitably, fulfilling blessings pronounced in Genesis 48:14–20. Through these boundaries, Ezekiel teaches that covenantal promises to Abraham's seed regarding land endure; despite exile and dispersion, the divine plan culminates in reestablishment. The precise measurements—

described in rods rather than cubits—serve as both technical details and symbols of divine provision: one rod equals six cubits, so readers understand that sacred spaces remain proportionate to human scale yet defined by divine precision (Ezekiel 40:3). The entire land is enveloped by the tribe of Dan, offering a northern border (Ezekiel 48:1), emphasizing that territorial integrity will be restored from Dan to Beersheba—echoing Abraham's original promise (Genesis 17:8). Borders meet the sea on the west and the Jordan River on the east (Ezekiel 47:18–20), signifying that the nation's geography embraces both agricultural fertility and potential trade routes. Notably, the city of the LORD, perhaps the future Jerusalem, occupies a distinct position within these tribal allotments (Ezekiel 48:35), teaching that city and temple remain focal despite wider land distribution. As water flows from the temple's threshold (Ezekiel 47:1–12), it irrigates the borderlands, reminding readers that the temple's blessings extend into every tribal territory, unifying them under God's life-giving presence. These geographical reorganizations underscore that tribal distinctives persist in the millennium, countering views that all distinctions vanish; yet unity prevails through shared worship. The vision encourages believers to anticipate how God reunites scattered tribes in a renewed land, carrying communal memories into a future era of holiness, which sets the stage for exploring how sacrificial rites function pedagogically in the restored temple.

**7.1.3 Memorial Sacrifices: Pedagogy or Propitiation?** In Ezekiel's millennial schema, sacrifices continue but function differently from pre-exilic rites, focusing more on memorial pedagogy than propitiatory atonement (Ezekiel 43:18–27). Daily offerings—two lambs each morning and evening—demonstrate consistent devotion rather than expiatory necessity, as Christ's once-for-all atonement will have already secured forgiveness (Hebrews 10:10–14). These sacrifices serve as continual reminders of God's presence and holiness, teaching future generations humility before divine majesty. Sabbath festivals include six lambs without blemish, translating Leviticus 23:3's pattern into an ongoing millennial rhythm where rest and worship remain inseparable (Ezekiel 45:21–22). Passover is observed "as a feast to the LORD" (Ezekiel 45:21), signaling that the church's celebration of the Lord's Supper will echo these early feasts but find deeper meaning in Christ's redemptive work. The Day of Atonement in Ezekiel's vision involves a sin offering of bulls for the leaders and people, indicating that the millennium acknowledges human imperfection even as sin's penalty has been paid; these offerings reinforce confession and communal restoration (Ezekiel 45:23–25). Unlike earlier sacrifices that covered sin temporarily (Leviticus 17:11), millennial sacrifices highlight Israel's covenant relationship with YHWH and train hearts toward grateful living rather than fear of condemnation. The grain offerings, oil, and drink offerings accompanying animal sacrifices (Ezekiel 45:24) teach that worship transcends mere bloodshed: all aspects of life—work, produce, fellowship—receive consecration. Periodic offerings during new moons and feast days (Ezekiel 45:17) ensure that temporal markers remain tied to sacred rhythms, countering secular calendrical drift. These sacrifices are also intergenerational teaching tools: infants conceived under millennial norms will grow learning about covenant faithfulness through ritual repetition (Deuteronomy 11:19). The priestly functions—selecting spotless animals, preparing altars, and ensuring ritual purity—demonstrate that divine standards extend into the millennium, maintaining continuity with Mosaic norms while pointing to ultimate fulfillment in Christ. Since Christ's sacrifice is central (Hebrews 9:12–14), these memorial offerings do not re-establish covenant on their own; rather, they keep memory alive, imprinting hearts with sacred history. This pedagogical emphasis highlights that even in a restored temple, worship remains formative: God shapes character through repeated gestures of gratitude and devotion. As this millennial pedagogy unfolds, attention turns to leadership structures, beginning with the Davidic prince and Zadokite priesthood, explored in the next section.

**7.1.4 Davidic Prince, Zadokite Priesthood, and Civil Governance** Ezekiel's description of the millennial leadership portrays a Davidic prince governing alongside the Zadokite priesthood, blending civil authority with liturgical stewardship (Ezekiel 45:22–25; 46:16–18). The prince, often understood as the Messiah or a type thereof, receives a portion of the land adjacent to the holy district for personal residence and maintenance, signifying that his civil duties are subordinate to the temple's spiritual functions. He provides the appointed offerings for burnt offerings, grain offerings, and drink offerings (Ezekiel 45:22–25), illustrating that political leadership remains intimately linked with worship. The prince's inheritance is not purely private: portions of his land help sustain the priests and Levites (Ezekiel 45:7–8), indicating that wealth circulates to support collective religious life. Under his governance, legal cases are judged "at the entrance of the gate of the house of the LORD" (Ezekiel 46:19), symbolizing that divine justice governs civil affairs. This model contrasts with secular governance, where royal authority often stands apart from cultic functions; in the millennium, Christ's rule merges judicial and liturgical responsibilities, reflecting Psalm 2:6–9's portrait of Messiah reigning from Zion with a rod of iron. The Zadokite priesthood, descended from Zadok who remained loyal to David (1 Kings 1:32–40), performs specialized liturgical roles, distinguishing them from Levites who guard and serve the temple (Ezekiel 44:15–16). Zadokites offer burnt offerings to atone for the people, teaching that priestly intercession remains necessary even when sin has been decisively defeated, emphasizing ongoing holiness (Ezekiel 44:15). Their role guards against unauthorized worship: congregants must pass through Levites to reach the priests, ensuring that purity and orthodoxy remain central (Ezekiel 44:10–13). Civil governance under the prince enforces holiness codes—proscriptions against idolatry, rules on impurity—parallel to Levitical law but enforced with messianic authority (Ezekiel 44:23–24). The prince's leadership embodies God's covenantal promise that a descendant of David will shepherd His people and govern with justice (Ezekiel 34:23–24). This union of political and religious responsibilities displaces any King-Priest dualism: in the millennium, the Prince functions as both ruler and liturgist, foreshadowing Christ's ultimate priesthood and kingship (Hebrews 7:1–3). As the city and temple function within a coherent governmental system, environmental renewal follows suit—all under Messianic oversight, preparing readers to examine how the temple's water flows nourish the land in the next subsection.

### 7.1.5 Environmental Renewal: River from the Threshold and Land Fertility

One of the most striking features of Ezekiel's vision is the river flowing from beneath the temple threshold, symbolizing divine life penetrating the land (Ezekiel 47:1–12). As the water reaches ankle depth, it begins to swell to knee depth, waist depth, and ultimately becomes a river too deep to cross (Ezekiel 47:3–5), signifying progressive overflow of God's blessings. This river serves as a life source: along its banks grow trees bearing fruit every month, their leaves offering healing (Ezekiel 47:12). This healing motif echoes Isaiah 35:6–7, where God's desert becomes a fertile field, indicating that millennial restoration encompasses physical and spiritual rejuvenation. Fish of various kinds teem in the river, assuring food supply and economic stability (Ezekiel 47:9). Gentiles will likely travel along this river, fishing in its waters without cost (Revelation 22:17), illustrating that God's blessings are not withheld from the nations. As the river progresses, the Dead Sea's saline waters are healed—its once barren shores become teeming with life (Ezekiel 47:8, 10), demonstrating that areas of prior judgment become centers of renewal. This environmental transformation suggests that ecological restoration in the millennium parallels covenantal healing—sin's curse retracts under divine authority (Genesis 3:17–19), restoring creation's original goodness (Romans 8:19–21). The temple's water thus functions like a sacramental symbol: God's presence issues forth from the sanctuary to renew all things. Irrigation channels branch off from the river, nourishing farmlands and villages (Ezekiel 47:11), integrating ritual spirituality with daily sustenance. Farmers reap bountiful harvests—barley in one month, wheat in another—underscoring that agricultural cycles align with new divine patterns (Ezekiel 45:11). The healed waters also point to eschatological life beyond the millennium: Revelation 22's river of life flows from God's throne, echoing Ezekiel's imagery, tying millennial renewal into ultimate new creation (Revelation 21:1–3). This detailed ecological vision reinforces that in the future kingdom, sacred space extends beyond the temple's walls to encompass all creation, encouraging believers to steward land faithfully now. As environmental renewal flows from the temple, communal rhythms—feasts, pilgrimages, and worship—emerge in response, which we examine in the final subsection.

**7.1.6 Feasts, Calendar, and Gentile Pilgrimage during the Millennium** In Ezekiel's millennial calendar, appointed feasts and pilgrimages maintain continuity with Mosaic observances while reflecting global participation (Ezekiel 45:21–25; 46:1–15). The Passover lambs are offered "as a feast to the LORD" on the fourteenth day of the first month (Ezekiel 45:21), demonstrating that remembrance of deliverance remains central. Unlike post-exilic practice where Passover often suffered neglect (2 Chronicles 30:1–27), millennial observance becomes universal and unbroken, signifying that all tribes return to covenant fidelity. The Feast of Weeks (Shavuot), marked a week after Passover, includes two wheat loaves offered to the LORD (Ezekiel 45:22), echoing Exodus 34:22's "feast of harvest." These agricultural celebrations connect worship with communal sustenance, teaching that thanksgiving arises from both spiritual and material provision. The Feast of Booths (Sukkot) occurs on the fifteenth day of the seventh month (Ezekiel 45:25), commemorating wilderness pilgrimage while pointing toward future rest (Leviticus 23:42–43). Nations streaming to Jerusalem for this feast (Zechariah 14:16–17) fulfill Isaiah 2:2's prophecy of Gentile pilgrimage, illustrating that millennial Jerusalem becomes a global worship center. Ezekiel also describes a monthly new moon offering (Ezekiel 46:1–3) featuring a single bull, six lambs, a ram, and grain offerings, ensuring that each month begins with communal consecration. These regular sacrifices cultivate rhythms of devotion, training hearts to orient time around divine presence. The Prince's provision—providing offerings, cooking, and supplying wine for each feast—demonstrates that leadership remains servant-oriented, coupling hospitality with holiness (Ezekiel 45:22–25). Gentiles who refuse to bring offerings face exclusion from Israel's land, a sobering reminder that participation in divine community requires recognition of God's ways (Ezekiel 47:23–24). Yet those who come "to worship" find welcome, indicating that millennial worship fosters both exclusivity in terms of covenant obedience and inclusivity through invitations to the nations. Pilgrims bring gifts in proportion to their resources—cattle, sheep, oil—highlighting that generosity flows from abundance and gratitude (Ezekiel 45:7–9). This pilgrimage economy supports Levites and priests, reinforcing that communal welfare intertwines with worship practices. Daily sacrificial rituals, monthly offerings, and annual festivals create a calendar steeped in covenant memory and eschatological hope, preparing the stage for contemplation of how postmillennialists spiritualize these temple patterns, which we explore in section 7.2.

## 7.2 Spiritualized Temple in Postmillennial Triumph

### 7.2.1 Global Worship and Moral Reform Postmillennialism envisions that as Christ's kingdom advances through the church, worship transcends physical buildings and moral reformation flows from a global proclamation of the gospel. When Jesus declared that

"true worshipers will worship the Father in spirit and truth" (John 4:23–24), He anticipated a spiritualized temple unconfined by masonry. Postmillennialists see modern missions—in media, literature, digital platforms—creating a global chorus of worship that aligns with Isaiah 56:7's promise that "My house will be called a house of prayer for all nations." As congregations in North America, Africa, and Asia intercede simultaneously—praying Psalm 122:6's directive to "pray for the peace of Jerusalem"—they prefigure Revelation 7:9's vision of "every nation, all tribes and peoples and languages" gathering before God's throne. This global worship context catalyzes moral reform: nations influenced by Christian ethics adopt legislation that upholds human dignity, reduces systemic injustice, and supports care for the vulnerable (Micah 6:8). For instance, laws addressing human trafficking often arise from church-led advocacy coalitions, demonstrating Jubilee principles (Leviticus 25:10) applied in contemporary settings. Educational institutions guided by biblical worldview principles—integrating faith with science, history, and the arts—shape generations to assess cultural trends through a kingdom lens (Matthew 24:14). As public policies reflect Scripture's concern for the orphan and widow (James 1:27), compassion ministries flourish, and churches partner with governments to create social insurance frameworks that echo Old Testament gleaning laws (Leviticus 19:9–10). This moral reformation is not limited to laws; it extends into social norms—reducing poverty through microfinance initiatives, promoting corporate ethics aligned with Proverbs 16:8's valorization of righteousness, and establishing media ethics committees that challenge dehumanizing content. Music, art, and literature become vehicles of sanctified creativity, resonating with Psalm 150's call to praise God with "trumpets and pipe and lyre," and reaching unchurched audiences through emotional resonance. Postmillennial thought holds that the beauty and truth revealed in art contribute to moral renewal, reflecting Psalm 19:1's declaration that creation declares God's glory. This spiritualized conception of temple thus integrates worship and societal ethics, illustrating that as Christian influence grows, a "temple-shaped" culture emerges—holy, just, and compassionate. As this cultural sacralization unfolds, postmillennialists see Pentecost's paradigm of a mobile sanctuary being realized, which leads into the next subsection.

**7.2.2 Pentecost as Portable Sanctuary: Spirit-Indwelt Communities** The day of Pentecost inaugurated a paradigm shift: the Holy Spirit's outpouring transformed believers into a living temple (Acts 2:1–4; 1 Corinthians 3:16). Postmillennialists interpret Pentecost not as a temporary phenomenon but as the ongoing mechanism that makes every faithful community a portable sanctuary. Jesus had predicted that the Spirit would dwell "with you and in you" (John 14:17), declaring that the believer's body becomes the sacred ground where God's presence resides. This indwelling sanctifies daily life—workplaces, schools, and homes become contexts for worship (Romans 12:1–2), blurring the lines between sacred and secular. Early Pentecostal communities exhibited signs—speaking in tongues, healing, communal sharing—exemplifying how God's presence cultivates communal holiness (Acts 2:42–47). Postmillennial thought sees these manifestations continuing throughout church history, with revivals serving as renewal of portable sanctuaries, purging congregations from moral decay and reorienting public influence toward kingdom values (Ecclesiastes 3:1–8). As Spirit-indwelt communities multiply—each local church embodying Christ's presence—God's tabernacle moves from a single hill in Jerusalem to hills and valleys across continents, fulfilling Ezekiel 11:16's vision of God being "no more in the midst of Israel's skyscraping stones." This makes house churches, neighborhood fellowships, and virtual gatherings valid loci of worship where God's glory manifests (Matthew 18:20). The Spirit's diverse gifts—prophecy, teaching, service—equip believers to serve as both priests and prophets in their spheres (Ephesians 4:11–13), ensuring that sanctity permeates every vocation. Communion liturgies, echoing the Lord's Supper (1 Corinthians 11:23–26), become focal moments where churches collectively reenact Christ's presence, affirming that portable sanctuaries are grounded in Eucharistic memory. As portable sanctuaries proliferate, public spaces—parks, stadiums, online forums—host worship gatherings, demonstrating that God's house extends beyond brick-and-mortar edifices. This diffusion of sacred space reforms cultural imaginaries, teaching societies to recognize divine presence in everyday life, thus laying groundwork for moral and civic transformations. The idea of Pentecost as portable sanctuary dovetails with postmillennial convictions about a Cathedral of Culture, the subject of the following subsection.

**7.2.3 Cathedral of Culture: Arts, Sciences, and Public Architecture as "Temple Service"** In postmillennial vision, as the kingdom advances, arts, sciences, and architecture become a collective "Cathedral of Culture," where the world itself reflects worship and sacrificial creativity (Romans 12:1). Artists—painters, musicians, poets—work not merely for entertainment but for sacramental purposes, channeling beauty to point hearts toward divine transcendence (Psalm 27:4). Philanthropic funding for arts centers in urban areas revives public spaces as modern "temples" where communities gather to encounter truth and beauty, paralleling Solomon's vision of the temple as a cultural center (1 Kings 7:1–12). Scientific research, when pursued under the assumption of Imago Dei, becomes an act of worship—exploring creation's laws reveals the Creator's wisdom (Romans 1:20). Christian-led universities champion interdisciplinary education that integrates faith with biology, engineering, and social sciences, training graduates to infuse technological innovation with ethical accountability (Colossians 3:17). Public architecture—civic buildings, libraries, concert halls—designed with principles of proportionality, symmetry, and openness becomes a physical testimony to order under God, echoing Proverbs 8:27–29's depiction of wisdom laying out the earth's foundations. Architects and urban planners collaborate with churches to create "sacred corridors," where greenbelts, community gardens, and public art installations foster spiritual reflection in everyday environments, anticipating Revelation 21:2's imagery of the heavenly city's beauty. Across continents, initiatives like "City of Peace" projects promote harmony, with murals and sculptures conveying biblical themes of reconciliation (2 Corinthians 5:18–19). In these cultural cathedrals, sacrificial offerings take the form of time, talent, and treasure— artists donate performances, scientists volunteer at educational workshops, and patrons fund community festivals—embodying Hebrews 13:15's call to "offer the sacrifice of praise to God." This reconstruction of culture into a unified temple service leverages media platforms—television, streaming, social media—to broadcast gospel-infused content, creating a digital nave where viewers participate in global worship. This cosmic temple concept underwrites postmillennial optimism, asserting that as culture's altar expands, society becomes increasingly oriented toward God's glory. Building on this cultural reorientation, postmillennial thought extends temple service into social justice, addressed next.

**7.2.4 Social Justice Altars: Sacrifice of Praise, Generosity, and Structural Mercy** Postmillennial ideology teaches that true worship extends beyond word and sacrament into tangible expressions of justice and mercy, forming "social justice altars" where sacrificial actions replace animal offerings. Proverbs 21:3—"To do righteousness and justice is more acceptable to the LORD than sacrifice"—underscores that ethical living itself constitutes worship. Churches establish benevolence ministries serving refugees, job training centers for the unemployed, and affordable housing projects for the homeless, offering resources that reflect Leviticus 19:18's command to "love your neighbor as yourself." These initiatives become public altars where believers lay down wealth and comfort, enacting Philippians 2:4's exhortation to consider others' interests. Community-sponsored clinics operate as healing altars, embodying Isaiah 61:1's proclamation that the good news invites healing for the brokenhearted. Nonprofit organizations led by faith-based coalitions advocate policy reforms—minimum wage hikes, criminal justice overhauls, environmental protections—mirroring Micah 6:8's call to "do justice, love kindness, and walk humbly." These structural reforms represent collective sacrifices, for advocates sacrifice time, influence, and sometimes personal safety to challenge ingrained systems of oppression. Annual social justice fairs and conferences become gatherings where "sacrifices of praise" (Hebrews 13:15) meet "sacrificial generosity" (2 Corinthians 8:1–5), teaching communities that worship is multidimensional. Educational workshops on ethical investing encourage congregants to divest from exploitative industries, paralleling Deuteronomy 24:14–15's protection for the poor in labor agreements. Through community gardens and fair-trade cooperatives, churches demonstrate a preferential option for the poor, fulfilling James 2:15–16's admonishment to meet physical needs. Youth ministries partner with local NGOs to combat human trafficking, raising awareness through art exhibits that confront societal apathy—reminiscent of Isaiah 58:6's call to "loose the bonds of wickedness" by confronting systemic evil. When congregations celebrate "Justice Sundays," they integrate testimonies of transformed lives with liturgies of confession—recognizing collective complicity in injustice—and call communities back to covenant faithfulness. These social justice altars position ministry not as charity but as prophetic worship, affirming Amos 5:24 that "let justice roll down like waters, and righteousness like an ever-flowing stream." As these societal altars proliferate, they reshape public perception of religion, moving worship from cloistered sanctuaries into civic centers. The concept of social justice altars thus illustrates how postmillennial thought spiritualizes temple functions into societal transformation, setting the stage for exploring global Sabbath rhythms and healing of nations in the subsequent section.

### 7.2.5 Worldwide Sabbath Rhythms and the Healing of Nations

An essential aspect of postmillennial temple spirituality involves reestablishing Sabbath rhythms on a global scale, facilitating rest, restoration, and collective worship. Genesis 2:3's observation that God "blessed the seventh day and made it holy" underscores rest as sacred action, not mere cessation of work. Postmillennial advocates encourage corporate practices such as "City Rest Days"—weekly interfaith events where businesses close briefly to promote reflection and community gatherings—fulfilling Isaiah 58:13's call to "call the Sabbath a delight." These rhythmic pauses allow neighborhoods to hold pop-up worship in parks, turning public squares into open-air sanctuaries where leaders recite Psalms (Psalm 92) and citizens share testimonies of God's faithfulness. In agricultural societies, Sabbath rest translates into land fallowing, reflecting Leviticus 25:4's instruction to allow fields to rest every seventh year, teaching environmental stewardship to modern farmers who observe regular crop rotations. On a national scale, postmillennial coalitions lobby for labor laws that guarantee workers paid time off for Sabbath or holy day observance, ensuring that worship remains accessible to all socioeconomic levels (Mark 2:27). Media outlets sponsor "Sabbath programming" with family-friendly content and worship services broadcast across time zones, reinforcing communal rest in a connected world. International prayer networks gather digitally every Sabbath to pray for global issues—poverty, pandemics, conflict—acknowledging Psalm 46:10's admonition to "be still, and know that I am God." These rhythms prepare hearts for healing at broader levels: as nations incorporate sabbatical principles— environmental rest, debt jubilees, work-life balance—they see reduced burnout, decreased debt cycles, and revitalized neighborhoods. Medical studies highlight that regular rest patterns improve mental health, reflecting the holistic intentions underlying Sabbath creation (Hebrews 4:9–10). Cities that adopt Sabbath principles report lower crime rates, as communal rest fosters social cohesion and reduces economic desperation. Observing Sabbath collectively also breaks down cultural barriers, as Jewish Shabbat, Christian Sunday, and Muslim Friday traditions harmonize into a shared ethos of rest, leading to enhanced interfaith cooperation. Through these weekly rhythms, postmillennialism envisions a society healed incrementally—physically, socially, spiritually— reflecting Jeremiah 31:25's promise that God "satisfies the weary soul and replenishes every languishing spirit." As nations discover the restorative power of Sabbath, they anticipate Ezekiel's vision of living waters flowing from the temple (Ezekiel 47:12), readying the world for an era of flourishing before Christ's return—a theme that transitions into envisioning renewed Jerusalem as metaphor for global flourishing in the next section.

**7.2.6 Future Convergence: Renewed Jerusalem as Metaphor for Civilizational Flourishing** Postmillennialism often employs renewed Jerusalem imagery—drawn from Isaiah 2:2 and Revelation 21:2—as a metaphor for civilizational flourishing that transcends geographic specificity. When Isaiah prophesied that "many peoples shall come and say, 'Come, let us go up to the mountain of the LORD,'" he envisioned a center of wisdom and worship that attracts nations, symbolizing a future epoch of shared ethical standards. Postmillennial readers apply this not only to the physical city but to cultural networks—academic institutions, arts councils, and think tanks—that serve as modern "Jerusalems," drawing the world to engage biblical truth. In this sense, "coming to Jerusalem" means aligning societal aspirations with covenantal justice (Jeremiah 1:10), nurturing a global center of theological and moral insight. Academic conferences on Christian ethics become pilgrimages for scholars seeking to integrate faith and public policy, mirroring Revelation 21:24's "kings of the earth bringing their glory into it." As healthcare systems adopt values of compassion and mercy rooted in Luke 10:30–37's Good Samaritan parable, they function as clinics of divine healing, prefiguring the new Jerusalem's healing leaves (Revelation 22:2). Technological hubs—Silicon Valley, Bangalore—when influenced by stewardship ethics (Genesis 1:28), become breeding grounds for innovations that alleviate suffering, echoing Isaiah 32:17's prophecy that righteousness brings peace and quietness. Financial centers that embrace biblical principles—fair wages, transparent transactions—reflect Isaiah 61:1–3's promise of "binding up the brokenhearted" through economic justice. In this metaphorical Jerusalem, public architecture—libraries, museums, concert halls—doubles as cultural temples, housing exhibits and performances that elevate human creativity toward divine reflection (Psalm 19:1). Cities hosting interfaith forums on peacemaking enact Zechariah 8:23's vision of outsiders seeking the Lord in Jerusalem, forging unity across ethnic lines. This symbiosis of renewed Jerusalem imagery with contemporary institutions anticipates a consolidated future where civilizational flourishing blossoms across all sectors—arts, sciences, politics—fulfilling Micah 4:1–2's vision of global peace rooted in God's law. By treating renewed Jerusalem as a broad metaphor rather than a strictly geographical entity, postmillennial thought preserves covenantal hope while embracing pluralistic participation, leading naturally into how amillennialists recast temple reality in Christ.

# 7.3 Christ as the True Temple in Amillennial Thought

### 7.3.1 Ecclesial Indwelling and Eschatological Fulfillment
Amillennial theology asserts that Christ's incarnation and ascension inaugurated a new temple where God dwells among His people through the Holy Spirit, fulfilling texts like John 2:21's declaration that Jesus' body is the temple. When Jesus breathed on the disciples and said, "Receive the Holy Spirit" (John 20:22), He signified that divine presence would henceforth inhabit believers' bodies, making each Christian a sacred dwelling (1 Corinthians 6:19–20). The book of Acts charts this shift: the seventy disciples return rejoicing that demons submit "in Jesus' name" (Luke 10:17), a foretaste of Christ's spiritual temple overcoming satanic strongholds among the nations. Pentecost's outpouring (Acts 2:1–4) establishes the ecclesial community as the new tabernacle of divine presence, synthesizing Old Testament temple patterns with Christ's priestly work (Hebrews 9:11–12). Amillennialists interpret Ephesians 2:19–22's vision of "living stones" built into a holy temple in the Lord as encapsulating how the church functions as both the visible temple and the ultimately consummated temple in heaven. This ecclesial indwelling transforms communal worship: wherever two or three gather in Jesus' name (Matthew 18:20), the temple presence emerges, making sacred space ubiquitous rather than confined to Jerusalem. As the church advances amid persecution, believers embody a prophetic temple presence, echoing Ezekiel's promise that

God's glory "will fill this house" (Ezekiel 43:5), now in the hearts of His people. This spiritualized temple anticipates the eschatological fulfillment described in Revelation 21:3, where "the dwelling place of God is with man," foreshadowing that individual and collective indwelling merge into one final, unmediated presence. Amillennial theology thus rejects any future physical temple rebuildings, insisting that Christ's one body stands forever. By identifying the church as the locus of divine presence, amillennialists equip believers to recognize sacred place wherever the Word is preached and sacraments are celebrated, transitioning into how Christ's sacrifice makes cultic rituals obsolete.

**7.3.2 "Once-for-All" Sacrifice and the Obsolescence of Cultic Ritual** Amillennialists hold that Christ's "once-for-all" sacrifice (Hebrews 7:27; 10:10) rendered all subsequent animal offerings obsolete, shifting the meaning of sacrifice from ritual to relational. The writer to the Hebrews emphasizes that the law's sacrificial system was "a shadow of the good things to come, not the realities themselves" (Hebrews 10:1). Ezekiel's vision of ongoing millennial sacrifices thus serves typologically lest Israel forget its need for Messiah; however, amillennialists argue that Christ's atonement fulfills worship once and for all (Hebrews 10:12–14), negating any future sacrificial cultic system. When Jesus declared from the cross, "It is finished" (John 19:30), He signaled that the price for sin had been paid in full, fulfilling Leviticus 17:11's principle that "the life of the flesh is in the blood." This definitive act transforms how believers understand covenant: no longer must priests slaughter animals to maintain atonement; instead, they trust in Christ's blood to purify consciences (Hebrews 9:13–14). Post-millennial and pre-millennial frameworks might retain sacrificial rituals pedagogically until Christ's return, but amillennial theology contends that ongoing sacrifices risk obscuring the sufficiency of Christ's work (Hebrews 9:11–12). Consequently, liturgical life centers on proclaiming Christ's accomplished work through preaching (1 Corinthians 1:21), celebrating the Eucharist as a remembrance of His body and blood (Luke 22:19–20), and practicing baptism as union with His death and resurrection (Romans 6:3–4). This shift moves sacrifice from the altar to the altar of the heart—Romans 12:1 calls believers to present themselves "as a living sacrifice, holy and acceptable to God," highlighting personal holiness as the new shrine activity. As a result, the church's identity as a royal priesthood (1 Peter 2:9) emerges, where each believer functions in priestly capacity—offering prayers, intercession, and good works as sacrifices pleasing to God (Philippians 4:18). This theological reorientation informs how congregations structure worship services, emphasizing the preached Word and celebrated sacraments over altar-based rituals, paving the way to explore how believers, as living stones, constitute a royal priesthood in everyday vocations.

### 7.3.3 Living Stones and Royal Priesthood: Everyday Vocations as Liturgy
Amillennial thought declares that each believer is a "living stone" built into a spiritual house (1 Peter 2:5), fulfilling Isaiah 66:1's assertion that "heaven is my throne, and the earth is my footstool," effectively dismantling any notion of a geographically bounded temple. As such, daily work becomes liturgy: farmers tilling fields function akin to Levites caring for temple grounds, transforming creation according to Genesis 2:15's mandate to steward the earth. Artists compose music and craft visual art as acts of worship, reflecting Colossians 3:17's injunction to do "whatever you do in word or deed, do all in the name of the Lord Jesus." Teachers, lawyers, and engineers interpret creation's order—mathematically, legally, mechanically—as echoing God's wisdom revealed in Proverbs 8:22–31, engaging every discipline with sacramental intentionality. This priesthood of all believers means that workplace decisions—business ethics, environmental policies—carry liturgical weight: choosing fair wages honors Deuteronomy 24:14–15's concern for the vulnerable, functioning as a spiritual offering. Entrepreneurs practicing generosity through profit-sharing demonstrate Hebrews 13:16's promise that "do good and share what you have, for such sacrifices are pleasing to God." When doctors treat patients with compassion, they enact Isaiah 53:4's depiction of the Servant bearing infirmities, situating medicine as a healing ministry. In this sense, secular vocation and sacred vocation converge; every profession becomes a sanctuary where God's presence dwells among those who serve faithfully. Marketplace evangelism, government service, and social entrepreneurship become acts of priestly intercession, bridging spiritual and material dimensions. The royal priesthood also carries communal responsibilities: believers counsel one another, encourage sanctification, and guard doctrine—priestly tasks once confined to Levitical classes now distributed among all saints (Hebrews 13:7). As the church gathers, communal worship flows

from these vocational liturgies, creating a temple unbounded by walls, built by faith and sustained by obedience. This priestly identity in everyday life points toward eschatological fulfillment, where every vocation converges in the presence of God, introducing the theme of suffering as sanctuary and martyrdom as heavenly altar imagery.

**7.3.4 Suffering as Sanctuary: Martyrdom, Witness, and Heavenly Altar Imagery** Amillennial theology often interprets suffering and martyrdom as a form of holy sacrifice, likening spilled blood to incense rising on a heavenly altar (Revelation 6:9–11; 8:3–4). When believers endure persecution for Christ's sake, they participate in Hebrews 13:12–13's notion of bearing Jesus' reproach, offering their lives as a sacrifice of witness. The book of Revelation portrays martyrs under the altar crying out, "How long, O Lord, holy and true, until you judge and avenge our blood?" (Revelation 6:10), imagery that associates martyrdom with worship in heaven—God's justice and mercy are vindicated on a cosmic altar. Stephen's death (Acts 7:54–60) models this, as his dying prayer echoes Jesus' compassion (Luke 23:34), demonstrating that martyrdom combines sanctified suffering with intercession. In modern contexts, when believers face imprisonment or violence, amillennial thought encourages congregations to view their testimony as contributing to the temple of witness, where spiritual altars rise through faithfulness under trial (1 Peter 4:14–16). Mission fields in hostile regions become sanctuaries of witness: medical professionals treating victims in conflict zones, despite personal risk, embody Leviticus 23:40's call to "rejoice before the Lord" by celebrating life amid death. Persecuted churches offering hospitality to the displaced create spaces where suffering itself becomes liturgical, as refugees encounter Christ's presence through sacrificial service (Matthew 25:35–40). Storytelling of contemporary martyrs—like those killed saving others—serves as sermon illustrations reminding congregations that the heavenly sanctuary receives their prayers as fragrant offerings (Revelation 8:3–4). When theologians reflect on 2 Corinthians 4:10–11, where Paul writes that dying body carries "Jesus' death" to make His life visible, they affirm that suffering constitutes sanctified priesthood rather than mere victimhood. Pastoral care in such contexts emphasizes that suffering refines faith, purifies motives (1 Peter 1:6–7), and strengthens the church's witness to the world. These realities challenge amillennial worship to integrate testimonies of persecution into liturgy—reading martyr narratives alongside Scriptures—ensuring that congregations understand suffering as an eschatological communion with Christ's own sacrifice (Philippians 3:10). In this way, suffering as sanctuary leads to envisioning the Eucharist as the ongoing Holy of Holies, mobile yet sacred, which is the theme of the next subsection.

**7.3.5 Eucharist as Mobile Holy of Holies: Presence without Geographic Limits** Amillennial theology identifies the Lord's Supper as the central locus of God's presence, replacing any future geographic Holy of Holies with a mobile sanctuary available wherever believers gather (1 Corinthians 11:23–26; Matthew 18:20). Jesus proclaimed that His blood is the "blood of the covenant, which is poured out for many for the forgiveness of sins" (Matthew 26:28), situating the Eucharist as the eschatological banqueting table where fellowship with God transpires. Early church practice—celebrating the Lord's Supper in homes, catacombs, and public squares—demonstrated that sacred space is where Christ's presence is recognized rather than within temple walls (Acts 2:46; Revelation 1:13). When Paul writes that "we, though many, are one bread and one body" (1 Corinthians 10:17), he underscores that the Eucharist unites diverse participants into a single living sanctuary. Amillennialists also observe that the "Holy of Holies" imagery shifts from physical separation to relational proximity; the curtain has been torn (Matthew 27:51), granting all believers access to God's presence. Consequently, every congregation's communion table functions as God's altar, a present fulfillment of Ezekiel 44:15's promise that priests minister "in order to stand before God." This mobile sacredness extends to digital gatherings: live-streamed communion services during pandemics manifested how indestructible the Holy of Holies has become when the Spirit transforms believers' hearts (John 4:21–24). Liturgy thus centers on Word and sacrament: preaching draws from Hebrews 4:12's "living and active" Word, and Communion enacts ongoing remembrance of Christ's once-for-all sacrifice (1 Corinthians 11:26). Liturgical design—whether in grand cathedrals or simple meeting rooms—emphasizes a central table, not a focal building, reminding worshipers that Christ's presence transcends architectural grandeur (John 14:23). This mobile Holy of Holies compels amillennial believers to see every place of gathering as a sacred locus, equipping them for mission in contexts that wield no literal temple site. As congregations experience this dynamic presence, they anticipate Christ's return when "the temple of God will be in their midst" once again, but fully realized without geographic constraints (Revelation 21:3). This eschatological reality—the consummated absence of a temple structure—prepares the way for apprehending the final consummation where no temple is needed, as explored in 7.3.6.

### 7.3.6 Consummated Communion: No Temple in the City (Revelation 21:22) Amillennialists hold that in the new heavens and new earth, worship reaches its apex, and no physical temple is necessary because God's presence dwells openly with humanity (Revelation 21:22; 22:3–5). John's vision portrays the New Jerusalem descending from heaven, illuminated by "the glory of God" rather than physical lamps (Revelation 21:23), conveying that the city itself becomes transparent to divine presence. This permanent communion moves beyond any spatial boundary, signaling the end of "holy place" demarcations. Isaiah 60:19–20 anticipated this: "The sun shall no longer be your light by day... instead the Lord will be your everlasting light, and your God will be your glory." The distinctiveness of the "holy of holies" thus dissolves—every street, home, and garden in the new creation participates in unbroken fellowship. In this consummated state, the Bereans' approach—examining all Scriptures to see if it is so (Acts 17:11)—culminates in seeing Christ face to face (1 Corinthians 13:12), rather than through analogies or symbols. The "tree of life" provides healing for nations (Revelation 22:2), integrating spiritual and physical restoration into one harmonious reality. These images fulfill Jeremiah 31:34's promise that God's people will know Him fully, with no need for intermediaries or temple rituals. The final disappearance of the temple also fulfills Daniel 9:27's prophecy of the abomination of desolation being reversed, as sacrilege is forever banished. Worship here is unmediated, as "they will see His face, and His name will be on their foreheads" (Revelation 22:4), embodying Hebrews 10:19–22's reality that all have direct access to the Father through Christ. Consequently, amillennial theology encourages believers to participate in this consummation now by cultivating communities that reflect the New Jerusalem's attributes—purity, justice, and perpetual worship—anticipating the day when temple spatiality gives way to eternal communion.

# 7.4 Typology, Continuity, and Discontinuity

**7.4.1 From Tabernacle to Heavenly Sanctuary** The progression from the wilderness tabernacle to the heavenly sanctuary encapsulates a typological trajectory spanning redemptive history (Exodus 25:8–9; Hebrews 8:1–5). The tabernacle, with its innermost Holy of Holies separated by a veil (Exodus 26:31–33), foreshadowed God's dwelling among His people while maintaining divine holiness. When Solomon built the temple, that earthly structure solidified central worship (1 Kings 6:1–38), yet prophets like Haggai (Haggai 2:6–9) pointed to a greater temple whose glory surpassed Solomon's. Ezekiel's exile visions expanded on this theme (Ezekiel 10:18–19; 11:22–23), teaching that God's glory, once departing the physical temple, would ultimately return. The book of Hebrews reveals that these earthly structures served as "copies and shadows" of heavenly realities (Hebrews 8:5), culminating in Christ's ascension where He entered the true heavenly sanctuary (Hebrews 9:24). Revelation's portrayal of the lamb-smiting shepherd entering the temple of heaven (Revelation 5:6) depicts the inaugurated fulfillment of tabernacle typology: the Lamb's body embodies both priest and offering. This typological continuity invites believers to see every tabernacle feature—altar, lampstand, ark—as pointing to Christ's redemptive work and ongoing priestly intercession (Hebrews 7:25). As typology unfolds, earthly discontinuities arise: the curtain rent at the crucifixion (Matthew 27:51) signals that the tabernacle and temple veil no longer separate God from His people; access becomes direct. Yet typology also anticipates ultimate continuity: Revelation 21:3 describes God's dwelling with humanity, fulfilling Exodus 25:8's original command to "make Me a sanctuary" in a permanent consummation. This theological movement underscores how each covenantal phase points forward while simultaneously receding in significance as the heavenly sanctuary's reality emerges.

**7.4.2 Garden, Mountain, City: Thematic Trajectory of Sacred Space** Sacred space in Scripture advances from a garden to a mountain to a city, each stage enriching the typological tapestry. Eden, as God's first sanctuary, provided unhindered communion between Creator and creature (Genesis 2:8–9), with Adam's role as priest tending to the garden (Genesis 2:15). Eden's lush vegetation and rivers flowing eastward (Genesis 2:10) prefigure Ezekiel's millennial river and John's river of life (Ezekiel 47:1–12; Revelation 22:1–2). After the flood, Noah's altar sacrifices (Genesis 8:20–22) fulfilled a priestly function despite the world's reordering, indicating that sacred acts continue even in a fallen environment. Mount Sinai emerges as the next locus, where Moses encounters God in cloud and fire (Exodus 19:16–20), and the Law is delivered, situating divine presence on a peak. Throughout Israel's history, Zion, the mountain of the LORD, becomes the city where God's temple dwells (Psalm 2:6; Psalm 48:1–2), merging mountain and city motifs. The prophetic visions of Isaiah 2:2–4 and Micah 4:1–4 expand Zion's influence to all nations, signaling a future point where mountains (plural) conflate into one mountain of the LORD. New Testament writers reinterpret this: Hebrews 12:22 places believers at "Mount Zion, the city of the living God," signifying a spiritual elevation rather than a physical ascent. Revelation's new Jerusalem combines mountain and city imagery—coming down from heaven like a bride (Revelation 21:2)—indicating that consummated sacred space embodies both edenic abundance and Zionic worship. This thematic trajectory teaches that God's presence adapts to human contexts—garden, mountain, city—while never abandoning relational intent; the end goal remains face-to-face fellowship. In each transition, sacrifice remains essential: from Abel's offering (Genesis 4:4) to altar sacrifices (Genesis 8:20) to temple offerings (Leviticus 1–7), culminating in Christ's once-for-all act (Hebrews 10:12). As sacred space evolves, worship adapts, teaching believers that location matters less than orientation to God's presence, preparing them to integrate these typologies into contemporary liturgical design and public worship practices.

### 7.4.3 Blood, Bread, and Praise: Evolution of Sacrificial Logic

Sacrificial logic in Scripture transitions from animal blood to symbolic bread and praise, tracing redemption's arc from Levitical rites to Eucharistic remembrance. Abel's offering of the "firstborn of his flock" (Genesis 4:4) typifies blood sacrifice as a means of acknowledging human sinfulness and God's holiness. After the flood, Noah's burnt offerings (Genesis 8:20–21) serve as thanksgiving collectively offered to the righteous God who spares creation. Abraham's near-sacrifice of Isaac (Genesis 22:1–18) introduces the concept of substitutionary sacrifice—Abraham provides a ram in Isaac's place—foreshadowing Christ's vicarious atonement. Mosaic law codifies blood theology: "without the shedding of blood there is no forgiveness" (Leviticus 17:11), teaching that life resides in blood and that sin demands a life-payment. Temple sacrifices under the Davidic monarchy elaborate on these rituals—thanksgiving, sin, and guilt offerings—each with specific purposes (Leviticus 7:12–38). Ezekiel's millennial temple scales back atonement offerings, emphasizing memorial aspects (Ezekiel 43:18–27), presaging the shift to once-for-all sacrifice in Christ (Hebrews 9:11–12). Jesus' declaration that He is the "bread of life" (John 6:35) transitions sacrificial logic from animal blood to spiritual sustenance—consuming His body imparts eternal life, signaling a new covenant (Luke 22:19). Paul reinterprets Passover symbolism in 1 Corinthians 5:7, proclaiming that "Christ, our Passover, has been sacrificed for us," indicating that the original lamb typology reaches its fullness in Christ. Praise emerges as a valid offering alongside or instead of blood: Psalm 50:14–15 encourages thanksgiving and fulfilling vows as sacrifices. The New Testament's emphasis on "praise through Jesus" (Hebrews 13:15) suggests that the community's vocal worship serves as liturgical sacrifice, transcending physical offerings. Revelation 5:8–9–10 portrays songs of "harps of gold" and incense of "golden bowls, which are the prayers of the saints," combining praise and prayer as spiritual offerings before God's throne. This evolution—blood, bread, and praise—highlights that sacrificial logic advances from external rituals to internal devotion, culminating in a worship centered on Christ's once-for-all act, guiding how the church conceives of liturgy and sacred offering in every age.

**7.4.4 Priests, Prophets, Kings—Christological Integration** The offices of priest, prophet, and king converge in Christ, offering a unified typology that redefines all leadership roles under His authority. Under the Old Testament system, priests mediated between God and people through sacrifices (Leviticus 16:6–10), prophets communicated divine revelation (1 Samuel 3:10), and kings governed according to God's statutes (1 Samuel 8:6–7). David's rule exemplified the integration of these functions—he wrote psalms (prophetic), led temple worship (priestly), and reigned under Yahweh's authority (kingship). Yet his successor Solomon, while wise, lacked prophetic authority, illustrating the separate nature of these offices. Amillennial theology sees Christ as the ultimate fulfillment of all three: as High Priest "after the order of

Melchizedek" (Hebrews 7:17), He offers Himself as the perfect sacrifice; as prophet, He speaks God's words to humanity (Hebrews 1:1–2); as King, He reigns from heaven (Revelation 19:16). This integration signifies that Christ transcends institutional offices, establishing a new order where priestly intercession, prophetic proclamation, and kingly governance all flow from His singular person and work. Under this model, believers share in these offices: 1 Peter 2:9 calls them a "royal priesthood," empowered to offer spiritual sacrifices and proclaim God's truth. The Great Commission (Matthew 28:18–20) invests the church with prophetic and kingly responsibilities—teaching nations and exercising Christ's delegated authority—while intercessory prayer (Colossians 4:2) enacts priestly ministry. Liturgies often reflect this triplex dimension: readings from Scripture (prophetic), prayers for the world (priestly), and creedal affirmations of Christ's reign (kingly leadership). This Christological integration undergirds amillennial critiques of segregating priesthood, prophecy, and kingship into isolated roles; in Christ's body, every member contributes to the unified mission. By embracing this typology, churches shape leadership development programs that cultivate pastoral, prophetic, and missional skill sets in each believer, preparing them for kingdom service. As this vision unfolds, it connects to hermeneutical considerations on how to read sacred texts—literally, figuratively, and anagogically—covered in section 7.4.5.

**7.4.5 Hermeneutical Tests: Literal, Figurative, and Anagogic Readings** Interpreting temple and sacrificial texts requires a hermeneutical strategy balancing literal, figurative, and anagogic dimensions. A strictly literal reading of Ezekiel's temple risks imposing physical reconstructions that fail to account for typological layers; yet a purely figurative approach may strip texts of historical grounding. Amillennialists propose a three-tiered reading: the literal sense (the plain meaning to Ezekiel's original audience), the figurative sense (how New Testament writers apply temple imagery to Christ and the church), and the anagogic sense (how these visions point to consummated reality in the new heavens and new earth). For example, literalists might insist on rebuilding an exact temple, while figurative readers see Ezekiel's prophecy as fulfilled in Christ's body (John 2:19–21). Anagogically, Ezekiel's river symbolizes eschatological life (Revelation 22:1–2). This multi-layered approach preserves text integrity while acknowledging canonical trajectory—

from Exodus 25's tabernacle, through Solomon's temple, to the heavenly reality described in Revelation. Psalm 118:22–23's cornerstone imagery demonstrates this multi-level reading: literally, a rejected stone in a building project; figuratively, Christ's rejection by Israel; anagogically, Christ as foundational in God's eternal city. Hermeneutical tests include examining authorial intent (Ezekiel's original context), canonical fulfillment (New Testament reinterpretations), and eschatological consummation (apocalyptic visions). Applying these tests ensures that interpretations align with the Bible's unified message without imposing extrabiblical schemes. As these methods sharpen understanding, they inform ethical and liturgical choices outlined in section 7.4.6.

**7.4.6 Ethical Payoff: Holiness Codes and Contemporary Worship Design** Holiness codes—dietary laws, Sabbath observance, purity regulations—point toward ethical principles that remain relevant when recast in spiritual terms. Leviticus 19:18's call to "love your neighbor as yourself" becomes a foundational ethic transcending cultic rituals, guiding social engagement. In worship design, communities draw on tabernacle patterns—centralization of Word and sacrament—to structure services that move congregants from preparation (confession) through proclamation (preaching) to response (communion), echoing Torah's progression from sacrifice to covenant affirmation. Architecture employs symbolic elements: north–south orientation reflects divine approaches, while incorruptible materials—wood overlaid with gold—affirm eternal values. Contemporary sanctuaries incorporate transparent ceilings or windows to symbolize Revelation 21:3's vision of God dwelling among people, encouraging congregations to view structural design as a form of ethical witness. Communion liturgies often feature prayers that link bread and wine to justice commitments—feeding the hungry and advocating for the oppressed—ensuring that sacramentality informs social responsibility. Deacons coordinate outreach ministries, equating service to "Hebrews 6:10" promises that God remembers service, integrating worship with action. As congregations design liturgies, sermon series trace temple themes— sermon on the altar's horns (Psalm 18:3) becomes a call to offer the "horns of our hands" in service (Isaiah 60:17). This convergence of ancient holiness codes and modern worship articulates how sacred space and ethical life coalesce, preparing believers to navigate historical developments and contemporary challenges discussed in the next chapter on historical trajectories and architectural embodiments.

# 7.5 Historical Trajectories and Architectural Embodiments

### 7.5.1 Second-Temple Judaism: Intertestamental Developments

After the Babylonian exile, Zerubbabel built a second temple under Persian authorization (Ezra 3:10–11), yet it lacked Solomon's grandeur, triggering prophetic lament and apostolic critique (Malachi 1:10; John 2:20). During the intertestamental period, successive rulers—the Ptolemies, Seleucids—competed for control over Jerusalem, influencing temple renovations under Hasmonean and Herodian dynasties (1 Maccabees 4:36–59; Josephus, *Antiquities* 15.11). The Hasmoneans expanded the temple precinct, while King Herod's renovation created the colossal Second Temple, adorned with Corinthian pillars and a golden Emperor's gate (Jewish Wars 5.193–205). These architectural changes reflected Hellenistic and Roman influences, blending pagan forms with Jewish sanctity, sparking debates among Pharisees, Sadducees, and Essenes about purity and appropriation. Intertestamental theologians—the Qumran community—emphasized temple purity, delineating strict membership criteria and envisioning an apocalyptic temple surpassing Herod's (The Community Rule). The apocryphal book of 1 Enoch describes visionary temples with angelic worship, indicating that second-temple priests developed elaborate eschatological expectations. Meanwhile, Greek philosophy permeated temple liturgy; synagogue readings incorporated Septuagint translations, fusing Hebrew prophecy with Hellenistic idioms. These developments prepared the stage for the New Testament's engagement: Jesus declared the temple's obsolescence (John 2:19; Mark 13:2), and Paul cited the destroyed temple as evidence of fulfilled prophecy (1 Corinthians 3:16–17). Post-canon scholars like Philo of Alexandria wove allegorical interpretations of the temple, foreshadowing patristic symbolic readings. Understanding these intertestamental shifts highlights the evolutionary nature of temple architecture and theology, leading into how early Christians repurposed sacred spaces in basilica forms.

**7.5.2 Early-Church Basilicas and Pilgrimage Sites** Following Constantine's conversion, Christian architecture shifted from house churches to purpose-built basilicas—long halls with apses—emulating Roman civic centers but reorienting the space toward liturgical action (Eusebius, *Life of Constantine*, 3.3). Old St. Peter's Basilica (c. 324 CE) in Rome set a precedent with its five-aisle plan, clerestory windows, and transept forming a cross shape, symbolizing Christ's sacrifice (Prof. Fergus Millar, *The Roman Empire and Its Neighbours*). Pilgrimage sites emerged: the Church of the Holy Sepulchre (c. 335 CE) enshrined Golgotha and the empty tomb, formalizing the geographical nexus of crucifixion and resurrection. In Jerusalem, the Mosaics of the Basilica of St. John Lateran (4th century) integrated Hebrew script and motifs, affirming continuity with Jewish temple symbolism. Monastic communities in Cappadocia carved rock-cut churches (6th–8th centuries) adorned with frescoes depicting biblical tabernacle imagery—incense, menorahs—translating temple concepts into carved stone. Pilgrims traveling via the Via Dolorosa retraced Jesus' Passion, creating a ritual geography that replaced the physical temple with experiential devotion along city streets. In North Africa, St. Augustine's basilica (late 4th century) incorporated porticos and atria serving catechumens, reflecting Jeremiah 7:4's critique of hollow sanctuaries by emphasizing inward transformation. Liturgical furniture—alters, ambones (pulpits), and baptisteries—became focal elements, each resonating with cultic functions: the altar symbolized Abraham's sacrifice (Genesis 22), the ambo signified prophetic proclamation (Amos 3:7), and the baptistery reflected cleansing akin to Levitical purification (Leviticus 16). These architectural evolutions illustrate how early Christians integrated temple typology into new forms, preparing congregations for worship without a centralized Jerusalem presence. As pilgrim infrastructure grew—hostels near holy sites, hospitality networks—prayer stations and relic veneration replaced sacrificial rites with commemorative acts, bridging millennia of temple heritage. This trajectory sets the stage for medieval cathedrals, relic cults, and the fusion of worship and power, which the next subsection will explore.

**7.5.3 Medieval Cathedrals, Relics, and Sacramental Space** The medieval era saw cathedral construction reach unprecedented scales—Notre-Dame de Paris (1163–1345) and Chartres Cathedral (c. 1194) exemplify Gothic innovations—flying buttresses, ribbed vaults, and stained-glass windows that transformed walls into luminous narratives akin to a "biblia pauperum" for semi-literate believers. These structures functioned as vertical lofting arms, directing worshipers' eyes heavenward, echoing Jacob's ladder in Genesis 28:12 as a conduit for divine-human encounter. The accumulation of relics—bones of martyrs, fragments of the True Cross—imbued cathedrals with sacramental potency akin to tabernacle presence (Hebrews 12:22–23), transforming each cathedral into a localized Holy of Holies. Pilgrims flocked to these sanctuaries—Chartres, Santiago de Compostela, Canterbury—creating economic networks and devotional hubs that mirrored Ezekiel's millennial vision of Gentile pilgrimage (Ezekiel 47:13; Zechariah 14:16). The liturgy became more elaborate: elaborated chants, processions, and drama reenactments (liturgical mysteries) conveyed biblical narratives in spatially immersive forms, reminiscent of temple processions (Exodus 40:17–38). Church councils regulated relic authentication and veneration, seeking to prevent idolatry while preserving historical continuity. Bishops functioned as Christ's vicars—priest, prophet, and king—whether carrying croziers or seated in cathedra, physically embodying ecclesiastical authority within the cathedral precincts (Ephesians 4:11–13). As secular powers grew, cathedrals symbolized civic identity—cities like Cologne and Milan rose around their cathedrals, reflecting unity between worship and government. Artistic programs—tapestries, frescoes, and illuminated manuscripts—reinforced cathedral teachings, resembling Jericho's walls inscribed with covenantal themes (Joshua 6:5). The rise of mendicant orders—Franciscans, Dominicans—shifted emphasis to itinerant ministry, reminding believers that the ultimate sanctuary resides in Christ, not in stone edifices. These medieval developments underscore how sacramental space evolves with culture while preserving foundational temple motifs, leading into Reformation iconoclasm and its repudiation of ornate spaces, addressed next.

### 7.5.4 Reformation Iconoclasm and the "Bare Stage" Sanctuary

The Protestant Reformation challenged medieval sacramental space, emphasizing the Word over symbols. Iconoclast movements in Zurich under Ulrich Zwingli (Huldrych Zwingli, *Sixty-Seven Articles*, 1523) and in England under Thomas Cranmer (42 Articles of Religion, 1553) saw removal of statues, stained glass, and altar rails, equating visual imagery with idolatry (Ezekiel 8:6–18).

Reformers argued that the gospel's purity required uncluttered worship spaces—"bare stage" sanctuaries—where only a pulpit, baptismal font, and communion table remained, aligning with John Calvin's assertion that "faith cannot be instituted apart from the ministry of the Word" (Institutes IV.10.4). This stripped environment aimed to mirror the tabernacle's functional simplicity in the wilderness rather than Solomon's ornate temple (1 Kings 6:14), signaling that true sanctity emanates from Christ's finished work, not vaulted ceilings. The Lutheran tradition maintained some liturgical elements—candles, vestments—to preserve continuity, reflected in the Augsburg Confession (XV)'s call for orderly ceremonies. Meanwhile, the Reformed tradition embraced total iconoclasm, focusing on preaching (2 Timothy 4:2) and congregational singing (Colossians 3:16), emphasizing direct access to God without priestly intermediaries. Churches like Geneva's St. Pierre Cathedral became hub for exhorted public scripture readings and sermons rather than sacramental drama. This "bare stage" design influenced colonial American meeting houses—simple timber frames with central pulpits—underscoring communal responsibility for worship (Hebrews 10:25). Architectural modifications— removal of cruciform plans, creation of centralized auditoria— reflected egalitarian ecclesiology, symbolizing that every believer shares in priestly ministry (1 Peter 2:9). The iconoclastic ethos underscored that sacred space is defined not by physical embellishments but by God's Word and Spirit, a principle that would later inform modern worship venues. As these stripped designs dominated Protestant realms, debates emerged over reintroducing aesthetic elements, setting the stage for modern expressions of sacred space in section 7.5.5.

**7.5.5 Modern Mega-Churches, Digital Venues, and the Question of Presence** The twentieth and twenty-first centuries have witnessed unprecedented shifts in sacred architecture and presence with mega-churches and digital venues redefining temple concepts. Mega-churches such as Lakewood Church in Houston and Saddleback Church in California incorporate arenas seating tens of thousands, outfitted with stadium-style seating, jumbo screens, and professional lighting, creating immersive worship environments that resemble secular concert halls more than traditional sanctuaries. This shift reflects a postmodern preference for experiential engagement: high-definition projection of scripture passages, contemporary praise bands, and sermon theaters facilitate multisensory worship, reminiscent of Ezekiel's temple vision where sensory elements signify divine glory (Ezekiel 43:2). Digital venues, born from pandemic-driven necessity, birthed virtual worship models—live-streamed services, online communion kits, and interactive chat-based prayer rooms—making sacred presence accessible to homebound or geographically distant believers (Matthew 18:20). Churches now invest in multimedia production teams, equating camera operators with Levites who safeguard and transmit divine presence. Virtual reality worship experiments allow avatars to enter simulated cathedral spaces, echoing Genesis 28:17's "This is none other than the house of God," albeit in digital form. Yet questions arise: Does digital participation constitute genuine sacred presence, or is physical proximity to other believers indispensable (Hebrews 10:24–25)? Hybrid models—simultaneous in-person and online gatherings—seek to integrate both, encouraging "digital ushers" to facilitate online fellowship as Levites distributed temple responsibilities. Architectural design in newer churches often incorporates flexible seating, networked video walls, and acoustic engineering, blurring distinctions between stage and sanctuary. Despite technological advances, the theological anchor remains that "where two or three are gathered" affirms presence, whether physical or virtual (Matthew 18:20). This reality challenges congregations to discern how corporate identity forms in digital contexts and how sacraments—baptism, communion—adapt when participants cannot gather physically (1 Corinthians 11:26). Modern debates over "megachurch syndrome"—consumerism, lack of pastoral intimacy—mirror Reformation tensions over form and substance. These contemporary developments illustrate how sacred space evolves in tandem with cultural and technological shifts, calling believers to test new forms against biblical temple principles as they navigate politicized dispute over holy-site custody and pilgrimage, a theme developed in section 7.5.6.

### 7.5.6 Archaeology, Tourism, and the Politics of Holy-Site Custody

Ezekiel's millennial temple and Solomon's ancient shrine remain subjects of archaeological inquiry, with digs at Jerusalem's Temple Mount and megasites in Qumran offering insights into sacred space's evolution. Excavations beneath the Dome of the Rock—traditionally overlaying the site of the First and Second Temples—reveal layers of Herodian masonry and unearth ritual baths (mikva'ot), highlighting how pilgrims purified before worship (David E. Johnson, "Mikva'ot in Jerusalem," *Bulletin of the American Schools of Oriental Research* 295). These findings feed both theological reflection and modern political debates, as Jewish, Christian, and Muslim claims converge on Mount Moriah (2 Chronicles 3:1; Genesis 22:2). Pilgrimage tourism to the Western Wall and Church of the Holy Sepulchre drives local economies, with permit systems and custodial arrangements reflecting complex interfaith agreements like the Status Quo accord (Derek Flood, *Political and Religious Rivalries at the Holy Sepulchre*). Archaeological discoveries outside Jerusalem—like Hezekiah's Siloam Tunnel and the Pool of Siloam—draw international pilgrims to lesser-known holy sites, illustrating how sacred history infuses contemporary geography. Security checkpoints, heritage site regulations, and UNESCO designations amplify tensions over who has authority to manage excavations and tourism, often leading to conflicts between state, religious authorities, and international bodies. Pilgrimage operators negotiate with Israeli, Palestinian, and Jordanian authorities, reflecting Zechariah 14:21's vision of the land offering ritual purity for all, yet current politics complicate access. Innovations like virtual tours of ancient temple reconstructions democratize pilgrimage, allowing global audiences to experience sacred spaces without physical travel, but raise questions about authenticity and commodification of holy sites. Academic institutions collaborate with local religious leaders to conduct "community archaeology," seeking to respect local sentiments while unveiling the strata of worship history, demonstrating Matthew 7:12's "do to others as you would have them do to you" ethos. These archaeological and touristic engagements remind believers that sacred space carries both spiritual weight and political ramifications, requiring wisdom to navigate covenantal heritage in a fractious modern context. As these historical and political factors converge, readers are prepared to see how sacrifice, ethics, and mission interconnect, which marks the transition to section 7.6.

# 7.6 Sacrifice, Ethics, and Contemporary Mission

### 7.6.1 Environmental Stewardship as Priestly Guardianship of Creation
Biblical temple narratives underscore humanity's role as caretakers—interpreted in Leviticus 25:23 as God's appointed

stewards—encouraging churches to embrace environmentalism as contemporary priestly service. Genesis 2:15 enjoins humankind to "till and keep" the garden, foreshadowing ecological responsibilities that extend beyond millennial visions into present-day ministry. Contemporary churches launch Creation Care teams, integrating "green Sabbath" initiatives—community garden projects and tree-planting events—that mirror Ezekiel's millennial river nourishing land (Ezekiel 47:12). These efforts align with Psalm 24:1–2's affirmation that "the earth is the Lord's," challenging congregations to view climate action as corporate worship. Seminaries incorporate eco-theology courses, teaching future pastors that biblical anthropology includes environmental ethics, drawing on Colossians 1:16's note that all things were created through Christ. Institutions adopt sustainable building practices—LEED-certified sanctuaries, solar panels, rainwater harvesting—showing that sanctuary spaces can reflect ecological holiness. Through partnerships with NGOs, churches sponsor clean water wells in developing regions, living out Psalm 23:2's fresh water symbolism in tangible relief. These environmental ministries also serve as evangelistic bridges: providing relief during natural disasters, they demonstrate Luke 10:34's compassion, opening hearts to the gospel. By framing environmentalism as priestly guardianship, congregations avoid extreme eco-paganism and instead situate creation care within a covenantal worldview that anticipates Ezekiel 47's flourishing earth. As believers act as ecological priests, they model how sacred space includes all creation, connecting to broader implications for holy land advocacy.

**7.6.2 Holy Land Advocacy: Peacemaking Principles for Sacred Geography** Churches today engage Holy Land advocacy by applying peacemaking principles rooted in biblical justice (Amos 5:24) to Israeli-Palestinian conflict. Drawing on Matthew 5:9's beatitude—"Blessed are the peacemakers"—followers of Jesus support nonviolent reconciliation initiatives that bring Jewish, Christian, and Muslim leaders together for dialogue. Organizations like the Israeli-Palestinian Bereaved Families Forum embody Micah 6:8's call to "act justly, love mercy," as families from both sides advocate for mutual recognition of suffering. Interfaith prayer gatherings at the Western Wall and Al-Aqsa compound reflect shared reverence for Genesis 22:2's "mount of the Lord," while emphasizing shared human dignity (Genesis 1:27). Churches partner with local NGOs providing vocational training to youth in the West Bank and Jerusalem's mixed neighborhoods, illustrating Luke 4:19's mission to "proclaim liberty to the captives" in socio-economic contexts. Pastors organize road trips that follow the Via Dolorosa and Shepherd's Field, combining pilgrimage with charitable acts—feeding refugees, visiting clinics—demonstrating Jeremiah 29:7's instruction to seek the welfare of the city. Academic conferences on biblical archaeology promote responsible research that respects both Jewish and Palestinian narratives, fostering Ephesians 4:2–3's "unity of the Spirit." Advocacy campaigns urge politicians to support two-state solutions or international frameworks ensuring justice, balancing God's love for all inhabitants (Joshua 24:15) with recognition of Israel's security needs. These efforts reflect 1 Peter 2:17's directive to "honor everyone, love the brotherhood, fear God, honor the emperor," adapting it to a context where multiple sovereignties overlap. By adopting these peacemaking principles, churches stake a prophetic claim on sacred geography, challenging worshipers to see holy land beyond boundaries and barriers, transitioning to reflect on animal sacrifice ethics.

### 7.6.3 Animal Sacrifice, Animal Rights, and Theological Anthropology

Modern debates over animal rights challenge traditional understandings of biblical sacrifice, prompting reexamination of theological anthropology concerning humanity's dominion role (Psalm 8:6). While Levitical codes prescribed animal offerings (Leviticus 1–7) to atone for sin, contemporary scholars ask whether these rites respect God's creation or perpetuate violence. Amillennialists observe that Christ's once-for-all sacrifice (Hebrews 10:10–14) renders ongoing animal offerings unnecessary, framing Old Testament sacrifices as temporary types rather than normative practice. Yet they caution against dismissing the sacrificial system's deeper message: that sin's penalty is severe, requiring death to restore broken relationships (Romans 6:23). In light of modern sensitivities, churches emphasize spiritual substitution rather than literal shedding of blood, focusing on ethical living as "sacrifices of praise" (Hebrews 13:15). Pastoral guidance instructs congregants to treat animals with compassion—reflecting Proverbs 12:10's assertion that "the righteous care for the needs of their animals"— while acknowledging that biblical contexts permitted sacrifice for atonement. Educational seminars on creation care include discussions on sustainable farming, ethical consumption, and stewardship of livestock, modeling Genesis 1:26–28's balanced dominion. Animal rescue ministries partner with veterinarians to reduce suffering, teaching communities that Christian love extends to all living beings (Matthew 10:29–31). This nuanced position avoids simplistic condemnation of biblical practices while affirming evolving moral understanding, paving the way to consider how urban planning and temple-shaped community spaces realize sacred space today.

### 7.6.4 Urban Planning and "Temple-Shaped" Community Spaces

Urban planners influenced by biblical principles seek to create "temple-shaped" community spaces—areas that foster relational worship, communal justice, and aesthetic beauty—mirroring the temple's role as a cultural pivot (Jeremiah 7:4; Romans 12:2). Projects like "City Sanctuaries" in São Paulo and Nairobi design mixed-use neighborhoods centered around public plazas where worship gatherings take place alongside markets, echoing Psalm 122:1–2's exhortation to pray for the peace of cities. These developments incorporate green corridors representing tree-of-life imagery (Revelation 22:2), providing parks where people gather for rest and reflection, embodying the Sabbath's restorative ethos (Mark 2:27). Worship spaces—multi-faith chapels, concert arenas— occupy central nodes, reflecting Isaiah 56:7's vision of a "house of prayer for all nations," while surrounding areas host clinics, schools, and community centers, illustrating Isaiah 58:7's integration of worship with compassion. Residential designs include communal courtyards that foster neighborly interaction, fulfilling Romans 12:10's call to "love one another with brotherly affection." Street designs minimize vehicular traffic in favor of pedestrian pathways, signifying holiness through slower, more intentional movement, akin to pilgrims approaching a temple (Psalm 42:1–2). Architects use light—skylights, translucent materials—to symbolize divine presence, recalling Revelation 21:23's "the Lamb is its light." Faith-based organizations collaborate with city councils to integrate ethical zoning laws—requiring affordable housing within gentrified neighborhoods—modeling Leviticus 25:10's Jubilee principles in modern context. Through participatory design workshops, community members co-create spaces that reflect shared values of justice (Micah 6:8) and beauty (Psalm 27:4), ensuring that "temple-shaped" spaces remain responsive to local cultures. These urban worship laboratories epitomize how sacred space can shape civic life, culminating in our discussion of interfaith dialogue on contested holy sites in the next subsection.

**7.6.5 Interfaith Dialogues on Mount Moriah: Jewish, Christian, Muslim Claims** Mount Moriah—site of Abraham's binding of Isaac (Genesis 22:2) and Solomon's temple (2 Chronicles 3:1)—serves as a focal point for interfaith dialogue, requiring nuanced engagement that honors Jewish, Christian, and Muslim connections. Jewish tradition identifies Moriah as the Temple Mount, where the First and Second Temples stood, sanctifying it as the holiest site in Judaism (Mishna, Yoma 1:1). Christians revere Moriah as the place where Jesus taught (Matthew 23:37–39) and as an eschatological center in Revelation 21:2–3. Muslims venerate it as Haram al-Sharif, the location of the Dome of the Rock and Al-Aqsa Mosque, where Muhammad's Night Journey ascended to heaven (Qur'an 17:1). Interfaith dialogues often convene at neutral venues, such as the King David Hotel's conference rooms, where clergy and scholars explore shared reverence while acknowledging divergent claims. Participants study Abraham's act of obedience (Genesis 22:9–10), recognizing that it prefigures Isaac's prophetic role for Jews and Ishmael's connection to Islam. Christian theologians emphasize Jesus' fulfillment of temple typology (John 2:19–21), seeking common ground with Jewish participants who see the temple's destruction (Matthew 24:1–2) as a divine chastisement yet hope for future restoration (Ezekiel 40–48). Muslim scholars contribute Qur'anic insights, referencing Abraham's significance as a patriarch of Islam (Qur'an 2:124–130), inviting dialogue on covenantal continuities. These conversations respect diverse hermeneutical lenses, examining texts like 2 Chronicles 3:1–2 and Qur'an 2:125–129, seeking applications for peace and mutual recognition. Practical outcomes include joint heritage preservation initiatives, where experts document and protect archaeological layers without endorsing exclusive claims. Tourism ministries collaborate with faith leaders to create guided tours that tell multi-layered narratives—Jeremiah 31:31–34's inclusive vision—highlighting how diverse traditions converge and diverge on Mount Moriah. Security protocols at the site, governed by the Status Quo, require representatives from all three faiths to negotiate access, illustrating John 13:35's vision of Christians loving neighbors as Christ commanded. As interfaith dialogue fosters deeper respect, it models how ancient sacred spaces can become platforms for reconciliation, concluding our exploration of ethics and mission by segueing into comparative synthesis in the following chapter.

## Conclusion

In surveying the biblical trajectory from tabernacle to heavenly city and the rich tapestry of Christian reflection on temple and sacrifice, one fact remains clear: all visions converge on the conviction that God desires to dwell with His people. Whether one looks forward to a millennial altar where rivers issue forth from a renewed sanctuary, hears the echo of global worship reforming moral structures, or finds Christ's presence sufficient wherever His followers gather, the underlying hope is the restoration of unbroken fellowship between Creator and creation. Debates over future animal offerings, rebuilt walls, and guarded courts reflect deeper questions about how divine holiness relates to human culture and how prophetic promises unfold. Yet even amid these differences, Scripture's refrain resounds: "Behold, the dwelling place of God is among mortals" (Revelation 21:3). As we leave behind detailed analyses of architecture, sacrifice, and sacred space, we carry forward a profound reminder that every liturgical gesture, ethical decision, and communal gathering participates in an ongoing story of reconciliation. In every age, the church remains called to embody the presence of the true Temple, anticipating the day when the veil is forever removed, and worship will be "unending, unhindered, and universal."

# Chapter 8 - Resurrection and Judgment

The Christian story reaches its climax in the twin realities of resurrection and judgment—events that define the destiny of every human soul and the renewal of all things. From the earliest promise that death would not have the final word (Genesis 3:15) to the apostolic affirmation that Christ's rising from the grave secures "new birth into a living hope" (1 Peter 1:3), Scripture weaves a tapestry of divine power that transforms mortality into immortality. This transformative promise finds expression in Jesus' own words: "Do not marvel at this, for an hour is coming when all who are in the tombs will hear his voice and come out" (John 5:28–29). Yet resurrection does not stand alone; it dovetails with the solemn reality of God's righteous judgment, when every secret deed—whether of oppression or mercy—will be laid bare before the throne (Ecclesiastes 12:14; Revelation 20:12). For believers, these truths generate both awe and comfort: awe at the holiness that demands accountability, and comfort in the assurance that Christ has conquered death on our behalf (1 Corinthians 15:54–57). Across history, Christians have wrestled with how to arrange these climactic events in the flow of God's redemptive work—debating whether the faithful rise before a thousand years of blessing, whether all await the final trumpet together, or whether Christ's current reign in heaven invites us to live in the tension of "already/not-yet" victory. In every case, these diverse interpretations sharpen the church's worship, ethics, and mission: if death is defeated, then suffering can be borne with hope, and if judgment is certain, then noble service and compassionate justice gain eternal significance. This chapter explores how different eschatological perspectives navigate the coming of resurrection and the manifestation of divine justice, revealing how these doctrines shape Christian hope and mobilize believers to live as citizens of a kingdom yet to be fully revealed.

# 8.1 Premillennial Two-Stage Resurrection

**8.1.1 Righteous Before the Millennium** Premillennialists teach that at Christ's second coming, believers who have died or been living are raised to reign with Him in the millennium, fulfilling Jesus' promise that "those who are considered worthy of taking part in that age and in the resurrection from the dead" will inherit eternal life (Luke 20:35–36). This first stage, often termed the "first resurrection," includes all who have believed in Christ throughout church history, from Abel onward (Hebrews 11). Paul describes this transformation when the dead in Christ will rise first and those alive will be "caught up" to meet the Lord in the air, ensuring that all the righteous enter the kingdom together (1 Thessalonians 4:16–17). Revelation 20:4–6 also situates this first resurrection before the millennium, noting that the souls of martyrs are "free from death" and "priests of God," indicating their exalted status even before the thousand-year reign begins. Since Daniel 12:2 speaks of "many who sleep in the dust of the earth" awakening, premillennialists interpret that as referring specifically to godly sleepers rising at Christ's return, distinguishing them from the wicked who come forth later. The righteous, clothed in imperishable bodies, will govern the earth under Christ's direct rule (Revelation 20:6), demonstrating justice and peace in a restored creation. During this millennial reign, these resurrected saints will guard against renewed rebellion, as Scripture warns that Satan is bound to prevent deception (Revelation 20:2). The resurrected righteous reign with Christ in a world free from direct demonic rule, fulfilling promises like Isaiah 11:9 that "the earth will be full of the knowledge of the LORD." Their glorified bodies will no longer experience death or suffering, echoing 1 Corinthians 15:54's declaration that death is swallowed up in victory. By entering the millennium in a state of resurrection, the righteous validate Christ's victory over the grave, preparing to administer divine rule until the final rebellion. As believers anticipate this first resurrection, their hope fuels present perseverance, knowing that present trials cannot compare with the glory yet to be revealed (Romans 8:18). This resurrection event establishes the righteous in a distinct phase of history, making way for the unredeemed dead to be raised after the millennium, which leads to examining the martyrs specifically.

**8.1.2 Tribulation Martyrs and the "First Resurrection" (Revelation 20:4–6)** Within the premillennial framework, a subset of believers experiences death during the seven-year tribulation, and their resurrection is uniquely associated with the first resurrection. Revelation 20:4–6 differentiates these martyrs as those who "had not worshiped the beast" and "had not received his mark," who live and reign with Christ a thousand years. Premillennialists hold that these martyrs will rise at Christ's return, even though some may have been raised or translated earlier during tribulation events (Daniel 12:1–2; Revelation 11:11–12). Their resurrection is immediate, bypassing the intermediate state to partake in the inaugural victory over death, demonstrating Christ's faithfulness to preserve His people through the end-time persecution (Matthew 24:9–13). The fact that they become "priests of God and of Christ" indicates that, in the millennium, they function in a priestly capacity, interceding for the nations and guiding spiritual life under Christ's headship (Revelation 20:6). Premillennialists emphasize that these tribulation servants—two witnesses (Revelation 11:3–12), the 144,000 Jewish evangelists (Revelation 7:1–8)—serve as catalysts for large-scale Jewish repentance, linking their martyrdom to Paul's picture of "a remnant chosen by grace" (Romans 11:5). Their resurrection celebrates divine vindication: Christ acknowledges their testimonies before assembling all nations at the judgment seat (Matthew 25:31–46). The resurrection of martyrs also fulfills Jesus' words that "the righteous will shine like the sun in the kingdom of their Father" (Matthew 13:43), indicating that their reward begins immediately at the millennium. By focusing on these martyrs, premillennialists underscore God's regard for those who endure opposition, confirming that no suffering for Christ is in vain (1 Corinthians

15:58). Their first resurrection serves as both a vindication and a warning: it highlights the blessings for obedience and the dire consequences for refusing allegiance to Christ's adversary. As this subset enters the millennium, attention soon turns to the resurrection of the wicked after the thousand years, which demands careful scrutiny.

**8.1.3 Wicked After the Millennium** Premillennialists teach that following the thousand-year reign, Satan is released to raise a final opposition, culminating in the resurrection of the wicked dead who face judgment (Revelation 20:7–10). At Christ's return, the wicked who have died or survived into the millennium remain in their mortal state, subject to death or aging until their subsequent resurrection. Daniel 12:2 anticipates this dual resurrection when "some to everlasting contempt and disgrace, but the wise to eternal life," marking a stark division. When Satan is loosed, he deceives the nations—Gog and Magog—and gathers them for battle, prompting divine judgment that consumes the rebels with fire from heaven (Revelation 20:9). Only then will the rest of the dead be raised to stand at the Great White Throne (Revelation 20:12). This second resurrection involves unbelievers, including tribulation survivors who refuse Christ and the numerous wicked whose lives spanned pre-tribulation, tribulation, and millennial periods. Their resurrection bodies, like the righteous, are imperishable yet destined for condemnation, underscoring that bodily resurrection itself does not guarantee salvation (John 5:28–29). The final defeat of Satan, coupled with the wicked's resurrection, ensures cosmic justice— sin's origins, agents, and adherents receive fitting retribution (Revelation 20:14–15). Premillennialists stress that this judgment vindicates God's holiness and moral governance, demonstrating that rebellion even after a thousand years of peace remains willful. The timing of this resurrection confirms a sequential pattern: first, the righteous inherit the kingdom, then the wicked arise to face the "second death" (Revelation 20:14). This sequence contrasts sharply with monolithic resurrection views, emphasizing that premillennialism retains a sharp temporal separation between the righteous and the wicked. As the wicked face final condemnation, consideration shifts to those millennial citizens who will pass into the new heavens and new earth, addressing whether they undergo a change or a secondary resurrection.

### 8.1.4 Millennium-Age Believers: Change or Second Raising? A
point of debate among premillennialists concerns believers who
enter the millennium alive and whether they experience bodily
change or a future resurrection. Some argue that living believers will
be "changed" at Christ's return, receiving glorified bodies instantly
so they can reign with resurrected saints (1 Corinthians 15:51–52),
thus eliminating any need for a subsequent resurrection. According
to this view, passage like 1 Corinthians 15 describes a
transformation rather than a post-millennial resurrection, implying
no second death for those glorified at the start of the millennium.
Others hold that millennial believers, though transformed, will still
participate in the first resurrection if they die during the thousand
years, receiving resurrection for glorified bodies in sequence with
the martyrs. This perspective preserves a clear two-stage pattern, as
Daniel 12:1–2 and Revelation 20:4–6 seem to imply distinct
resurrections for different groups. Regardless of the mechanism,
believers living at the millennium's dawn share in the blessings of
the first resurrection, whether by immediate change or by later
bodily raising. Their immortality reflects Jesus' promise that
"whoever lives and believes in me shall never die" (John 11:26),
anticipating an era where death no longer incurs power. The precise
timing of transformation—whether instantaneous at "the sound of
the last trumpet" that signals the first resurrection (1 Corinthians
15:52) or spread across a millennial era—remains debated, yet all
affirm that these believers do not face the second death. Their
continuity into the millennial reign illustrates God's gracious intent
to allow faithful servants to witness the kingdom directly, fulfilling
Luke 12:43's promise that the faithful servant stands "ready" for the
master's return. As these millennium-age saints fulfill
administrative and worship roles, their status contrasts with the
wicked's inevitable resurrection and judgment after the millennium,
which brings the final conflagration.

### 8.1.5 Satan's Release, Gog-Magog, and the Final Conflagration
After a thousand years of righteous rule, premillennialism posits that
Satan is released from his prison to test the nations labeled Gog and
Magog, initiating a final rebellion (Revelation 20:7–9). This event
echoes Ezekiel 38–39's prophecies against Gog, recontextualized in
the end-time landscape where tribulation survivors and nonbelievers
follow Satan one last time. The assembled armies surround the
beloved city—symbolic of Christ's millennial capital—until divine

fire descends, consuming them and thwarting Satan's final scheme. This cataclysmic judgment demonstrates that even a restored creation can rebel, highlighting human depravity and spiritual agency (Romans 1:21–23). Immediately following this revolt, Scripture records a great white throne judgment where the wicked dead are raised and judged, culminating in casting them into the lake of fire (Revelation 20:11–15). The final conflagration, often termed the "second death," consummates divine justice, dissolving all vestiges of rebellion as fire and brimstone eradicate the works of darkness (2 Peter 3:7–10). This cosmic purging also refines creation for the new heavens and new earth (Revelation 21:1), reminiscent of 2 Peter 3's purifying fire motif that both purges and prepares. Premillennialists assert that the final conflagration verifies Revelation 20:14's declaration that death and Hades themselves are thrown into the lake of fire, eradicating sin's last foothold. While some view this as annihilation, most historic premillennialists affirm eternal conscious punishment, arguing that a literal lake of fire aligns with Christ's warnings (Matthew 25:41–46) and Paul's depiction of everlasting destruction (2 Thessalonians 1:9). The inevitability of this final conflagration underscores the stakes of spiritual decisions, prompting both reverence and urgency in evangelism. As fire consumes all unclean elements, attention turns to how Daniel's and Paul's writings help harmonize this chronology with the unfolding plan, addressed in the next subsection.

**8.1.6 Chronological Harmonization with Daniel 12 and 1 Corinthians 15** Premillennialists seek to harmonize Daniel 12's description of "many who sleep in the dust of the earth shall awake" with Paul's teaching on the order of resurrection in 1 Corinthians 15. Daniel 12:2 seems to indicate that the righteous rise first to "everlasting life," while the wicked rise to "shame and everlasting contempt," prompting debate over whether these refer to two separate chronological events or a simultaneous general resurrection. Premillennial chronology resolves this by describing two distinct resurrections: the righteous at Christ's coming (Luke 14:14; 1 Thessalonians 4:16), correlating with Daniel 12:2's first phrase, and the wicked after the millennium, fulfilling the latter phrase. Paul's "last trumpet" sequence (1 Corinthians 15:52) is understood to mark the instant transformation or resurrection of the righteous at the parousia, aligning with Revelation 11:15's "seventh trumpet" pronouncement of Christ's kingdom. This trumpet motif recurs when trumpets summon martyrs to life (Revelation 11:15–19) and when the heavenly host unleashes wrath, indicating a consistent apocalyptic pattern. By situating Daniel's prophecy within the broader sequence—first resurrection, millennial reign, second resurrection—premillennialists maintain canonical harmony: texts like Matthew 25:31–46 and John 5:28–29 function within this timeline without contradiction. This chronological framework underscores how God's plan unfolds in progressive stages: sealing, wrath, millennial peace, final rebellion, and ultimate new creation. Such harmonization also addresses divergent interpretations of terms like "everlasting contempt" (Daniel 12:2) and "perish" (John 3:16), ascribing them to second resurrection judgment rather than immediate post-mortem condemnation. Through this synthesis, premillennialism preserves both Daniel's and Paul's emphases on bodily resurrection, validating the certainty of life after death for the righteous and the irrevocable fate of the wicked. This comprehensive sequence equips believers to live in anticipation of each eschatological milestone, setting the stage for contrasting these views with the singular resurrection models of postmillennialism and amillennialism.

## 8.2 Postmillennial and Amillennial Single Resurrection

### 8.2.1 Timing at the Last Trumpet (1 Corinthians 15:52; 1 Thessalonians 4:16) Both postmillennialists and amillennialists hold that there will be a single general resurrection of all the dead at Christ's return, marked by the sounding of the last trumpet. Paul's words in 1 Corinthians 15:52—"in a moment, in the twinkling of an eye, at the last trumpet. For the trumpet will sound, and the dead will be raised imperishable"—provide the primary textual basis. Likewise, 1 Thessalonians 4:16–17 depicts the Lord descending with a loud command, the voice of the archangel, and the trumpet of God, where those who have died in Christ rise first to meet the Lord. Postmillennialists interpret "last trumpet" as a chronological indicator that follows the golden-age triumph of the gospel but precedes the final judgment. They do not envision a separate tribulation resurrection but see these texts as describing the singular moment when Christ gathers all—righteous and wicked—for immediate resurrection and judgment. Amillennialists likewise

affirm that there is no intermediate resurrection but instead an eschatological event where every individual stands before Christ. The Last Trumpet's function across both views communicates that God's timeline moves inexorably toward this culminating blast, which shatters the permanence of death (1 Corinthians 15:26). Since Christ's parousia is visible to all, the trumpet becomes a universal summons difficult to miss, underscoring the public nature of the resurrection. Postmillennialists often tie this event to Matthew 24:30–31, where Jesus says the Son of Man will send His angels "with a loud trumpet call" to gather His elect, indicating that the resurrection and rapture are one and the same. Amillennialists emphasize that the "dead in Christ" rising first refers to the righteous dead among all the dead, demonstrating that resurrection order is based on salvation status but occurs in the same event. Both camps reject a secret rapture separate from general resurrection, arguing that Christ's return and the trumpet blast are public and visible (John 5:28–29). Recognizing this single trumpet moment leads to evaluating the nature of the resurrected bodies believers will receive, a topic we develop next.

**8.2.2 Nature of Glorified Bodies: Continuity and Transformation** Postmillennial and amillennial theologians agree that resurrection bodies share both continuity with our present bodies and radical transformation into glorified existence. Paul's discourse in 1 Corinthians 15:42–44 explains that "the body that is sown perishable is raised imperishable... sown in dishonor, raised in glory... sown in weakness, raised in power... is sown a natural body, raised a spiritual body," indicating a continuity of personal identity—"sown" and "raised" refer to the same "body" yet transformed. Postmillennialists see these verses as affirming that glorified bodies will resemble Christ's resurrection body; still recognizable yet endowed with supernatural attributes— incorruption, immortality, glory, adaptability to every environment without fatigue. They point to Luke 24:39, where the risen Jesus invites Thomas to touch His hands and side, showing continuity of physicality even as He passes through locked doors (John 20:19). Amillennialists emphasize that "spiritual" does not mean immaterial but that the body is governed by Spirit instead of flesh, making it imperishable while retaining real, tangible qualities. The glorified body will not be subject to pain, aging, or sickness, as Isaiah 25:8 prophesies that God will "swallow up death forever." Such bodies possess the ability to travel instantly across distances (John 20:19–26) and perhaps reflect the "glory of God" in luminous form (Matthew 17:2). Additionally, post- and amillennialists affirm that interpersonal relationships—marriage, friendship, familial bonds—will be deepened rather than erased, since Jesus said in heaven people will be "like the angels" in not marrying but existing in perpetual union with God's family (Matthew 22:30), suggesting continuity of community even as earthly institutions cease. The transition to glorified state will leave no memory of sin or shame, aligning with Romans 8:29's promise to conform believers to the image of God's Son. Neither group expects reptilian or ethereal ghosts; rather, resurrection bodies will be tangible enough to eat (Luke 24:41–43) while being unfettered by material constraints. This biblical synthesis informs pastoral reassurance, as bereaved families trust that loved ones continue in conscious fellowship with Christ (Philippians 1:23). With the transformed body in view, discussion shifts to how resurrection shapes present "already/not-yet" experiences of victory over death.

### 8.2.3 "Already/Not-Yet" Victory over Death (John 5:24–29)

Both postmillennial and amillennial traditions emphasize the "already/not-yet" paradigm regarding resurrection and judgment, stressing that believers experience victory over death spiritually now while awaiting physical consummation at the last trumpet. Jesus' words in John 5:24—"whoever hears my word and believes him who sent me has eternal life. He does not come into judgment but has passed from death to life"—indicate that believers possess eternal life before bodily resurrection, marking a present deliverance from death's penalty. Paul further underscores this in Romans 6:9: "Christ, having been raised from the dead, dies no more; death no longer has dominion over him." Consequently, post- and amillennialists teach that believers partake in Christ's resurrection power now through regeneration and sanctification (Romans 6:4). They cite passages like 2 Corinthians 1:9–10 where Paul finds relief "from deadly peril" as a foretaste of future deliverance. The future resurrection thus secures and confirms the already-given eternal life, illustrating that present suffering and tribulation cannot sever believers from the love of God that raised Christ (Romans 8:35–39). This duality equips Christians to stand firm in persecution, knowing that a bodily resurrection awaits beyond the grave (Philippians 3:20–21). Postmillennialists see societal advances as partial manifestations of this victory, contending that ethical and cultural reforms reflect Christ's triumph over darkness (Colossians 1:13–14). Amillennialists stress that while death remains a present reality—"the wages of sin is death" (Romans 6:23)—its sting is removed by spiritual union with Christ (1 Corinthians 15:55). This realization transforms funeral liturgies from lament over loss to celebration of victory, anchoring hope in resurrection certainty. As the chapter transitions to universal standing before Christ, these "already/not-yet" convictions confirm that final resurrection fulfills what has been accomplished at the cross.

### 8.2.4 Universal Standing Before Christ: Sheep–Goats Paradigm

Postmillennial and amillennial views share that the general resurrection leads immediately into universal judgment, employing the sheep–goats paradigm to illustrate separation based on deeds (Matthew 25:31–46). At the "Son of Man coming in His glory," all nations gather, and Christ sits on His glorious throne, a scene reminiscent of Daniel 7:13–14's Son of Man enthronement. The "sheep" on Christ's right, representing the righteous, inherit the kingdom because they clothed the naked, fed the hungry, and visited the imprisoned, evidencing faith's fruit (Matthew 25:35–36). The "goats" on the left, the unrighteous, face "eternal punishment" for failing to demonstrate compassion, underscoring that final judgment evaluates deeds as a verification of professed faith (2 Corinthians 5:10). Postmillennialists interpret this as indicating that Christ's kingdom impact among nations will result in moral accountability— even nations achieving positive reforms will be judged on how they've respected human dignity. Amillennialists emphasize that since all stand before Christ, there is no intermediate heavenly tribunal for believers (bema seat) versus bowl-of-wrath judgment for the damned; rather, all appear once before Christ's throne, attesting to a single resurrection and judgment event. They also note that this audience includes believers who may face additional "rewards" or "loss" based on works, even though their salvation is secure (1 Corinthians 3:12–15). The sheep–goats motif thus clarifies that the final verdict distinguishes between those who lived out the love of Christ and those who did not, demonstrating that faith necessarily expresses itself in compassion. This universal standing underscores the egalitarian aspect of judgment: Jew and Gentile, rich and poor, bond and free—no one escapes accounting for stewardship. As the crowd disperses according to verdict, focus shifts to how Israel's corporate resurrection hope (Romans 11:15) intersects with this universal paradigm in each eschatological view.

**8.2.5 Relation to Israel's "Life from the Dead" (Romans 11:15) in Each View** Romans 11:15's statement that "if their rejection brought reconciliation to the world, what will their acceptance be but life from the dead" carries different emphases for post- and amillennialists regarding corporate Israel's eschatological hope. Postmillennial interpreters see this passage as anticipating a future turning of ethnic Israel after the fullness of Gentile inclusion, emphasizing that Israel's national conversion will correspond with a broader spiritual resurrection influencing global blessing. They argue that this "life from the dead" symbolizes expansive gospel fruit when Jewish communities awaken to Messiah's identity, triggering accelerated kingdom growth. In contrast, amillennialists interpret "life from the dead" as corporate election's spiritual revitalization rather than literal national resurrection separate from the church. They understand Paul's olive-tree metaphor (Romans 11:16–24) to signify that Gentile inclusion provokes Jewish believers to jealousy, leading to a believing remnant entering the eschatological community. Both approaches affirm that Israel's restoration involves resurrection imagery, but postmillennialism highlights a future national miracle, while amillennialism emphasizes present spiritual continuity in the church's life. Premillennialists, though outside this subsection's scope, would read Romans 11 as combining both: a partial present restoration and an ultimate national resurrection during the first resurrection. The theological nuance here affects how churches pray for and engage Jewish communities: postmillennialists advocate mission strategies anticipating mass conversion events, while amillennialists focus on individual regeneration as part of the church's ongoing life. In both perspectives, Romans 11 propels congregations toward intercessory prayer—"Lord, send revival to Zion"—and contextualized outreach, ensuring that Israel's "life from the dead" remains a living hope rather than abstract doctrine. With corporate Israel's role clarified, attention turns to pastoral concerns as believers face death, grief, and martyrdom amid expectancy, detailed next.

**8.2.6 Pastoral Consolation: Bereavement, Martyrdom, and Hope** In both postmillennial and amillennial frameworks, pastoral care surrounding death and bereavement emphasizes the certainty of resurrection and the comfort found in Christ's victory over the grave. When a believer dies, congregations read 1 Thessalonians 4:15–18 at funerals, assuring mourners that the deceased are "with the Lord" until the Lord returns. Counseling ministries draw from Romans 8:38–39's affirmation that nothing can separate believers from Christ's love, applying it to situations of grief, loss, and martyrdom. In contexts of persecution, pastors encourage families of martyrs by citing Revelation 6:9–11, where souls under the altar cry out for justice, reminding them that deceased Christians live on as priests in heaven (Revelation 20:6). This heavenly identity offers solace, as it assures that even instrumental violence contributes to the believer's witness rather than annihilation. Prayer groups devote time to intercede for captive or suffering brothers and sisters with the expectation that they will "receive the crown of life" if they remain faithful (James 1:12). Preachers underscore 1 Corinthians 15:55— "O death, where is your victory? O death, where is your sting?"— demonstrating that even the final enemy has lost its ultimate power. For families grappling with unexpected or traumatic deaths—car accidents, wars, refugee crises—pastors emphasize that physical separation is temporary: Philippians 1:21's "to live is Christ, to die is gain" reframes loss as gain in Christ's eternal presence. Youth ministries create support networks where young people can share stories of grief and doubting faith, promoting open dialogue anchored in 2 Corinthians 1:3–4's promise that "God of all comfort" ministers in affliction. As congregations celebrate memorial services, they incorporate testimonies of transformed lives— illustrating that the gospel's power transcends death—providing tangible hope that fosters resilience. This pastoral response encourages believers to press on in mission, knowing their labors for Christ stand beyond the grave (1 Corinthians 15:58). With these pastoral concerns addressed, reflection shifts to how corporate judgment scenes encompass both resurrected saints and unsaved multitudes, as outlined in the following section.

## 8.3 Great White Throne and Bema Seat

### 8.3.1 Scope of Judgment: Angels, Nations, and Individual Believers
Biblical texts present multiple faceted judgments: the Great White Throne for the wicked (Revelation 20:11–15), the Bema Seat or Judgment Seat of Christ for believers (2 Corinthians 5:10),

and angelic judgments (1 Corinthians 6:3). Postmillennial and amillennial frameworks see these as aspects of the same universal judicial event or closely linked proceedings. At the Great White Throne, all the dead—small and great—stand before God, as earthly status carries no weight in heaven (Revelation 20:12). This scene encompasses every unsaved soul resurrected to face condemnation, underscoring God's impartial justice (Romans 2:11). Nations are included, fulfilling Matthew 25:31–46's sheep–goats separation, where collective corporate responsibility is evaluated—"Depart from me, you cursed… for I was hungry and you gave me no food" (Matthew 25:41–43). Angels, once cast from their first estate through rebellion, stand judged alongside humanity, for Jude 1:6 insists that they are "kept in eternal chains under gloomy darkness" awaiting final judgment. Paul's statement that "we must all appear before the judgment seat of Christ" (2 Corinthians 5:10) applies primarily to believers, indicating that their works will be evaluated for reward rather than for salvation. Some postmillennial interpreters see the Bema Seat as a separate event prior to the Great White Throne, occurring immediately after resurrection to assign rewards—crowns, positions in the kingdom—while amillennialists often merge the assessments, noting that both saved and unsaved stand before Christ's throne to receive either eternal life or wrath. The scope thus ranges from personal deeds to corporate ideologies, integrating individual moral accountability with broader social responsibilities. Judgment sits on "books" opened—scrolls of deeds, Book of Life—signifying exhaustive records of every action (Revelation 20:12). This holistic scope means that all realms— personal, communal, even demonic—fall under divine scrutiny, concluding that no hidden sin goes unnoticed (Ecclesiastes 12:14). As this universal scope clarifies, understanding the instruments of judgment—books, scrolls, and the Book of Life—becomes critical to grasp the mechanics of final verdicts.

**8.3.2 Books, Scrolls, and the Book of Life** Revelation 20:12 describes "books" opened at the Great White Throne, including the Book of Life and books recording deeds. Postmillennialists teach that these books symbolize comprehensive divine record-keeping— every word, deed, and thought is accounted for (Matthew 12:36–37). The Book of Life lists those whose names have been written before the foundation of the world (Revelation 13:8), indicating that salvation was planned eternally rather than decided post-mortem.

During judgment, those whose names are absent are "thrown into the lake of fire," signifying eternal separation. Books of deeds serve as evidence, providing a transparent basis for judgment—illustrating the principle that "God will bring every work into judgment" (Ecclesiastes 12:14). Amillennialists tend to emphasize that the righteous need not fear these deeds-accounts, for Christ's intercession eclipses condemnation (Hebrews 7:25). Postmillennialists, focusing on moral transformation in history, see the opened books as vindication of societal reforms—or exposure of injustice—underscoring that communal repentance can alter how society's story is written in divine archives. The law, once a "tutor" to bring people to Christ (Galatians 3:24), becomes judge, revealing sin's breadth and depth. Psalm 139:16's assertion that God's eyes saw "my unformed substance" and recorded "in your book all the days that were formed" expands this record-keeping to prenatal life, reinforcing that divine scrutiny begins from conception. Ancient Near Eastern parallels—Mesopotamian scribal archives—help illuminate how record metaphors would have resonated with Biblical audiences, revealing God as both divine scribe and just judge. This understanding sets the stage for discussing rewards and degrees of glory, since the opened books inform how outcomes are determined.

### 8.3.3 Rewards and Degrees of Glory

While the Great White Throne assigns eternal destinies to the wicked, the Bema Seat evaluates believers for rewards, not salvation (2 Corinthians 5:10; 1 Corinthians 3:12–15). Postmillennialists emphasize that rewards—crowns (stephanos)—signal recognition for faithful service: an "incorruptible crown" for disciplined living (1 Corinthians 9:24–25), a "crown of righteousness" for longing the Lord's appearance (2 Timothy 4:8), and a "crown of life" for enduring trials (James 1:12). Amillennialists likewise affirm varied crowns, noting that "many rooms" in the Father's house (John 14:2) suggests a spectrum of positional privilege within the one eternal kingdom. Degrees of glory derive from Paul's description in 1 Corinthians 15:40–41: celestial bodies compared to the sun, terrestrial to the moon, and "those are of the stars," implying that resurrected bodies radiate differing intensities of glory based on faithfulness. Similarly, 2 Corinthians 5:10 asserts that each receives "what is due for what he has done," indicating calibrated recompense. Postmillennialists stress that societal reforms and Christian influence on culture align with these rewards, as believers' global impact yields greater crowns, exemplifying Isaiah 49:8's notion that "in the time of my favor I answer you, and in the day of salvation I help you." Amillennialists emphasize that all crowns are temporary symbols, eventually surrendered to Christ (Revelation 4:10–11), underscoring that ultimate satisfaction arises from worship rather than reward retention. Yet rewards function to motivate holiness (1 John 3:3), informing present ethics: faithfulness in small tasks equates to broader kingdom responsibilities (Luke 19:17). The degrees of glory also foster communal encouragement: those whose ministries seem small receive assurance that "an abundant entrance" is prepared in the age to come (2 Peter 1:11). As believers reflect on these future rewards, attention naturally shifts to the fate of the wicked—second death and the lake of fire—concluding that just recompense awaits every soul.

**8.3.4 Second Death, Lake of Fire, and Theories of Eternal Punishment** At the Great White Throne judgment, the wicked face the "second death," defined as "the lake of fire" (Revelation 20:14–15). Postmillennialists generally interpret this as eternal conscious punishment, drawing from Jesus' teaching that the lake is "prepared for the devil and his angels" (Matthew 25:41), implying permanent separation from God. They reject annihilationism, since Scriptural language—"the smoke of their torment goes up forever and ever" (Revelation 14:11)—suggests unending experience. Amillennialists similarly affirm eternal conscious punishment, regarding Revelation's imagery as literal or best understood through apocalyptic symbolism that conveys infinite torment rather than finite annihilation. Conditionalists or annihilationists argue that terms like "destroy" (apollymi) sometimes mean "ruin" rather than "eternal torment," but mainstream post- and amillennial interpreters hold that Scripture's cumulative witness supports perpetual suffering for unrepentant souls (Mark 9:48). This view underscores divine holiness: a God who is infinitely just cannot undermine His own standards by reducing the punishment for infinite sin against infinite worth. The lake of fire's description—"the second death" (Revelation 20:14)—leads to the theological question of immortality: since immortality is "brought to light through the gospel" (1 Timothy 6:16–17), the wicked remain immortal only to suffer eternal separation. Debates over degrees of punishment—whether varied torments correspond to offenses—refer back to Luke

12:47–48's "greater sin, greater punishment," indicating proportional justice. Jesus warns about Gehenna as a place "where their worm does not die and the fire is not quenched" (Mark 9:48), evoking the perpetual nature of punishment. This sobering doctrine fuels urgency in evangelism: if eternal ruin awaits, proclamation of the gospel becomes a matter of life and death (Romans 10:9–10). As discussions of the lake of fire conclude, focus turns to how public verdicts vindicate God's justice and address the problem of evil, examined next.

**8.3.5 Public Vindication of God's Justice and the Problem of Evil**
The Great White Throne functions as God's cosmic court, publicly demonstrating that divine judgments are righteous and transparent, resolving questions about His justice and the problem of evil. When the "books" are opened and every secret deed laid bare (Revelation 20:12), it shows that God's judgments are based on comprehensive knowledge, affirming passages like Psalm 139:1–4, which declare that God knows all thoughts and intentions. The public nature of judgment vindicates God before creation: when the heavens and earth flee, and no place is found (Revelation 20:11), every being acknowledges God's sovereign deliberation. This satisfies prophetic desires for righteousness to be displayed before all nations (Psalm 96:10). The problem of evil—why a good God permits suffering— finds partial resolution as the final resurrection and judgment reveal all causes and effects, ensuring that victims receive justice and evildoers face retribution (Revelation 22:12). God's justice addresses cosmic scale injustices—martyrdom, genocide, systemic oppression—demonstrating that no crime against humanity remains unaccounted for (Jeremiah 31:15–17). This vindication also comforts believers, assuring them that "the righteous will shine" and "they will judge the world" (Daniel 12:3; 1 Corinthians 6:2–3), indicating that long-suffering faithfulness will not be in vain. Additionally, public vindication invites worship: when the living know that God's judgments are true and righteous (Revelation 19:1), all creation joins in praise. This culminates in Revelation 5:12–13's doxology before the Lamb, as every creature acknowledges God's holiness. Having seen God's justice publicly affirmed, the community can move toward worship and service, but also face the challenge of reconciliation and restoration—cepts that shape liturgical echoes, explored next.

**8.3.6 Liturgical Echoes: Confession, Absolution, and Anticipatory Verdicts** Judgment motifs resonate in Christian liturgy through confession and absolution, prefiguring the final verdict by offering believers assurance of divine mercy. In many traditions, the service begins with corporate confession—"I confess to almighty God..."—mirroring Micah 6:8's call to "seek justice," acknowledging sin before a holy God. The pastor then pronounces absolution—"Your sins are forgiven in the name of Christ"— echoing Romans 8:1's declaration: "There is therefore now no condemnation for those who are in Christ Jesus." These liturgical acts function as anticipatory glimpses of the Great White Throne's outcomes, as forgiven believers experience preliminary verdicts of righteousness (Matthew 6:14–15). Penitential rites, such as Ash Wednesday, utilize ashes to remind worshipers of mortality—"You are dust, and to dust you shall return" (Genesis 3:19)—prompting reflection on resurrection hope. Communion liturgy often includes prayers acknowledging unworthiness, followed by Christ's promise that "whoever comes to me I will never cast out" (John 6:37), anchoring believers in a forgiveness that transcends final judgment. Psalms like Psalm 51 ("Create in me a clean heart...") give vocal expression to repentance, anticipating Revelation's vision where washed robes signify victory (Revelation 7:14). Baptism functions as a public declaration of being "buried with Christ... raised to walk in newness of life" (Romans 6:4), symbolizing both past forgiveness and future resurrection. Easter liturgies re-enact the empty tomb's triumph, serving as Sunday-by-Sunday reminders that the final verdict has already been rendered in Christ's resurrection (1 Corinthians 15:13–14). Homilies frequently draw on Revelation's universal judgment scenes to exhort ethical living: "Blessed are you who are invited to the marriage supper of the Lamb" (Revelation 19:9), prompting readiness. These liturgical echoes sustain congregations in both humble confession and bold anticipation, bridging current worship with future eschatological realities, leading naturally into reflections on intermediate state and degrees of reward.

# 8.4 Intermediate State and "Souls Under the Altar"

### 8.4.1 Paradise vs. Hades: Conscious Experience before the Resurrection Both postmillennial and amillennial theologians teach that between death and the resurrection lies an intermediate state where souls experience conscious existence, either in "Paradise" for the righteous or "Hades" for the wicked. Luke 23:43 reveals that Jesus assured the thief on the cross he would be with Him in Paradise on that day, indicating immediate conscious fellowship with Christ post-mortem. Similarly, Philippians 1:23–24 conveys Paul's desire to "depart and be with Christ," suggesting no unconscious "soul sleep" theology. Conversely, the rich man in Luke 16:23, conscious in Hades and in torment, confirms that the unrighteous remain aware of their state. Early church fathers—Justin Martyr, Irenaeus—affirmed this dichotomy, with some church councils condemning the idea of soul sleep as incompatible with Tertullian's view that souls await bodily reunification. The parable of Lazarus and the rich man further indicates an impassable chasm between the blessed and the condemned (Luke 16:26). Postmillennialists hold that believers in Paradise await bodily resurrection, enjoying fellowship with angels and hearing God's praises, as reflected in Revelation 6:9–11 where souls of martyrs under the altar ask, "How long until you judge the inhabitants of the earth?" Amillennialists similarly teach that the intermediate state involves conscious fellowship with Christ or conscious separation, but they emphasize that this state is provisional, awaiting the final, general resurrection at the last trumpet. The intermediate state offers hope and accountability: believers comfort the grieving through assurance that loved ones are "present with the Lord" (2 Corinthians 5:8), while also reminding the living of the urgency of evangelism, given the reality of immediate assignment upon death. Understanding this preparatory phase clarifies why funerals include committal services praying for the departed's soul "to be bound in the bonds of life," reinforcing that human souls do not vanish at death. With souls in an awaiting condition, theological nuances arise—such as the state of "sacred slept saints" in Revelation 7—leading to historical considerations in the next subsection.

### 8.4.2 Historical Development: Sheol, Bosom of Abraham, and Patristic Views

The concept of the intermediate state develops from the Old Testament Sheol to New Testament depictions of Abraham's bosom and then nuances in patristic theology. In the Hebrew Scriptures, Sheol was the place of the dead, a shadowy realm where both righteous and wicked descended (Psalm 6:5; Ecclesiastes 9:10). Yet passages like 1 Samuel 2:6 suggest two compartments within Sheol—one for the godly, one for the wicked—hinting at early distinctions. By Jesus' time, Jewish thought had evolved to include Hades and Paradise divisions, as evidenced by Luke 16's parable and the Book of Enoch's elaborations on spiritual regions. Church fathers like Augustine, in *City of God* (Book 22), affirmed that the righteous's souls ascended to a place of comfort, while the wicked remained in torment. Some Eastern Fathers—Origen and Gregory of Nyssa—explored more allegorical readings, focusing on the soul's purification rather than physical places. Augustine countered soul sleep (per Aristotelian influence), arguing in *On the Soul and Its Origin* that the soul remains conscious after death. Cyril of Alexandria described Paradise as "a blessed state… awaiting the first resurrection," providing a catechetical foundation for medieval views. In contrast, Reformers like Luther and Calvin reaffirmed immediate entrance into Christ's presence for believers, rejecting purgatorial intermediary states that developed in medieval Catholicism. The medieval notion of Purgatory built atop these foundations, proposing that some souls undergo cleansing before attaining paradise. Both postmillennial and amillennial teachers largely reject Purgatory, citing Luke 23:43's "today" promise and 2 Timothy 1:18's statement that Paul's spirit is with Christ. The Protestant emphasis on "justification by faith" asserts that no further purification is necessary, supporting the doctrine of immediate resurrection reward or punishment. As these historical trajectories show, understanding ancient and patristic views helps clarify contemporary debates on post-mortem consciousness, transitioning next into contrasting theories of post-mortem purification.

### 8.4.3 Purgation, Rest, or Sleep? Comparative Theological Proposals

The intermediate state's nature incites debates: some propose that believers undergo purification (purgation), others that they rest spiritually, and still others that they "sleep" unconsciously. Purgatorial views, held by Roman Catholicism and some Eastern Orthodoxy strands, assert that certain venial sins remain at death and must be cleansed before seeing God (1 Corinthians 3:15). They cite 1 Corinthians 15:29's reference to baptism for the dead and 2 Maccabees 12:46 to justify prayers aiding departed souls. Postmillennialists and amillennialists, however, typically reject these arguments, emphasizing that Christ's atonement on the cross cleanses completely, leaving no residue requiring additional purification (Hebrews 10:14). "Soul sleep" theories, which claim the dead are unconscious until resurrection, find little favor among mainstream Protestants, as Scriptures like Philippians 1:23 and Luke 23:43 indicate awareness after death. Instead, most hold to "rest" models where faithful souls rest in Christ (Revelation 14:13) yet remain conscious, anticipating future resurrection. Some Eastern traditions nuance this as "intermediate repose," suggesting a peaceful state but with awareness. The Covenant theology tradition asserts that the interlude is a restful enjoyment of God's presence for the righteous (Revelation 6:9–11), while the wicked await final judgment in conscious torment. Socinian and Christadelphian groups advocate soul sleep, but their readings of texts like Ecclesiastes 9:5 ("the dead know nothing") are countered by broader New Testament data indicating consciousness. Comparative theological analyses must weigh biblical texts' nuances, historical theology's witness, and philosophical presuppositions about consciousness. While debates continue, the pastoral priority for both postmillennial and amillennial believers is to offer comfort and hope, recognizing that the intermediate state—whatever its precise nature—prepares souls for the final resurrection. With these perspectives in mind, focus shifts to how martyrs' intercession in Revelation underscores the interim presence of souls in worship contexts.

**8.4.4 Martyrs' Intercession (Revelation 6:9–11) and Its Eschatological Significance** Revelation 6:9–11 depicts martyrs under the altar crying out for God's justice, illuminating how they function in an intercessory capacity within the intermediate state. These souls, rather than resting passively, actively witness to God's righteousness, appealing for vindication of their blood—even as Christ intercedes for believers forever (Hebrews 7:25). Postmillennial interpreters view this as God acknowledging their pleas, since the ongoing progress of the gospel partly depends upon the perseverance of such testimonies. Amillennialists likewise emphasize that these martyrs demonstrate the continuity of worship in heaven, as Hebrews 12:1–2 describes a "cloud of witnesses" surrounding the faithful on earth, encouraging them to "run with endurance." The martyrs' posture under the altar evokes Genesis 8:20, where Noah builds an altar to offer burnt offerings after the flood, signifying renewal that emerges from sacrifice. Their petitions echo Psalm 94:1's cry for divine vengeance against the wicked, revealing that God's moral government will not leave injustices unpunished. The fact that they are told to "rest a little longer" until the full number of their fellow servants and brothers are martyred (Revelation 6:11) indicates that martyrdom continues until the appointed times, linking earthly suffering with eschatological purposes. This teaching encourages believers to see suffering not as meaningless but as contributing to the final consummation of God's redemptive plan. As long as martyrs rise in worship, their intercession aligns with Romans 8:34's assertion that the risen Christ presents them before the Father, affirming that their witness transcends temporal limits. Reflecting on their intercession shapes how the church prays for persecuted communities, recognizing that prayers of the faithful echo those of martyr saints. With this corporate vision of martyrs' intercession, attention turns to how these beliefs influence funeral rites and pastoral care, securing hope against nihilism and fear, themes developed at the conclusion of this chapter.

## 8.5 Degrees of Reward and Punishment (moved per previous outline order)

### 8.5.1 "Many Rooms" and Varied Stewardship (John 14:2; Luke 19:17–19)
Jesus' promise that He goes to prepare "many rooms" in His Father's house (John 14:2) suggests that the afterlife will accommodate diverse levels or capacities of glory among believers. Postmillennialists often interpret these rooms as signifying varied responsibilities in Christ's kingdom—those who faithfully stewarded their talents receive expanded authority (Luke 19:17–19). Amillennialists likewise emphasize that stewardship correlates with rewards; in Jesus' parable, the servant with five talents receives five cities to rule, illustrating proportional recompense (Luke 19:17). This principle underscores that divine economy is relational and merit-based, not equalistic; each believer's fidelity yields a reward commensurate with one's faithfulness (Matthew 25:21, 23). The

"many rooms" metaphor portrays the intermediate joy of dwelling with Christ while awaiting full participation in the final eschaton. As a pastoral application, this encourages congregations to invest spiritual capital—time, gifts, resources—into kingdom work, knowing that such investments hold eternal value (1 Corinthians 3:12–15). This vision also guards against complacency, reminding believers that entering the house of the Father involves ongoing growth rather than static enjoyment. While all who trust Christ share in the same eternal life, degrees of prominence, influence, and service reflect how they labored during the church age. These spatial distinctions thus serve to motivate holiness and discipleship, transitioning into a discussion of specific crowns saints receive.

**8.5.2 Crowns: Incorruptible, Righteousness, Life, Glory, and Shepherding** The New Testament mentions several crowns (stéphanoi) that believers may earn, each symbolizing a particular aspect of faithful service. The incorruptible crown (διάβρωσις) rewards athletes who practice self-discipline (1 Corinthians 9:24–25), reminding believers that spiritual disciplines—prayer, fasting, study—produce eternal fruit. The crown of righteousness goes to those who eagerly anticipate the Lord's return (2 Timothy 4:8), encouraging eschatological hope to inform present ethics. The crown of life is promised to those who endure trials and persecution (James 1:12; Revelation 2:10), testifying that steadfastness under suffering yields ultimate vindication. A crown of glory is given to "shepherds" who eagerly care for Christ's flock (1 Peter 5:4), affirming pastoral and mentoring ministries. Additionally, Revelation 4:4 and Revelation 6:2 depict elders wearing many crowns, suggesting a culmination of all reward types, signifying that heavenly knighthood transcends earthly titles. Postmillennialists highlight that these crowns reflect tangible expressions of different callings—missionaries, pastors, ethicists—demonstrating how various ministries contribute to kingdom expansion. Amillennialists note that crowns remain secondary to Christ's worthiness, to be laid at His feet (Revelation 4:10), preventing pride and cultivating humility. Crown imagery motivates believers to pursue excellence in service, as Luke 19:17's "well done" commendation glows brighter with every crown received. Although metaphorical, the crowns communicate that spiritual achievements have real, imperishable value (1 Corinthians 9:25). By wearing these crowns in heaven, believers display the manifold wisdom of God working through diverse giftedness (Ephesians 3:10). With crowns in view, reflection moves to how God's justice addresses the fate of the unredeemed, illuminating theories of eternal punishment and the second death.

### 8.5.3 Justice for the Oppressor: Greater Stripes for Greater Light (Luke 12:47–48) Jesus teaches in Luke 12:47–48 that those who know their Lord's will and fail to act will be beaten with many stripes, while those ignorant will receive fewer, illustrating divine principle of proportional justice. Postmillennialists interpret this to mean that societal leaders who grasp Christian ethics yet enact oppression face more severe judgment than those living under ignorance, reinforcing the moral accountability of power. Amillennialists also affirm this principle, noting that privilege brings proportionate responsibility (James 3:1), so ministers and gifted leaders face stricter judgment for sloppy handling of doctrine or failure to shepherd well. This principle clarifies why rewards differ: more light equals greater expectation, as Romans 2:12–13 indicates those who sin without law perish, but those with the law judged by the law find justification in obedience. In judgment, those who persecuted the church during the tribulation or suppressed the gospel suffer intensified wrath (Revelation 6:9–11). This proportional framework aligns with Jesus' teaching that losing even one's life for His sake yields greater reward (Mark 8:35). Similarly, those who influenced more souls for Christ's kingdom will receive larger "spheres" of service, consistent with parables of talents and minas (Matthew 25; Luke 19). Conversely, religious leaders who used scriptural knowledge to mislead will receive heavier condemnation, fulfilling Matthew 23:14's woes. This concept underscores perfect justice: divine metrics account for both deeds and motives (1 Corinthians 4:5), so no act of cruelty or self-serving ministry goes unnoticed. As believers reflect on proportional justice, they are prompted to steward light faithfully, transitioning to consider divergent views on the fate of the unredeemed—the annihilationist, eternal torment, and conditional immortality debates.

### 8.5.4 Annihilationism, Eternal Conscious Torment, and Conditional Immortality Within broader evangelicalism, theories of final punishment diverge: traditionalists assert eternal conscious torment, annihilationists argue for eventual destruction of the wicked, and conditionalists propose that only believers receive

immortality, with unbelievers ceasing to exist. Premillennialists predominantly favor eternal conscious torment, citing Revelation 14:11's "smoke of their torment goes up forever and ever" as indicating unending suffering. Postmillennial and amillennial advocates likewise often affirm this view, drawing on Christ's warnings about "eternal fire" (Matthew 25:41) and "outer darkness" (Matthew 8:12). Annihilationists appeal to verses like Matthew 10:28—"fear him who can destroy both soul and body in hell"— arguing that "destroy" implies cessation rather than everlasting torment. Conditionalists reference Romans 2:7's promise that those who seek glory, honor, and immortality will be granted life, implying that immortality is not inherent but conditional upon faith. Amillennialists counter that texts like Revelation 20:14–15 speak of "second death," indicating ongoing existence in separation, not mere nonexistence. Postmillennialists argue that categorical language— "eternal punishment" (Matthew 25:46)—demands an unending state. Debates often hinge on Greek terms—aiōnios (eternal) and oligōs (little)—fueling scholarly contention over duration semantics (Robert A. Morey, *Death and the Afterlife*). These divergent views impact worship and evangelism: fear of eternal conscious torment can motivate urgency but risks borderline terrorism, whereas annihilationism may diminish the seriousness of sin's consequences. Conditional immortality poses pastoral challenges regarding loss of loved ones' continued consciousness. Each view strives to balance divine justice with divine love, and congregations often navigate these tensions pastorally, ensuring that preaching remains faithful to Scripture's witness. As punishment theories are considered, reflection moves to envisioning emotional realities in eternity, including whether envy or memory persists, explored next.

**8.5.5 Emotional Architecture of Heaven: Envy, Memory, and Perfect Joy** The diversity of reward and punishment evokes questions about emotional life in eternity: Will believers feel envy toward those with greater crowns? Does memory of earthly failures persist? Postmillennialists and amillennialists affirm that in the new heavens and new earth, "sin will be no more" (Revelation 21:4), implying that emotions aligned with sin—envy, regret—are eradicated. Isaiah 65:17–25's depiction of abundant life, longevity, and harmony suggests that human emotions will be healed and perfected. The doctrine of the beatific vision (1 John 3:2) posits that beholding God face to face eclipses all lesser desires, filling believers' souls with unspeakable joy. While early Reformers like Calvin affirmed that selective remembrance endures to magnify God's grace—serving as an eternal testimony to divine mercy—they insisted that shaming memories vanish, consistent with Revelation 21:4's "no more death, mourning, crying, or pain." Postmillennialists often emphasize that cultural achievements—architekturally "cathedrals of culture"—find fulfillment in eternal expression of creativity without sin's distortions, indicating that memory of good persists as ongoing celebration. Amillennialists highlight 1 Corinthians 2:9, where Paul says that "what no eye has seen… God prepared for those who love him," implying that eternal joy transcends all present comprehension. The mutual fellowship among saints—the "great cloud of witnesses" (Hebrews 12:1)—fosters perfect community, eliminating loneliness and jealousy. Yet the concept of degrees of glory (1 Corinthians 15:41) suggests that believers experience profound satisfaction relative to their service, not through comparison but through recognition of God's unique calling on each life. As emotion and memory intertwine in the eschaton, ethical motivation sharpens: knowing that deeds done in the flesh bear fruit beyond measure encourages sacred vocation, bridging to discussions of cosmic re-creation in the next section.

**8.5.6 Motivating Holiness without Works-Righteousness** A balanced understanding of degrees of reward guards against works-righteousness by emphasizing that salvation remains by grace through faith (Ephesians 2:8–9) even as rewards are "by works" (1 Corinthians 3:14–15). Postmillennialists teach that good works flow from gratitude, with believers serving out of love—"the fruit of the Spirit" (Galatians 5:22–23)—rather than compulsion. Amillennialists reinforce that while "the righteous live by faith" (Habakkuk 2:4), faith without works is dead (James 2:17), so the Bema Seat evaluates faith's authenticity manifested through service. This dynamic avoids legalism by clarifying that works contribute to reward, not salvation, aligning with Matthew 5:16's principle that good deeds glorify the Father. Pastors can help congregations resist pride by pointing to Philippians 3:8, where Paul considers all his works "loss for the sake of Christ." In counseling, ministers reassure that believers condemned vestiges of sin need not evoke shame, for Christ's righteousness covers, but admonish that faithfulness still matters, promoting sanctification (1 Thessalonians 4:1–2). This balance frames evangelistic urgency: sharing the gospel remains paramount for eternal destiny, while encouraging believers to live in ways that build eternal significance. As discussions of degrees of reward conclude, attention naturally turns to the final cosmic renewal—new heavens and new earth—signified by universal transformation.

## 8.6 New Heavens and New Earth: Cosmic Re-Creation

**8.6.1 Resurrection of Creation: Romans 8 and 2 Peter 3 in Dialogue** Paul teaches in Romans 8:19–21 that creation itself "eagerly waits for the revealing of the sons of God" and will be "set free from its bondage to corruption," while Peter depicts a cosmic cleansing by fire that precedes "a new heaven and a new earth" (2 Peter 3:10–13). Postmillennialists interpret the "revealing" as the church's flourishing mission bringing societal alignment with God's purposes, which in turn purifies creation progressively—ethical public policies, environmental rehabilitation, humanitarian care prefigure this fulfillment. Amillennialists see the present sufferings of creation—ecological destruction, natural disasters—as reminders of Eden's curse, with ultimate reversal at the final conflagration (Revelation 21:1). In both views, the new creation completes the resurrection program: the perfected Earth becomes fitting for indwelling humanity reshaped in Christ's image (Romans 8:29). Isaiah 65:17's prophecy of former things passing away presents the new heavens and new earth not as a complete annihilation but as re-creative transformation, compatible with Revelation 21:5's "Behold, I am making all things new." By highlighting continuity—righteous seeds inhabiting renewed land—these passages assure believers that God's salvific work extends beyond souls to all domains, culminating in unbroken divine presence. As restoration echoes Genesis 1's original creation, devotees anticipate environmental redemption alongside personal resurrection, informing how stewardship today aligns with future consummation (Matthew 6:10). This cosmic perspective transitions to the specific contours of environmental continuity within God's renewed order.

**8.6.2 Environmental Continuity: Culture, Art, and Nations' Glory (Revelation 21:24–26)** Revelation 21:24–26 describes nations walking by the light of the New Jerusalem, bringing their glory and honor into it—a vision implying that ethnic and cultural identities endure within God's redeemed order. Postmillennialists speak of cultures as instruments of kingdom expression, with art and music reflecting divine beauty rather than merely secular creativity (Exodus 35:31–35). Amillennialists correlate this with Isaiah 66:22–23, where new heavens and new earth feature preserved distinctions among Israel's tribes yet ascend in worship "from one Sabbath to another." These texts confirm that cultural contributions—poetry, architecture, scientific exploration—persist under Christ's lordship, informing how believers engage arts and sciences today. Environmental continuity further suggests that agricultural rhythms will resume without the curse, as Ezekiel 47:12's life-giving river imagery implies stunning restoration of ecosystems. This continuity makes possible sustained cosmopolitan collaboration: musicians from diverse heritages join choirs, architects design structures that reflect a holistic worldview, and educators curate knowledge that honors each culture's legacy. Revelation's image of no night (Revelation 21:25–27) indicates an absence of sin's darkness, echoing Jesus' teaching that "in My Father's house are many rooms" (John 14:2), where nations gather to shine in unified worship. This vision encourages believers to treat cultural artifacts—textiles, languages, folk practices—as sacred gifts, not idols, stewarding them for eschatological value. As this section prepares for final eschatological features, reflection turns to symbolic elements like no sea and no night, signifying chaos banished, addressed next.

**8.6.3 No Sea, No Night: Symbolism of Chaos Banished** Revelation 21:1 explicitly states, "there was no longer any sea," symbolizing the removal of chaotic forces represented by the sea in biblical imagery (Isaiah 57:20; Revelation 13:1). Postmillennial interpreters highlight that this symbolizes the final quelling of evil powers—political turbulence, demonic influence—indicating that God's reign will render the sea's instability null. Amillennialists connect this to Revelation 22:5's "no night there," affirming perpetual light that precludes fear, ignorance, and sin's darkness. The absence of sea and night suggests that the factors which once threatened life—violent storms, darkness concealing wrongdoing—will be no more, as the Lamb's light governs entirely. This elimination of chaos aligns with Ezekiel 37's vision of valleys dry turning lush under Spirit's breath, illustrating God's capacity to transform death into life. In this reign, even natural elements cease to perpetuate harm; the sea's barrenness and the night's cover are replaced by transparency and righteousness. Jesus' statement that "the woman clothed with the sun" in Revelation 12 emphasizes that the cosmic woman—God's people—operate in full illumination, no longer vulnerable to the serpent's darkness. By recognizing the eschatological banishment of chaos, believers gain confidence that God's cosmic order will prevail, making present sufferings temporary when measured against future incorruptibility. As this vision unfolds, the next consideration is the beatific vision—seeing God face to face and its implications.

### 8.6.4 Beatific Vision and Unmediated Presence (1 John 3:2)

Amillennialists and postmillennialists affirm that the apex of the new heavens and new earth is the beatific vision—believers seeing God "face to face" (1 Corinthians 13:12), experiencing unmediated communion. John's promise that "we will be like Him" (1 John 3:2) suggests that glorified humans share in God's nature without sin tarnishing the likeness (2 Peter 1:4). Postmillennial teaching often emphasizes that earthen temples—as in Ezekiel 47's life-giving river—prefigure this consummation, when God's embodiment pervades all creation (Revelation 21:3). Amillennial thought affirms that the nuptial imagery of the marriage supper of the Lamb (Revelation 19:9) culminates in eternal fellowship with God and one another, fulfilling Jesus' prayer "that they may all be one" (John 17:21). The vision of God's unmediated presence surpasses every earthly blessing, as seen in Isaiah 33:17's promise to "look upon Zion, the city of our solemnities" and behold God's beauty, marking complete satisfaction. This perfect fellowship eliminates longing and anxiety: "there will be no more night" (Revelation 21:25), affirming that believers rest in God's direct radiance. This vision motivates present worship practices: knowing that "we see in a mirror dimly" now (1 Corinthians 13:12) prompts worshipers to approach God with reverence. As this consummated communion paints the horizon of hope, reflection turns to the marriage supper of the Lamb and eternal Sabbath rhythms.

### 8.6.5 Marriage Supper of the Lamb and Eternal Sabbath

Revelation 19:7–9 portrays the marriage supper of the Lamb, where the Bride—redeemed saints—dines with Christ, anticipating Luke 12:36's commendation for servants "ready and dressed for service," emphasizing preparedness. Postmillennialists see in this banquet a symbol of cultural unity, as diverse nations gather in celebration, foreshadowing a future where human creativity and fellowship find supreme expression in God's presence. Amillennialists connect the summer of feasting to Isaiah 25:6–9's prophetic portrayal of a feast on the mountain, where God "will swallow up death forever," showing that the marriage banquet reverses Genesis' curses. This eternal Sabbath begins as a consummated rest (Hebrews 4:9–10), where labor ends and worship persists unceasingly—exemplified in Revelation 22:3's "they shall reign forever and ever," indicating both rule and rest. As Shabbat provided Israel with weekly rest (Exodus 20:8–11), the eschatological Sabbath involves perpetual rest in God's presence, transcending temporal cycles. The imagery of feasting underscores that salvation is relational and celebratory, not merely judicial; justification that completes in sight leads to joy (Zephaniah 3:17). This eternal banquet mirrors Christ's institution of the Lord's Supper "until he comes" (1 Corinthians 11:26), reinforcing that present Eucharistic celebrations prefigure the marriage feast. Participation in this future event motivates ethical hospitality now, as believers practice open tables, reflecting Hebrews 13:2's call to show hospitality "for thereby some have entertained angels unaware." The marriage supper and Sabbath thus shape present worship and community life, preparing hearts for the new creation. With this consummation in view, we proceed to consider how Scripture locates this hope within various eschatological frameworks, especially regarding timing and reward discussions in the following section.

**Conclusion**

As the echoes of the resurrection trumpet fade into the vision of the final courtroom, two realities remain fixed in Scripture: death's hold is broken, and every life will ultimately stand before God's righteous scrutiny. Whether one envisions a staged raising, a single grand summoning, or a spiritual participation now with bodily transformation later, the underlying assertion is unwavering: in Christ's final victory, "death will be swallowed up in victory" (1 Corinthians 15:54). This hope transforms our present existence—infusing suffering with purpose, giving urgency to witness, and inviting us into proactive justice as foretaste of the great reversal to come. Judgment, with its open books and public vindication of divine holiness, reminds us that no act of mercy or cruelty escapes notice, compelling believers to embody grace and truth (John 1:14) until the consummation. As we await the renewal of heaven and earth, our hearts align with the apostle's longing that "this perishable body may be clothed with the imperishable" (2 Corinthians 5:4), trusting that the same power that raised Christ "will also give life to your mortal bodies" (Romans 8:11). In embracing these realities, the church stands as a living testimony that the grave is not its final chapter and that the love of God, poured out through Christ's sacrifice, secures both resurrection and verdict for all who believe. In light of this assurance, every sermon, every act of compassion, and every breath of worship becomes a prelude to the day when the saints—clothed in imperishable life—will gather before the Lamb in unbroken fellowship, and the curtain will finally fall on sin's long reign.

# Chapter 9 - The Nature and Scope of Christ's Reign

From Eden's promise of a reigning seed (Genesis 3:15) to Revelation's vision of every creature acknowledging His sovereignty (Revelation 5:13), Scripture unfolds a grand portrait of Jesus as King—one whose authority spans heaven and earth, spirit and matter, the present age and the age to come. His kingship does not merely inaugurate a future utopia; it shapes our present vocation, our families, and even the way we engage art, science, and governance. Throughout history, believers have disagreed over whether His rule will be exercised from a literal throne in Jerusalem or whether it already reigns invisibly in human hearts, affecting cultures and institutions. Yet across every perspective, the central affirmation remains that Christ's enthronement transforms how we view work, worship, relationships, and society. As we explore His reign, we discover that it is at once a binding of cosmic forces, a renewal of creation's rhythms, and a call to ethical service—blurring the lines between "sacred" and "secular" as all spheres bend toward His lordship.

# 9.1 Paradigms of Kingship: Political vs. Spiritual

**9.1.1 Territorial Governance in Premillennialism** Premillennial interpreters envision Christ's royal office as a tangible monarchy headquartered in Jerusalem, fulfilling the angel's promise that He will sit on "the throne of His father David" (Luke 1:32–33). They point to Zechariah 14, where living waters flow from Zion while the nations keep the Feast of Booths, as evidence that political borders, annual diplomacy, and pilgrimage rhythms endure inside a renovated earth. Isaiah's description of highways from Egypt and Assyria (Isa 19:23–25) is read literally: trade corridors, travel permits, and regional alliances flourish under messianic arbitration. Administratively, resurrected saints function as provincial governors—"You have made them a kingdom and priests, and they shall reign on the earth" (Rev 5:10)—while surviving mortals repopulate territories and learn righteousness in real time (Isa 2:3–4). Economic justice issues from a royal edict that balances land inheritance (Ezek 47:13–23) with Jubilee rhythms, ensuring no family sinks beneath generational poverty. Arab, African, and Asian peoples contribute regional abundance—cedars of Lebanon, frankincense from Sheba, ships of Tarshish—depicting a global supply chain sanctified by covenant (Isa 60:5–13). Disputes over water rights or crime are adjudicated by Christ's infallible word, turning plowshares into pruning hooks of prosperity. Animal predation ceases, signaling ecological order that mirrors political order (Isa 11:6–9). Critics of this literalist vision ask how resurrected administrators coexist with still-mortal citizens; premillennialists answer that glorified bodies serve as pedagogical icons of life beyond death, drawing nations toward faith. In this way territorial governance complements priestly mediation, anticipating cosmic renewal explored later in the chapter.

**9.1.2 Cultural Leaven in Postmillennialism** Postmillennial thought locates Christ's reign primarily in the church's Spirit-empowered advance, saturating cultures until "the earth will be full of the knowledge of the LORD as the waters cover the sea" (Hab 2:14). Rather than descending to seize political thrones by force, Jesus rules through converted hearts that reshape institutions from the inside out (Matt 13:33). The arts catch this leaven first: painters echo covenant symbolism, poets critique idolatry, architects frame civic plazas around Sabbath rest, all bearing witness that beauty must serve the King (Ps 27:4). Legal systems absorb biblical notions of due process and restorative justice, so statutes against usury, slavery, and profiteering emerge not by coercion but by conscience (Deut 24; Jas 5:1–6). Universities reform curricula to integrate theology with biology and ethics, cultivating graduates who prize wisdom above market triumph (Prov 1:7). Technological innovation bends toward neighbor love—clean-energy grids, open-source medicine—mirroring Isaiah's prophecy that inventions will no longer destroy (Isa 2:4). National foreign policy orients toward peacemaking alliances reminiscent of Solomon's shipping consortium with Hiram (1 Kgs 10). Postmillennialists admit the process is gradual and reversible—apostasy can retard progress— but the arc bends steadily upward because Christ "must reign until He puts all enemies under His feet" (1 Cor 15:25). Thus political structures remain important, yet they grow out of cultural fermentation rather than abrupt imposition. This leavening paradigm in turn invites reflection on amillennial assertions of Christ's present heavenly enthronement.

**9.1.3 Heavenly Session in Amillennialism** Amillennial expositors anchor kingship in Jesus' ascension and session "at the right hand of the Majesty on high" (Heb 1:3), arguing that His throne is presently active though veiled to human sight. Psalm 110's oracle—"Sit at my right hand until I make your enemies your footstool"—frames history as the progressive extension of a rule already inaugurated. Consequently, earthly governments come and go, but the church's worship each Lord's Day is a diplomatic gathering in the heavenly court (Heb 12:22–24). Sacraments function as royal seals: baptism signifies citizenship; the Eucharist renews allegiance to the enthroned Prince (1 Cor 11:26). Social transformations occur, yet amillennialists resist utopian charts, insisting that wheat and weeds mature together until the harvest (Matt 13:30). Persecution, therefore, is not evidence of Christ's absence but proof that the dragon knows "his time is short" (Rev 12:12). Spiritual warfare replaces geographic conquest; intercession dethrones principalities more effectively than swords (Eph 6:12–18). The kingdom is "already/not-yet"—present in righteousness and peace (Rom 14:17) but awaiting public manifestation at the parousia. This heavenly-session paradigm tempers triumphalism, fosters patient endurance, and bridges naturally into a comparative look at how saints and martyrs administer justice in the age to come.

### 9.1.4 Mediator-King: Prophetic and Priestly Dimensions of Royal Office

All three frameworks affirm that Christ fuses Davidic sovereignty with prophetic proclamation (Deut 18:15) and priestly intercession (Ps 110:4). He rules not merely by decree but by teaching Torah from Zion (Isa 2:3), cleansing consciences by His blood (Heb 9:14), and sending Spirit-borne gifts to equip His body (Eph 4:7–12). Whether one highlights territorial courts, cultural committees, or heavenly liturgy, the king's authority remains integrally pedagogical and sacrificial, shaping his citizens' minds and purifying their worship. This integrative lens prepares the way for evaluating the nitty-gritty of kingdom administration—duration, geography, and daily governance.

## 9.2 Duration, Geography, and Administration

### 9.2.1 The Role of Saints and Martyrs

Premillennialists designate resurrected saints as regional governors who share Davidic authority, echoing Christ's promise, "You will rule over ten cities" (Luke 19:17). Tribulation martyrs, in particular, hold priestly portfolios—teaching nations the liturgy of atonement (Rev 20:4–6). Postmillennialists redefine the same promise vocationally: saints exercise influence through law courts, laboratories, and literature, "judging" not by coercion but by paradigmatic excellence (1 Cor 6:2–3). Amillennial thought sees martyr-witness as the church's hidden scepter; their prayers under the altar accelerate the kingdom's advance (Rev 6:9–11). Across all views, sainthood entails stewardship: whether on refurbished earth or in unseen heaven, believers participate in governance that reconciles creation to its Maker (2 Cor 5:18–20). This participation frames subsequent questions of law, justice, and worship.

### 9.2.2 Law, Justice, and Worship Patterns

In a premillennial horizon, Isaiah 2:3–4 becomes public policy: international disputes are arbitrated at Jerusalem's tribunal, where Torah scrolls inform legal precedents. Agricultural tithe laws (Lev 27:30–34) translate into fair-trade regulations; Sabbath statutes govern labor rhythms. Postmillennial settings apply the Sermon on the Mount to civic codes—enemy-love informs restorative justice; oath integrity reforms contractual law (Matt 5). Amillennial worship centers on Word and sacrament; weekly gatherings rehearse final judgment by confessing sin and receiving absolution (1 John 1:9). Regardless of chronology, justice and worship intertwine: lawful order protects true worship, while true worship forms virtuous citizens (Ps 72). Such reciprocity extends into economics and infrastructure.

**9.2.3 Economic Flourishing and Social Order** Premillennial epochs feature Edenic harvests—"the plowman overtakes the reaper" (Amos 9:13)—supported by equitable land redistribution (Ezek 48). Postmillennial projections anticipate technological breakthroughs guided by stewardship ethics: waste-free manufacturing and energy grids that restore rather than exploit (Gen 2:15). Amillennial analysts emphasize spiritual contentment: godliness with contentment is great gain (1 Tim 6:6), inoculating societies against material idolatry even as they innovate. In each scheme, Christ's reign subverts scarcity mentalities, producing generosity that echoes the early church's koinonia (Acts 4:32–35). Economic vitality, in turn, funds festival calendars that sustain cultural memory.

**9.2.4 Feasts, Calendar, and Sacred Timekeeping** Premillennial calendars re-institute Passover, Tabernacles, and New-Moon offerings (Ezek 45–46), now interpreted through the Lamb's finished work (John 1:29). Postmillennial cultures baptize civic holidays—art festivals, environmental sabbaths—into doxological rhythms, fulfilling Colossians 3:17's mandate that every activity honor Christ. Amillennial praxis retains the Lord's Day as eschatological hinge, a weekly micro-advent that trains saints to anticipate consummation (Rev 1:10). Thus time itself becomes liturgy, shaping how communities build infrastructure and plan urban design.

**9.2.5 Infrastructure, Technology, and Urban Design under the King** Premillennial Jerusalem features a river from the temple threshold irrigating arid regions (Ezek 47), complemented by terrace agriculture and renewable energy derived from restored ecosystems. Postmillennial planners envisage "kingdom smart-cities" where green roofs offset carbon, public art catechizes citizens, and digital systems foster transparency rather than surveillance. Amillennial theologians caution against idolizing progress yet applaud technologies that alleviate suffering, framing them as firstfruits of Romans 8 liberation. Infrastructure thereby materializes kingdom values—accessibility, beauty, harmony with creation—pointing toward global security.

### 9.2.6 Conflict Resolution and Global Security in a Messianic Age

Premillennial texts portray Christ settling territorial quarrels with immediate verdicts—iron-scepter justice deters rebellion (Ps 2:9). Postmillennial optimism foresees international mediation agencies shaped by biblical peacemaking (Matt 5:9), converting military economies into humanitarian enterprises. Amillennial realism maintains that spiritual conflict remains until the parousia, yet believes gospel proclamation restrains evil (2 Thess 2:6–8). Across frameworks, the result is a security rooted not in fear but in covenant fidelity, leading naturally into a discussion of cosmic renewal and the flowering of eschatological shalom.

## 9.3 Cosmic Renewal and Eschatological Shalom

### 9.3.1 Creation's Liberation from Futility

Paul's vision of creation "groaning" (Rom 8:19–22) finds discrete expression in each millennial map. Premillennial renewal unfolds in two stages: millennium and new earth. During the thousand-year reign, deserts bloom (Isa 35:1–2), carnivores turn herbivorous, signaling incremental healing that culminates in fire-purged new creation (2 Pet 3:10–13). Postmillennialists depict liberation as culturally mediated—sustainable agriculture, species preservation, pollution reduction—arguing that as the gospel penetrates societies, environmental stewardship follows. Amillennial expositors view liberation metaphorically realized now in sacramental life—baptismal waters and Eucharistic bread already redeem matter—while awaiting full transfiguration at Christ's appearing. This ecological hope undergirds the next theme: universal knowledge of the Lord.

### 9.3.2 Universal Knowledge of the LORD

Jeremiah's new-covenant oracle—"They shall all know me, from the least to the greatest" (Jer 31:34)—anchors an intellectual renaissance under Christ's reign. Premillennialists expect annual pilgrimages to Zion where Torah instruction radiates (Mic 4:2); linguistics and law harmonize around Hebrew rootage yet respect ethnic dialects (Zeph

3:9). Postmillennial thinkers highlight digital translation projects, open-access theological libraries, and arts curricula that make biblical worldview ubiquitous, so that toddlers recite psalms as easily as the alphabet. Amillennialism contends the promise is spiritually fulfilled in the church's global expansion—house churches in high-rise apartments, roadside sacraments under mango trees—yet remains incomplete until the veil lifts at the parousia (1 Cor 13:12). In all views, knowledge is covenantal, fusing intellect and devotion, which paves the way for exploring how cosmic warfare concludes and peace permeates creation.

**9.3.3 Cosmic Warfare Defeated: Powers, Principalities, and Peace** Premillennial chronology reserves one last uprising—Gog and Magog—before Satan's final defeat (Rev 20:7–10), illustrating that liberation involves decisive military victory. Postmillennial confidence claims the cross already disarmed principalities (Col 2:15); residual skirmishes recede as gospel light expands. Amillennial theology stresses ongoing conflict yet celebrates that martyr-blood is the church's seed; every faithful witness tightens the enemy's chain (Rev 12:11). In each case, Christ's reign terminates cosmic insurgency, fulfilling Isaiah 9:7's promise of endless peace. Once warfare ends, ecological and social harmonies flourish.

**9.3.4 Ecology, Biodiversity, and the Return of Edenic Harmony** Wolves dwell with lambs, toddlers handle serpents (Isa 11:6–9), and polluted rivers become fisheries teeming like the Mediterranean (Ezek 47:10). Postmillennial agendas translate such images into wildlife corridors, reforestation campaigns, and ocean-cleanup alliances spearheaded by Christian NGOs. Amillennial worshipers support these projects as signs but not guarantees, trusting ultimate harmony to Christ's appearing (Rom 8:21). Biodiversity thus becomes a sacrament of future glory, training humanity to steward rather than strip-mine creation. This stewardship segues into planetary Sabbath.

**9.3.5 Sabbath Rest as Planetary Rhythm** Leviticus 25 prescribes sabbatical years; premillennial ages reinstate them globally so soils recuperate, mirroring Edenic rest. Postmillennial society institutionalizes "green sabbaths," corporate shutdowns that refresh workers and ecosystems alike, testifying that man was not made for profit but for communion (Mark 2:27). Amillennial spirituality frames Sunday worship as weekly firstfruits of ultimate Sabbath (Heb 4:9). As rest becomes rhythmic, the cosmos hums in synchronized worship.

**9.3.6 Liturgical Life of a Renewed Cosmos** Finally, the entirety of creation becomes doxology: mountains clap (Isa 55:12), streets resound with multilingual psalms (Rev 7:9–10), and celestial bodies shine with unshadowed glory (Rev 21:23). Premillennial festivals assemble tribes on limestone plazas; postmillennial symphonies pipe hymns through global networks; amillennial saints gather at one table stretching from catacomb to catwalk. The convergence of political, cultural, and cosmic dimensions in Christ's reign demonstrates that every atom, anthem, and affection belongs to the King—foreshadowing the next chapter's focus on kingdom ethics lived out in daily vocations.

# 9.4 Kingdom Ethics and Human Vocation

**9.4.1 Work, Creativity, and Cultural Mandate** Human labor finds its ultimate meaning under Christ's reign because every task reflects God's creative and redemptive purposes (Genesis 1:28). Postmillennialists observe that as the gospel permeates societies, work increasingly aligns with kingdom values—honesty, diligence, and service—transforming factories, farms, and offices into venues of worship (Colossians 3:23). In a premillennial scenario, resurrected entrepreneurs and artisans leverage supernatural insight to unlock sustainable technologies, building cities that glorify God's craftsmanship (Isaiah 65:21–22). Amillennial interpreters stress that Christian vocation consistently participates in God's ongoing economy even now, for believers "work heartily, as for the Lord" (Colossians 3:23), anticipating that their labor will bear fruit "in the Lord" (1 Corinthians 15:58). Artists paint murals that narrate redemption motifs, musicians compose hymns that echo Psalm 150's call to praise, and architects design structures that point every eye upward (Psalm 27:4). Even mundane tasks—cooking, driving, bookkeeping—become liturgical gestures when done "in Jesus' name" (Colossians 3:17). Creativity becomes an act of stewardship, exercising dominion in ways that honor the Creator rather than exploit creation (Genesis 2:15). As technological frontiers expand, Christian engineers who design water filtration systems reflect Isaiah 58:11's promise that God will "satisfy your desires with good
303

things." Writers, educators, and entrepreneurs foster innovation that rescues the vulnerable from poverty and disease, fulfilling Micah 6:8's call to "do justice, love kindness, and walk humbly." Under Christ's future administration, vocational callings will no longer be tainted by sin or frustration; instead, every profession will cohere with the flourishing of creation (Romans 8:19–21). This understanding flows into how family and marriage function as sanctified spheres under the King's authority.

**9.4.2 Family, Marriage, and Generational Blessing** The institution of family participates in Christ's reign because marriage images the covenantal bond between Christ and the church (Ephesians 5:25–27). Postmillennial optimism expects that as cultures embrace biblical marriage, families become "little kingdoms" modeling submission, love, and sacrificial service, nurturing children who "walk in the truth" (3 John 1:4). Premillennial visions foresee multigenerational households living under one roof, where grandparents relay covenant promises from Genesis 17:7 to grandchildren around a communal table, echoing Deuteronomy 6:7's command to teach children diligently. Amillennialists emphasize that the church is God's family now (Galatians 6:10), and marital fidelity serves as a witness that "the two become one flesh" (Mark 10:8). In a renewed earth, couples will no longer face divorce or relational strife, embodying Matthew 19:6's promise that God "joins" and no human can separate. Children will grow without fear of abandonment, secure in the generational covenant so that "your children shall all be taught by the LORD" (Isaiah 54:13). Parenting will involve cultivating both character and spiritual formation, integrating Proverbs 22:6's instruction to "train up a child" with Deuteronomy 11:18–21's emphasis on loving obedience to God's law. Extended kin networks will coordinate to care for widows, orphans, and the aged, fulfilling James 1:27's depiction of pure religion. Households will function as basic units of church administration, with family devotions becoming corporate worship mini-congregations (Joshua 24:15). These transformed familial structures lay the groundwork for robust educational initiatives in Christ's kingdom.

**9.4.3 Education and the Diffusion of Wisdom** In the kingdom age, educational enterprises will operate under Christ's instruction that "all Scriptures... are able to make you wise for salvation" (2

Timothy 3:15), expanding into robust disciplines that integrate biblical truth with every field. Postmillennial theorists anticipate a renaissance of Christian scholarship—colleges and universities founded on Proverbs 1:7's principle that "the fear of the LORD is the beginning of knowledge"—producing graduates who shape law, science, and arts through the lens of Christ's lordship. Premillennial accounts envision seminary-like academies in millennial Jerusalem where resurrected theologians tutor students both in ancient Hebrew exegesis and in celestial realities unavailable earlier (1 Corinthians 13:12). Amillennialists emphasize current church-based education—catechisms, Bible studies, and apprenticeship models—rehearsing John 17:17's "sanctify them by Your truth; Your word is truth" until the final consummation. In each view, curriculum includes theology, ethics, environmental stewardship, and vocational skills, empowering learners to steward creation wisely (Genesis 2:15) and to serve society as salt and light (Matthew 5:13–16). Literacy and critical thinking flourish as families and institutions prioritize Deuteronomy 6:7's mandate to teach children at all times. Technology enhances access: digital Torah scrolls, virtual simulations of millennial agriculture, and interactive liturgical rehearsals prepare saints for the age to come. Adult education programs equip older believers to mentor youth, modeling Titus 2:3–5's pattern of generational discipleship. By diffusing wisdom across every societal sector, education under Christ's reign secures cultural renewal that leads into how healthcare reflects the King's healing touch.

### 9.4.4 Healthcare, Healing, and the Ministering King

The physician's hands become extensions of Christ's own healing touch, fulfilling Luke 4:18's proclamation that the anointed One "heals the brokenhearted" and "proclaims release to the captives." Postmillennial advocates point to medical missions, Christian hospitals, and biomedical research guided by Matthew 25:36's rubric—"I was sick and you visited Me"—as present signs of future millennial health. In a premillennial context, even mortal wounds will be restored because "the leaves of the tree are for the healing of the nations" (Revelation 22:2), and cities will host clinics where diseases vanish at a sword's blast or divine decree (Isaiah 35:5–6). Amillennial theology emphasizes that in both heaven and earth, healing flows from Christ's atoning work (1 Peter 2:24), so believers experience spiritual and physical relief simultaneously in sacraments and prayer (James 5:14–16). Hospice ministries echo pastoral care, combining Kingdom proclamation with palliative relief, offering glimpses of future resurrection's eradication of pain (Revelation 21:4). Occupational therapy and disability accommodations in today's churches prefigure a time when "no resident will say, 'I am sick'" (Isaiah 33:24). Mission hospitals in remote regions demonstrate God's justice in action by offering free surgeries to the poor, anticipating millennial abundance when "morning by morning He will awaken; He will awaken my ear to hear as the learned" (Isaiah 50:4). Mental health care, rooted in Psalm 34:18's assurance that "the LORD is near to the brokenhearted," underscores that Christ's reign mends both soul and body. This holistic healing ethos sets the stage for economic justice, explored next.

### 9.4.5 Social Equity, Wealth Distribution, and Jubilee Principles
Under Christ's reign, economic structures align with Jubilee laws (Leviticus 25:8–55), ensuring that land and wealth cycles prevent generational poverty. Postmillennial economists highlight fair-trade cooperatives and microfinance programs inspired by Leviticus 25:35's call to "help your brother" when he lacks. Premillennial frameworks expect enforced land redistribution every fifty years, with Jubilee proclamations echoing through renovated courts (Lev 25:10), restoring ancestral inheritance and wiping out debt. Amillennial thought teaches that while literal Jubilees are not reinstated now, Christian mutual aid networks serve as anticipatory signs of God's mercy (Acts 2:44–45). Across all views, banking systems evolve to prohibit usury (Exodus 22:25), complementing economies that prioritize human dignity over profit (1 Timothy 6:10). Legislation mandates living wages, guided by Deuteronomy 24:15's command that "you shall give him his wages on his day," resulting in diminished exploitation and increased hospitality ministries. Land trusts preserve affordable housing, embodying Micah 2:2's denunciation of land grabbing, while Christian coalitions lobby for policies that tax excess wealth for social investment. Nonprofit organizations function as stewards of resource flows, fulfilling Proverbs 19:17's promise that "he who is generous to the poor lends to the LORD." In metropolitan megachurches, benevolence funds support the homeless, reflecting Isaiah 58:7's emphasis on loosening the chains of injustice. As social equity takes root, households and businesses collaborate to eliminate

slums and slaveries, ushering systemic peace that leads us into the role of art and music as devotional service.

**9.4.6 Art, Music, and Storytelling as Royal Service** Creative expressions become acts of worship under Christ's reign because God fashioned creation with aesthetic intention (Psalm 19:1) and invites humanity to join the cosmic choir (Revelation 5:13). Postmillennialists note that Christian artists create murals depicting kingdom themes in public squares, while film and theater companies produce narratives that affirm redemption rather than despair. In a premillennial horizon, architects sculpt sanctuaries whose columns and color schemes reflect heavenly geometry (Revelation 21:16–17), and minstrels summon multitudes to seaside amphitheaters for praise that resounds through mountain valleys (Psalm 98:4–6). Storytellers craft saga-like histories that chart the arc of redemption from Eden to the new creation, fulfilling God's command to "tell of His glory among the nations" (Psalm 96:3). In amillennial practice, church choirs incorporate global musical traditions—African drums, Latin chorales, Asian stringed instruments—anticipating Revelation 7:9's vision of a worshiping multitude "from every tribe and tongue." Poets offer meditations on God's beauty, weaving theological nuance with evocative language that stirs hearts toward holiness (Psalm 45:1). Visual artists in catacombs reinterpret iconographic motifs—lamb, vine, olive tree—reminding believers of continuity with early martyrs (Revelation 7:14). Liturgical dancers trace redemptive movements across altars, enacting Hosea 6:3's hope that we "know the LORD" as surely as the dawn. Filmmakers produce documentaries that accompany missions, capturing orphan care and anti-trafficking work as anticipatory glimpses of Isaiah 11:6's harmony. In all these creative endeavors, art and music serve as royal liturgies that reveal God's character, transforming secular spaces into sanctuaries of praise, thus culminating our survey of vocational ethics under Christ's reign.

# 9.5 Worship, Sacraments, and Liturgy in Christ's Kingdom

**9.5.1 Temple, Table, and Throne: Converging Symbols** In every millennial vision, the motifs of temple, table, and throne converge to shape worship, sacraments, and cosmic authority. Premillennialists regard Ezekiel's millennial temple (Ezekiel 40–48) as a literal structure where blessings flow like rivers (Ezekiel 47:1–12), yet they also affirm that the marriage supper of the Lamb (Revelation 19:9) fulfills Passover's typology, transforming tables into foretaste of unbroken fellowship. Postmillennial interpreters see the Lord's Supper as a present-day expression of kingdom table fellowship, bridging diverse cultures as they share bread and cup "in remembrance of me" (Luke 22:19), pointing forward to banquets where "every nation, tribe, people, and language" gather (Revelation 7:9–10). Amillennial theology emphasizes that the church is the new temple (1 Corinthians 3:16–17), where Spirit and Word replace stone and sacrifice; Sunday worship functions as "little Epiphanies" of Christ's enthroned presence (Rev 1:12–16). In this paradigm, earthly sanctuary architecture—be it cathedral or community hall— becomes the threshold where heaven intersects earth (Matthew 18:20). Icons, banners, and liturgical furnishings all reflect heavenly reality, shaped by Revelation 4's description of the throne room's splendor. Baptismal fonts resemble laver bowls from Solomon's temple (1 Kings 7:23–26), symbolizing entrance into a royal priesthood (1 Peter 2:9). Pulpit design often mimics Solomon's lectern, conveying the prophet's voice that echoes David's rule (2 Samuel 23:20–23). Across these expressions, the thesis remains consistent: Christ's reign informs how the church gathers around throne, table, and temple in every generation.

### 9.5.2 Eucharistic Kingship: Meal as Covenant Administration

The Lord's Supper stands as a primary locus of Christ's kingdom rule within the church, administering covenantal promises through visible signs. Postmillennialists assert that each Eucharistic celebration anticipates a future age of universal shalom, as participants "proclaim the Lord's death until he comes" (1 Corinthians 11:26), thereby invoking scriptural injunctions about covenant renewal (Jeremiah 31:31–34). In premillennial frameworks, this meal connects directly with millennial Passover celebrations, signaling that bread and wine become memorials of Christ's atonement until Israel's restoration. Amillennial interpreters emphasize that the Eucharist inaugurates the heavenly feast, as Jesus declared, "I will not drink again of this fruit of the vine until that day when I drink it new in the kingdom of God" (Mark 14:25), underscoring that this sacrament transcends time and space. Liturgies often feature readings from Revelation 5:8–10 to frame communion as an entry into the throne room banquet. Catechists teach that when believers eat the bread and drink the cup, they "participate in the body and blood of Christ" (1 Corinthians 10:16), thus receiving spiritual nourishment that equates to royal commission. This Eucharistic kingship affirms that the meal is not only remembrance but also active participation in the reign of the resurrected Son, forging unity among participants "until the day of Christ" (Philippians 1:10). As the community departs from this table, they embody kingdom ethics until the Lord's return.

### 9.5.3 Music of the Kingdom: Psalms, Hymns, and New Songs
Worship under Christ's rule resonates with diverse musical expressions—ancient psalms, contemporary hymns, and prophetic "new songs" (Psalm 96:1; Revelation 5:9). Premillennial congregations will incorporate millennial Jerusalem melodies—Hebrew chants refined by resurrected Levites—while also integrating global languages as nations stream to Zion (Isaiah 66:18). Postmillennialists commission composers to write orchestral symphonies that evoke cosmic worship, blending styles from every continent to fulfill Revelation 7:9's portrait of universal praise. Amillennial parishes often adopt multigenerational hymnals that bridge classical and contemporary song, reflecting Colossians 3:16's exhortation to "let the word of Christ dwell in you richly" through psalm, hymn, and spiritual song. Music ministers view their craft as royal service, offering "sacrifices of praise" (Hebrews 13:15) that reinforce doctrinal truths. Gospel choirs, handbell ensembles, and ethnic drum circles all contribute to a tapestry of worship that mirrors diverse crowns worn by saints in heaven (Revelation 4:4). Theologically, melodies carry eschatological weight: each refrain anticipates cosmic harmony when lions and lambs lie together (Isaiah 11:6–9), transcending present dissonance. As worshipers raise voices in unison, they enact prophetic drama—"lift up your voices with strength" (Psalm 81:1)—revealing that every note anticipates the day when Jesus receives all authority—and all praise—as King of kings.

### 9.5.4 Pilgrimage and Festival in a Global Capital
In symbolism and practice, pilgrimages and festivals will characterize worship in Christ's capital. Premillennial projections imagine throngs traveling highways—some on foot, others via resurrected chariots—to appear before the Messiah during appointed feasts (Zechariah 14:16).

Global pilgrimage logistics include lodging for nomadic desert tribes, floating dock cities for coastal pilgrims, and pastoral host families in villages along the routes. Postmillennial celebrations echo this by encouraging annual "Kingdom Week" events, where congregations gather for Earth Day–inspired creation care, cultural fairs, and gospel assemblies, illustrating Jeremiah 31:12's promise that "they shall come and sing aloud on the height of Zion." Amillennial communities foster local "pilgrim Sundays" where believers walk neighborhood routes, praying for homes and workplaces, imitating Psalm 122:1–2's call to "pray for the peace of Jerusalem." Festivals incorporate liturgical drama, processions, and communal feasts, aligning with Luke 15's imagery of banquet restored after lost sons return. Scholars working on virtual reality pilgrimages produce simulations of millennial temple rituals so those unable to travel can connect digitally—a nod to Isaiah 56:6's invitation that "foreigners who join themselves to the LORD" are welcome. As these festivals knit nations together in worship, they strengthen bonds that transcend geographic borders and prepare hearts for the final consummation, bridging naturally into the role of language and praise.

**9.5.5 Language, Translation, and Multilingual Praise** Under Christ's reign, language barriers fall away so that every tongue joins in worship. Premillennialists reference Zephaniah 3:9, predicting a day when God will "restore to the peoples a pure language," enabling seamless liturgical exchange. They envision resurrected prophets translating Hebrew psalms into Aramaic, Greek, and Arabic in real time, perhaps through Spirit-infused stroking of scrolls. Postmillennial advocates anticipate digital translation tools so effective they resemble "tongues of fire" from Pentecost (Acts 2:3–8), allowing simultaneous global livestream worship with subtitles in thousands of dialects. Amillennial ministers note that Revelation 7:9's depiction of "a great multitude that no one could number, from every nation, tribe, people and language" already emboldens churches to incorporate multilingual hymns—Spanish, Swahili, Mandarin—each voice echoing Ephesians 2:19's "members of God's household." Translation work becomes sacred stewardship, ensuring Bible versions like the World English Bible, Luganda, and Hindi reach remote villages. Glossolalia practices in some charismatic churches foreshadow the Tower of Babel's reversal, celebrating unity without erasing cultural distinctives (Acts

2:1–11). Seminaries teach exegesis alongside hermeneutics of cross-cultural communication, preparing students to preach the gospel to minority language groups. Multilingual praise bands assemble—flute, djembe, sitar, violin—blending timbres that anticipate Revelation 15:3's declaration, "Great and marvelous are Your deeds." As language facilitates worship unity, attention turns to how covenantal identity shapes interfaith dynamics in the expanded kingdom.

## 9.6 Israel, the Nations, and Inter-faith Relations

### 9.6.1 Zion's Primacy or Parity?—Viewpoints Compared
Debates about whether Jerusalem retains a singular, preeminent role or becomes one trustee among many global centers animate kingdom discussions. Premillennialists insist that "Zion" remains the epicenter of divine governance, as described in Isaiah 2:3 and Micah 4:2, where "many peoples... say, 'Come, let us go up to the mountain of the LORD.'" They maintain that all nations pilgrimage there annually, affirming Judah's headship and Christ's Davidic throne (2 Samuel 7:12–16). Postmillennial voices critique this exclusivity, proposing that all Christian communities become "Zions" in miniature (Psalm 132:13–14), distributing spiritual capital globally and honoring Revelation 21:24's image that "the nations walk by its light." Amillennialists hold that while earthly Jerusalem no longer monopolizes divine presence (John 4:21–24), Zion's spiritual reality persists in local congregations that incarnate New Jerusalem virtues (Hebrews 12:22). In practice, premillennial worship calendars revolve around actual festivals in restored Jerusalem; postmillennial churches host local "kingdom convocations"; amillennial assemblies declare that any gathered community embodies Zion (Psalm 84:5). Each view negotiates Old Testament prophecies about Zion's primacy with New Testament reinterpretations, yet all concur that Christ's reign gathers and blesses nations, setting the stage for considering gentile inclusion and diversity.

### 9.6.2 Gentile Inclusion and Cultural Diversity
Genesis 12:3's promise that "all peoples on earth will be blessed through you" finds varied application under each framework. Premillennial models foresee gentile tribes bringing tribal gifts—Ophir gold, Sheba frankincense—into Jerusalem's courts, reflecting Pharaoh's Sub-

Saharan worship in Egypt (Gen 41:45) but now turning to Messiah's throne. Postmillennialists emphasize that as the church sports multiethnic leadership—African bishops, Asian theologians, European lay elders—global inclusion demonstrates the gospel's efficacy in breaking down dividing walls (Eph 2:14). Amillennial readings stress that "in Christ there is neither Jew nor Greek" (Gal 3:28), so cultural diversity enriches rather than dilutes covenant identity. Hymnbooks include choirs that sing Handel's "Hallelujah" in Swahili, Mandarin, and Portuguese, illustrating that gentile voices occupy worship sanctuaries once reserved for Jewish Temple music (Psalm 150:3–5). Educational programs teach church history from Ethiopian eunuch to Korean church plant, revealing how gentile inclusion broadens covenantal scope. Fellowship meals feature dishes—doro wat, ceviche, samosas—as sacramental participation in God's promise to Abraham, foreshadowing Revelation 7:9's great multitude clad in white. Recognizing cultural distinctives as gifts, rather than obstacles, undergirds mission strategies that respect local customs while proclaiming gospel unity. This inclusive posture leads into questions about covenantal identity after the consummation.

### 9.6.3 Covenantal Identity after the Consummation Biblical texts hint that post-consummation, ethnic distinctions persist but become ordered under shared allegiance to the Lamb (Zechariah 14:16–19; Revelation 21:24–26). Premillennialists teach that tribal banners from Judah, Ephraim, and Levi once more unfurl beside banners representing gentile lineages—akin to the twelve tribes plus nations depicted in Revelation 7. Postmillennial thinkers suggest that national histories become chapters in a global narrative where each people's unique heritage contributes to communal worship "before the throne" (Rev 7:9–10). Amillennial interpreters highlight that Revelation's portrayal of "no temple" (Rev 21:22) and universal priests (Rev 1:6) means covenant identity transcends ethnicity while preserving flourishing diversity. In this consummated community, descendants of Abraham still receive particular honor—"the servant of the LORD is blessed" (Isaiah 53:11)—even as Jeremiah 31:33's prophecy of covenant written on hearts extends to all. Genealogists trace family lines as historical footnotes rather than as prerequisites for worship access, reflecting Romans 11:16's imagery of olive branches. Educational archives in the New Jerusalem contain scrolls chronicling each people's journey, not for hierarchy but to celebrate

God's redemptive faithfulness. These covenantal configurations pave the way for diplomatic, trade, and shared prosperity considerations.

**9.6.4 Diplomacy, Trade, and Shared Prosperity** Under Christ's universal reign, international relations assume a sacramental dimension where diplomacy becomes stewardship of peace (Matthew 5:9). Premillennial assemblies convene nation-states at Zion's council chambers, where laws reflect God's statutes as interpreted by resurrected judges trained in Torah and gospel wisdom (Deut 17:18–20). Trade caravans from Tarshish to the East Indies bear luxury goods alongside daily essentials, ensuring equitable distribution and fulfilling Isaiah 60:5's image of nations coming to Zion's light with gold and frankincense. Postmillennial economists anticipate that as Christian values permeate market ethics, fair trade pacts and microloan programs eliminate systemic poverty, resembling Acts 4:32–35's early church economy. Amillennial dialogues envision ongoing global commerce regulated by moral imperatives—"love your neighbor as yourself" (Mark 12:31)—transmuting profit motives into kingdom provisioning. Embassies in Jerusalem reflect Ephesians 2:19's "members of the household of God," where envoys negotiate border disputes through mutual deference rather than unilateral force. Banking systems align with Jubilee debt remission, and stock markets adopt transparency inspired by Proverbs 20:10's warning against dishonest scales. Even global tourism centers on pilgrimage, with travel agencies arranging sacred journeys that mimic ancient caravans but now promote ecumenical encounter. This vision of shared prosperity segues into how Christ's kingdom addresses religious pluralism and ethical persuasion.

**9.6.5 Religious Pluralism, Conversion, and the Ethics of Persuasion** In every millennial view, Christ's reign ultimately unifies worship, yet the process of conversion and inter-faith engagement raises complex ethical considerations. Premillennial policies prohibit coercion: passages like Revelation 14:9–11 warn against forced worship of the beast, prompting millennial judges to defend freedom of conscience to preach Christ's lordship (John 14:6). Postmillennial ethics affirm that conversion should arise from love-driven witness—"let your light shine before others" (Matthew 5:16)—rather than political fiat. Amillennial churches emphasize

John 4:23–24's call for worship "in spirit and truth," maintaining that respectful dialogue precedes proclamation. Missionaries navigate religious plurality by building bridges through shared moral concerns—child and refugee welfare—mirroring James 2:15–16's compassion ethic before articulating theological distinctives. In academic symposia, theologians debate truth claims using reasoned discourse and scriptural evidence, embodying 1 Peter 3:15's "gentleness and respect." Muslim, Hindu, and Buddhist neighbors may attend open-air gospel concerts, encountering "good news" in cultural idioms before profundities of incarnation. In the premillennial era, these dialogues expand to global councils where representatives of all faiths witness final kingship before acknowledging Christ's supremacy (Philippians 2:10–11). This cultivated ethos of persuasion informs next how pilgrim nations receive and disperse "kingdom gifts."

**9.6.6 Pilgrim Nations and the Flow of the "Kingdom Gifts" (Isaiah 60; Revelation 21)** Isaiah 60's prophecy that "nations shall come to your light, and kings to the brightness of your rising" (Isaiah 60:3) and Revelation 21:24's vision of "kings of the earth bringing their glory into" the New Jerusalem anticipate a global exchange of resources, wisdom, and worship. Premillennial passages depict tribal delegations traveling to Jerusalem bearing gold, frankincense, and myrrh, which are then dispersed to sustain global relief efforts—mimicking royal tithes that maintain temple functions (Ezekiel 45:8–12). Postmillennial communities organize "Kingdom Expos," where artisans from every country exhibit crafts that reflect their culture's gift to the unified worshiper, embodying 1 Peter 4:10's call to serve others through God-given gifts. Amillennial theologians celebrate digital platforms where knowledge of God spreads instantaneously, so that a seminary lecture in Nairobi enhances liturgy in São Paulo, realizing Psalm 67:2's desire that "your way [be] known on earth, your saving power among all nations." Economic aid flows from wealthier to poorer districts as an expression of love in action (2 Corinthians 8:1–5). Educational materials—Bible translations, musical scores, commentaries—offer spiritual gifts that cross linguistic borders, fulfilling Revelation 7:9–10's multilingual praise. Hospitality networks host pilgrims at Immanuel Hotels, ensuring that "no widow or orphan remains unprovided for" (James 1:27). As pilgrim movements cultivate reciprocity—nations receiving and giving kingdom gifts—they model the eschatological unity where every tribe contributes to a global canticle, culminating the chapter on Christ's reign and preparing the reader for future explorations of contested questions and pastoral implications.

## 9.7 Contested Questions and Emerging Syntheses

### 9.7.1 Literal vs. Figurative Rule—Can the Divide Be Bridged?
Scholarship wrestles with whether prophecies describing mountains flowing with wine and rivers of living water (Amos 9:13; John 4:14) should be taken literally or figuratively. Premillennial expositors often insist on corporeal fulfillment—vineyards on resurrected hills, springs gushing from reconstructed temple foundations (Ezekiel 47:1–12). Postmillennial voices propose a mediated reading: wine symbolizes joyful worship and social festivity under kingdom ethics (Isaiah 25:6), while rivers of living water represent the Spirit's outpouring (John 7:38). Amillennialists advocate typological interpretations: living water promises refer to ongoing sacramental life, not a physical stream (John 4:10–11). Emerging mediators suggest a "both/and" approach: certain promises find temporal expressions today—renewable agriculture, community festivals—while ultimate consummation awaits literal restoration (Revelation 21:1–4). This bridging tactic fosters hermeneutical humility, inviting readers to weigh genre, context, and canonical shape before definitive stances, setting the path for discussing temporal metrics next.

### 9.7.2 Temporal Metrics: "Thousand Years," "Short Time," or Eternal Now?
The phrase "thousand years" in Revelation 20:2–7 has sparked debate about whether it denotes a literal millennium or a symbolic era of indefinite duration. Premillennialists uphold a chronological millennium—Christ's kingdom spans exactly one thousand years—after which final rebellion erupts (Revelation 20:7). Postmillennial interpreters read "thousand years" numerically but view it as a hyperbolic metaphor for a prolonged period of gospel advance, during which Christ's subjective reign manifests in human history, not confined to a calendar. Amillennialists argue that the term is figurative, signifying the entire church age—that indeterminate epoch from Pentecost until parousia (Luke 11:29–30). A mediating proposal links Revelation 20's "short time" (Rev 12:12) with Daniel 12:7's "a time, times, and half a time," suggesting the biblical economy deploys both symbolic and literal metrics, varying

by context. Recognizing these flexible temporal frameworks encourages respect for ecclesial diversity and nuance in eschatological teaching, prompting further inquiry into how geography and polity fit alongside time.

**9.7.3 Geo-political Center or Distributed Presence?** The question of whether Jerusalem or the totality of converted communities functions as Christ's geo-political seat remains unresolved. Premillennialists point to Zechariah 8:3—"I will dwell in the midst of Jerusalem"—underscoring the city's enduring preeminence. Postmillennial voices counter by highlighting Matthew 24:14's universal mandate—"This gospel of the kingdom will be proclaimed as a witness to all nations"—indicating a decentralized network of influence that transcends physical capital. Amillennialists interpret 1 Peter 2:5—"You yourselves like living stones are built into a spiritual house"—suggesting that Christ dwells in every congregation, making each gathering a focal point of reign (John 14:23). Innovative proposals merge these views, envisioning an eschatological "distributed Jerusalem" where localized centers parallel circuit-riding bishops of old, all accountable to a resurrected head in heaven (Eph 1:22–23). Such syntheses invite fresh ecumenical conversations on ecclesial polity, preparing enclosure for exploring covenantal models that moderate between discontinuity and continuity.

**9.7.4 Progressive Covenantalism and Other Mediating Models** Progressive Covenantalism (PC) argues that God's covenants unfold progressively—from Edenic promise to Abrahamic land, Davidic kingship, and New Covenant fulfillment—while upholding continuity with each previous stage. PC proponents maintain that promises to Israel find partial spiritual realization in the church but await consummate fulfillment in the new creation (2 Cor 1:20). They propose that millennium expectations, whether temporal or symbolic, derive from God's unfolding covenantal plan rather than discrete dispensations. This mediating framework allows premillennialist temple hopes to inform social ethics today, while embracing amillennial emphases on spiritual reign. Other models— such as "inaugurated eschatology"—similarly blend realized and future aspects of Christ's reign, equipping churches to adopt kingdom practices now without neglecting future consummation. These proposals encourage humility and dialogue, setting the stage

316

for assessing how creedal formulations articulate kingdom convictions across ages.

**9.7.5 The Kingdom in Ecumenical Creeds and Contemporary Confessions** Historical creeds—the Apostles', Nicene, and Athanasian—affirm Christ's eternal kingship ("He ascended into heaven and is seated at the right hand of God the Father Almighty"). Yet they offer little detail on earthly administration, reflecting imperial contexts wary of condoning papal temporal power. Reformed confessions—Westminster, Belgic, and London Baptist Confessions—add nuance by asserting that Christ's kingdom extends invisibly across the world and visibly in the church. Contemporary declarations—Lausanne Covenant, Manila Manifesto—often emphasize cultural transformation without prescriptive millennial timelines, indicating a convergence toward post- and amillennial consensus. Emerging global confessions negotiate language that honors Israel's future while affirming Gentile inclusion, illustrating ongoing ecumenical negotiation on kingdom scope. These creedal anchors enable theologians to trace continuity across centuries, preparing readers for cutting-edge research in AI-enhanced exegesis and virtual reality kingdom studies.

**Conclusion**

Reflecting on Christ's rule reveals a dynamic tapestry: one moment He reigns from a heavenly throne, the next He guides us through sacramental signs at our communion tables, and simultaneously His kingdom advances through acts of mercy and justice in our neighborhoods. Whether His reign will one day manifest in visible political structures or operate mainly through Spirit-transformed hearts, its inexorable reach touches every aspect of human life— from the songs we sing to the laws we uphold, from the way we educate our children to how we steward the earth. In light of His comprehensive sovereignty, our call is to live as ambassadors of a kingdom that transcends geopolitical boundaries, cultivates cultural flourishing, and anticipates cosmic renewal. With each step of faithful obedience—whether in family, business, or community— we participate in the unfolding drama of a King who will one day draw every tribe, tongue, and nation into His perfect, unshakable reign.

# Chapter 10 - Comparative Analysis and Critique

As Christians, we draw from a shared repository of Scripture, creeds, and historic confessions, yet find ourselves reading the same passages in divergent ways when it comes to how and when Christ's promised kingdom breaks into history. Across centuries, interpreters have wrestled with how to hold together biblical promises of a future reign, the present activity of the Spirit, and the unfolding drama of redemption. Some envision a dramatic, earthbound throne where resurrected saints govern nations under Christ's visible rule. Others see gospel-prompted cultural transformation as the primary manifestation of kingdom advance. Still others emphasize that Christ's reigning power is already at work in a spiritual reality often hidden from human eyes. These differences do not arise from mere quibbles over dates or symbolic details—they flow from deeper questions about how we read apocalyptic images, how we relate Old Testament covenants to New Testament fulfillment, and how we understand the church's mission in the world. By setting each perspective side by side, we can celebrate shared convictions—such as Christ's bodily resurrection, the certainty of final judgment, and God's unshakable sovereignty—while also recognizing where interpretive commitments lead us to divergent hopes, emphases, and priorities. Confronting these differences honestly, with charitable respect and careful reasoning, enriches our grasp of Scripture and equips us to serve faithfully in a world still longing for ultimate restoration.

## 10.1 Hermeneutical Consistency

**10.1.1 Textual Literalism vs. Symbolic Realism** Evaluating millennial frameworks requires attention to the degree of literalism applied to apocalyptic texts. Premillennialists often adopt a predominantly literal approach to Revelation 20, interpreting the "thousand years" as an actual chronological period during which Christ will visibly reign on earth. They insist that vivid images— such as Satan's binding (Revelation 20:2–3), resurrected bodies (Revelation 20:4), and millennial cities—point to real, physical realities rather than mere symbols. By contrast, postmillennialists and amillennialists lean toward symbolic realism, understanding many of these images as metaphors for God's spiritual rule or as typological representations of broader redemptive truths. They might read the "binding" of Satan as a description of Christ's victory at the cross that limits demonic power (Colossians 2:15) rather than expecting a future angelic imprisonment. Yet, even among symbolic readers, there is often disagreement over how much metaphor to allow. For example, some postmillennial thinkers will interpret the "resurrection" of martyrs under the altar (Revelation 6:9–11) not as a literal bodily raising but as a portrayal of Christ's vindication of persecuted saints through gospel expansion. Amillennialists might view the "sea" disappearing in Revelation 21:1 as the end of chaos rather than the geographical draining of oceans. In contrast, those committed to literalism argue that symbolic readings risk allegorizing away predictive prophecy. They appeal to Luke 24:27, where Jesus interprets "all the Scriptures" in relation to Himself, suggesting that a historical-grammatical method yields more accurate exegesis. Yet symbolic realists counter that genre-sensitive exegesis demands recognizing apocalyptic literature's heavy reliance on imagery and metaphor, as seen in Daniel's visions (Daniel 7–12). They point out that Jesus often taught in parables (Matthew 13:34–35), setting a precedent for non-literal language. Both approaches seek fidelity to Scripture, but they diverge in handling tensions between plain reading and recognizing figurative elements. This tension shapes each model's ability to remain consistent: literalists must account for implausible scenarios—e.g., resurrected reptiles coexisting peacefully with children (Isaiah 11:6)—while symbolic realists must guard against minimizing future hope into mere spiritualization. Transitioning from literal versus symbolic concerns, readers must also consider how many interpretive lenses or "lenses" each framework employs, which we examine next.

**10.1.2 Single-Lens vs. Multi-Lens Reading Strategies** Some interpreters adhere to a single-lens hermeneutic, treating every prophecy as forecasted future history or, alternately, as always already fulfilled in Christ's first coming. This monolithic approach facilities internal consistency but can flatten the text's richness. For instance, a strictly futurist reading finds all of Revelation's judgments still to occur, whereas a strictly preterist angle locates most events in the first century. Premillennialists typically follow a futurist approach, concentrating much of Revelation's narrative in a future timeline after the church age. Postmillennialists often adopt a historicist lens, seeing Revelation's seals, trumpets, and bowls as unfolding across church history. Amillennialists frequently prefer a preterist-cum-symbolic lens, situating many passages in first-century events (e.g., Jerusalem's fall in AD 70) while allowing for timeless theological truths. Multi-lens readers argue that prophetic texts sometimes have layered fulfillments—an "already" component for original recipients and a "not-yet" aspect for ultimate consummation. They point to Jesus' own words regarding the "sign of Jonah" (Matthew 12:39–40), which carried immediate meaning to Nineveh's repentance but also foreshadowed Christ's death, burial, and resurrection. In a similar vein, Old Testament prophecies about a new covenant (Jeremiah 31:31–34) have both initial fulfillment in Christ and an eschatological consummation in the new heavens and new earth (Revelation 21:1–5). The single-lens camp warns that mixing lenses risks forcing artificial harmonizations; but multi-lens proponents respond that genre, redemptive progression, and canonical context justify layered interpretation. Premillennialists critique historicists for seeing modern European monarchs as the Four Horsemen or Antichrist, while postmillennialists point out that strict futurism can detach texts from their first-century contexts. Amillennialists maintain that Jesus' warning not to add or subtract from prophecy (Revelation 22:18–19) cautions against over-literalizing symbolic imagery. Judicious multi-lens readers seek to honor both the original setting and the Scriptures' telos, ensuring that neither immediate nor ultimate horizons are disregarded. As we move from lens strategies, it becomes vital to discern how genre-sensitive exegesis influences each model's hermeneutical consistency.

### 10.1.3 Genre-Sensitive Exegesis of Apocalyptic Literature

Apocalyptic writings—Daniel, Ezekiel, Zechariah, and Revelation—employ symbolic visions, angelic-mediators, and cosmic imagery that set them apart from straightforward narrative or epistolary genres. A genre-sensitive approach emphasizes understanding these books' unique conventions: layered symbolism, numeric codes, cyclical structure, and dynamic recapitulation. Premillennialists often argue that Revelation's structure still progresses chronologically, even if some scenes overlap. They interpret trumpets and bowls as sequences rather than cycles, believing Revelation 8–11 delves deeper into certain seal judgments rather than resetting the timeline. Postmillennialists, embracing historicism, map trumpets to specific historical events—e.g., the first trumpet corresponding to the Huns' invasions—arguing that such mapping reveals God's providential orchestration across church history. Amillennialists emphasize that Revelation's molten throne room (Revelation 4) and eschatological temple (Revelation 21) function as literary frames rather than sequential occurrences. They note that John's vision leaps frequently between heaven and earth—e.g., Revelation 4–5's heavenly scenes and Revelation 6's earthly seizure—indicating thematic rather than strictly chronological progression. Critics of genre sensitivity point out that identifying a passage as "poetic literature" risks excusing inconsistent literal interpretation. Conversely, those who ignore genre risk imposing a literal timeline onto texts meant to convey theological truths rather than precise future histories. For example, symbolic leanness applies when apocalyptic imagery draws from Daniel's beasts but does not necessitate identical fulfillment patterns. Recognizing genre-specific markers—like shift indicators ("And I saw"), hyperbole, and allusion—helps prevent naive readings that conflate every image with a physical object. This genre sensitivity further highlights the importance of reading Revelation in its first-century cultural context—ancient Roman imperial symbolism, Jewish

321

temple allusions, and early Christian persecution realities—which informs whether an image should be understood historically, futuristically, or both. Having addressed genre issues, the next step is exploring how the entire canon interrelates through progressive revelation and intertextual echoes.

### 10.1.4 Canonical Intertextuality and Progressive Revelation
Understanding the role of one biblical text in light of another is essential for consistency. Premillennialists highlight intertextual threads such as Jesus' identification as "the root and offspring of David" (Revelation 22:16), tying back to 2 Samuel 7's Davidic covenant. They also trace progressive revelation from Genesis 49's blessing of Judah to Isaiah's Suffering Servant (Isaiah 53) to Micah's prophecy about a ruler from Bethlehem (Micah 5:2) to Revelation's Rider on a White Horse (Revelation 19:11–16). Postmillennialists note how Paul's "already/not yet" motif (Romans 13:11–12; 2 Corinthians 6:2) synthesizes Old Testament promises with New Testament fulfillment, arguing that the same progressive horizon informs millennial hope. They see Isaiah's "wolf dwelling with lamb" (Isaiah 11:6–9) as both a future reality and a present ethical call to promote peace and environmental justice. Amillennialists point to typology, where the crossing of the Red Sea prefigures baptism (1 Corinthians 10:1–2) and Jesus as the antitype of Adam (Romans 5:14). They assert that genealogical chains— from Abraham through Isaac, Jacob, Judah, to David—culminate in Christ (Matthew 1:1–17), with progressive layers of covenant building toward the new covenant (Jeremiah 31:31–34). Critics of canonical intertextuality warn against proof-texting, yet those who ignore such connections risk undercutting the organic unity of Scripture. Recognizing that God "spoke in many portions and in many ways" (Hebrews 1:1) aids interpreters in appreciating how later revelation clarifies earlier shadows. For example, if Ezekiel's restored temple (Ezekiel 40–48) anticipates ultimate spiritual reality, the literal temple concept requires recalibration. Thus, participants in each millennial camp evaluate whether their method honors both inner-biblical commentary and the trajectory toward consummation, leading into the value of extra-biblical sources in hermeneutics.

### 10.1.5 Use of Second-Temple and Patristic Sources
Second-Temple literature (1 Enoch, 2 Esdras, Jubilees) and patristic writings (Justin Martyr, Irenaeus, Hippolytus) provide windows into how

early Jews and Christians interpreted apocalyptic visions. Premillennialists draw heavily on Irenaeus (Against Heresies 5.32.2), who defended a literal millennium in which resurrected martyrs reign. They also reference the Similitudes of Enoch's descriptions of a millennial kingdom of righteousness to argue that early Jewish apocalypticists anticipated a physical reign of God's anointed. Postmillennialists, while acknowledging these sources, caution that pseudepigraphal texts often contain speculative theology not authoritative for later churches. They note that church fathers like Augustine (City of God 20.7) adapted premillennial language to emphasize a symbolic reign of the church rather than a terrestrial kingdom. Amillennialists lean heavily on Chrysostom and Gregory the Great, who spiritualized prophetic texts to emphasize the soul's ongoing struggle rather than awaiting a future earthly monarchy. Yet the danger arises when interpreters regard patristic consensus as normative—given that early fathers held diverse eschatological views. Recognizing that patristic writers operated with limited manuscripts and differing philosophical presuppositions encourages critical use of these sources. Second-Temple texts must be appreciated for their historical setting within Jewish apocalyptic culture, but not as part of the canonical revelation. By filtering these writings through the lens of Solomon's admonition—"there is no new thing under the sun" (Ecclesiastes 1:9)—readers can guard against adopting every extrabiblical detail. Balanced engagement with early interpretations enriches hermeneutical consistency without abdicating responsibility to Scripture alone (1 Thessalonians 2:13). Reflecting on extra-biblical insights sets the stage for examining each model's internal strengths and blind spots.

**10.1.6 Strengths, Blind Spots, and "Flex Points" in Each Model**
Each hermeneutical system exhibits areas of consistency and vulnerability. Premillennial strength lies in its willingness to treat Scripture's prophetic text as predictive history, preserving the future hope of bodily resurrection and Christ's visible reign. Yet it risks "proof-text" overreach, such as insisting on a fully literal fulfillment for every symbolic vision, even when surrounding context suggests metaphor. Postmillennialism's strength is its integration of the "already/not yet" tension, enabling believers to celebrate present gospel progress without losing sight of future consummation. However, it sometimes overstretches cultural optimism,

underestimating the persistence of evil and human folly. Amillennialism excels at prioritizing Christ's current heavenly kingship and viewing Scripture through the unity of redemptive history. Its blind spot can be a tendency toward excessive spiritualization that downplays the promise of new heavens and new earth. Flex points—interpretive hinge topics—include whether Revelation's "binding of Satan" (Revelation 20:2–3) applies to Christ's first advent, or whether it refers to a future binding. Another flex point concerns how to interpret "all nations" consistently: is it instantaneous at the parousia (Matthew 24:30–31) or a progressive process reaching its zenith in the millennium? Recognizing these flex points allows each model to refine its hermeneutical approach while maintaining fidelity to Scripture's multifaceted witness. As these strengths and blind spots come into view, readers are better prepared to assess doctrinal coherence and how each eschatology interlocks with core Christian teachings in the next major section.

## 10.2 Doctrinal Coherence

**10.2.1 Soteriology: Grace, Faith, and Kingdom Entrance** Any viable millennial view must harmonize its eschatological timeline with the gospel's teaching on salvation by grace through faith (Ephesians 2:8–9). Premillennialists stress that entrance into the millennial kingdom requires belief in Christ prior to the millennium, often citing Isaiah 2:3's "come and let us walk in the light of the LORD," which indicates a faith-based participation. They contend that the first resurrection involves only those who have "overcome" by faith (Revelation 20:6), suggesting a continuity between soteriology and future reward. However, critics argue that this poses a tension: if salvation depends solely on grace, how can overcoming imply an additional merit-based qualification for the millennium? Premillennial authors respond by distinguishing justification from glorification—salvation grants eternal life, while overcoming demonstrates sanctification and qualifies for millennial rewards (Revelation 2:26–28). Postmillennial theology likewise upholds justification by faith, interpreting the spread of the gospel as evidence of God's saving grace at work across nations (Matthew 28:19–20). They argue that social reforms flow not from human morality alone but from transformed hearts regenerating societies (Romans 12:2). Yet they must guard against implying that cultural change becomes coercive in proclaiming grace. Amillennialism emphasizes that "those who have believed in Christ" experience the "first resurrection" spiritually now (John 5:24), making them citizens of Christ's kingdom despite earthly trials. They uphold Christ's declaration, "My sheep hear my voice...and they follow me" (John 10:27), as the operative soteriological paradigm rather than linking entrance to a future timeline. The challenge for amillennialists is to articulate how present spiritual transformation fully anticipates future glorification without diminishing the role of faith. In all three views, grace remains primary, but each must carefully maintain that faith alone justifies while works demonstrate faith's authenticity (James 2:17). As soteriology interacts with millennial expectations, the church's identity—ecclesiology—naturally emerges as the next point of doctrinal coherence.

**10.2.2 Ecclesiology: Israel–Church Relations and Covenant Identity** Covenantal relationships between Israel and the church pose significant questions for doctrinal harmony. Premillennialists hold a distinction between national Israel and the church, affirming that God's promises to Israel (land, kingdom, priesthood) will be fulfilled literally in a future millennial restoration (Romans 11:26–27). They teach that the church participates in God's plan but is not a substitute for Israel's unique covenants (Galatians 3:28–29). Critics contend that this dual-covenant framework risks bifurcating God's people and fragmenting soteriological unity. Proponents respond that Romans 11 itself depicts olive tree imagery where Gentile believers are grafted in but native branches (Israel) undergo a future casting away and re-grafting, preserving both continuity and distinction. Postmillennialists often speak of typological continuity: the church inherits the blessings promised to Israel, and ethnic distinctions lose their covenantal significance (Ephesians 2:14–16). They tend to spiritualize land promises as membership in the new covenant community and view modern Israel's political state as extraneous to biblical prophecy. Critics warn that this undermines God's faithfulness to Israel and dismisses Old Testament covenants. To address this, postmillennial writers highlight passages like 1 Peter 2:9–10, where believers are described as God's chosen people, and argue that the church comprises true Israel. Amillennialists embrace a covenantal framework that sees the church as the new Israel, the fulfillment of God's redemptive plan (Galatians 6:16). They interpret promises of land and temple as typological foreshadowings of Christ's presence among His people (John 2:19–21). However, they contend that ethnic Israel still has a remnant faith that transcends dispensational timelines (Romans 11:5). Opponents caution that this view risks negating God's specific commitments to ethnic Israel, but amillennial defenders point to passages like Jeremiah 31:31–34—where a new covenant is guaranteed to Israel and Judah—as evidence that the church's identity first emerges from Israel's spiritual redefinition. Each model must articulate how covenantal identity shapes ecclesial boundaries, leading directly into the next discussion on how each view integrates eschatology.

### 10.2.3 Eschatology: Resurrection, Judgment, and New Creation

Doctrinal coherence demands that each millennial framework align with the biblical teaching on bodily resurrection (1 Corinthians 15:42–44), the final judgment (Matthew 25:31–46), and the establishment of a new heavens and new earth (Revelation 21:1–5). Premillennialists emphasize a two-stage resurrection (1 Thessalonians 4:16–17; Revelation 20:4–6) and see the millennium as an intermediate era distinct from the ultimate new creation. They assert that the Great White Throne judgment (Revelation 20:11–15) follows the millennium and precedes the final re-creation. Critics argue that separating eras introduces discontinuities in God's redemptive plan, but advocates highlight passages like Daniel 12:2 as implying sequential resurrections. Postmillennialists teach a single resurrection for all at Christ's return, linking 1 Corinthians 15:52's "last trumpet" with the parousia (1 Thessalonians 4:16). They claim that the millennium represents a long period of gospel triumph leading to a collective resurrection-judgment event. Amillennialists agree on the single resurrection but interpret the millennium symbolically as the present church age under Christ's spiritual reign. They see Revelation 20:4–6 as describing the spiritual state of believers reigning with Christ now, rather than as a future earthly reign. Each group points to 2 Peter 3:13 to affirm that regardless of the timing, "we are awaiting new heavens and a new earth in which righteousness dwells." The diversity of eschatological details requires each model to demonstrate compatibility with core tenets like the bodily nature of resurrection (Philippians 3:21) and the reality of eternal destinies (Matthew 25:46). Any perceived tension must be resolved by appealing to Scripture's progressive revelation—recognizing that New Testament texts both clarify and expand on Old Testament hope. As we examine eschatological coherence, the kingly office of Christ and its doctrinal ramifications—Christology—naturally emerge as an essential next topic.

**10.2.4 Christology: Mediator-King, Prophet, and Priest** Each millennial vision portrays Christ's offices—prophet, priest, and king—in nuanced ways. Premillennialism accentuates Christ's kingly role in a future earthly rule, affirming direct fulfillment of Messianic titles like "Prince of Peace" (Isaiah 9:6) and "Root of Jesse" (Isaiah 11:10). They maintain that Christ's priestly atonement (Hebrews 7:27) laid the foundation for a future temple sacrifice system in the millennium, where resurrected saints serve as priests (Revelation 20:6). Postmillennialists stress that Christ's kingship is already advancing through the church's influence, projecting His prophetic word into societal structures (Matthew 28:18–20). They highlight Hebrews 4:15–16 and 1 John 2:1–2 to show that Christ functions as both high priest and advocate even now, ensuring believers' confidence until His return. Amillennial theorists emphasize that Christ's prophetic and priestly offices continue seamlessly; His once-for-all sacrifice (Hebrews 10:10) permanently mediates our access to the Father (Hebrews 9:24). They focus on passages like John 17:24 and Revelation 1:13 to situate Christ's priestly, intercessory ministry seated at God's right hand, demonstrating that His reign is heavenly and timeless. At the same time, all three schools affirm Christ's prophetic function, as Isaiah 61:1's anointing extends through the Spirit's empowerment for proclamation across ages. While distinctions arise regarding the visible manifestation of kingship, none denies that Christ's triune office undergirds all redemptive activity. Reconciling these emphases reveals that Christ's kingship involves both present spiritual rule (Colossians 1:13) and future visible dominion (1 Corinthians 15:24–25). Solid Christological foundations thus ensure that no eschatological view deviates from the gospel's core claims about who Jesus is. This Christological consensus further shapes how each perspective understands the Spirit's work in bringing about kingdom life, which we explore next.

**10.2.5 Pneumatology: Spirit's Role in Present and Future Ages** The Holy Spirit's role binds soteriology, ecclesiology, and eschatology together across all millennial models. Premillennialists teach that the Spirit indwells believers now to guarantee a future heavenly inheritance (Ephesians 1:13–14), and they look forward to the Spirit's pouring out during the tribulation (Joel 2:28–29) as a sign of the coming kingdom's fullness. Postmillennialists focus on the Spirit's present ministry through the church in equipping saints for mission (Acts 1:8) and fostering societal transformation through gifts like prophecy, teaching, and healing (1 Corinthians 12:7–11). They interpret Joel's prophecy as already fulfilled at Pentecost, catalyzing incremental advances in righteousness and justice. Amillennialists emphasize that the Spirit's ever-present work—convicting of sin, guiding into truth, and sustaining spiritual life (John 16:8–13)—constitutes the true "kingdom power" since Christ's ascension. They highlight passages like Romans 8:9, which assert that those in whom the Spirit dwells belong to Christ, indicating that "kingdom citizenship" is a present reality. While premillennialists anticipate a special outpouring during end-times, even they stress that the Spirit's restraining activity currently restrains sin (2 Thessalonians 2:7). Critics of fuller realized-pneumatic views caution against negating future prophetic or miraculous works, but advocates respond by pointing to John 14:12–14—suggesting that Spirit-empowered signs persist until Christ's return. Each perspective must affirm that the Spirit's work bridges present experience with future hope, enabling believers to live "in the Spirit" while awaiting bodily resurrection (Romans 8:11). These pneumatological affirmations secure doctrinal coherence as the discussion moves toward addressing specific tensions and harmonizations next.

**10.2.6 Doctrinal Tensions and Harmonization Attempts** No millennial framework is hermetically sealed; each faces internal tensions. For premillennialism, the challenge lies in maintaining that God's kingdom is both "already" inaugurated at the first advent (Luke 17:21) and not "not yet" until after the tribulation. They respond by positing a two-phase reign: an invisible, spiritual rule now and a visible, earthly reign later. Critics argue that this creates a confusing bifurcation of the one kingship of Christ. Postmillennialists wrestle with balancing optimism about gospel progress against biblical realism about sin's persistence (Galatians 5:17). Their harmonization often rests on emphasizing that partial advances do not guarantee linear progress but reflect God's sovereignty unfolding through complex human history. Amillennialists face critique for appearing to spiritualize New

Testament promises of millennial blessings (e.g., Isaiah 65:17), but they argue that typology and covenantal fulfillment provide sufficient continuity without denying eschatological future. All three schools strive to maintain the coherence of salvation history—from fall to consummation—while offering meaningful pathways for the church's mission now. Each harmonization attempt relies on overarching biblical-theological frameworks—redemptive-historical, covenantal, or dispensational—to contextualize particular texts. This structural cohesion prepares the ground for evaluating how doctrinal distinctions impact practical ministry objectives, which we address in the next major section on pastoral and missional outcomes.

## 10.3 Pastoral and Missional Outcomes

### 10.3.1 Ethical Motivation: Holiness, Justice, and Stewardship

Each millennial stance fosters certain ethical emphases among believers. Premillennial congregations often emphasize personal holiness and readiness, reflecting Christ's warning to "keep watch" because the Son of Man comes at an hour you do not expect (Matthew 24:42–44). The expectation of a future literal rule contributes to an ethic of separation—resisting cultural compromise—while encouraging sacrificial service to "endure to the end" (Matthew 24:13). Critics note that such separation can yield withdrawal from social engagement, but premillennial proponents contend that loving one's neighbor requires proclaiming impending judgment (2 Peter 3:9). Postmillennial communities tend to channel ethical energy into social reform, interpreting "bring on the day of the Lord" as partnering with God to advance justice (Amos 5:24). They support initiatives like anti-trafficking legislation, environmental sustainability, and educational equity as anticipatory signs of the millennial kingdom. Opponents worry that focusing on cultural progress risks idolatry of social structures, but advocates respond by affirming dependence on the Holy Spirit's guidance (John 16:13). Amillennial pastors stress that holiness unfolds through spiritual disciplines—prayer, fasting, study—to manifest Christ's reign within hearts, which naturally extends to just and faithful stewardship of creation (Psalm 24:1). They foster an ethic of faithful presence rather than utopian blueprinting, citing Jesus' call to "love your enemies" (Matthew 5:44) as a primary mark of kingdom ethics. Each view's ethical motivations shape congregational priorities: some emphasize evangelism to avert devastation, others political advocacy to accelerate righteousness, and still others personal spiritual formation as the seedbed of societal transformation. These approaches set the stage for how worship forms and liturgical practices develop in each community.

**10.3.2 Worship Practices and Liturgical Form** Theological perspective on Christ's reign profoundly influences worship styles. Premillennial churches often incorporate eschatological liturgy—regular readings of Revelation texts, antiphonal psalms forecasting Zion's future, and responsive prayers petitioning for Christ's audible return (1 Thessalonians 4:16). They may utilize visual elements—sand tables depicting Jerusalem's topography—to remind worshipers of a coming physical kingdom. Critics charge this can distract from present spiritual realities, but supporters argue that future hope galvanizes present faithfulness. Postmillennial congregations might prioritize corporate praying for societal institutions—schools, governments, markets—to reflect Isaiah 58's call for righteous influence. Their worship includes songs celebrating social action, testimonies of community outreach, and sermons that highlight communal transformation. Opponents suggest this risks reducing worship to social activism, but advocates believe that proclamation and demonstration remain inseparable (James 2:18). Amillennial worship services stress Christ's current heavenly enthronement by focusing on Word and sacrament—proclaiming Jesus as the Lamb who was slain yet lives (Revelation 5:12–13). The frequency and style of communion can reflect an anticipation of the marriage supper of the Lamb (Revelation 19:9) rather than a strictly futuristic setting. This sacramental orientation fosters deep reverence and a sense of participation in the already inaugurated kingdom. Each liturgical form demands vigilance to ensure that eschatological motifs do not become overshadowed by cultural or temporal enthusiasms. As worship feeds mission and morality, pastoral care in suffering and hope emerges as a critical dimension to consider next.

**10.3.3 Counseling, Suffering, and Hope** Pastoral care needs vary according to eschatological conviction. In premillennial contexts, suffering believers often find comfort in promises of a future literal restoration where "He will wipe away every tear" (Revelation 21:4).

Counseling focuses on end-time perseverance, encouraging those facing persecution by highlighting tribulation-martyr rewards (Revelation 20:4). Critics argue that overemphasis on future vindication can lead to acquiescence in present injustices; supporters counter that caring for temporal suffering does not negate eternal hope. Postmillennial counselors remind congregants that societal transformation is a present possibility, so they can process grief through engagement in community initiatives—providing tangible relief and long-term improvement (Luke 10:30–37). Clients struggling with despair may find purpose in pursuing justice and militate structural sin. However, if societal conditions appear stagnant, hope can wane; pastors must carefully balance ambition with realistic expectations. Amillennial practitioners focus on Christ's presence in suffering—"He was pierced for our transgressions" (Isaiah 53:5)—offering believers immediate comfort through the Spirit's fellowship (2 Corinthians 1:3–4) rather than solely promising future change. They draw on Revelation's heavenly sanctuary imagery to reassure that a better, eternal environment awaits (Hebrews 8:1–2). Each approach shapes pastoral strategies: home visitations in premillennial churches incorporate eschatological Scripture readings, postmillennial communities might channel grief into advocacy projects, while amillennial caregivers emphasize present spiritual consolation through prayer and sacrament. Mastering these nuances informs how churches mobilize hope to counter despair, leading into the topic of evangelism and cultural engagement.

### 10.3.4 Evangelism, Social Reform, and Cultural Engagement

Eschatology frames evangelistic methods and priorities. Premillennial advocates often lean heavily on preaching judgment and Christ's imminent return (2 Peter 3:10), using urgency as a catalyst for conversion. They see themselves as calling a lost world out of darkness before the next cataclysmic events unfold (Matthew 24:14). Critics caution that this approach can foster fear-based or superficial repentance, but proponents reply that only clear presentation of consequences motivates genuine conversion (Luke 16:23–24). Postmillennial campaigns integrate evangelism with social reform, believing that gospel proclamation should simultaneously address spiritual and material needs (Matthew 25:35–40). Their conviction that Christ is building His kingdom leads them to invest in education, political lobbying, and environmental stewardship, trusting that hearts open when minds witness Christian ethics in action. Opponents charge this can blur the boundary between gospel and social gospel, but advocates insist that New Testament apostles practiced both proclamation (Acts 2:36–38) and benevolent deeds (Acts 2:44–45). Amillennial practitioners typically focus on personal discipleship—mentoring and small groups—embedding evangelistic efforts within community relationships (1 Peter 3:15). They emphasize that spiritual transformation precedes and informs any cultural engagement. While some critique this as too individualized, supporters argue that somber clarity about judgment (John 3:36) yields deeper, lasting faith. Irrespective of model, effective evangelism requires contextualization that honors local cultures (1 Corinthians 9:22–23), consistent with Christ's incarnational method. These varying emphases on preaching versus societal action produce distinct missional profiles that condition how churches view their role in the world. As mission strategies evolve, so too does the potential for either triumphalist overreach or despairing passivity, which we analyze next.

### 10.3.5 Risk of Triumphalism or Despair in Each View

Eschatological convictions can become theological malaises if unbalanced. Premillennial congregations risk triumphalism if they regard themselves as the only true remnant insulated from worldly apostasy; such an attitude can foster elitism and disengagement from societal needs. Conversely, they may despair if global events fail to align with timetables they expect—leading to disillusionment or conspiracy-minded speculation. To guard against these, some preachers encourage humility, reminding believers that "no one knows the day or hour" (Matthew 24:36), urging readiness without date-setting. Postmillennialism's unquestioned optimism in gospel progress can lead to triumphalism—assuming that social gains inevitably herald the millennium—or to despair if expected cultural shifts stall or reverse. Pastors in these contexts must balance hope with realism, acknowledging that "the gates of Hades will not overcome" (Matthew 16:18) even when visible progress seems negligible. Amillennial churches face the opposite peril: by emphasizing spiritual victory now, congregants can become complacent or self-satisfied, ignoring pressing injustices, or can slip into pessimism, believing the world is too corrupt to change. To offset this, responsible amillennial teachers stress the urgency of faithfulness in small matters (Matthew 25:14–30) and the biblical call to "sorrow as one who has no hope" (1 Thessalonians 4:13). Each argument underscores that no eschatological model guarantees health without vigilance. Recognizing these pitfalls leads us to examine concrete examples of how diverse communities embody or falter in their millennial convictions.

**10.3.6 Case Studies from Global Church Contexts** Real-world illustrations reveal how eschatological emphases unfold in diverse cultures. In a Nigerian megachurch steeped in premillennial conviction, Sunday services brim with prophetic preaching on imminent tribulation, leading to vigorous evangelistic outreaches and relief efforts for persecuted congregations in neighboring regions. While membership soars, critics note that the focus on future doom sometimes eclipses sustained community development. In India, a postmillennial-affiliated network of churches has partnered with local NGOs to build schools, clean water wells, and micro-enterprise programs for Dalit populations. These acts accompany gospel proclamation, leading to significant church growth among previously unreached caste groups. Yet some suggest that emphasis on social reforms occasionally eclipses evangelistic proclamation, potentially muddying theological clarity. In Eastern European denominations influenced by amillennial theology, worship centers on deep expository preaching, catechesis, and sacramental devotion. Parishioners sustain quiet resistance to corrupt social structures, embodying Christ's suffering servant ethos (Philippians 2:5–8). Observers note that this approach fosters strong internal community but sometimes lacks visible public impact. In Latin America, charismatic groups blend elements from each model: they anticipate literal millennial breakthroughs while simultaneously engaging in vibrant social ministries and emphasizing present Spirit power. This hybrid model testifies to the complexity of ministering in culturally plural contexts. Across these case studies, we see that contextual dynamics mediate how eschatology drives ethics, worship, and mission. Understanding these real-life expressions underscores the need for balanced, contextually sensitive application, paving the way for identifying shared convictions and enduring disagreements in Chapter 10's next sections.

# 10.4 Common Ground and Irreconcilable Differences

### 10.4.1 Core Nicene-Trinitarian Affirmations Across premillennial, postmillennial, and amillennial perspectives, foundational Nicene-Trinitarian doctrines serve as bedrock commitments. All three traditions assert that the Father is unbegotten, the Son is "begotten, not made," and the Spirit proceeds from the Father (John 1:1; John 15:26). They agree that Christ is "of one substance with the Father," fully divine and fully human, who took on flesh to redeem sinners (Philippians 2:6–8; Colossians 2:9). Believers in every millennial camp confess that the Spirit indwells the church, uniting members into one body (1 Corinthians 12:13). These shared convictions guard against heretical views such as Arianism, which denied Christ's full divinity, and Pelagianism, which minimized the Spirit's role in regeneration. Each model upholds the Trinity's coequal unity, emphasizing that God's work of salvation—from election to glorification—flows through the Father's plan, the Son's atoning death, and the Spirit's sanctifying ministry (Ephesians 1:3–14). This common ground ensures that disagreements over earthly or spiritual reign do not compromise the gospel's core: that God saves by grace through faith in Christ, empowered by the Spirit. Even as future timelines diverge, every community prays in Jesus' name confident that the triune God hears and answers (John 14:13–14). The Nicene Creed stands as a unifying text, invoked interchangeably in liturgies, catechisms, and confessionals across these traditions. Its language guards against subordinationism or modalism, providing a shared theological vocabulary whenever Christ's nature or the Spirit's work is taught (Matthew 28:19). Because the three models consider Christ's fellowship with the Father and Spirit as essential, they likewise agree that the promises of resurrection and reign must be understood within the framework of the Triune God's redemptive covenant. This consensus sets the stage for addressing deeper convictions about resurrection and final judgment, which follow Nicene affirmation.

### 10.4.2 Shared Convictions on Resurrection and Final Judgment
Despite divergent timetables, all three frameworks affirm the historic, bodily resurrection of Jesus as the guarantee of future

resurrection for believers (1 Corinthians 15:20–23). They teach that Christ's resurrection broke the bonds of death and inaugurated a new creation, paving the way for every person's future bodily raising (1 Thessalonians 4:16–17). Each model insists that just as Christ rose in a tangible body, so too will the saints rise to live forever in glorified bodies (Philippians 3:20–21). They agree that the final judgment is a universal event in which every individual stands before Christ to give account, whether for entrance into blessing or condemnation (Matthew 25:31–46; Revelation 20:11–15). Sinners receive eternal separation—"eternal punishment" (Matthew 25:46)—while the righteous inherit "eternal life" (Daniel 12:2; John 5:28–29). Although premillennialism places a specific millennium between Christ's return and the Great White Throne, postmillennialism and amillennialism embed the millennium differently, they nonetheless concur that a Great White Throne judgment awaits after resurrection. All three assert that no secret sin or hidden thought escapes God's scrutiny (Psalm 139:1–4; Ecclesiastes 12:14). In pastoral teaching, ministers from every camp draw on Revelation 20 and 2 Corinthians 5:10 to underscore accountability and hope. They affirm that resurrection and judgment are motivated by God's justice, love, and mercy—mercy extended to those in Christ (Ephesians 2:4–5), justice executed toward evildoers (Romans 2:5–8). Freedoms about chronology do not alter the binding reality that Christ's resurrection secures believers' future, nor the inescapable truth that every life is evaluated. This shared conviction about resurrection and judgment functions as a theological safety net, ensuring that differences in millennial sequencing do not undermine belief in the resurrection's centrality. With these convictions as a foundation, models can maintain unity around what happens after death even while disagreeing about intervening stages.

**10.4.3 Hermeneutical Principles Held in Unity** In addition to Nicene and eschatological agreements, the models share basic hermeneutical commitments to certain interpretive principles. All affirm that Scripture alone is the supreme authority for faith and practice (2 Timothy 3:16–17). They recognize the importance of historical-grammatical exegesis: interpreting the Bible by considering authorial intent, literary genre, and historical context. Each model endorses the value of comparing Scripture with Scripture, using well-established passages to clarify more obscure texts (Isaiah 28:10; 1 Peter 1:10–12). They also agree that Christ is the hermeneutical key to the entire Bible (Luke 24:27; John 5:39–40), meaning that Old Testament promises must be read in light of Christ's life and teaching. While methods vary—some leaning more literal, others more typological—they concur that indiscriminate allegorization is unfaithful (2 Peter 1:20–21). All three stress the role of the Holy Spirit in guiding faithful interpretation (John 16:13), acknowledging that no purely neutral reader exists apart from divine illumination. They accept the necessity of using ancient manuscripts, textual criticism, and canonical boundaries to guard doctrinal integrity. Even as they diverge on the millennium's specifics, they maintain unity over basic presuppositions: that the Bible is God-breathed, inerrant in the original autographs, and sufficient for equipping the church. This shared hermeneutical bedrock prepares them to weigh differences without accusing one another of outright heresy. Recognizing these common interpretive commitments sets the stage for appreciating the remaining irreconcilable debates—especially regarding millennium timing and temple expectations.

**10.4.4 Non-Negotiables: Millennium Timing and Temple Expectation** Despite broad agreements, certain core disagreements remain irreducible, most notably the timing of the millennium and expectations regarding a future temple. Premillennialists insist on a literal thousand-year reign in which a physical temple is rebuilt, animal sacrifices resume, and David's throne in Jerusalem is occupied (Isaiah 2:2–4; Ezekiel 40–48). Postmillennialists generally reject a literal temple and chronology, viewing temple references as symbols of spiritual realities within the church (Hebrews 8:1–5) or as fulfilled in Christ's person and work (John 2:19–21). Amillennialists similarly spiritualize temple imagery, seeing Christ's body and the church as the true temple (1 Corinthians 3:16–17; Ephesians 2:19–22). Premillennialists view postponing temple expectations as a denial of God's specific promises to Israel (Jeremiah 33:14–18), but postmillennialists argue those promises find fulfillment in Christ rather than in earthly structures. Amillennialists add that Christ's declaration "destroy this temple, and in three days I will raise it up" (John 2:19) indicates a pattern of typological fulfillment rather than repeated physical rebuilding. Defenders of each viewpoint maintain that their position best harmonizes Old and New Testament witnesses without forcing undue literalism or undue allegory. Because these positions involve canonical passages—Daniel's "seventy weeks" prophecy (Daniel 9:24–27) and Ezekiel's temple vision—they stand as non-negotiable for adherents: accepting a different timetable or temple expectation touches core identity. These intractable differences prompt respectful dialogue rather than personal division, once shared commitments have been affirmed. As these debates persist, both sides benefit from examining the methodological assumptions that shape their convictions, which leads naturally into the next section on methodological considerations.

**10.4.5 Terminology Clashes and Talking Past One Another** A recurring obstacle to fruitful conversation arises when differing eschatological camps use the same terms—"kingdom," "millennium," "binding of Satan"—but assign divergent meanings. Premillennialists speak of "rapture" as a discrete, future event, while amillennialists often consider it synonymous with the general resurrection. Postmillennialists sometimes refer to an "age of peace" as a symbolic description of gospel influence, but premillennialists hear those words and expect a literal, global cessation of war. Similarly, "millennium" in premillennial circles connotes a future chronological period, whereas post- and amillennialists treat it as flexible symbolism. These terminological clashes can lead to misunderstandings, where one side accuses the other of denying obvious biblical truths, when in fact they simply interpret the same term differently. To overcome this, some suggest using clarifying qualifiers—"premillennial millennium," "symbolic millennium," "ethical millennium"—to specify referent frameworks. All three camps agree that clear definitions are essential: "resurrection" signifies bodily raising, "spiritual/written law" points to moral imperatives, and "temple" varies between stone edifice or Christ himself. When communicators fail to clarify their terms, they talk past one another, leading to entrenched categories where no actual disagreement exists substantively. Having recognized how language issues exacerbate division, we proceed to opportunities for ecumenical agreement and statements that might bridge divides.

**10.4.6 Prospects for Constructive Ecumenical Statements** Despite substantive differences, there is growing interest in crafting ecumenical statements focusing on shared convictions while allowing diversity in non-essential matters. Early efforts like the Lausanne Covenant emphasize affirming Christ's lordship over history without specifying millennial timelines, enabling cooperation in evangelism (Matthew 28:19–20). More recent dialogues produce joint documents—such as "A Common Hope for the Future"—where theologians from diverse backgrounds affirm the certainty of Christ's return, bodily resurrection, and final judgment, while agreeing to disagree on millennium specifics. These statements often restate the primacy of the gospel, the call to social justice, and the ethics of humble dialogue—principles rooted in Philippians 2:1–5 and Ephesians 4:1–6. By focusing on what Paul terms "that which makes for peace and building up" (Romans 14:19), ecumenical efforts seek to minimize distractive controversy over chronology or temple typology. Constructive statements may explicitly reserve millennium questions as "areas requiring further research," encouraging continued academic collaboration without schism. Churches adopting such statements commit to mutual respect, recognizing that at least two or three witnesses (Matthew 18:20) provide a valid ecclesial basis for conviction without silencing dissenters. With these ecumenical strands in view, the next major theme explores methodological considerations that underlie hermeneutical and doctrinal stances.

## 10.5 Methodological Considerations

### 10.5.1 Historical-Critical vs. Theological Reading Priorities One major methodological fault line exists between those who emphasize historical-critical approaches and those who prioritize theological or canonical readings. Proponents of historical-critical exegesis argue that understanding the original audience and authorial intent is essential; they focus on Sitz im Leben—how Daniel addressed 6th-century BC exiles or how Revelation comforted late first-century Asian churches under Domitian. They emphasize textual criticism, source criticism, and form criticism to reconstruct the earliest forms of biblical books. Critics assert that historical-critical methods can undermine faith by suggesting multiple redaction layers or authorial anonymity. In contrast, theological approaches posit that Scripture must be read as a coherent whole, shaped by progressive revelation from Genesis through Revelation, with Christ as interpretive center. Such theologians stress canonical unity, seeing texts like Isaiah 2:2–4 as linked seamlessly to Revelation 21:1–4 rather than emphasizing discrete historical contexts. Both camps agree on the value of

context, but they diverge on weighting. Historical-critical advocates warn that ignoring context leads to eisegesis—reading one's own ideas into the text. Theological readers contend that overly secular historical methods discount divine inspiration, risking reductive naturalism. Some mediators propose integrated methodologies: starting with historical-critical tools to understand original meaning, then advancing to canonical-theological reflection to discern contemporary application (Luke 24:27). By combining the discipline of historical inquiry with reverent devotion to Scripture's theological witness, interpreters can honor both exegetical integrity and doctrinal faithfulness. As methods shape conclusions, next we examine how underlying philosophical presuppositions influence interpretive outcomes.

**10.5.2 Role of Philosophical Presuppositions (e.g., Realism, Idealism)** Beyond surface methodology lies a substratum of philosophical commitments that subtly guide interpretation. Realist presuppositions assume biblical texts refer to a concrete external reality—a historical person or future event—leading interpreters to favor literal readings of prophecy. Premillennialists often adopt this realism: if Scripture speaks of a golden city with walls 144 cubits thick (Revelation 21:17), they expect some actual counterpart in the new heavens and new earth. Idealist presuppositions, common among amillennialists, assume that biblical narratives primarily convey timeless spiritual truths, leading to symbolic or typological readings. They argue that focusing on timeless principles prevents conflating scripture with secular chronologies. Pragmatists or reader-response theorists, occasionally reflected in postmillennial circles, emphasize the reader's experience and the community's discernment of text, focusing on how texts function to inspire social transformation regardless of historical referents. Each philosophical stance highlights certain aspects while downplaying others: realism safeguards fidelity to objective revelation but risks rigid literalism; idealism protects against naïve literalism but may neglect real historical trajectories; pragmatism invites practical application but can neglect doctrinal boundaries. Recognizing these underlying worldviews helps explain why interpreters come to divergent conclusions on the same passage (Matthew 13:13). As interpreters become aware of their presuppositions, they can test them against Scripture's claim to be "God-breathed" (2 Timothy 3:16) and to interpret itself through progressive revelation. Awareness of presuppositions lays a foundation for understanding how Scripture, Tradition, Reason, and Experience interplay in interpretive work, the focus of our next subsection.

### 10.5.3 Interplay of Scripture, Tradition, Reason, and Experience
Interpretation does not occur in a vacuum; rather, it engages a dynamic interplay among Scripture, church tradition, reason, and personal experience. In the Wesleyan quadrilateral, Scripture functions as primary norm, but tradition—witness of church fathers and ecumenical creeds—provides a guardrail against erratic interpretations. Premillennialists often appeal to patristic witness, citing figures like Irenaeus and Justin Martyr, while post- and amillennialists point to Augustine and Chrysostom to affirm spiritual readings. Reason contributes by assessing coherence and logical consistency: if a given millennial model yields self-contradictions or theological incoherence, reason flags the problem. Experience resonates in communal context—if believers observe that gospel advance yields social fruit, that may lend credence to postmillennial hopes. Critics argue that experience can mislead, especially if emotions or cultural trends shape beliefs more than biblical truth. Defenders counter that God's Spirit works in community, guiding discernment through shared experience (Acts 15:28). Tradition can both preserve orthodoxy and ossify innovation, requiring a careful balance so neither Scripture nor new insights are compromised. Reading Scripture in conversation with tradition and reason helps avoid doctrinal aberrations: for example, abandoning literal resurrection contradicts apostolic teaching and creedal affirmations (1 Corinthians 15; Nicene Creed). Yet uncritically accepting ancient traditions without testing against the full canon can perpetuate outdated errors. As interpreters navigate these four authorities, they might utilize an oblique hermeneutic: affirming that Scripture interprets Scripture, harnessing tradition as a lens, applying reason to detect logical coherence, and acknowledging that experience shapes pastoral urgency. Understanding this interplay aids in evaluating which millennial claims rest on robust engagement with all four, and which rely disproportionately on one. Having outlined this quadrilateral, the next concern is how cultural contexts influence eschatological imagination.

### 10.5.4 Cultural Contexts Shaping Eschatological Imagination
The cultural milieu in which interpreters live influences how they

envision the kingdom. Renaissance and Enlightenment optimism fueled postmillennial confidence in human progress, leading interpreters like Jonathan Edwards to see America as a harbinger of millennial transformation. Conversely, 20th-century wars and existential crises gave rise to pessimistic amillennial readings, where cosmic conflict and clergy-focused spirituality eclipsed social optimism. Contemporary global concerns—climate change, pandemics, political polarization—shape how believers expect God's future intervention: some premillennialists interpret these crises as clear signposts of imminent tribulation (Matthew 24:6–8), while postmillennialists see them as opportunities for gospel-based solutions to flourish. Amillennial Christians might take a middle path: advocating for societal engagement but remaining skeptical about temporal fixes, recalling Paul's warning against trusting princes (Psalm 146:3). Similarly, in regions experiencing persecution, believers often prefer literalist eschatologies that promise vindication and restoration, whereas more privileged contexts foster hope in gradual reform. Cultural pressures also affect whether congregations emphasize personal piety or social activism. In Sub-Saharan Africa, for instance, a theology of suffering and martyrdom often finds resonance with premillennial promises of restoration. In Western Europe, where secularism is ascendant, amillennial focuses on personal sanctification and ecclesial renewal gain traction. Recognizing these cultural influences prevents interpreters from assuming that their own imaginations alone capture biblical possibilities. As interpreters evaluate cultural conditioning, they must ask: does a reading faithfully reflect Scripture or merely mirror local anxieties or hopes? This leads to examining ethical implications of methodological choices, our next area of focus.

**10.5.5 Ethical Implications of Method Choices** Methodological decisions carry ethical ramifications in how believers live and act. A literalist approach that views the world as rapidly falling apart might discourage investment in social institutions, leading to disengagement or fatalism (Matthew 24:12). Conversely, a purely idealist stance that reduces crises to spiritual metaphors might undercut practical responses—e.g., neglecting poverty alleviation or climate care—and inadvertently silence God's call to care for creation (Genesis 2:15). An integrated method that perceives literal and symbolic elements can foster balanced ethics: working for social justice while recognizing ultimate restoration comes from God

341

alone. Moreover, methods that overemphasize experience as a hermeneutical authority may elevate subjective feelings above objective biblical truth, leading to moral relativism. In contrast, methods that rigidly clothe themselves in tradition without questioning outdated or harmful applications can perpetuate injustices—such as ignoring systemic racism or gender inequities under the guise of doctrinal fidelity. Ethical reading thus demands humility: interpreters must ask whether their approach promotes love, justice, and mercy—core biblical values—or whether it facilitates pride, indifference, or partisan agendas. Proponents of kingdom ethics argue that eschatological expectation influences behavior: hope in renewal motivates environmental stewardship, while fear of judgment spurs evangelistic outreach. Failing to account for these ethical implications risks creating eschatologies divorced from real-world concerns. As this section has shown, methodological choices ripple into practical consequences, preparing us to outline guidelines for fair comparative work in the next subsection.

**10.5.6 Guidelines for Fair Comparative Work** To evaluate multiple millennial models responsibly, interpreters should adopt a set of guiding principles. First, they must define terms clearly to avoid equivocation. If "millennium" can mean literal or symbolic, authors should specify which they intend, thereby preventing misunderstandings. Second, they should employ charitable language: when critiquing another view, describe it in its strongest form—"steel-manning"—and refrain from caricature or ad hominem attacks. Third, comparisons should rely on primary texts rather than relying solely on secondhand summaries; reading an opponent's key passages firsthand reduces misrepresentation. Fourth, scholars should acknowledge degrees of uncertainty—distinguishing between essential doctrines and secondary suppositions—so that areas of genuine agreement can be emphasized over peripheral disputes. Fifth, they should integrate historical development: recognizing that views evolved over centuries rather than appearing fully formed in one era. For instance, the premillennialism of Irenaeus differs significantly from modern dispensational premillennialism, and acknowledging this nuance fosters accuracy. Sixth, comparative studies must consider cultural contexts that shape interpretations, understanding that a reading from 19th-century England may not transfer seamlessly to contemporary Asia. Seventh, researchers should rely on interdisciplinary resources—archaeology, sociology, literary studies—to enrich, correct, or confirm textual insights. Finally, they should cultivate humility, realizing that no human exegete attains complete exhaustiveness; thus, inviting ongoing conversation rather than drawing unchallengeable conclusions. With these guidelines, comparative theologians can produce balanced evaluations of hermeneutical strategies, doctrinal coherence, and missional implications. Having established methodological guardrails, the chapter moves on to explore historical trajectories and reception of each view in the following sections.

## Conclusion

In surveying these varied visions, one truth emerges clearly: no single human scheme exhausts the mystery of God's unfolding purposes. Each approach—whether we place greater weight on a literal future reign, on present spiritual transformation, or on a symbolic reading of apocalyptic poetry—reflects sincere efforts to honor the biblical witness. Yet each also faces tensions: a literal reign must grapple with symbolic language; a symbolic reign must answer the plain teaching about resurrection bodies; a present-spiritual reign must hold fast to future hope without dissolving it into mere idealism. By acknowledging both the strengths and blind spots in each framework, believers can engage in dialogue that sharpens our understanding of Scripture rather than hardening us into tribes of irreconcilable "millennium camps." At the heart of every perspective remains the conviction that Jesus Christ, risen and enthroned, is building His kingdom in all its dimensions—personal, communal, cosmic. As we continue to learn from one another, may our shared longing for the day when God's reign is fully realized motivate us toward worship, service, and hope, trusting that "the mystery that has been kept hidden for ages and generations, but now has been revealed to his saints" (Colossians 1:26) will one day be seen in all its fullness.

www.ingramcontent.com/pod-product-compliance
Lightning Source LLC
LaVergne TN
LVHW051357080426
835508LV00022B/2864